Beginner's Guide for DATA ANALYSIS using R PROGRAMMING

Revised Edition

Dr. Jeeva Jose
Associate Professor, Department of Computer Applications
Baselios Poulose II Catholicos College (BPC)
Piravom - 686 664, Ernakulam District, Kerala, India

KHANNA BOOK PUBLISHING CO. (P) LTD.
Publisher of Engineering and Computer Books
4C/4344, Ansari Road, Darya Ganj, New Delhi-110002
Phone : 011-23244447-48 **Mobile:** +91-9910909320
E-mail : contact@khannabooks.com
Website : www.khannabooks.com

Price: ₹ 450.00

ISBN: 978-93-86173-45-4

Beginner's Guide to Data Analysis using R Programming
by Jeeva Jose

First Edition: 2018
Revised Edition: 2019
Reprint: 2023, 2025

To view complete list of books, Please scan the QR Code:

KPH

Published by:
Khanna Book Publishing Co. (P) Ltd.
CIN: U22110DL1998PTC095547

Visit us at: **www.khannabooks.com**
Write us at: **contact@khannabooks.com**

Printed in Bharat.

Preface

R is basically a programming language that combines standard programming capabilities with statistical analysis. This is a powerful language used widely for data analysis and statistical computing. This was originally developed by statisticians as an open-source alternative to expensive suites of statistical software like SAS and MATLAB. It is liked as Excel, able to execute sophisticated analyses and produce publication quality graphs and tables.

This language was created by Ross Ihaka and Robert Gentleman at the University of Auckland, New Zealand. R is named after the first names of the creators. The project was conceived in 1992 and a stable version or R was released in 2000. R is supported by the R Foundation for Statistical Computing. R language is freely available under the GNU General Public License and widely used among statisticians and data miners.

R Programming is free and open-source meaning anyone can examine the source code. This helps everyone to fix bugs and add features without help of vendor. R can be considered as a computer program as well as a statistical programming language. R programs will work on Windows, Macintosh or Linux.

The source code for the R software environment is written primarily in C, R and FORTRAN. R and its libraries implement a wide variety of statistical and graphical techniques. This includes linear and nonlinear modeling, classical statistical tests, time-series analysis, classification, clustering and others. R is easily extensible through functions and extensions. Many of R's standard functions are written in R itself, which makes it easy for users to follow the algorithmic choices made.

R Programming allows integrating with other languages (C/C++, Java, Python) and enables to communicate with many data sources like Excel, Access, SAS, Stata, SPSS, Minitab etc.

For computationally intensive tasks, C, C++ and FORTRAN code can be linked and called at run time. Advanced users can write C, C++, Java, .NET or Python code to manipulate R objects directly. R has stronger object-oriented programming facilities than most statistical computing languages.

R is very flexible and can be used to carry out unusual or non-standard procedures and is quick to adopt new procedures and innovations. It has libraries for almost everything that has been tried with other languages. It also has excellent graphics with a wide range of possibilities.

Another strength of R is static graphics, which can produce publication-quality graphs, including mathematical symbols. Dynamic and interactive graphics are available through additional packages. Rd package of R provides LaTeX like documentation format which is used to supply comprehensive documentation. Commonly used Graphical Integrated Development Environment for R is RStudio.

Many organizations are using R programming extensively. **Facebook** uses R for analyzing the Facebook status updates, its social network graph and for predicting colleague interactions. **Ford Motor Company** uses R for statistical analysis and data-driven decision support. **Google** uses R to calculate ROI on advertising campaigns, to predict economic activity, to analyze effectiveness of advertisement and to improve the efficiency of online advertising. In **Foursquare,** R is important part of the technology stack behind their famed recommendation engine. Statisticians at **John Deere** use R for time series modeling and geospatial analysis in a reliable and reproducible way. These results are then integrated with Excel and SAP. Insurance giant **Lloyd's** uses R for creating motion charts for providing analysis to investors. **Microsoft** uses R in their video gaming brand **Xbox** for matchmaking service. They also use R as a statistical engine in their **Azure** machine language framework. **Mozilla**, the foundation behind the **Firefox web browser** uses R to visualize Web activity. R is used in the news cycle at **The** *New York Times* to crunch data and prepare graphics before they go to print or online. **Thomas Cook**, a Tours and Travel company uses R for prediction and fuzzy logic to automate price settings of their last-minute offers. **National Weather Service** provides weather forecasts and warnings to US Government uses R to generate graphics for flood forecasting. R is part of **Twitter**'s Data Science toolbox for sophisticated statistical modeling and is used to monitor the user experience on the site. The fourth largest bank in Australia **ANZ Bank** use R for its credit risk modeling and analysis. **Uber**, the transportation company is using R for their statistical analysis. **Airbnb** a hospitality service company uses R for scale data science.

All programs provided in this book is tested in R3.4.2 version for Windows. This book helps you to study R programming as a tool in statistics for data analysis. The readers of this book are expected to have basic knowledge of statistics. Hope you all enjoy reading this book.

Acknowledgement

First and foremost I thank God Almighty for providing me knowledge, support, wisdom, information and strength to complete the authoring of this book.

The director of Khanna Book Publishing House Mr. Mukul Seth deserves special acknowledgement for placing confidence on me by asking to author a book on R programming. My sincere thanks to the editorial team for the immense support provided at every phase of the activity with their valuable guidance.

I thank my students, friends, relatives, parents and colleagues who eagerly waited for my new book and motivated for the successful completion.

The management and staff of BPC College, Kerala, India where I am serving as a professor encouraged me and supported me with resources whenever I required.

I am deeply indebted to my husband Vijo Mathew for lovingly motivating me, providing inputs, critical suggestions and coordinating various activities for me to successfully release this book. My two sons Samuel and Solomon should be appreciated for their patience and taking pride about their mother for authoring this book on R programming.

Dr. Jeeva Jose

Content

1 Introduction

R is an open source programming language and software environment for statistical computing and graphics that is supported by the R Foundation for Statistical Computing. R language is widely used among statisticians and data miners for developing statistical software and data analysis. R was created by Ross Ihaka and Robert Gentleman at the University of Auckland, New Zealand and is currently developed by the R Development Core Team. R is named partly after the first letter of the names of two R authors. The project was conceived in 1992, with an initial version released in 1995 and a stable beta version in 2000.

R language was inherited from a language called S. The source code for the R software environment is written primarily in C, Fortran and R. The core of R is an interpreted computer language which allows branching and looping as well as modular programming using functions. R allows integration with the procedures written in C, C++, .Net, Python or FORTRAN languages for efficiency.

R is freely available under the GNU General Public License and pre-compiled binary versions are provided for various operating systems like Linux, Windows and Mac. While R has a command line interface, there are several graphical front-ends available.

1.1 Features of R

R has a wide variety of statistical and programming features which made it the world's most widely used statistics programming language. It is the first choice of data scientists for statistical analysis and modeling. R is supported by a vibrant and talented community of contributors. R is used in education, scientific and in mission critical business applications. Following are the features of R.

(a) R is a well-developed, simple and effective programming language which includes decision making, flow control, recursive functions, input and output methods.

(b) R has an effective data handling and storage facility which is important for statistical analysis.

(c) R provides a variety of operators for calculations on arrays, lists, vectors and matrices.

(d) R provides a large, coherent and integrated collection of packages and tools for data analysis.

(e) R provides graphical facilities for plotting a wide variety of graphs and charts for data analysis including mathematical symbols. Dynamic and interactive graphics are available through additional packages.

(f) R and its libraries implement a wide variety of statistical and graphical techniques, including linear and nonlinear modelling, classical statistical tests, time-series analysis, classification, clustering and others.

(g) R is easily extensible through functions and extensions. R community is noted for its active contributions in terms of packages. For computationally intensive tasks, C, C++ and Fortran code can be linked and called at run time. Advanced users can write C, C++, Java, .NET or Python code to manipulate R objects directly.

(h) Since R was inherited from a language called S, R has stronger object-oriented programming facilities than most statistical computing languages.

1.2 How to Install R

(a) Windows Installation

We can download the Windows installer version of R from R-3.4 for Windows (32/64 bit) and save it in a local directory. As it is a Windows installer (.exe) with a name "R-version-win.exe", we can just double click and run the installer accepting the default settings. If our Windows is 32-bit version, it installs the 32-bit version. But if our Windows operating system is 64-bit, then it installs both the 32-bit and 64-bit versions.

After installation we can locate the icon to run the program in a directory structure "C:\Program Files\R\R3.4.2\bin\i386\Rgui.exe" under the Windows Program Files. Clicking this icon brings up the R-GUI which is the R console to do R Programming. All the programs in this book are tested using R3.4.2 version for Windows.

(b) Linux Installation

R is available as binary for many versions of Linux at the location R Binaries. The instruction to install Linux varies from flavor to flavor. However, we can use **yum** command to install R as follows.

```
$ yum install R
```

Above command will install core functionality of R programming along with standard packages. Still if we need additional package, then we can launch R prompt as follows.

```
$ R
```

1.3 How to Run R

(a) R Command Prompt

From the command prompt, we can run our first R program. At the command prompt, type the following.

```
> first_str<-"Hello World!"
> first_str
```

The output will be

```
[1] "Hello World!"
```

Here first statement defines a string variable `first_str`, where we assign a string "Hello World!" and then next statement `first_str` is being used to print the value stored in variable `first_str`.

(b) R Script File

Usually, we will write our programs in script files and then we execute those scripts at our command prompt with the help of R interpreter called `Rscript`. We will write the following code in a text file called `test.R` as follows.

```
#Test Program in R
str <- "Hello World!"
str
```

Save the above code in a file `test.R` and execute it at the command prompt as given below.

```
$ Rscript test.R
```

When we run the above program, it produces the following result.

```
[1] "Hello, World!"
```

(c) Using GUI

Use the same file `test.R`. From the File menu select "Open Script". Open the script file `test.R` and select the text. Select the right button of the mouse and click the option "Run line or selection". The output will be displayed as follows.

```
> #Test Program in R
> str <- "Hello World!"
> str
[1] "Hello World!"
```

1.4 Comments in R

Comments are included in our R program for better understanding. They are ignored by the interpreter while executing the actual program. Single comment is written using # at the beginning of the statement as follows.

```
#Test Program in R
```

R does not support multi-line comments as in C or Python.

1.5 Reserved Words

Reserved words in R programming are a set of words that have special meaning and cannot be used as an identifier (variable name, function name etc.). The list of reserved words can be viewed by typing `?reserved` or `help(reserved)` at the R command prompt. Following Table 1.1 shows a list of reserved words in R.

Table 1.1: Reserved Words in R

if	else	repeat	while	function
for	in	next	break	TRUE
FALSE	NULL	Inf	NaN	NA
NA_integer_	NA_real_	NA_complex_	NA_character_	...

Among these words, `if, else, repeat, while, function, for, in, next` and `break` are used for conditions, loops and user defined functions. They form the basic building blocks of programming in R. `TRUE` and `FALSE` are the logical constants in R. `NULL` represents the absence of a value or an undefined value. `Inf` is for "Infinity". For example, when 1 is divided by 0, `Inf` is displayed. `NaN` is for "Not a Number". For example, when 0 is divided by 0 we get `NaN`. `NA` stands for "Not Available" and is used to represent missing values.

R is a case sensitive language. For example, `TRUE` and `True` are not the same. While the first one is a reserved word denoting a logical constant in R, the latter can be used as a variable name.

1.6 Identifiers

The unique name given to a variable like function or objects is known as an identifier. Following are the rules for naming an identifier.

1. Identifiers can be a combination of letters, digits, period (.) and underscore (_).
2. It must start with a letter or a period. If it starts with a period, it cannot be followed by a digit.
3. Reserved words in R cannot be used as identifiers.

Examples of some valid identifiers are `total, Sum, .date.of.birth, Sum_of_two, Rank2`

Examples of some invalid identifiers are `tot@l, 2um, _prod, TRUE, .0wl`

Earlier versions of R used underscore (_) as an assignment operator. So, the period (.) was used extensively in variable names having multiple words. Current versions of R support underscore as a valid identifier but it is good practice to use period as word separators. For example, `a.variable.name` is preferred over `a_variable_name` or alternatively we could use camel case as `aVariableName`.

1.7 Constants

Constants or literals, as the name suggests, are entities whose value cannot be altered. Basic types of constants are numeric constants and character constants. There are built-in constants also.

All numbers fall under this category. They can be of type integer, double or complex. We can check the type of constants with the `typeof()` function. Numeric constants followed by `L` are regarded as integer and those followed by `i` are regarded as complex.

Example

```
> typeof(3)
```

```
[1] "double"
> typeof(3L)
[1] "integer"
> typeof(3i)
[1] "complex"
```

Character constants can be represented using either single quotes (') or double quotes (") as delimiters.

Example

```
> typeof("Apple")
[1] "character"
> typeof('mango')
[1] "character"
```

Some of the built-in constants defined in R along with their values is shown below.

Example

```
> LETTERS
[1]"A" "B" "C" "D" "E" "F" "G" "H" "I" "J" "K" "L" "M" "N" "O" "P" "Q"
"R" "S"
[20] "T" "U" "V" "W" "X" "Y" "Z"
> letters
[1] "a" "b" "c" "d" "e" "f" "g" "h" "i" "j" "k" "l" "m" "n" "o" "p" "q"
"r" "s"
[20] "t" "u" "v" "w" "x" "y" "z"
> pi
[1] 3.141593
>month.name
[1] "January"   "February"  "March"     "April"     "May"       "June"
[7] "July"      "August"    "September" "October"   "November"  "December"
> month.abb
[1] "Jan" "Feb" "Mar" "Apr" "May" "Jun" "Jul" "Aug" "Sep" "Oct" "Nov"
"Dec"
```

But it is not good to rely on these, as they are implemented as variables whose values can be changed. Following example illustrates this.

```
> pi
[1] 3.141593
> pi<-20
> pi
[1] 20
```

1.8 Variables

A variable provides us with named storage that our programs can manipulate. A variable in R can store an atomic vector, group of atomic vectors or a combination of many R objects. A valid variable name consists of letters, numbers and the dot or underline characters. The rule for naming a variable is same as that of any identifier which is already discussed in Section 1.6.

The variables can be assigned values using leftward, rightward and equal to operator. The values of the variables can be printed using `print()` or `cat()` function. The `cat()` function combines multiple items into a continuous print output.

Example

```
#Assignment using equal operator.
variable.1 = c(1,2,3)
#Assignment using leftward operator.
variable.2 <- c("Lotus","Rose")
#Assignment using rightward operator.
c(FALSE,1) -> variable.3
variable.1
cat("variable.1 is ", variable.1 ,"\n")
cat("variable.2 is ", variable.2 ,"\n")
cat("variable.3 is ", variable.3 ,"\n")
```

Output

```
[1] 1 2 3
variable.1 is  1 2 3
variable.2 is  Lotus Rose
variable.3 is  0 1
```

In the above example, `variable.1, variable.2` and `variable.3` are vector data types. Data types will be discussed in Chapter 2. The vector `c(FALSE,1)` has a mix of logical and numeric class. So logical class is converted to numeric class by making `FALSE` as 0. Hence the output appears as `variable.3 is 0 1`.

In R, there is no declaration for a variable like in C or Java. It gets the data type of the R - object assigned to it. So R is called a dynamically typed language, which means that we can change a variable's data type of the same variable again and again when using it in a program. We can get the data type of a variable using `class()` function. The following example illustrates this.

Example

```
var_1 <- 10L
cat("The class of var_1 is ",class(var_1),"\n")
var_1 <- 20+10i
cat("The class of var_1 is ",class(var_1),"\n")
```

```
var_1 <- 90.86
cat("The class of var_1 is ",class(var_1),"\n")
var_1 <- "Good Morning"
cat("The class of var_1 is ",class(var_1),"\n")
```

Output

```
The class of var_1 is integer
The class of var_1 is complex
The class of var_1 is numeric
The class of var_1 is character
```

We can find all variables in a workspace using the `ls()` function. The following illustrates the use of `ls()` function.

Example

```
> print(ls())
[1] "a"            "add"          "b"            "c"            "churnTest"
[6] "churnTrain"   "ds"           "k"            "mdat"         "USArrests"
[11] "VADeaths"     "var.1"        "var.2"        "var.3"        "var_1"
[16] "variable.1"  "variable.2"  "variable.3"
```

The `ls()` function can also be used to match the variable names with patterns. In the example given below, the `ls()` function matches for the variables begin with "v".

Example

```
> print(ls(pattern="v"))
[1] "var.1"        "var.2"        "var.3"        "var_1"        "variable.1"
[6] "variable.2" "variable.3"
```

Variables can be deleted by using the `rm()` function. We can delete the variable `variable.3`. On printing the value of the variable `variable.3`, error is thrown.

Example

```
> rm(variable.3)
```

1.9 Operators

R has several operators to perform tasks including arithmetic, logical and bitwise operations. R provides following types of operators. They are

1. Arithmetic Operators
2. Relational Operators
3. Logical Operators
4. Assignment Operators
5. Miscellaneous Operators

1.9.1 Arithmetic Operators

These operators are used to carry out mathematical operations like addition, subtraction, multiplication, division, modulus, integer division and exponentiation. Table 1.2 shows a list of arithmetic operators available in R. The arithmetic operators are applied for vectors. Even if we give a single value, it is considered as a vector with length one.

Table 1.2: Arithmetic Operators in R

Operator	Description
+	Adds two vectors.
–	Subtracts second vector from the first vector.
*	Multiplies first vector with the second vector.
/	Divide the first vector with the second vector.
%%	Gives the remainder of the first vector divided with the second vector.
%/%	The result of division of first vector with second vector. Only the quotient will be taken.
^	The first vector raised to the exponent of second vector.

Example Program

```
a<-c(10,20,30,40)
b<-c(2,2,4,3)
cat("Sum=",(a+b),"\n")
cat("Difference=",(a-b),"\n")
cat("Product=",(a*b),"\n")
cat("Quotient=",(a/b),"\n")
cat("Remainder=",(a%%b),"\n")
cat("Integer Division=",(a%/%b),"\n")
cat("Exponentiation=",(a^b),"\n")
```

Output

```
Sum= 12 22 34 43
Difference= 8 18 26 37
Product= 20 40 120 120
Quotient= 5 10 7.5 13.33333
Remainder= 0 0 2 1
Integer Division= 5 10 7 13
Exponentiation= 100 400 810000 64000
```

1.9.2 Relational Operators

Relational operators are used to compare between values. Each element of the first vector is compared with the corresponding element of the second vector. The result of comparison is a boolean value. Table 1.3 shows a list of relational operators available in R.

Table 1.3: Relational Operators in R

Operator	Description
<	Checks whether each element of the first vector is less than the corresponding element of the second vector. `TRUE` or `FALSE` is returned for each comparison.
>	Checks whether each element of the first vector is greater than the corresponding element of the second vector. `TRUE` or `FALSE` is returned for each comparison.
<=	Checks whether each element of the first vector is less than or equal to the corresponding element of the second vector. `TRUE` or `FALSE` is returned for each comparison.
>=	Checks whether each element of the first vector is greater than or equal to the corresponding element of the second vector. `TRUE` or `FALSE` is returned for each comparison.
==	Checks whether each element of the first vector is equal to the corresponding element of the second vector. `TRUE` or `FALSE` is returned for each comparison.
!=	Checks whether each element of the first vector is not equal to the corresponding element of the second vector. `TRUE` or `FALSE` is returned for each comparison.

Example Program

```
a<-c(10,20,30,40)
b<-c(25,2,30,3)
cat(a,"Less Than",b,(a<b),"\n")
cat(a,"Greater Than",b,(a>b),"\n")
cat(a,"Less Than or Equal To",b,(a<=b),"\n")
cat(a,"Greater Than or Equal To",b,(a>=b),"\n")
cat(a,"Equal To",b,(a==b),"\n")
cat(a,"Not Equal To",b,(a!=b),"\n")
```

Output

```
10 20 30 40 Less Than 25 2 30 3 TRUE FALSE FALSE FALSE
10 20 30 40 Greater Than 25 2 30 3 FALSE TRUE FALSE TRUE
10 20 30 40 Less Than or Equal To 25 2 30 3 TRUE FALSE TRUE FALSE
10 20 30 40 Greater Than or Equal To 25 2 30 3 FALSE TRUE TRUE TRUE
10 20 30 40 Equal To 25 2 30 3 FALSE FALSE TRUE FALSE
10 20 30 40 Not Equal To 25 2 30 3 TRUE TRUE FALSE TRUE
```

1.9.3 Logical Operators

Logical operators are applicable only to vectors of type logical, numeric or complex. All numbers greater than 1 are considered as logical value TRUE. Table 1.4 shows the logical operators available in R. Each element of the first vector is compared with the corresponding element of the second vector. The result of comparison is a Boolean value. Operators & and | perform element-wise operation producing result having length of the longer operand. But && and || examines only the first element of the operands resulting into a single length logical vector.

Table 1.4: Logical Operators in R

Operator	Description
!	Logical NOT. Takes each element of the vector and gives the opposite logical value.
&	Element-wise logical AND. It combines each element of the first vector with the corresponding element of the second vector and gives an output TRUE if both the elements are TRUE.
&&	Logical AND. It takes first element of both the vectors and gives TRUE only if both the elements are TRUE.
|	Element-wise logical OR. It combines each element of the first vector with the corresponding element of the second vector and gives an output TRUE if one of the elements is TRUE.
||	Logical OR. It takes first element of both the vectors and gives an output TRUE if one of the elements is TRUE.

Example Program

```
a<-c(0,20,30,56)
b<-c(2,2,30,0)
cat(a,"Logical NOT",(!a),"\n")
cat(a,"Element-wise Logical AND",b,(a&b),"\n")
cat(a,"Logical AND",b,(a&&b),"\n")
cat(a,"Element-wise Logical OR",b,(a|b),"\n")
cat(a,"Logical OR",b,(a||b),"\n")
```

Output

```
0 20 30 56 Logical NOT TRUE FALSE FALSE FALSE
0 20 30 56 Element-wise Logical AND 2 2 30 0 FALSE TRUE TRUE FALSE
0 20 30 56 Logical AND 2 2 30 0 FALSE
0 20 30 56 Element-wise Logical OR 2 2 30 0 TRUE TRUE TRUE TRUE
0 20 30 56 Logical OR 2 2 30 0 TRUE
```

1.9.4 Assignment Operators

These operators are used to assign values to variables or vectors. Table 1.5 shows the list of assignment operators available in R with their description. The operators <- and = can be used, almost interchangeably, to assign values to a variable in the same environment. The <<- operator is used for assigning values to variables in the parent environments (more like global assignments). The rightward assignments, although available are rarely used.

Table 1.5: Assignment Operators in R

Operator	Description
<-, <<-, =	Leftwards assignment
->, ->>	Rightwards assignment

Example Program

```
#Leftwards Assignment
var.a=c(0,20,TRUE)
var.b<-c(0,20,TRUE)
var.c<<-c(0,20,TRUE)
var.a
var.b
var.c
#Rightwards Assignment
c(1,2,TRUE)->v1
c(1,2,TRUE)->>v2
v1
v2
```

Output

```
[1] 0 20 1
[1] 0 20 1
[1] 0 20 1
[1] 1 2 1
[1] 1 2 1
```

1.9.5 Miscellaneous Operators

These operators are used for specific purpose. They are not used for mathematical or logical computation. Table 1.6 shows the list of miscellaneous operators available in R with their description.

Table 1.6: Miscellaneous Operators in R

Operator	Description
:	Colon. It creates a range of numbers in sequence for a vector.
%in%	This operator is used to check whether an element belongs to a vector. The result will be a boolean value either `TRUE` or `FALSE`.
%*%	This operator is used to multiply a matrix with its transpose which will be discussed in the forthcoming Chapter.

Example Program for Colon(:) Operator

```
var1<-3:9
var1
```

Output

```
[1] 3 4 5 6 7 8 9
```

Example Program for Miscellaneous Operator (%in%)

```
a=2
b=3
var<-3:10
a%in%var
b%in%var
```

Output

```
[1] FALSE
[1] TRUE
```

Example program for miscellaneous operator (%*%) will be discussed in the forthcoming Chapter.

1.10 Operator Precedence

When multiple operators are used in a single expression, we need to know the precedence of these operators to understand the sequence of operation that will take place. Precedence defines the order of execution, i.e., which operator gets the higher priority. It is possible to have multiple operators of same precedence in an expression. In such case the order of execution is determined through associativity. The precedence and associativity of operators in R from highest to lowest is given in Table 1.7. Most of the operators have left to right associativity while some of them have right to left associativity.

Table 1.7: Operator Precedence and Associativity in R

Operator	Description	Associativity
^	Exponent	Right to Left
-x, +x	Unary minus, Unary plus	Left to Right
%%	Modulus	Left to Right
*, /	Multiplication, Division	Left to Right
+, -	Addition, Subtraction	Left to Right
<, >, <=, >=, ==, !=	Relational Operators	Left to Right
!	Logical NOT	Left to Right
&, &&	Logical AND	Left to Right
|, ||	Logical OR	Left to Right
->, ->>	Rightward assignment	Left to Right
<-, <<-	Leftward assignment	Right to Left
=	Leftward assignment	Right to Left

1.11 Strings

Strings are created in R by writing any value within a pair of single quote or double quotes. However, internally R stores every string within double quotes, even if we create them with single quote. The quotes at the beginning and end of a string should be both double quotes or both single quotes. They cannot be mixed. Another feature of string is that double quotes can be inserted into a string starting and ending with single quote. Similarly single quote can be inserted into a string starting and ending with double quotes. String or character handling functions will be explained in Chapter 4.

Example Program

```
s<-"Hello World"
s
r<-'Good Morning'
r
```

Output

```
[1] "Hello World"
[1] "Good Morning"
```

1.11.1 Reading Strings

We can read strings from a keyboard using the `readline()` function. It lets the user to enter a one-line string at the terminal. The syntax for `readline()` function is as follows.

`value<- readline(prompt="string")` where the argument `prompt` is printed in front of the user input.

Example Program

```
print(n<- readline(prompt="Enter a name: "))
```

Output

```
Enter a name: Jeeva
[1] "Jeeva"
```

1.12 Conclusion

This Chapter gives an introduction to R programming. Features of R programming, how to install R in Windows and Unix, how to run R programs and how to give comments in R are also explained in this Chapter. The fundamental building blocks of R programming which includes reserved words, constants, identifiers and variables are explained with examples. Various operators which include arithmetic operators, relational operators, logical operators, assignment operators and miscellaneous operators are illustrated with examples. The precedence and associativity of operators, creation of strings and how to read strings from the terminal are also well explained in this Chapter.

2 Data Types & Operations

2.1 Introduction

There are several basic R data types that are of frequent occurrence in routine R calculations. Variables are nothing but reserved memory locations to store values. When we create a variable we reserve some space in memory. Variables can be classified as basic data types and R objects. Basic data types in R includes numeric, integer, complex, logical and character.

The variables are assigned with R objects and the data type of the R object becomes the data type of the variable. There are many types of R objects. The frequently used ones are

— Vectors
— Lists
— Matrices
— Arrays
— Factors
— Data Frames

Based on the data type of a variable, the operating system allocates memory and decides what can be stored in the reserved memory. In most of the programming languages like C, C++ and Java we need to declare the variables before using it. But in R, the variables are not declared as some data type.

2.2 Basic Data Types

2.2.1 Numeric

Decimal values are called numeric in R. It is the default computational data type. If we assign a decimal value to a variable `x` as follows, `x` will be of numeric type. Furthermore, even if we assign an integer to a variable `y`, it is still being saved as a numeric value and not an integer. We can use the function named `class()` to know the data type of a variable. The variable `y` can be tested whether it is an integer using the function `is.integer()`.

Example Program

```
x=10.9
```

```
x
y=5
y
class(x)              #displays the data type of x
class(y)              #displays the data type of y
is.integer(x)         #checks whether x is integer data type
is.integer(y)         #checks whether y is integer data type
```

Output

```
[1] 10.9
[1] 5
[1] "numeric"
[1] "numeric"
[1] FALSE
[1] FALSE
```

2.2.2 Integer

In order to create an integer variable in R, we invoke the `as.integer` function. We can be assured that `y` is indeed an integer by applying the `is.integer` function. We can coerce a numeric value into an integer with the same `as.integer` function. We can also parse a string for decimal values in the same way. But it is erroneous to parse a non-decimal string. Boolean values like `TRUE` and `FALSE` can be coerced to 1 and 0 using the `as.integer` function.

Example Program

```
x=as.integer(3)
x
class(x)                  #displays the data type of x
is.integer(x)             #checks whether x is integer data type
y=as.integer(3.23)        #coerced to integer
y
z=as.integer("7.81")      #coerced to integer
z
as.integer(TRUE)          #coerced to integer
as.integer(FALSE) #coerced to integer
```

Output

```
[1] 3
[1] "integer"
```

```
[1] TRUE
[1] 3
[1] 7
[1] 1
[1] 0
```

2.2.3 Complex

A complex value in R is defined via the pure imaginary value i. A complex number will be of the form `a+bi`, where `a` is the real part and `b` is the imaginary part.

Example Program

```
x=5+4i
x
class(x)            #displays the data type of x
is.complex(x)       #checks whether x is complex data type
y=as.complex(3)     #coerced to complex
y
```

Output

```
[1] 5+4i
[1] "complex"
[1] TRUE
[1] 3+0i
```

2.2.4 Logical

A logical value is often created via comparison between variables. The two logical values are `TRUE` and `FALSE`. `TRUE` can be coerced to 1 and `FALSE` can be coerced to 0.

Example Program

```
x = 1; y = 2
z = x > y
z                 #prints the logical value
class(z)          #displays the data type of z
as.logical(1)     #coerced to TRUE
as.logical(0)     #coerced to FALSE
```

Output

```
[1] FALSE
[1] "logical"
```

```
[1] TRUE
[1] FALSE
```

2.2.5 Character

A character object is used to represent string values in R. We convert objects into character values with the `as.character()` function. Both single quotes and double quotes can be used to represent strings. Strings and string manipulating functions are discussed in Chapter 4.

Example Program

```
x="abc"
y=as.character(7.8)
x
y
class(y) #displays the data type of y
```

Output

```
[1] "abc"
[1] "7.8"
[1] "character"
```

2.3 Vectors

Vector is a basic data structure in R. It contains elements of the same type. The data types can be logical, integer, double, character, complex or raw. Members in a vector are officially called components.

2.3.1 Creating Vectors

When we use a single value in R, it becomes a vector. For multiple elements vector, we can create the vector in several ways. The type of a vector can be found using `typeof()` function and length of a vector can be retrieved using `length()` function.

(a) colon (:) operator

If we want to create a vector of consecutive numbers, the : operator is very useful.

Example Program

```
x <- 1:7       #creates a vector from 1 to 7
x
x<-2.5:10.5    #creates a vector from 2.5 to 10.5
x
x<-2.5:4.7     #creates a vector from 2.5 to 4.5
x
```

Output

```
[1] 1 2 3 4 5 6 7
[1] 2.5 3.5 4.5 5.5 6.5 7.5 8.5 9.5 10.5
[1] 2.5 3.5 4.5
```

(b) c() function

Vectors can be created using `c()` function. Since, a vector must have elements of the same type, this function will try and coerce elements to the same type, if they are different. Coercion is from lower to higher types from logical to integer to double to character.

Example Program

```
x<-c(10,2.5, TRUE)            #all elements are coerced to double
x
typeof(x)                     #prints the type of x
x<-c(1,2.8,TRUE,"apple") #all elements are coerced to character
x
typeof(x)
length(x)                     #retrieves the length of vector x
```

Output

```
[1] 10.0 2.5 1.0
[1] "double"
[1] "1" "2.8" "TRUE" "apple"
[1] "character"
[1] 4
```

(c) sequence (seq) operator

More complex sequences can be created using the `seq()` function, like defining number of points in an interval, or the step size.

Example Program

```
x<-seq(2, 3, by=0.2)      # creates a vector from 2 to 3 with step size 0.2
x
x<-seq(1, 5, length=3)     # creates a vector with length 3
x
```

Output

```
[1] 2.0 2.2 2.4 2.6 2.8 3.0
[1] 1 3 5
```

2.3.2 Combining Vectors

Vectors can be combined via the function c. For example, the following two vectors n and m are combined into a new vector containing elements from both vectors. When the two vectors are combined, the numeric values are being coerced into character strings. This is necessary so as to maintain the same primitive data type for members in the same vector.

Example Program

```
n = c(2, 3, 4)
m = c("a", "b", "c", "d")
c(n, m) #combining vectors
```

Output

```
[1] "2" "3" "4" "a" "b" "c" "d"
```

2.3.3 Accessing Vector Elements

Elements of a vector can be accessed using vector indexing. The vector used for indexing can be logical, integer or character vector. We retrieve values in a vector by declaring an index inside a single square bracket "[]" operator.

(a) Integer Vector as Index

In R, vector index starts from 1 whereas in most programming languages index starts from 0. Since the vector index is 1-based, we can use the index position 3 for retrieving the third member. Unlike other programming languages, the square bracket operator returns more than just individual members. In fact, the result of the square bracket operator is another vector, and s[3] is a vector slice containing a single member "c".

We can also use negative integers to return all elements except that those specified. But we cannot mix positive and negative integers while indexing and real numbers, if used, are truncated to integers. If an index is out-of-range, a missing value will be reported via the symbol NA.

Example Program

```
s = c("a", "b", "c", "d", "e")
s[3]        #retrieves a vector slice at index 3
s[-3]       #negative index returns all elements except at index 3
s[10]       #out of range index
```

Output

```
[1] "c"
[1] "a" "b" "d" "e"
[1] NA
```

A new vector can be sliced from a given vector with a numeric index vector, which consists of member positions of the original vector to be retrieved. The following example shows how to retrieve a vector slice containing the second and third members of a given vector s. The index vector allows duplicate values. Hence the following example retrieves a member twice in one operation. The index vector can even be out-of-order. In the below example is a vector slice with the order of first and second members reversed. To produce a vector slice between two indexes, we can use the colon operator ":". This can be convenient for situations involving large vectors.

Example Program

```
s = c("a", "b", "c", "d", "e")
s[c(2, 3)]          # retrieves second and third members
s[c(2, 3, 3)]       # retrieves third member twice
s[c(2, 1, 3)]       # retrieve members in the order second, first and third
s[2:4]              # retrieve members from second to fourth
```

Output

```
[1] "b" "c"
[1] "b" "c" "c"
[1] "b" "a" "c"
[1] "b" "c" "d"
```

(b) Logical Vector as Index

When we use a logical vector for indexing, the position where the logical vector is TRUE is returned. This feature also helps to filter vectors based on conditions.

Example Program

```
s = c(1,2,3,-5,-6)
s[c(TRUE,FALSE,FALSE,TRUE,FALSE)]        # retrieve members at index where
TRUE
s[s<0]                                   # retrieve members less than zero
s[s>0]                                   # retrieve members greater than
zero
```

Output

```
[1] 1 -5
[1] -5 -6
[1] 1 2 3
```

(c) Character Vector as Index

This type of indexing is useful when dealing with named vectors. We can name each elements of a vector. For example, the following variable v is a character string vector with three members. We now name the first member as First, second member as Second and third member as Third. Then we can retrieve the member by its name. Furthermore, we can reverse the order with a character string index vector.

Example Program

```
v=c("Jack","Joe","Tom")
v
names(v)=c("First","Second","Third")
names(v)
#retrieves the second member with its name
v["Second"]
#reverse the order of the character string index
v[c("Third","First","Second")]
```

Output

```
[1] "Jack" "Joe"  "Tom"
[1] "First" "Second" "Third"
    Second
    "Joe"
    Third First Second
    "Tom" "Jack"  "Joe"
```

2.3.4 Modifying Vectors

We can modify a vector using the assignment operator. The techniques discussed above can be used to access specific elements and modify them. If we want to truncate the elements, we can use reassignments.

Example Program

```
x=c(10,20,30,40,50,60)
x
x[2] <- 90          # modify 2nd element
x
x[x<30] <- 5        # modify elements less than 30
x
x <- x[1:4]         # truncate x to first 4 elements
x
```

Output

```
[1] 10 20 30 40 50 60
[1] 10 90 30 40 50 60
```

```
[1] 5 90 30 40 50 60
[1] 5 90 30 40
```

2.3.5 Deleting Vectors

We can delete a vector by simply assigning a `NULL` to it. Following example illustrates this.

Example Program

```
x=c(10,20,30,40,50,60)
x
x <- NULL   # assigning NULL
x
```

Output

```
[1] 10 20 30 40 50 60
NULL
```

2.3.6 Vector Arithmetic & Recycling

Vector arithmetic involves addition, subtraction, multiplication, division, modulus, integer division and exponentiation. Two vectors of same length can be added, subtracted, multiplied, divided, find the modulus, perform integer division or find the power giving the result as a vector output. We have already discussed this in arithmetic operators of Chapter 1.

The recycling rule is that if the two vectors are of equal length then there is no issue. But if the lengths are different, the shorter one is recycled or repeated until its length is equal to that of the longer one. This recycling process will give a warning if the longer vector is not an integral multiple of the shorter one. Following program illustrates this.

Example Program

```
x=c(10,20,30)
x
y=c(1,2,3)
y
x+y
x+1          #1 is recycled to (1,1,1)
y+c(4,5)     #c(4,5) is recycled to c(4,5,4) with a warning
```

Output

```
[1] 10 20 30
[1] 1 2 3
[1] 11 22 33
[1] 11 21 31
[1] 5 7 7
```

```
Warning message:
In y + c(4, 5) :
  longer object length is not a multiple of shorter object length
```

2.3.7 Vector Element Sorting

Sorting of vectors can be done using the `sort()` function. By default, it sorts in ascending order. To sort in descending order we can pass `decreasing=TURE`. Vector is immutable which means that the original vector is not affected after sorting. The original vector remains unchanged and only a sorted version of it is returned.

Example Program

```
x=c(7,1,8,3,2,6,5,2,2,4)
sort(x)                                # sort in ascending order
sort(x,decreasing=TRUE)                # sort in descending order
x                                      # vector x remains unaffected
flowers=c("lotus","rose","jasmine","daisy","lilly")
#sorting of strings
sort(flowers)                          # sort in ascending order
sort(flowers,decreasing=TRUE)          # sort in descending order
flowers                                # vector x remains unaffected
```

Output

```
[1] 1 2 2 2 3 4 5 6 7 8
[1] 8 7 6 5 4 3 2 2 2 1
[1] 7 1 8 3 2 6 5 2 2 4
[1] "daisy"   "jasmine" "lilly"   "lotus"   "rose"
[1] "rose"    "lotus"   "lilly"   "jasmine" "daisy"
[1] "lotus"   "rose"    "jasmine" "daisy"   "lilly"
```

2.3.8 Reading Vectors

We can use `readline()` function to take input from the user (terminal). This function will return a single element character vector. If we want integers, we need to do appropriate conversion using the function `as.integer()`. Similarly, we can convert character vector to double, boolean, complex etc. using the function `as.double(), as.logical(), as.complex()` respectively.

Example Program

```
my.name <- readline(prompt="Enter name: ")
my.age <- readline(prompt="Enter age: ")
# convert character into integer
my.age <- as.integer(my.age)
```

```
my.bool<-readline(prompt="Enter(TRUE/FALSE): ")
# convert character into boolean
my.bool<- as.logical(my.bool)
my.name
my.age
my.bool
```

Output

```
[1] "Jeeva"
[1] 38
[1] TRUE
```

Note: Each `readline()` statement should be executed line by line to read the inputs. Multiple selection of `readline()` statements will not work.

2.4 Lists

A list is a generic vector containing other objects. Lists are the R objects which contain elements of different types like – numbers, strings, vectors and another list inside it. A list can also contain a matrix or a function as its elements.

2.4.1 Creating Lists

List can be created using the `list()` function. For example, the following variable n is a list containing three vectors and a numeric value 3.

Example Program

```
# creation of list
n = list(c(2, 3, 5),c("a", "b", "c", "d", "e"), c(TRUE, FALSE, TRUE,
FALSE, FALSE),3)
n
```

Output

```
[[1]]
[1] 2 3 5
[[2]]
[1] "a" "b" "c" "d" "e"
[[3]]
[1] TRUE FALSE TRUE FALSE FALSE
[[4]]
[1] 3
```

2.4.2 Accessing List Elements

Lists can be accessed in similar fashion to vectors. Integer, logical or character vectors can be used for indexing. Elements of the list can be accessed by the index of the element in the list. We retrieve a list slice with the single square bracket "[]" operator. With an index vector, we can retrieve a slice with multiple members. We can assign names to list members, and reference them by names instead of numeric indexes. A named list member can also be referenced directly with the "$" operator. The following example illustrates this.

Example Program

```
n = list(c(2, 3, 5),c("a", "b", "c", "d", "e"), c(TRUE, FALSE, TRUE,
FALSE, FALSE),3)
n[2]
n[c(2:4)]
n[-2]             # using negative integer to exclude second component
n[c(TRUE,FALSE,FALSE)]  # index using logical vector
names(n)=c("First","Second","Third","Fourth")
n[c("Second","Fourth")] # index using character vector(names)
names(n)=c("First","Second","Third","Fourth")
#using $ for referencing a member
n$Fourth
```

Output

```
[[1]]
[1] "a" "b" "c" "d" "e"
[[1]]
[1] "a" "b" "c" "d" "e"
[[2]]
[1] TRUE FALSE TRUE FALSE FALSE
[[3]]
[1] 3
# using negative integer to exclude second component
[[1]]
[1] 2 3 5
[[2]]
[1] TRUE FALSE TRUE FALSE FALSE
[[3]]
[1] 3
# index using logical vector
```

```
[[1]]
[1] 2 3 5
[[2]]
[1] 3
# index using character vector(names)
$Second
[1] "a" "b" "c" "d" "e"
$Fourth
[1] 3
#using $ for referencing a member
[1] 3
```

In order to reference a list member directly, we have to use the double square bracket "[[]]" operator. In the following example, the object n[[2]] is the second member of n. In other words, x[[2]] is a copy of n. We can modify its content directly.

Example Program

```
n = list(c(2, 3, 5),c("a", "b", "c", "d", "e"), c(TRUE, FALSE, TRUE,
FALSE, FALSE),3)
n[2]
n[[2]][1]="z"
n[[2]]        #value changed
```

Output

```
[[1]]
[1] "a" "b" "c" "d" "e"
#value changed
[1] "z" "b" "c" "d" "e"
```

2.4.3 Updating List Elements

We can add, delete and update list elements. We can add and delete elements only at the end of a list. But we can update any element. Following program illustrates this.

Example Program

```
n = list(c(2, 3, 5),c("a", "b", "c", "d", "e"), c(TRUE, TRUE),3)
# add element at the end of the list.
n[5] <- "New element"
n[5]
# remove the last element.
n[5] <- NULL
```

```
# print the 5th Element.
n[5]
# update the 3rd Element.
n[3] <- c("rose")
n
```

Output

```
[[1]]
[1] "New element"
# remove the last element.
[[1]]
NULL
# update the 3rd Element.
[[1]]
[1] 2 3 5
[[2]]
[1] "a" "b" "c" "d" "e"
[[3]]
[1] "rose"
[[4]]
[1] 3
```

2.4.4 Merging Lists

We can merge many lists into one list by placing all the lists inside one `list()` function. Following program illustrates this.

Example Program

```
m=list(c(2, 3, 5))
n=list(c("a", "b", "c"))
k=list(c(TRUE,FALSE,TRUE))
# merges three lists into one single list
merged.lis=c(m,n,k)
merged.lis
```

Output

```
[[1]]
[1] 2 3 5
[[2]]
```

```
[1] "a" "b" "c"
[[3]]
[1] TRUE FALSE TRUE
```

2.4.5 List to Vector Conversion

A list can be converted to a vector so that the elements of the vector can be used for further manipulation. All the arithmetic operations on vectors can be applied after the list is converted into vectors. To do this conversion, we use the `unlist()` function. It takes the list as input and produces a vector.

Example Program

```
# create list1 and list2.
list1 <- list(1:5)
list1
list2 <-list(11:15)
list2
# convert the lists to vectors.
v1 <- unlist(list1)
v2 <- unlist(list2)
v1
v2
# now add the vectors
result <- v1+v2
result
```

Output

```
[1] 1 2 3 4 5
[1] 11 12 13 14 15
[1] 12 14 16 18 20
```

2.5 Matrices

A matrix is a collection of data elements arranged in a two-dimensional rectangular layout. The following is an example of a matrix with 2 rows and 3 columns.

$$A = \begin{bmatrix} 2 & 4 & 3 \\ 1 & 5 & 7 \end{bmatrix}$$

They contain elements of the same atomic types. Though we can create a matrix containing only characters or only logical values, they are not of much use. We use matrices containing numeric elements to be used in mathematical calculations.

2.5.1 Creating Matrices

The basic syntax for creating a matrix in R is as follows.

```
matrix(data, nrow, ncol, byrow, dimnames)
```

where `data` is the input vector which becomes the data elements of the matrix, `nrow` is the number of rows to be created, `ncol` is the number of columns to be created, `byrow` is a logical clue and `dimname` is the names assigned to the rows and columns. If `byrow` is `TRUE`, then the input vector elements are arranged by row. Providing value for both dimensions is not necessary. If one of the dimensions is provided, the other is inferred from length of the data. We can also define names to rows and columns of a matrix by passing a 2 element list as argument to the function `dimnames()`.

Example Program

```
# elements are arranged by row.
M <- matrix(c(1:12), nrow = 4, byrow = TRUE)
M
# elements are arranged by column.
N <- matrix(c(1:12), nrow = 4, byrow = FALSE)
N
# define the column and row names.
rnames = c("r1", "r2", "r3", "r4")
cnames = c("c1", "c2", "c3")
P <- matrix(c(1:12), nrow = 4, byrow = TRUE,
dimnames = list(rnames, cnames))
P
```

Output

```
# elements are arranged by row.
     [,1] [,2] [,3]
[1,]    1    2    3
[2,]    4    5    6
[3,]    7    8    9
[4,]   10   11   12
 # elements are arranged by column.
     [,1] [,2] [,3]
[1,]    1    5    9
[2,]    2    6   10
[3,]    3    7   11
[4,]    4    8   12
```

```
# define the column and row names.
   c1 c2 c3
r1  1  2  3
r2  4  5  6
r3  7  8  9
r4 10 11 12
```

Another way of creating a matrix is by using functions `cbind()` and `rbind()`. If we are using `cbind()` function, elements will be filled column-wise and `rbind()` function fills the matrix elements row-wise.

Example Program

```
# elements will be filled column-wise
M=cbind(c(1,2,3),c(4,5,6))
M
# elements will be filled row-wise
N=rbind(c(1,2,3),c(4,5,6))
N
```

Output

```
# elements filled column-wise
     [,1] [,2]
[1,]    1    4
[2,]    2    5
[3,]    3    6
# elements filled row-wise
     [,1] [,2] [,3]
[1,]    1    2    3
[2,]    4    5    6
```

We can also create a matrix from a vector by setting its dimension using `dim()`.

Example Program

```
M=c(1,2,3,4,5,6)
# matrix creation with the dimensions passed
dim(M)=c(2,3)
M
```

Output

```
# matrix created with the dimensions passed
```

```
     [,1] [,2] [,3]
[1,]    1    3    5
[2,]    2    4    6
```

2.5.2 Accessing Matrix Elements

Matrix elements can be accessed in three different ways.

(a) Integer Vector as Index

An element at the mth row and n^{th} column of a matrix P can be accessed by the expression P[m, n]. Here m and n are vectors. We can use negative integers to specify rows or columns to be excluded. If any field inside the bracket is left blank, it selects all. For example the entire m^{th} row of matrix P can be extracted as P[m,]. Similarly, the entire n^{th} column of matrix P can be extracted as P[,n]. We can also extract more than one rows or columns at a time.

Example Program

```
M <- matrix(c(1:12), nrow = 4, byrow = TRUE)
M                   # matrix M
M[2, 3]             # element at 2nd row, 3rd column
M[2, ]              # the 2nd row
M[ ,3]              # the 3rd column
M[,]                # selects the entire matrix
M[ ,c(1,3)]         # the 1st and 3rd columns
M[c(3,2),]          # the 3rd and second row
M[c(1,2),c(2,3)]# the 1st and 2nd row & 2nd and 3rd column
M[-1,]              # select all rows except first
```

Output

```
# matrix M
     [,1] [,2] [,3]
[1,]    1    2    3
[2,]    4    5    6
[3,]    7    8    9
[4,]   10   11   12
# element at 2nd row, 3rd column
[1] 6
# the 2nd row
[1] 4 5 6
# the 3rd column
[1] 3 6 9 12
```

```
# selects the entire matrix
     [,1] [,2] [,3]
[1,]    1    2    3
[2,]    4    5    6
[3,]    7    8    9
[4,]   10   11   12
# the 1st and 3rd columns
     [,1] [,2]
[1,]    1    3
[2,]    4    6
[3,]    7    9
[4,]   10   12
# the 3rd and second row
     [,1] [,2] [,3]
[1,]    7    8    9
[2,]    4    5    6
# the 1st and 2nd row & 2nd and 3rd column
     [,1] [,2]
[1,]    2    3
[2,]    5    6
# select all rows except first
     [,1] [,2] [,3]
[1,]    4    5    6
[2,]    7    8    9
[3,]   10   11   12
```

Here the result after indexing is given as a vector. This behavior can be avoided by using the argument `drop = FALSE` while indexing.

Example Program

```
M <- matrix(c(1:12), nrow = 4, byrow = TRUE)
M                           # matrix M
M[2,,drop=FALSE ]           # the 2nd row as 1X3 matrix
```

Output

```
# matrix M
     [,1] [,2] [,3]
[1,]    1    2    3
```

```
[2,]    4    5    6
[3,]    7    8    9
[4,]   10   11   12
# the 2nd row as 1X3 matrix
     [,1] [,2] [,3]
[1,]    4    5    6
```

It is possible to index a matrix with a single vector. While indexing in such a way, it acts like a vector formed by stacking columns of the matrix one after another. The result is returned as a vector.

Example Program

```
M <- matrix(c(1:12), nrow = 4, byrow = TRUE)
M[1:4]        #retrieves the first 4 elements
M[c(3,6,8)] #retrieves the third, sixth and eighth elements
```

Output

```
#retrieves the first 4 elements column-wise
[1] 1 4 7 10
#retrieves the third, sixth and eighth elements
[1] 7 5 11
```

(b) Logical Vector as Index

Two logical vectors can be used to index a matrix. In such situation, rows and columns where the value is `TRUE` is returned. These indexing vectors are recycled if necessary and can be mixed with integer vectors.

Example Program

```
M <- matrix(c(1:12), nrow = 4, byrow = TRUE)
# retrieves elements of 1st and 3rd row & 1st and 2nd column
M[c(TRUE,FALSE,TRUE),c(TRUE,TRUE,FALSE)]
# the 2 element logical vector is recycled to 3 element vector
M[c(TRUE,FALSE),c(2,3)]
```

Output

```
# retrieves elements of 1st and 3rd row & 1st and 2nd column
     [,1] [,2]
[1,]    1    2
[2,]    7    8
[3,]   10   11
# the 2 element logical vector is recycled to 3 element vector
```

```
     [,1] [,2]
[1,]    2    3
[2,]    8    9
```

It is also possible to index using a single logical vector where recycling takes place if necessary. `M[c(TRUE, FALSE)]` will give the output as

```
[1] 1 7 2 8 3 9
```

In the above example, the matrix M is treated as vector formed by stacking columns of the matrix one after another, i.e., `(1,2,3,4,5,6,7,8,9,10,11,12)`. The indexing logical vector is also recycled and thus alternating elements are selected.

Logical vector indexing of a matrix can be used for filtering elements. Following program illustrates this.

Example Program

```
M <- matrix(c(1:12), nrow = 4, byrow = TRUE)
M
M[M>4]      #filter elements greater than 4
M[M%%2!=0] #filter odd elements from M
```

Output

```
     [,1] [,2] [,3]
[1,]    1    2    3
[2,]    4    5    6
[3,]    7    8    9
[4,]   10   11   12
#filter elements greater than 4
[1] 7 10 5 8 11 6 9 12
#filter odd elements from M
[1] 1 7 5 11 3 9
```

(c) Character Vector as Index

If we assign names to the rows and columns of a matrix, then we can access the elements by names. This can be mixed with integer or logical indexing.

Example Program

```
M <- matrix(c(1:12), nrow = 4, byrow = TRUE,
dimnames=list(c("r1","r2","r3","r4"),c("c1","c2","c3")))
M
M["r2", "c3"]          # element at 2nd row, 3rd column
M[,"c1"]               # elements of the column named c1
```

```
M[TRUE,c("c1","c2")] # elements of all rows & columns c1 and c2
M[2:3,c("c1","c3")]  # elements of 2nd and 3rd row & columns c1 and c3
```

Output

```
# matrix M
   c1 c2 c3
r1 1 2 3
r2 4 5 6
r3 7 8 9
r4 10 11 12
# element at 2nd row, 3rd column
[1] 6
# elements of the column named c1
r1 r2 r3 r4
 1 4 7 10
# elements of all rows & columns c1 and c2
   c1 c2
r1 1 2
r2 4 5
r3 7 8
r4 10 11
# elements of 2nd and 3rd row & columns c1 and c3
   c1 c3
r2 4 6
r3 7 9
```

2.5.3 Matrix Arithmetic

Various mathematical operations are performed on the matrices using the R operators. The result of the operation is also a matrix. The dimensions (number of rows and columns) should be same for the matrices involved in the operation.

Example Program

```
# create two 2x3 matrices.
matrix1 <- matrix(c(10,20,30,40,50,60), nrow = 2)#matrix 1
matrix1
matrix2 <- matrix(c(1,2,3,4,5,6), nrow = 2)       #matrix 2
matrix2
# add the matrices.
```

```
sum <- matrix1 + matrix2
cat("Result of addition","\n")
sum
# subtract the matrices
difference <- matrix1 - matrix2
cat("Result of subtraction","\n")
difference
# multiply the matrices.
product <- matrix1 * matrix2
cat("Result of multiplication","\n")
product
# divide the matrices
quotient <- matrix1 / matrix2
cat("Result of division","\n")
quotient
```

Output

```
#matrix 1
      [,1] [,2] [,3]
[1,]   10   30   50
[2,]   20   40   60
#matrix 2
     [,1] [,2] [,3]
[1,]    1    3    5
[2,]    2    4    6
Result of addition
     [,1] [,2] [,3]
[1,]   11   33   55
[2,]   22   44   66
Result of subtraction
     [,1] [,2] [,3]
[1,]    9   27   45
[2,]   18   36   54
Result of multiplication
     [,1] [,2] [,3]
[1,]   10 90 250
[2,]   40 160 360
```

```
Result of division
     [,1] [,2] [,3]
[1,]   10   10   10
[2,]   10   10   10
```

In the above example, matrix multiplication is done element-wise. The real matrix multiplication will be discussed in the forthcoming Section 2.5.5.

2.5.4 Matrix Manipulation

We can combine assignment operator with the above learned methods for accessing elements of a matrix to modify it. We can modify a single element or elements based on a condition. Following program illustrates this.

Example Program

```
matrix1 <- matrix(c(10,20,30,40,50,60), nrow = 3)#matrix1 of order 3X2
matrix1
matrix1[2,2] <- 100      #modifies single element at 2,2
matrix1
matrix1[matrix1<40] <- 0 #modify elements less than 40
matrix1
```

Output

```
     [,1] [,2]
[1,]   10   40
[2,]   20   50
[3,]   30   60
#modifies single element at 2,2
     [,1] [,2]
[1,]   10 40
[2,]   20 100
[3,]   30 60
#modify elements less than 40
     [,1] [,2]
[1,]    0 40
[2,]    0 100
[3,]    0 60
```

We can add row or column using `rbind()` and `cbind()` function respectively. Similarly, it can be removed through reassignment.

Example Program

```
matrix1 <- matrix(c(10,20,30,40,50,60), nrow = 3)#matrix1 of order 3X2
matrix1
cbind(matrix1, c(1, 2, 3))              # add column
rbind(matrix1,c(1,2))                   # add row
print(matrix1 <- matrix1[1:2,])         # removes last row
```

Output

```
#matrix1 of order 3X2
     [,1] [,2]
[1,]   10   40
[2,]   20   50
[3,]   30   60
# add column
      [,1] [,2] [,3]
[1,]   10   40    1
[2,]   20   50    2
[3,]   30   60    3
# add row
      [,1] [,2]
[1,]   10   40
[2,]   20   50
[3,]   30   60
[4,]    1    2
# removes last row from matrix1
      [,1] [,2]
[1,]   10   40
[2,]   20   50
```

Dimension of matrix can be modified as well, using the `dim()` function.

Example Program

```
matrix1 <- matrix(c(10,20,30,40,50,60), nrow = 3)#matrix1 of order 3X2
matrix1
dim(matrix1)<-c(2,3)          # dimension changed to 2X3
matrix1
```

Output

```
#matrix1 of order 3X2
     [,1] [,2]
```

```
[1,]    10    40
[2,]    20    50
[3,]    30    60
# dimension changed to 2X3
     [,1] [,2] [,3]
[1,]    10    30    50
[2,]    20    40    60
```

2.5.5 Matrix Operations

(a) Matrix Multiplication

Two matrices A of order MXN and B of order PXQ are eligible for multiplication only if N is equal to P. The resultant matrix will be of the order MXQ. Matrix multiplication is performed using the operator A %*% B where A and B are two matrices.

Example Program

```
# create two matrices.
#matrix1 of order 3X2
matrix1 <- matrix(c(10,20,30,40,50,60), nrow = 3)
matrix1
#matrix2 of order 2X3
matrix2 <- matrix(c(1,2,3,4,5,6), nrow = 2)
matrix2
# multiply the matrices.
product <- matrix1%*% matrix2 #product matrix of order 3X3
cat("Result of multiplication","\n")
product
```

Output

```
#matrix1 of order 3X2
     [,1] [,2]
[1,]    10    40
[2,]    20    50
[3,]    30    60
#matrix2 of order 2X3
     [,1] [,2] [,3]
[1,]     1     3     5
[2,]     2     4     6
```

```
Result of multiplication
     [,1] [,2] [,3]
[1,] 90 190 290
[2,] 120 260 400
[3,] 150 330 510
```

(b) Transpose

In linear algebra, the transpose of a matrix is an operator which flips a matrix over its diagonal, that is it switches the row and column indices of the matrix by producing another matrix denoted as A^T or A'. This can be done with the function `t()` in R.

Example Program

```
#matrix1 of order 3X2
matrix1 <- matrix(c(10,20,30,40,50,60), nrow = 3)
matrix1
t(matrix1)  #transpose of the matrix
```

Output

```
#matrix1 of order 3X2
     [,1] [,2]
[1,]   10   40
[2,]   20   50
[3,]   30   60
#transpose of the matrix
     [,1] [,2] [,3]
[1,]   10   20   30
[2,]   40   50   60
```

(c) Outer Product

The outer product $U \otimes V$ is equivalent to a matrix multiplication UV^T, provided that U is represented as a m × 1 column vector and V as a n × 1 column vector (which makes V^T a row vector). This is achieved in R using the operator U %o% V where U and V are two matrices.

Example Program

```
#matrix 1 of order 3X2
matrix1 <- matrix(c(10,20,30,40,50,60), nrow = 3)
matrix1
matrix2 <- matrix(c(1,2,3,4,5,6), nrow = 2)#matrix 2 of order 2X3
matrix2
matrix1%o%matrix2   #outer product
```

Output

```
#matrix 1 of order 3X2
     [,1] [,2]
[1,]   10   40
[2,]   20   50
[3,]   30   60
#matrix 2 of order 2X3
     [,1] [,2] [,3]
[1,]    1    3    5
[2,]    2    4    6
#outer product
, , 1, 1
     [,1] [,2]
[1,]   10   40
[2,]   20   50
[3,]   30   60
, , 2, 1
     [,1] [,2]
[1,]   20   80
[2,]   40  100
[3,]   60  120
, , 1, 2
     [,1] [,2]
[1,]   30  120
[2,]   60  150
[3,]   90  180
, , 2, 2
     [,1] [,2]
[1,]   40  160
[2,]   80  200
[3,]  120  240
, , 1, 3
     [,1] [,2]
[1,]   50  200
[2,]  100  250
[3,]  150  300
```

```
, , 2, 3
     [,1] [,2]
[1,]   60  240
[2,]  120  300
[3,]  180  360
```

(d) Cross Product

Cross product of two matrices A and B is calculated as A'B where A' is the transpose of A. This is implemented in R using the function `crossprod(A,B)`. The cross product of a matrix to itself is calculated as A'A and is implemented using the function `crossprod(A)`.

Example Program

```
A <- matrix(c(10,20,30,40), nrow = 2)#matrix A of order 2X2
A
B <- matrix(c(1,2,3,4), nrow = 2)#matrix B of order 2X2
B
crossprod(A,B)        #cross product of A and B
crossprod(A)          #cross product of A to itself
```

Output

```
#matrix A of order 2X2
     [,1] [,2]
[1,]   10   30
[2,]   20   40
#matrix B of order 2X2
     [,1] [,2]
[1,]    1    3
[2,]    2    4
#cross product of A and B
     [,1] [,2]
[1,] 50 110
[2,] 110 250
#cross product of A to itself
     [,1] [,2]
[1,] 500 1100
[2,] 1100 2500
```

(e) Diagonal Matrix

In R, the function `diag(A)` returns a vector containing the elements of the principal diagonal. An identity matrix of the order KXK can be created using the function `diag(k)`, if `k` is a scalar. The diag(x,k) function creates diagonal matrix with elements of x in the principal diagonal where x is a vector and k is a scalar.

Example Program

```
A<-matrix(1:9,nrow=3)#matrix A of order 3X3
A
diag(A)          #prints the diagonal elements
diag(3)          #creates an identity matrix of order 3
diag(c(1,2,3),3)#creates a matrix of order 3 with diagonal elements 1,2,3
```

Output

```
#matrix A of order 3X3
     [,1] [,2] [,3]
[1,]    1    4    7
[2,]    2    5    8
[3,]    3    6    9
#prints the diagonal elements
[1] 1 5 9
#creates an identity matrix of order 3
     [,1] [,2] [,3]
[1,]    1    0    0
[2,]    0    1    0
[3,]    0    0    1
#creates a matrix of order 3 with diagonal elements 1,2,3
     [,1] [,2] [,3]
[1,]    1    0    0
[2,]    0    2    0
[3,]    0    0    3
```

(f) Row Sum and Column Sum

We can find the sum of each row as well as sum of each column in a matrix. The function rowSums(A) returns the sum of rows of matrix A as a vector. Similarly colSums(A) returns the sum of columns of matrix A as a vector.

Example Program

```
A<-matrix(1:9,nrow=3)#matrix A of order 3X3
A
rowSums(A)          #prints the row sum of A
colSums(A)          #prints the column sum of A
```

Output

```
#matrix A of order 3X3
     [,1] [,2] [,3]
[1,]    1    4    7
[2,]    2    5    8
[3,]    3    6    9
#prints the row sum of A
[1] 12 15 18
#prints the column sum of A
[1] 6 15 24
```

(g) Row Means and Column Means

We can find the mean of each row as well as mean of each column in a matrix. The function `rowMeans(A)` returns the mean of rows of matrix A as a vector. Similarly `colMeans(A)` returns the mean of columns of matrix A as a vector.

Example Program

```
A<-matrix(1:9,nrow=3)#matrix A of order 3X3
A
rowMeans(A)          #prints the row mean of A
colMeans(A)          #prints the column mean of A
```

Output

```
     [,1] [,2] [,3]
[1,]    1    4    7
[2,]    2    5    8
[3,]    3    6    9
#prints the row mean of A
[1] 4 5 6
#prints the column mean of A
[1] 2 5 8
```

(h) Eigen Values and Eigen Vectors

The eigen values and eigen vectors of a matrix can be found out using the function `eigen(A)` where A is a matrix. `$values` gives the eigen values and `$vectors` gives the eigen vectors for A.

Example Program

```
A<-matrix(1:9,nrow=3)#matrix A of order 3X3
A
```

```
y<-eigen(A)
y    #prints the eigen values and eigen vectors of A
```

Output

```
     [,1] [,2] [,3]
[1,]    1    4    7
[2,]    2    5    8
[3,]    3    6    9
#prints the eigen values and eigen vectors of A
$values
[1] 1.611684e+01 -1.116844e+00 -5.700691e-16
$vectors
           [,1]       [,2]       [,3]
[1,] -0.4645473 -0.8829060  0.4082483
[2,] -0.5707955 -0.2395204 -0.8164966
[3,] -0.6770438 0.4038651 0.4082483
```

(i) Inverse

We can find the inverse of a matrix using the function `solve(A)`, where A is a square matrix. The function `solve(A, B)` in R returns matrix x in the equation B = Ax (i.e., $A^{-1}B$) where A and B are two matrices compatible for multiplication.

Example Program

```
A<-matrix(1:4,nrow=2)   #matrix A of order 2X2
A                       #matrix A
solve(A)                #prints the Inverse of A
B<-matrix(1:2, nrow=2)  #matrix B of order 2X1
B                       #matrix B
solve(A,B)              #prints the Inverse of A multiplied with B
```

Output

```
#matrix A
     [,1] [,2]
[1,]    1    3
[2,]    2    4
#prints the Inverse of A
     [,1] [,2]
[1,]   -2  1.5
```

```
[2,]      1 -0.5
#matrix B of order 2X1
#matrix B
     [,1]
[1,]    1
[2,]    2
#prints the Inverse of A multiplied with B
     [,1]
[1,]    1
[2,]    0
```

2.6 Arrays

Arrays are R data objects which can store data in more than two dimensions. Arrays can store only same data type. For example, if we create an array of dimension (2, 4, 5) then it creates 5 rectangular matrices each with 2 rows and 4 columns.

2.6.1 Creating Arrays

An array is created using the `array()` function. It takes vectors as input. The function `dim()` defines the dimension of an array or use the values in the `dim` parameter to create an array.

Example Program

```
v1=c(1,2,3)
v2=c(10,20,30,40,50,60)
A<-array(c(v1,v2),dim=c(3,3,2))#creates 2 3X3 matrix
A
```

Output

```
, , 1
     [,1] [,2] [,3]
[1,]    1   10   40
[2,]    2   20   50
[3,]    3   30   60
, , 2
     [,1] [,2] [,3]
[1,]    1   10   40
[2,]    2   20   50
[3,]    3   30   60
```

We can give names to the rows, columns and matrices in the array by using the `dimnames` parameter.

Example Program

```
v1=c(1,2,3)
v2=c(10,20,30,40,50,60)
column.names <- c("COL1","COL2","COL3")
row.names <- c("ROW1","ROW2","ROW3")
matrix.names <- c("Matrix1","Matrix2")
#creates 2 3X3 matrix with rows, columns and matrices named
A<-array(c(v1,v2),dim=c(3,3,2),dimnames = list(row.names,column.names,
matrix.names))
A
```

Output

```
, , Matrix1
     COL1 COL2 COL3
ROW1    1   10   40
ROW2    2   20   50
ROW3    3   30   60
, , Matrix2
     COL1 COL2 COL3
ROW1    1   10   40
ROW2    2   20   50
ROW3    3   30   60
```

2.6.2 Accessing Array Elements

In R programming, we can use the index position to access the array elements. Using index we can access or alter each and every individual element present in an array. Index value starts at 1 and ends at n where n is the size of a matrix, row or column. The syntax is `array_name[row_position, column_position, matrix_level]`.

For example, we declared an array of two matrices of size 6 rows * 4 columns. To access or alter 1st value use `array_name[1, 1, 1]`, to access or alter 2nd row 3rd column value at 1st Matrix level then use `array_name[2, 3, 1]` and to access the 6th row 4th column in 2nd matrix level then use `array_name[6, 4, 2]`.

Example Program

```
# accessing R array elements
A <- array(1: 24, dim = c(3, 4, 2))
A
# access the elements of 1st row and 2nd column in matrix 1.
```

```
A[1, 2, 1]
# access the elements of 3rd row and 4th column in matrix 2.
A[3, 4, 2]
# access only the 3rd row in first matrix.
A[3, , 1]
# access only the 4th column in second matrix.
A[, 4, 2]
# access the complete first matrix.
A[ , , 1]
# access the complete second matrix.
A[ , , 2]
```

Output

```
, , 1
     [,1] [,2] [,3] [,4]
[1,]    1    4    7   10
[2,]    2    5    8   11
[3,]    3    6    9   12
, , 2
     [,1] [,2] [,3] [,4]
[1,]   13   16   19   22
[2,]   14   17   20   23
[3,]   15   18   21   24
# access the elements of 1st row and 2nd column in matrix 1.
 [1] 4
# access the elements of 3rd row and 4th column in matrix 2.
 [1] 24
# access only the 3rd row in first matrix.
 [1] 3 6 9 12
# access only the 4th column in second matrix.
 [1] 22 23 24
# access the complete first matrix.
     [,1] [,2] [,3] [,4]
[1,]    1    4    7   10
[2,]    2    5    8   11
[3,]    3    6    9   12
```

```
# access the complete second matrix.
     [,1] [,2] [,3] [,4]
[1,]   13   16   19   22
[2,]   14   17   20   23
[3,]   15   18   21   24
```

We can access subset of multiple items from the array with the help of R Vector. Negative index positions are used to omit those values from array as in vectors and matrices.

Example Program

```
# accessing R array elements
A <- array(1: 24, dim = c(3, 4, 2))
A
# access the elements of 1st, 2nd row and 3rd, 4th column in matrix 1.
A[c(1, 2), c(3, 4), 1]
# access all the elements of 2nd and 3rd row in matrix 2.
A[c(2, 3), , 2]
# access all the elements of 1st and 4th column in matrix 1.
A[ , c(1, 4), 1]
# access all the elements except 2nd row and 3rd column in matrix 2.
A[-2, -3, 2]
```

Output

```
, , 1
     [,1] [,2] [,3] [,4]
[1,]    1    4    7   10
[2,]    2    5    8   11
[3,]    3    6    9   12
, , 2
     [,1] [,2] [,3] [,4]
[1,]   13   16   19   22
[2,]   14   17   20   23
[3,]   15   18   21   24
# access the elements of 1st, 2nd row and 3rd, 4th column in matrix 1.
     [,1] [,2]
[1,]    7   10
[2,]    8   11
# access all the elements of 2nd and 3rd row in matrix 2.
```

```
      [,1] [,2] [,3] [,4]
[1,]   14   17   20   23
[2,]   15   18   21   24
# access all the elements of 1st and 4th column in matrix 1.
      [,1] [,2]
[1,]    1   10
[2,]    2   11
[3,]    3   12
# access all the elements except 2nd row and 3rd column in matrix 2.
      [,1] [,2] [,3]
[1,]   13   16   22
[2,]   15   18   24
```

2.6.3 Array Element Manipulation

Since an array is made up of matrices in multiple dimensions, the operations on elements of array are carried out by accessing elements of the matrices. We can do calculations across the elements in an array using the `apply()` function. Following is the syntax of the `apply()` function.

```
apply(x, margin, func)
```

where `x` is an array, `margin` is the name of the data set used and `func` is the function to be applied across the elements of the array.

Example Program

```
v1=c(1,2,3)
v2=c(10,20,30,40,50,60)
A<-array(c(v1,v2),dim=c(3,3,2))#creates 2 3X3 matrix
A
B<-apply(A,c(1),sum)  # finds the row sum of all matrices
B
C<-apply(A,c(2),sum)  # finds the column sum of all matrices
C
```

Output

```
, , 1
      [,1] [,2] [,3]
[1,]    1   10   40
[2,]    2   20   50
[3,]    3   30   60
, , 2
```

```
     [,1] [,2] [,3]
[1,]    1   10   40
[2,]    2   20   50
[3,]    3   30   60
# finds the row sum of all matrices
[1] 102 144 186
# finds the column sum of all matrices
[1] 12 120 300
```

2.6.4 Array Arithmetic

We can perform arithmetic operation on arrays. To perform the arithmetic operations, we need to convert the multi-dimensional matrix into one-dimensional matrix.

Example Program

```
v1=c(1,2,3)
v2=c(10,20,30,40,50,60)
A<-array(c(v1,v2),dim=c(3,3,2))#creates 2 3X3 matrix
A
mat.A <- A[, , 1]  #retrieves first matrix
mat.B <- A[, , 2]  #retrieves second matrix
mat.A+mat.B        #addition
mat.A-mat.B        #subtraction
mat.A*mat.B        #elementary multiplication
mat.A/mat.B        #elementary division
```

Output

```
, , 1
     [,1] [,2] [,3]
[1,]    1   10   40
[2,]    2   20   50
[3,]    3   30   60
, , 2
     [,1] [,2] [,3]
[1,]    1   10   40
[2,]    2   20   50
[3,]    3   30   60
#addition
```

```
     [,1] [,2] [,3]
[1,]    2   20   80
[2,]    4   40  100
[3,]    6   60  120
#subtraction
     [,1] [,2] [,3]
[1,]    0    0    0
[2,]    0    0    0
[3,]    0    0    0
#elementary multiplication
     [,1] [,2] [,3]
[1,]    1  100 1600
[2,]    4  400 2500
[3,]    9  900 3600
#elementary division
     [,1] [,2] [,3]
[1,]    1    1    1
[2,]    1    1    1
[3,]    1    1    1
```

2.7 Factors

Factor is a data structure used for fields that takes only predefined, finite number of values or categorical data. They are used to categorize the data and store it as levels. They can store both strings and integers. They are useful in the columns which have a limited number of unique values. For example, a data field such as marital status may contain only values from single, married, separated, divorced, or widowed. In such case, we know the possible values beforehand and these predefined, distinct values are called levels. They are useful in data analysis for statistical modeling.

2.7.1 Creating Factors

We can create a factor using the function `factor()` by taking vector as input. Levels of a factor are inferred from the data if not provided. Following example illustrates how to create a factor. We can check if a variable is a factor or not, using `class()` function. Similarly, levels of a factor can be checked using the `levels()` function. The function `str()` retrieves the structure of the factor.

Example Program

```
# factor creation
x <- factor(c("single", "married", "married", "single","divorced"))
x
class(x)
```

```
levels(x)
str(x)
```

Output

```
[1] single   married  married  single   divorced
Levels: divorced married single
[1] "factor"
[1] "divorced" "married"  "single"
Factor w/ 3 levels "divorced","married",..: 3 2 2 3 1
```

Here, we can see that factor x has five elements and three levels. Factors are closely related with vectors. In fact, factors are stored as integer vectors. This is clearly seen from its structure. The levels are stored in a character vector and the individual elements are actually stored as indices.

2.7.2 Accessing Factor Components

Accessing components of a factor is very much similar to that of vectors. We can access the factor components by using integer vector or logical vector. Negative integers are used to avoid an index.

Example Program

```
x <-  factor(c("single",  "married",  "married",  "single","divorced"))#
factor creation
x
x[3]            # access 3rd element
x[c(2, 4)]      # access 2nd and 4th element
x[-1]           # access all but 1st element
x[c(TRUE, FALSE, FALSE, TRUE)] # using logical vector
```

Output

```
[1] single   married  married  single   divorced
Levels: divorced married single
# access 3rd element
[1] married
Levels: divorced married single
# access 2nd and 4th element
[1] married single
Levels: divorced married single
# access all but not 1st element
[1] married  married  single   divorced
Levels: divorced married single
```

```
# using logical vector
[1] single   single   divorced
Levels: divorced married single
```

2.7.3 Modifying Factors

Components of a factor can be modified using simple assignments. However, we cannot choose values outside of its predefined levels.

Example Program

```
# factor creation
x <- factor(c("single", "married", "married", "single","divorced"))
x
x[2] <- "divorced"      # modify second element
x
x[3] <- "widowed"       # cannot assign values outside levels
x
levels(x)<- c(levels (x)), "widowed")
#add new level
x[3]<-"widowed"
x
```

Output

```
[1] single   married  married  single   divorced
Levels: divorced married single
# modify second element
[1] single   divorced married  single   divorced
Levels: divorced married single
# cannot assign values outside levels
Warning message:
In `[<-.factor`(`*tmp*`, 3, value = "widowed") :
  invalid factor level, NA generated
[1] single   divorced <NA>     single   divorced
Levels: divorced married single
# add new level
[1] single   divorced widowed  single   divorced
Levels: divorced married single widowed
```

The order of the levels in a factor can be changed by applying the factor function again with new order of the levels.

Example Program

```
# factor creation
x <- factor(c("single", "married", "married", "single","divorced"))
x
# order of levels are changed
y<-factor(c("single","married","married", "single","divorced"),levels=c(
"single","married","divorced"))
y
```

Output

```
[1] single   married married single   divorced
Levels: divorced married single
# order of levels are changed
[1] single   married married single   divorced
Levels: single married divorced
```

We can generate factor levels by using the `gl()` function. It takes two integers as input which indicates how many levels and how many times each level. Following is the syntax of `gl()` function.

```
gl(n, k, labels)
```

where `n` is an integer giving the number of levels, `k` is an integer giving the number of replications and `labels` is a vector of labels for the resulting factor levels. Following program illustrates this.

Example Program

```
x <- gl(3,2,labels=c("single", "married","divorced"))
x
```

Output

```
[1] single  single  married married divorced divorced
Levels: single married divorced
```

2.8 Data Frames

A data frame is used for storing data tables. It is a list of vectors of equal length. A data frame is a table or a two-dimensional array-like structure in which each column contains values of one variable and each row contains one set of values from each column. Following are the characteristics of a data frame.

(a) The column names should be non-empty.

(b) The row names should be unique.

(c) The data stored in a data frame can be of numeric, factor or character type.

(d) Each column should contain same number of data items.

2.8.1 Creating Data Frames

We can create data fames using the function `data.frame()`.The top line of the table called the **header** contains the column names. Each horizontal line afterward denotes a **data row**, which begins with the name of the row, and then followed by the actual data. Each data member of a row is called a **cell**. We can get the names of the header using the function `names()`, number of rows using the function `nrow()` and number of columns using the function `ncol()`. The `length()` function returns the length of the list which is same as that of number of columns. The structure of a data frame can be retrieved using `str()` function. The statistical summary and nature of the data can be obtained by applying `summary()` function. Following example illustrates this.

Example Program

```
x<-data.frame("roll"=1:2,"name"=c("Jack","Jill"),"age"=c(20,22))
x              # data frame
names(x)       # retrieves header names
nrow(x)        # retrieves the number of rows
ncol(x)        # retrieves the number of columns
str(x)         # retrieves the structure of x
summary(x)     # retrieves the statistical summary of x
```

Output

```
# data frame
  roll name age
1    1 Jack  20
2    2 Jill  22
#retrieves header names
[1] "roll" "name" "age"
# retrieves the number of rows
[1] 2
# retrieves the number of columns
[1] 3
# retrieves the structure of x
'data.frame':   2 obs. of  3 variables:
 $ roll: int  1 2
 $ name: Factor w/ 2 levels "Jack","Jill": 1 2
 $ age : num  20 22
# retrieves the statistical summary of x
      roll          name        age
 Min.   :1.00   Jack:1   Min.   :20.0
```

```
 1st Qu.:1.25   Jill:1   1st Qu.:20.5
 Median :1.50            Median :21.0
 Mean   :1.50            Mean   :21.0
 3rd Qu.:1.75            3rd Qu.:21.5
 Max.   :2.00            Max.   :22.0
```

2.8.2 Accessing Data Frame Components

Components of data frame can be accessed like a list or like a matrix.

(a) Accessing like a List

We can use either [[or $ operator to access columns of data frame. Accessing with [[or $ is similar.

Example Program

```
x<-data.frame("roll"=1:2,"name"=c("Jack","Jill"),"age"=c(20,22))
x              # data frame
# retrieves the value for the column name "name" as list
x$name
# retrieves the value for the column name "name" as list
x[["name"]]
# retrieves the value for the third column name as list
x[[3]]
```

Output

```
# data frame
  roll name age
1    1 Jack  20
2    2 Jill  22
# retrieves the value for the column name "name" as list
[1] Jack Jill
Levels: Jack Jill
# retrieves the value for the column name "name" as list
[1] Jack Jill
Levels: Jack Jill
# retrieves the value for the third column name as list
[1] 20 22
```

(b) Accessing like a Matrix

Data frames can be accessed like a matrix by providing index for row and column. We can use the [] for indexing. This will return us a data frame unlike the other two [[and $ will reduce it into a vector. We can use the `head()` function to display first `n` rows. Negative numbers for the index are also allowed in data frames.

Example Program

```
x<-data.frame("roll"=1:3,"name"=c("Jack","Jill","Tom"),"age"
=c(20,22,23))
x                          # data frame
# retrieves the value for the column name "name"
x["name"]
# retrieves the value for first and second column
x[1:2,]
# retrieves the value for all rows and 2nd and 3rd column
x[,2:3]
# retrieves the values for 1st and 2nd row & 2nd and 3rd column
x[c(1,2),c(2,3)]
x[,-1]                     # retrieves the values except the first column
x[-1,]                     # retrieves the values except the first row
x[x$age>21,]               # retrieves the rows whose age>21
head(x,2)                  # retrieves the first two rows
```

Output

```
# data frame
  roll name age
1    1 Jack  20
2    2 Jill  22
3    3  Tom  23
# retrieves the value for the column name "name"
  name
1 Jack
2 Jill
3  Tom
# retrieves the value for first and second column
  roll name age
1    1 Jack  20
2    2 Jill  22
# retrieves the value for all rows and 2nd and 3rd column
  name age
```

```
1 Jack  20
2 Jill  22
3  Tom  23
# retrieves the values for 1st and 2nd row & 2nd and 3rd column
  name age
1 Jack  20
2 Jill  22
# retrieves the values except the first column
  name age
1 Jack  20
2 Jill  22
3  Tom  23
# retrieves the values except the first row
  roll name age
2    2 Jill  22
3    3  Tom  23
# retrieves the rows whose age>21
  roll name age
2    2 Jill  22
3    3  Tom  23
# retrieves the first two rows
  roll name age
1    1 Jack  20
2    2 Jill  22
```

2.8.3 Modifying Data Frames

Data frames can be modified like we modified matrices through reassignment.

Example Program

```
x<-data.frame("roll"=1:3,"name"=c("Jack","Jill","Tom"),"age"
=c(20,22,23))
x                    # data frame
x[1,"age"] <- 25     # modifies the first age to 25
x
```

Output

```
# data frame
  roll name age
```

```
1     1 Jack  20
2     2 Jill  22
3     3  Tom  23
# modifies the first age to 25
  roll name age
1     1 Jack  25
2     2 Jill  22
3     3  Tom  23
```

A data frame can be expanded by adding columns and rows. We can add the column vector using a new column name. Columns can also be added using the `cbind()` function. Similarly rows can be added using the `rbind()` function. Data frame columns can be deleted by assigning `NULL` to it. Similarly, rows can be deleted through reassignments.

Example Program

```
x<-data.frame("roll"=1:3,"name"=c("Jack","Jill","Tom"),"age"
=c(20,22,23))
x                    # data frame
#adding a new column bloodgroup
print(x$bloodgroup<-c("A+","B-","AB+"))
#adding a new column using cbind()
print(x<-cbind(x,city=c("Delhi","Mumbai","Chennai")))
#adding a new row using rbind()
print(x<-rbind(x,c(4,"Jack",24,"B+","Delhi")))
```

Output

```
# data frame
  roll name age
1     1 Jack  20
2     2 Jill  22
3     3  Tom  23
#adding a new column bloodgroup
[1] "A+"  "B-"  "AB+"
#adding a new column using cbind()
  roll name age bloodgroup    city
1     1 Jack  20         A+   Delhi
2     2 Jill  22         B-  Mumbai
3     3  Tom  23        AB+ Chennai
#adding a new row using rbind()
```

```
  roll name age bloodgroup    city
1    1 Jack  20         A+   Delhi
2    2 Jill  22         B-  Mumbai
3    3  Tom  23        AB+ Chennai
4    4 Jack  24         B+   Delhi
```

2.8.4 Aggregating Data

It is relatively easy to collapse data in R using one or more `by` variables and a defined function. When using the `aggregate()` function, the `by` variables must be in a list, even if there is only one column. The function can be built-in functions like `mean, max, min, sum` etc. or user provided function.

Example Program

```
y<-data.frame("roll"=1:11,
"name"=c("Jack","Jill","Jeeva","Smith","Bob","Smith","John","Mathew","C
harles","Zen","Yug"),
"age"=c(20,20,30,21,19,21,19,18,22,25,21),
"marks"=c(100,98,99,75,80,90,88,43,87,43,89))
# Data Frame Y
y
# mean marks for each age
aggdata <-aggregate(y$marks,list(m=y$age),mean)
aggdata
# max marks for each age
aggdata <-aggregate(y$marks,list(m=y$age),max)
aggdata
# sum of marks for each age
aggdata <-aggregate(y$marks,list(m=y$age),sum)
aggdata
```

Output

```
# Data Frame Y
   roll    name age marks
1     1    Jack  20   100
2     2    Jill  20    98
3     3   Jeeva  30    99
4     4   Smith  21    75
5     5     Bob  19    80
```

```
6      6   Smith  21     90
7      7    John  19     88
8      8  Mathew  18     43
9      9 Charles  22     87
10    10     Zen  25     43
11    11     Yug  21     89
# mean marks for each age
   m        x
1 18 43.00000
2 19 84.00000
3 20 99.00000
4 21 84.66667
5 22 87.00000
6 25 43.00000
7 30 99.00000
# max marks for each age
   m   x
1 18  43
2 19  88
3 20 100
4 21  90
5 22  87
6 25  43
7 30  99
# sum of marks for each age
   m   x
1 18  43
2 19 168
3 20 198
4 21 254
5 22  87
6 25  43
7 30  99
```

2.8.5 Sorting Data

To sort a data frame in R, use the `order()` function. By default, sorting is ascending. We can sort in descending order by giving the sorting variable a minus sign in front. Following program illustrates this.

Example Program

```
x<-data.frame("roll"=1:11,
"name"=c("Jack","Jill","Jeeva","Smith","Bob","Smith","John","Mathew","C
harles","Zen","Yug"),
"age"=c(20,22,30,28,30,21,19,18,25,25,29))
# Data Frame
x
# sort by name
newdata <- x[order(x$name),]
newdata
# sort by age and within sort by name
newdata <- x[order(x$age,x$name),]
newdata
#sort by name(ascending) and within age(descending)
newdata <- x[order(x$name,-x$age),]
newdata
```

Output

```
# Data Frame
   roll    name age
1     1    Jack  20
2     2    Jill  22
3     3   Jeeva  30
4     4   Smith  28
5     5     Bob  30
6     6   Smith  21
7     7    John  19
8     8  Mathew  18
9     9 Charles  25
10   10     Zen  25
11   11     Yug  29
# sort by name
   roll    name age
5     5     Bob  30
9     9 Charles  25
1     1    Jack  20
3     3   Jeeva  30
```

```
2     2     Jill  22
7     7     John  19
8     8   Mathew  18
4     4    Smith  28
6     6    Smith  21
11   11      Yug  29
10   10      Zen  25
# sort by age and within sort by name
   roll     name age
8     8   Mathew  18
7     7     John  19
1     1     Jack  20
6     6    Smith  21
2     2     Jill  22
9     9  Charles  25
10   10      Zen  25
4     4    Smith  28
11   11      Yug  29
5     5      Bob  30
3     3    Jeeva  30
#sort by name(ascending) and within age(descending)
   roll     name age
5     5      Bob  30
9     9  Charles  25
1     1     Jack  20
3     3    Jeeva  30
2     2     Jill  22
7     7     John  19
8     8   Mathew  18
4     4    Smith  28
6     6    Smith  21
11   11      Yug  29
10   10      Zen  25
```

2.8.6 Merging Data

We can merge two data frames (datasets) horizontally, by using the `merge()` function. In most cases, we can join two data frames by one or more common key variables (i.e., an inner join). There are different types of join like inner join, outer join, left outer join, right outer join and cross join.

Following are the points to be kept in mind while performing join operation.

1. An inner join of two data frames df1 and df2 returns only the rows in which the left table have matching keys in the right table.
2. An outer join of two data frames df1 and df2 returns all rows from both tables, join records from the left which have matching keys in the right table.
3. A left outer join (or simply left join) of two data frames df1 and df2 returns all rows from the left table, and any rows with matching keys from the right table.
4. A right outer join of two data frames df1 and df2 returns all rows from the right table, and any rows with matching keys from the left table.
5. A cross join of two data frames df1 and df2 returns a result set which is the number of rows in the first table multiplied by the number of rows in the second table.

Example Program

```
df1 = data.frame(CustomerId = c(1:6), Product = c(rep("Toaster", 3), rep("Radio", 3)))
df2 = data.frame(CustomerId = c(2, 4, 6), State = c(rep("Alabama", 2), rep("Ohio", 1)))
#Data Frame df1
df1
#Data Frame df2
df2
#inner join
merge(df1, df2, by = "CustomerId")
#outer join
merge(x = df1, y = df2, by = "CustomerId", all = TRUE)
#left outer join
merge(x = df1, y = df2, by = "CustomerId", all.x = TRUE)
#right outer join
merge(x = df1, y = df2, by = "CustomerId", all.y = TRUE)
#cross join
merge(x = df1, y = df2, by = NULL)
```

Output

```
#Data Frame df1
  CustomerId Product
1          1 Toaster
2          2 Toaster
3          3 Toaster
```

```
4           4   Radio
5           5   Radio
6           6   Radio
#Data Frame df2
  CustomerId   State
1          2 Alabama
2          4 Alabama
3          6    Ohio
#inner join
  CustomerId Product   State
1          2 Toaster Alabama
2          4   Radio Alabama
3          6   Radio    Ohio
#outer join
  CustomerId Product   State
1          1 Toaster    <NA>
2          2 Toaster Alabama
3          3 Toaster    <NA>
4          4   Radio Alabama
5          5   Radio    <NA>
6          6   Radio    Ohio
#left outer join
  CustomerId Product   State
1          1 Toaster    <NA>
2          2 Toaster Alabama
3          3 Toaster    <NA>
4          4   Radio Alabama
5          5   Radio    <NA>
6          6   Radio    Ohio
#right outer join
  CustomerId Product   State
1          2 Toaster Alabama
2          4   Radio Alabama
3          6   Radio    Ohio
#cross join
   CustomerId.x Product CustomerId.y   State
```

```
1           1 Toaster         2 Alabama
2           2 Toaster         2 Alabama
3           3 Toaster         2 Alabama
4           4   Radio         2 Alabama
5           5   Radio         2 Alabama
6           6   Radio         2 Alabama
7           1 Toaster         4 Alabama
8           2 Toaster         4 Alabama
9           3 Toaster         4 Alabama
10          4   Radio         4 Alabama
11          5   Radio         4 Alabama
12          6   Radio         4 Alabama
13          1 Toaster         6    Ohio
14          2 Toaster         6    Ohio
15          3 Toaster         6    Ohio
16          4   Radio         6    Ohio
17          5   Radio         6    Ohio
18          6   Radio         6    Ohio
```

The `rep()` function is used for replication of data which will be discussed in Chapter 4.

2.8.7 Reshaping Data

R provides a variety of methods for reshaping data prior to analysis. Two important functions for reshaping data are the `melt()` and `cast()` functions. These functions are available in `reshape` package. Before using these functions, make sure that the package is properly installed in our machine. We will discuss more about packages in Chapter 4. We can "melt" the data so that each row is a unique id-variable combination. Then we can "cast" the melted data into any shape we would like. Following example illustrates this.

Example Program

```
y<-data.frame("id"=c(1,2,1,2,1),"age"=c(20,20,21,21,19),
"marks1"=c(80,60,70,80,90),
"marks2"=c(100,98,99,75,80))
# Data Frame Y
y
# melting data mdata=melt(y,id=c("id","age"))
mdata=melt(y,id=c("id","age"))
```

```
mdata
#cast the melted data
#cast(data, formula, function)
#mean marks for each id
markmeans <- cast(mdata,id~variable, mean)
markmeans
#mean marks for each age
agemeans <- cast(mdata, age~variable, mean)
agemeans
```

Output

```
# Data Frame Y
  id age marks1 marks2
1  1  20    80    100
2  2  20    60     98
3  1  21    70     99
4  2  21    80     75
5  1  19    90     80
# melting data mdata=melt(y,id=c("id","age"))
   id age variable value
1   1  20   marks1    80
2   2  20   marks1    60
3   1  21   marks1    70
4   2  21   marks1    80
5   1  19   marks1    90
6   1  20   marks2   100
7   2  20   marks2    98
8   1  21   marks2    99
9   2  21   marks2    75
10  1  19   marks2    80
#cast the melted data
#cast(data, formula, function)
#mean marks for each id
  id marks1 marks2
1  1     80   93.0
2  2     70   86.5
#mean marks for each age
```

```
  age marks1 marks2
1  19     90     80
2  20     70     99
3  21     75     87
```

2.8.8 Subsetting Data

The `subset()` function is the easiest way to select variables and observations. In the following example, we select all rows that have a value of age greater than or equal to 20 or age less than 10. Similarly we select all rows with name="Smith" or name="John".

Example Program

```
x<-data.frame("roll"=1:11,
"name"=c("Jack","Jill","Jeeva","Smith","Bob","Smith","John","Mathew","C
harles","Zen","Yug"),
"age"=c(20,22,30,28,30,21,19,18,25,25,29))
# Data Frame X
x
# subset(x, age >= 25 & age < 30,select=c(roll,name,age))
newdata <- subset(x, age >= 25 & age < 30,select=c(roll,name,age))
newdata
# subset(x, name=="Smith" | name=="John",select=roll:age)
newdata <- subset(x, name=="Smith" | name=="John",select=roll:age)
newdata
```

Output

```
# Data Frame X
   roll    name age
1     1    Jack  20
2     2    Jill  22
3     3   Jeeva  30
4     4   Smith  28
5     5     Bob  30
6     6   Smith  21
7     7    John  19
8     8  Mathew  18
9     9 Charles  25
10   10     Zen  25
11   11     Yug  29
```

```
# subset(x, age >= 25 & age < 30,select=c(roll,name,age))
   roll    name age
4     4   Smith  28
9     9 Charles  25
10   10     Zen  25
11   11     Yug  29
# subset(x, name=="Smith" | name=="John",select=roll:age)
  roll   name age
4    4 Smith  28
6    6 Smith  21
7    7  John  19
```

2.9 Data Type Conversion

We can convert one data type to another data type as in any programming language. We have already seen this in basic data types of R in the beginning of this Chapter. We can convert any basic data type to numeric using the function `as.numeric()`. Similarly `as.integer()` converts to integer, `as.character()` converts to character, `as.logical()` converts to logical and `as.complex()` converts to complex data types. The following Table 2.1 illustrates the possibility of converting from one data type to another.

Table 2.1: Various Data Type Conversion

	to one long vector	to matrix	to data frame
from vector	c(x,y)	cbind(x,y) rbind(x,y)	data.frame(x,y)
from matrix	as.vector(mymatrix)		as.data.frame(mymatrix)
from data frame		as.matrix(myframe)	

2.10 Conclusion

This Chapter gives a detailed explanation of all the data types including the basic data types as well as the advanced ones. The basic data types include numeric, integer, character, logical and complex. Advanced data types include vectors, lists, matrices, arrays, factors and data frames. The operations on vectors include creating vectors, combining vectors, accessing vector elements, modifying vectors, deleting vectors, vector arithmetic & recycling, vector element sorting and how to read vectors from the terminal are illustrated with example programs. The list data structure includes various operations like creating the list, accessing list elements, updating list elements, merging lists and list to vector conversion. Another important data structure is the matrix. Various operations on matrix like creating matrices, accessing matrix elements, matrix arithmetic, matrix manipulation and matrix algebra operations are explained. The array data structure is well explained with its operations namely creating arrays, accessing array elements, array element manipulation and array arithmetic. Another important data structure is factor. Various operations on factor include factor creation, accessing factor components and modifying factors. The data structure called data frame is illustrated with its operations namely creating data frames, accessing data frame components and modifying data frames. Other operations on data frames like aggregating data, sorting data, merging data, reshaping data and subsetting data are well explained with examples. Finally, data type conversion in R is discussed. All data structures are illustrated with ample number of examples and solved programs which imparts any student an in depth knowledge in data types of R.

3 Flow Control

Decision making structures are used by the programmer to specify one or more conditions to be evaluated or tested by the program. A statement or statements need to be executed if the condition is TRUE and optionally other statements to be executed if the condition is FALSE.

3.1 Decision Making

R provides the following types of decision making statements which includes *if* statement, *if...else* statement, *nested if...else* statement, *ifelse()* function and *switch* statement.

3.1.1 *if* Statement

An *if* statement consists of a boolean expression followed by one or more statements. The syntax of *if* statement is as follows.

```
if(boolean_expression) {
   // statement(s) will execute if the boolean expression is true.
}
```

If the `boolean_expression` evaluates to `TRUE`, then the block of code inside the *if* statement will be executed. If `boolean_expression` evaluates to `FALSE`, then the first set of code after the end of *if* statement (after the closing curly brace) will be executed. Here, `boolean_expression` can be a logical or numeric vector, but only the first element is taken into consideration. In the case of numeric vector, zero is taken as `FALSE`, rest as `TRUE`. Figure 3.1 illustrates the flow chart for *if* statement.

Example Program

```
x <- 10
if(x > 0){
   cat(x,"is a positive number\n")
}
```

Output

```
10 is a positive number
```

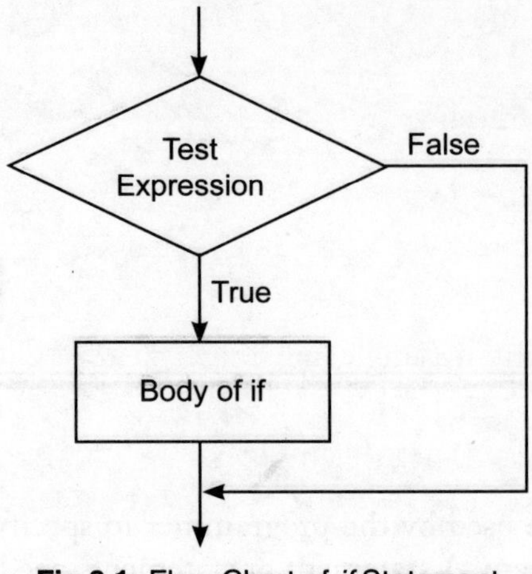

Fig.3.1: Flow Chart of *if* Statement

3.1.2 *if...else* Statement

An *if* statement can be followed by an optional *else* statement which executes when the boolean expression is `FALSE`. The syntax of *if...else* statement is as follows.

```
if(boolean_expression) {
   // statement(s) will execute if the boolean expression is true.
} else {
   // statement(s) will execute if the boolean expression is false.
}
```

If the `boolean_expression` evaluates to be `TRUE`, then *if* block of code will be executed, otherwise *else* block of code will be executed. Figure 3.2 shows the flow chart for *if...else* statement.

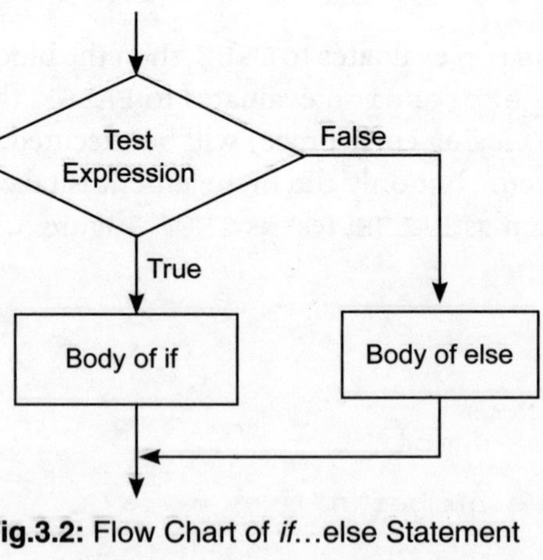

Fig.3.2: Flow Chart of *if*...else Statement

Example Program

```
x <- -5
if(x > 0){
```

```
  cat(x,"is a positive number\n")
} else {
  cat(x,"is a negative number\n")
}
```

Output

```
-5 is a negative number
```

We can write the *if…else* statement in a single line if the *if* and *else* block contains only one statement as follows.

```
if(x > 0)cat(x,"is a positive number\n") else cat(x,"is a negative number\n")
```

3.1.3 Nested *if...else* Statement

An *if* statement can be followed by an optional *else if...else* statement, which is very useful to test various conditions using single *if...else if* statement. We can nest as many *if...else* statement as we want. Only one statement will get executed depending upon the boolean_expression. The syntax for nested *if…else* is shown below.

```
if(boolean_expression 1) {
  // executes when the boolean_expression 1 is true.
} else if(boolean_expression 2) {
  // executes when the boolean_expression 2 is true.
} else if( boolean_expression 3) {
  // executes when the boolean_expression 3 is true.
} else {
  // executes when none of the above condition is true.
}
```

Example Program

```
x <-19
if (x < 0) {
  cat(x,"is a negative number")
} else if (x > 0) {
  cat(x,"is a positive number")
} else
  print("Zero")
```

Output

```
19 is a positive number
```

3.1.4 *ifelse()* Function

Most of the functions in R take vector as input and output a resultant vector. This vectorization of code, will be much faster than applying the same function to each element of the vector individually. There is an easier way to use *if...else* statement specifically for vectors in R programming. We can use *ifelse()* function instead which is the vector equivalent form of the *if...else* statement. Following is the syntax of *ifelse()* function.

```
ifelse(boolean_expression,x,y)
```

Here, `boolean_expression` must be a logical vector (or an object that can be coerced to logical). The return value is a vector with the same length as `boolean_expression`. This returned vector has element from `x` if the corresponding value of `boolean_expression` is `TRUE` or from `y` if the corresponding value of `boolean_expression` is `FALSE`. For example, the i-th element of result will be `x[i]`, if `boolean_expression[i]` is `TRUE` else it will take the value of `y[i]`. The vectors `x` and `y` are recycled whenever necessary.

Example Program

```
a = c(5,7,2,9)
ifelse(a %% 2 == 0,"even","odd")
```

Output

```
[1] "odd"  "odd"  "even" "odd"
```

In the above example, the `boolean_expression` is `a %% 2 == 0` which will result into the vector `(FALSE,FALSE,TRUE,FALSE)`. Similarly, the other two vectors in the function argument gets recycled to `("even","even","even","even")` and `("odd","odd","odd","odd")` respectively. Hence the result is evaluated accordingly.

3.1.5 *switch* Statement

A *switch* statement allows a variable to be tested for equality against a list of values. Each value is called a case, and the variable being switched on is checked for each case. The basic syntax for creating a switch statement in R is as follows.

```
switch(expression, case1, case2, case3....)
```

If the value of expression is not a character string, it is coerced to integer. We can have any number of case statements within a switch. Each case is followed by the value to be compared to and a colon. If the value of the integer is between 1 and nargs()–1 (the max number of arguments) then the corresponding element of case condition is evaluated and the result is returned.

If expression evaluates to a character string then that string is matched (exactly) to the names of the elements. If there is more than one match, the first matching element is returned. No default argument is available.

Example Program

```
switch(2,"red","green","blue")
switch("color", "color" = "red", "shape" = "square", "length" = 5)
```

Output

```
[1] "green"
[1] "red"
```

If the value evaluated is a number, that item of the list is returned. In the above example, `"red","green","blue"` form a three item list. The `switch()` function returns the corresponding item to the numeric value evaluated. In the above example, `green` is returned. The result of the statement can be a string as well. In this case, the matching named item's value is returned. In the above example, `"color"` is the string that is matched and its value `"red"` is returned.

3.2 Loops

In general, statements are executed sequentially. The first statement in a function is executed first, followed by the second, and so on. Loops are used in programming to repeat a specific block of code. R provides various looping structures like *for* loop, *while* loop and *repeat* loop.

3.2.1 *for* Loop

A *for* loop is a repetition control structure that allow us to efficiently write a loop that needs to execute a specific number of times. A *for* loop is used to iterate over a vector in R programming. The syntax of *for* loop is as follows.

```
for (value in sequence) {
   statements
}
```

Here, `sequence` is a vector and `value` takes on each of its value during the loop. In each iteration, `statements` are evaluated. Figure 3.3 shows the flow chart of a *for* loop.

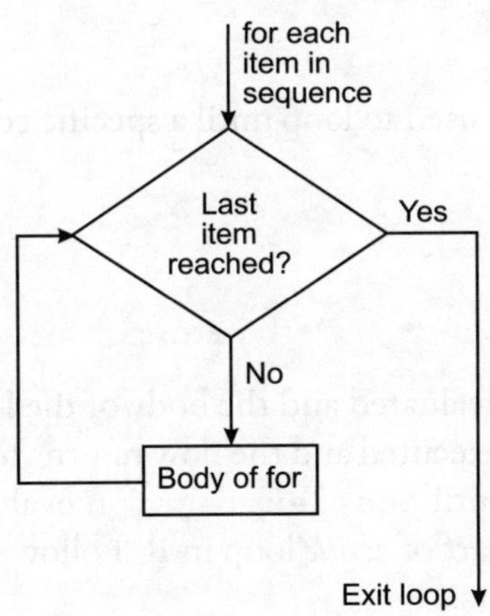

Fig.3.3: Flow Chart of *for* Loop

The following program illustrates the working of *for* loop to count the number of even numbers from a vector.

Example Program

```
x <- c(2,5,3,9,8,11,6)
count <- 0
for (val in x) {
    if(val %% 2 == 0)  count = count+1
}
cat("No: of even numbers in", x,"is", count,"\n")
```

Output

```
No: of even numbers in 2 5 3 9 8 11 6 is 3
```

The *for* loop in R is flexible that they are not limited to integers in the input. We can pass character vectors, logical vectors, lists or expressions. Following program illustrates this.

Example Program

```
v<-c("a","e","i","o","u")
for(vowel in v) print(vowel)
```

Output

```
[1] "a"
[1] "e"
[1] "i"
[1] "o"
[1] "u"
```

3.2.2 *while* Loop

In R programming, while loops are used to loop until a specific condition is met. The syntax of *while* loop is as follows.

```
while (test_expression)
{statement
}
```

Here, `test_expression` is evaluated and the body of the loop is entered if the result is `TRUE`. The statements inside the loop are executed and the flow returns to evaluate the `test_expression` again. This is repeated each time until `test_expression` evaluates to `FALSE`, in which case, the loop exits. Figure 3.4 is the flow chart of *while* loop in R. Following program illustrates how to find the sum of first five natural numbers.

Example Program

```
# sum of first 5 natural numbers
num = 5
sum = 0
```

```
# use while loop to iterate until zero
while(num > 0) {
        sum = sum + num
        num = num - 1
       }
cat("The sum is", sum,"\n")
```

Output

```
The sum is 15
```

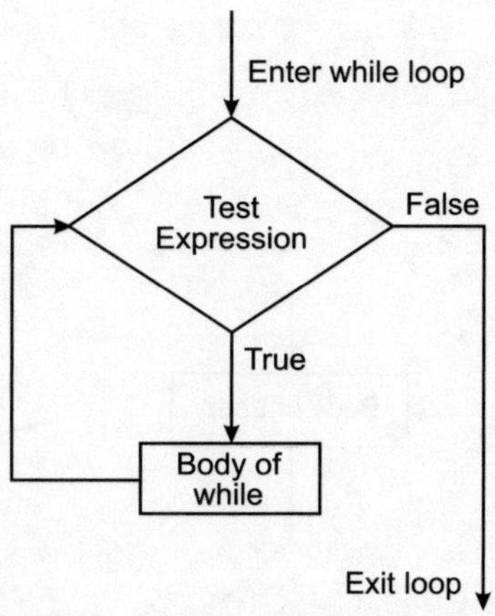

Fig.3.4: Flow Chart of *while* Loop

3.2.3 *repeat* Loop

A *repeat* loop is used to iterate over a block of code multiple number of times. There is no condition check in *repeat* loop to exit the loop. We must ourselves put a condition explicitly inside the body of the loop and use the *break* statement to exit the loop. Otherwise it will result in an infinite loop. *break* statement will be discussed in the next Section. Following is the syntax of *repeat* loop. Figure 3.5 shows the flow chart of *repeat* loop.

```
repeat {
   statements
if(condition) {
      break
   }
}
```

Example Program

```
#prints numbers from 1 to 5
x <- 1
```

```
repeat {
   print(x)
   x = x+1
   if (x > 5){
        break
   }
}
```

Output

```
[1] 1
[1] 2
[1] 3
[1] 4
[1] 5
```

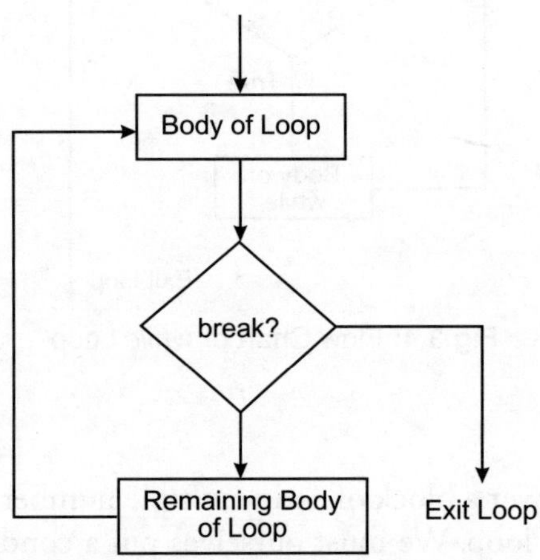

Fig.3.5: Flow Chart of *repeat* Loop

3.3 Loop Control Statements

Loop control statements are also known as jump statements. Loop control statements change execution from its normal sequence. When execution leaves a scope, all automatic objects that were created in that scope are destroyed. The loop control statements in R are *break* statement and *next* statement.

3.3.1 *break* Statement

A *break* statement is used inside a loop (repeat, for, while) to stop the iterations and flow the control outside of the loop. In a nested looping situation, where there is a loop inside another loop, this statement exits from the innermost loop that is being evaluated. Figure 3.6 shows the flow chart of *break* statement. The syntax of *break* statement is as follows.

```
break
```

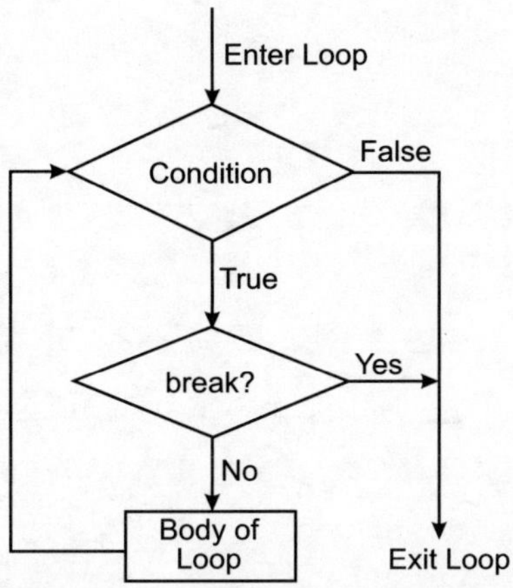

Fig.3.6: Flow Chart of *break* Statement

Example Program

```
x <- 1:10
for (val in x) {
    if (val == 3){
        break
    }
    print(val)
}
```

Output

```
[1] 1
[1] 2
```

In the above example, we iterate over the vector x, which has consecutive numbers from 1 to 10.

Inside the *for* loop we have used an if condition to break if the current value is equal to 3. We can see from the output that the loop terminates when it encounters the *break* statement.

3.3.2 *next* Statement

A *next* statement is useful when we want to skip the current iteration of a loop without terminating it. On encountering *next*, the R parser skips further evaluation and starts next iteration of the loop. Figure 3.7 shows the flow chart of *next* statement. This is equivalent to the *continue* statement in C, Java and Python. The syntax of *next* statement is as follows.

```
next
```

Example Program

```
x <- 1:10
for (val in x) {
```

```
    if (val == 3){
        next
    }
    print(val)
}
```

Output

```
[1] 1
[1] 2
[1] 4
[1] 5
[1] 6
[1] 7
[1] 8
[1] 9
[1] 10
```

In the above example, we use the *next* statement inside a condition to check if the value is equal to 3. If the value is equal to 3, the current evaluation stops (value is not printed) but the loop continues with the next iteration.

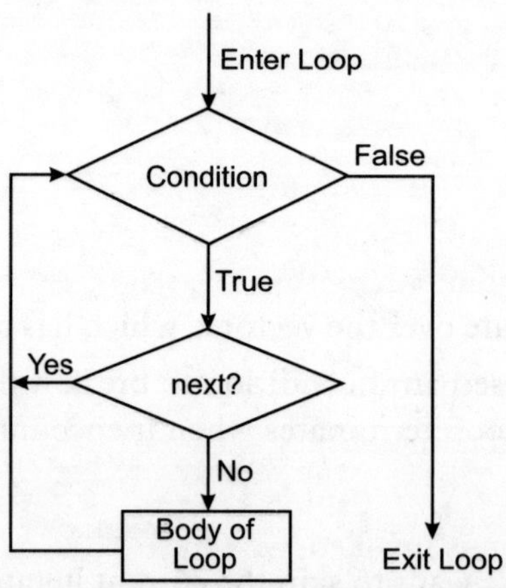

Fig.3.7: Flow Chart of *next* Statement

3.4 Conclusion

This Chapter focuses on decision making, loops and loop control statements. Decision making statements include *if* statement, *if...else* statement, nested *if...else* statement, *ifelse()* function and *switch* statement. Looping structures are explained in detail which includes *for* loop, *while* loop and *repeat* loop. The loop control statements namely *break* and *next* are also explained in this Chapter. All sections have ample number of examples and solved programs.

4 Functions & Packages

Functions are used to logically break our code into simpler parts which become easy to maintain and understand. A function is a set of statements organized together to perform a specific task. R has a large number of built-in functions and the user can create their own functions. A function is an object, with or without arguments. The function in turn performs its task and returns control to the interpreter as well as any result which may be stored in other objects.

4.1 Function Definition

The reserved word `function` is used to declare a function in R. Following is the syntax of function definition.

```
func_name <- function (argument) {
   statement
}
```

Here, we can see that the reserved word `function` is used to declare a function in R. The statements within the curly braces form the body of the function. These braces are optional if the body contains only a single expression. Finally, this function object is given a name by assigning it to a variable, `func_name`. The statements within the curly braces form the body of the function. These braces are optional if the body contains only a single expression.

Following are the components of a function in R.

Function name – This is the actual name of the function. It is stored in R environment as an object with this name.

Arguments – When a function is invoked, we can pass values to the argument. Arguments are optional. A function may or may not contain arguments. The arguments can also have default values.

Function body – The function body contains a collection of statements that defines what the function does.

4.2 Function Calling

We can create user-defined functions in R. They are specific to what a user wants and once created they can be used like built-in functions. Following is an example which shows how to create a function and how to call a function in R.

Example Program

```
#function to print x raised to the power y
power <- function(x,y) {
   result <- x^y
   cat(x,"raised to the power", y, "is", result,"\n")
                          }
#Function Calling
power(2,3)
```

Output

```
2 raised to the power 3 is 8
```

Here, the arguments used in the function declaration x and y are called formal arguments and those used while calling the function are called actual arguments.

4.2.1 Function without Arguments

It is possible to create a function in R without arguments. Following program illustrates this.

Example Program

```
#function to print the square of numbers from 1 to 5
square <- function() {
   for (i in 1:5) cat("Square of",i,"is",(i*i) ,"\n")
                      }
#Function Calling
square()
```

Output

```
Square of 1 is 1
Square of 2 is 4
Square of 3 is 9
Square of 4 is 16
Square of 5 is 25
```

4.2.2 Function with Named Arguments

In the above function call in Section 4.2, the argument matching of formal arguments to the actual arguments takes place in positional order. This means that, in the call `power(8,2)`, the formal arguments x and y are assigned 8 and 2 respectively. We can also call the function using named arguments.

When calling a function in this way, the order of the actual arguments doesn't matter or we can pass the arguments in a shuffled order. For example, all the function calls given below are equivalent.

Example Program

```
power(2,3)
power(x=2,y=3)
power(y=3,x=2)
```

Output

```
2 raised to the power 3 is 8
2 raised to the power 3 is 8
2 raised to the power 3 is 8
```

Further we can use named and unnamed arguments in a single function call. In such case, all the named arguments are matched first and then the remaining unnamed arguments are matched in a positional order.

Example Program

```
power(x=2,3)
power(2,y=3)
```

Output

```
2 raised to the power 3 is 8
2 raised to the power 3 is 8
```

4.2.3 Function with Default Arguments

We can assign default values to arguments in a function in R. This is done by providing an appropriate value to the formal argument in the function declaration. The function named `power` discussed above is defined with a default value for `y` in the following example program. If no value is passed for `y`, then the default value is taken. If a value is passed for `y`, then the default value will be overridden.

Example Program

```
#function to print x raised to the power y
power <- function(x,y=2) {
   result <- x^y
   cat(x,"raised to the power", y, "is", result,"\n")
                              }
#Function Calling
power(2)
power(2,3)
```

Output

```
2 raised to the power 2 is 4
2 raised to the power 3 is 8
```

4.3 Built-in Functions

There are several built-in functions available in R. These functions can be directly used in user written programs. The built-in functions can be grouped into mathematical functions, character functions, statistical functions, probability functions, date functions, time functions and other useful functions. We will see one by one.

4.3.1 Mathematical Functions

Some of the commonly used mathematical functions and their purpose are illustrated with examples.

1. **`abs()`** - This function computes the absolute value of numeric data. The syntax is `abs(x)`, where `x` is any numeric value, array or vector.

   Example Program

```
abs(-1)
abs(20)
#Absolute value of vector
x <- c(-2,4,0,45,9,-4)
abs(x)
#Matrix x
x <- matrix(c(-3,5,-7,1,-9,4),nrow=3,ncol=2,byrow=TRUE)
x
#Absolute value of first row
abs(x[1,])
#Absolute value of first column
abs(x[,1])
```

   Output

```
[1] 1
[1] 20
#Absolute value of vector
[1] 2 4 0 45 9 4
#Matrix x
     [,1] [,2]
[1,]   -3    5
[2,]   -7    1
[3,]   -9    4
#Absolute value of first row
[1] 3 5
#Absolute value of first column
```

```
abs(x[,1])
[1] 3 7 9
```

2. **`sin(),cos() and tan()`**-The function `sin()` computes the sine value, `cos()` computes the cosine value and `tan()` computes the tangent value of numeric data in radians. The syntax is `sin(x)`, `cos(x)` and `tan(x)` where `x` is any numeric value, array or vector.

Example Program

```
sin(10)
cos(90)
tan(50)
x <- c(-2,4,0,45,9,-4)
#sin value of vector
sin(x)
#cosine value of vector
cos(x)
#tangent value of vector
tan(x)
#Matrix x
x <- matrix(c(-3,5,-7,1,-9,4),nrow=3,ncol=2,byrow=TRUE)
x
#sin value of first row
sin(x[1,])
#cos value of first row
cos(x[1,])
#tan value of first row
tan(x[1,])
```

Output

```
[1] -0.5440211
[1] -0.4480736
[1] -0.2719006
#sin value of vector
[1] -0.9092974 -0.7568025  0.0000000  0.8509035  0.4121185  0.7568025
#cosine value of vector
[1] -0.4161468 -0.6536436  1.0000000  0.5253220 -0.9111303 -0.6536436
#tangent value of vector
[1] 2.1850399 1.1578213 0.0000000 1.6197752 -0.4523157 -1.1578213
#Matrix x
     [,1] [,2]
[1,]   -3    5
```

```
[2,]   -7    1
[3,]   -9    4
#sin value of first row
[1] -0.1411200 -0.9589243
#cos value of first row
[1] -0.9899925 0.2836622
#tan value of first row
[1] 0.1425465 -3.3805150
```

3. **`asin(), acos() and atan()`** - The function `asin()` computes the inverse sine value of numeric data in radians. The syntax is `sin(x)`, where `x` is any numeric value, array or vector. Similarly the function `acos()` computes the inverse cosine value of numeric data in radians and `atan()` computes the inverse tangent value of numeric data in radians.

   Example Program

   ```
   asin(1)
   acos(1)
   atan(50)
   ```

   Output

   ```
   [1] 1.570796
   [1] 0
   [1] 1.550799
   ```

4. **`exp(x)`** - This function computes the exponential value of a number or number vector, e^x.

   Example Program

   ```
   x=5
   exp(x)
   x<-c(1,2,3)
   exp(x)
   ```

   Output

   ```
   [1] 148.4132
   [1] 2.718282 7.389056 20.085537
   ```

5. **`ceiling()`** – This function returns the smallest integer larger than the parameter. The syntax is `ceiling(x)` where `x` is a numeric variable or vector.

   Example Program

   ```
   x <- 2.5
   ceiling(x)
   x <- c(3.5, 2.67, 6.2)
   ceiling(x)
   ```

Output

```
[1] 3
[1] 4 3 7
```

6. **`floor()`** – This function returns the largest integer not greater than the giving number. The syntax is `floor(x)` where `x` is numeric variable or a vector.

   Example Program

   ```
   x <- 2.5
   floor(x)
   x <- c(3.5, 2.67, 6.2)
   floor(x)
   ```

   Output

   ```
   [1] 2
   [1] 3 2 6
   ```

7. **`round()`** - This function returns the integer rounded to the giving number. The syntax is `round(x, digits=n)` where `x` is numeric variable or a vector and `digit` specifies the number of digits to be rounded.

   Example Program

   ```
   x <- 2.5878888
   round(x,3)
   x <- c(3.509899, 2.67231, 6.299982)
   round(x,2)
   ```

   Output

   ```
   [1] 2.588
   [1] 3.51 2.67 6.30
   ```

8. **`trunc()`** - This function returns the integer truncated with decimal part. The syntax is `trunc(x)` where `x` is numeric variable or a vector.

   Example Program

   ```
   x <- 2.99
   trunc(x)
   x <- c(3.509899, 2.67231, 6.299982)
   trunc(x)
   ```

   Output

   ```
   [1] 2
   [1] 3 2 6
   ```

9. **`signif(x,digits=n)`** - This function rounds the values in its first argument to the specified number of significant digits. The syntax is `signif(x, digits=n)` where `x` is numeric variable or a vector and `digit` specifies the number of significant digits.

Example Program

```
x <- 2.5878888
signif(x,3)
x <- c(3.509899, 2.67231, 6.299982)
signif(x,2)
```

Output

```
[1] 2.59
[1] 3.5 2.7 6.3
```

10. **`sqrt()`** - This function computes the square root of a numeric vector. The syntax is `sqrt(x)` where `x` is numeric, complex vector or array.

Example Program

```
x <- 25
sqrt(x)
x <- c(9, 64, 81)
sqrt(x)
```

Output

```
[1] 5
[1] 3 8 9
```

11. **`log()`, `log10()`, `log2()`, `log(x, b)`** - `log()` function computes natural logarithms for a number or vector. `log10()` computes common logarithms with base 10. `log2()` computes binary logarithms or logarithms with base 2. `log(x,b)` computes logarithms with base `b`.

Example Program

```
#Natural Logarithm of 5
log(5)
#Logarithm to Base 10 of 5
log10(5)
#Logarithm to Base 2 of 5
log2(5)
#Logarithm to Base 3 of 5
log(5,base=3)
x<-c(10,20,30)
```

```
#Natural Logarithm
log(x)
#Logarithm to Base 10
log10(x)
#Logarithm to Base 2
log2(x)
#Logarithm to Base 3
log(x,base=3)
```

Output

```
#Natural Logarithm of 5
[1] 1.609438
#Logarithm to Base 10 of 5
[1] 0.69897
#Logarithm to Base 2 of 5
[1] 2.321928
#Logarithm to Base 3 of 5
[1] 1.464974
#Natural Logarithm
[1] 2.302585 2.995732 3.401197
#Logarithm to Base 10
[1] 1.000000 1.301030 1.477121
#Logarithm to Base 2
[1] 3.321928 4.321928 4.906891
#Logarithm to Base 3
[1] 2.095903 2.726833 3.095903
```

12. **`max()` and `min()`** - `max()` function computes the maximum value of a vector and `min()` function computes the minimum value of a vector.

Example Program

```
x<-c(10,289,-100,8000)
#Maximum value
max(x)
#Minimum value
min(x)
```

Output

```
#Maximum value
```

```
[1] 8000
#Minimum value
[1] -100
```

13. **`beta()` and `lbeta()`** - `beta()` function returns the beta value and `lbeta()` function returns the natural logarithm of the beta function. Beta function is calculated as follows. `B(a,b) = Γ(a)Γ(b)/Γ(a+b)`. The syntax is `beta(a,b)` and `lbeta(a,b)` where `a,b` are non-negative numeric vectors.

Example Program

```
beta(4,9)
lbeta(4,9)
x <- c(3,6, 4)
y <- c(7,4, 12)
beta(x,y)
```

Output

```
[1] 0.0005050505
[1] -7.590852
[1] 0.0039682540 0.0019841270 0.0001831502
```

14. **`gamma()`** - This function returns the gamma function `Γx`. The syntax is `gamma(x)` where `x` is a numeric vector.

Example Program

```
x=5
gamma(x)
x<-c(1,2,3)
gamma(x)
```

Output

```
[1] 24
[1] 1 1 2
```

15. **`factorial()`** - This function computes factorial of a number or a numeric vector. The syntax is `factorial(x)` where `x` is a number or numeric vector.

Example Program

```
x=5
factorial(x)
x<-c(1,2,3,4)
factorial(x)
```

Output

```
[1] 120
[1] 1 2 6 24
```

4.3.2 Character Functions

These functions are used for string handling operations like extracting characters from a string, extracting substrings from a string, concatenation of strings, matching strings, inserting strings, converting strings from one case to another and so on. The following illustrates each function with examples.

1. **`agrep()`** - This function searches for approximate matches to pattern within each element of the string. The syntax is as follows.

   ```
   agrep(pattern, x, ignore.case=FALSE, value=FALSE, max.distance=0.1, useBytes=FALSE)
   ```

   where `pattern` is the string to be matched, `x` is the string vector, `ignore.case`: if `TRUE`, ignore case, `value`: if `TRUE`, return the matching elements vector, else return the indices vector, `max.distance` is the maximum distance allowed for a match (expressed either as integer, or as a fraction of the pattern length times the maximal transformation cost) and `useBytes`: should the comparison be character-by-character (the default) or byte-by-byte.

   Example Program

   ```
   x <- c("R language","and","SAND")
   agrep("an",x)
   agrep("an",x, ignore.case=TRUE)
   agrep("uag",x, ignore.case=TRUE)
   agrep("uag",x, ignore.case=TRUE, max=1)
   agrep("uag",x, ignore.case=TRUE, max=2)
   ```

   Output

   ```
   [1] 1 2
   [1] 1 2 3
   [1] 1
   [1] 1
   [1] 1 2 3
   ```

2. **`char.expand()`** - This function seeks for a unique match of its first argument among the elements of its second. If successful, it returns this element; otherwise, it performs an action specified by the third argument. The syntax is as follows.

   ```
   char.expand(input, target, nomatch = stop("no match"), warning())
   ```

   where `input` is the character string to be expanded, `target` is the character vector with the values to be matched against, `nomatch` is an R expression to be evaluated in case expansion was not possible and `warning` function prints the warning message in case there is no match. The match string searches only in the beginning.

Example Program

```
x <- c("sand","and","land")
char.expand("an",x,warning("no expand"))
char.expand("a",x,warning("no expand"))
char.expand("xx",x,warning("no expand"))
```

Output

```
[1] "and"
[1] "and"
[1] NA
Warning message:
In eval(nomatch) : no expand
```

In the below example both "an" and "a" begins only in the string "and", even though sand and land contains the string "and".

3. **`charmatch()`** - This function finds matches between two arguments and returns the index position. Following is the syntax

```
charmatch(x, table, nomatch = NA_integer_)
```

where `x` gives the values to be matched, `table` gives the values to be matched against and `nomatch` gives the (integer) value to be returned at non-matching positions.

Example Program

```
charmatch("an",c("and","sand"))
charmatch("an",c("end","and","sand"))
charmatch("an","sand")
```

Output

```
[1] 1
[1] 2
[1] NA
```

4. **`charToRaw()`** - This function converts character to ASCII or "raw" objects. Following is the syntax of this function.

```
charToRaw(x)
```

where `x` is the character to be converted.

Example Program

```
x <- charToRaw("a")
x
```

```
y<-charToRaw("AB")
y
```

Output

```
[1] 61
[1] 41 42
```

5. **`chartr()`** - This function is used for character substitutions. Following is the syntax of this function.

   `chartr(old, new, x)`

   where `old` is the old string to be substituted, `new` is the new string and `x` is the target string.

   Example Program

```
x <- "apples are red"
x
chartr("a","g",x)
```

   Output

```
[1] "apples are red"
[1] "gpples gre red"
```

6. **`dQuote()`** - This function is used for putting double quote on a text. The syntax is `dQoute(x)` where `x` is the string.

   Example Program

```
x <- '2013-06-12 19:18:05'
dQuote(x)
```

   Output

```
[1] ""2013-06-12 19:18:05""
```

7. **`format()`** - Numbers and strings can be formatted to a specific style using `format()` function. The basic syntax for `format()` function is as follows.

```
format(x, digits, nsmall, scientific, width, justify = c("left",
"right", "centre", "none"))
```

   where `x` is the vector input, `digits` is the total number of digits displayed, `nsmall` is the minimum number of digits to the right of the decimal point, `scientific` is set to `TRUE` to display scientific notation, `width` indicates the minimum width to be displayed by padding blanks in the beginning and `justify` is the display of the string to `left, right or center.`

   Example Program

```
result <- format(23.123456789, digits = 9)
```

```
print(result)
# Display numbers in scientific notation.
result <- format(c(6, 13.14521), scientific = TRUE)
print(result)
# The minimum number of digits to the right of the decimal point.
result <- format(23.47, nsmall = 5)
print(result)
# Format treats everything as a string.
result <- format(6)
print(result)
# Numbers are padded with blank in the beginning for width.
result <- format(13.7, width = 6)
print(result)
# Left justify strings.
result <- format("Hello", width = 8, justify = "l")
print(result)
# Justfy string with center.
result <- format("Hello", width = 8, justify = "c")
print(result)
```

Output

```
[1] "23.1234568"
[1] "6.000000e+00" "1.314521e+01"
[1] "23.47000"
[1] "6"
[1] "  13.7"
[1] "Hello   "
[1] " Hello  "
```

8. **gsub()** – This function replaces all matches of a string, if the parameter is a string vector, returns a string vector of the same length and with the same attributes (after possible coercion to character). Elements of string vectors which are not substituted will be returned unchanged (including any declared encoding). Following is the syntax.

   ```
   gsub(pattern, replacement, x, ignore.case = FALSE)
   ```

   where `pattern` is the string to be matched, `replacement` is the string for replacement, `x` is the string or string vector and `ignore.case`: if `TRUE`, ignores case.

   Example Program

   ```
   x <- "apples are red"
   gsub("are","were",x)
   ```

Output

```
[1] "apples were red"
```

9. **`nchar()& nzchar()`** – This function determines the size of each elements of a character vector. `nzchar()` tests whether elements of a character vector are non-empty strings. The syntax of both the functions are as follows.

```
nchar(x, type = "chars", allowNA = FALSE)
nzchar(x)
```

where `x` is a character vector, `type` is `bytes, chars` or `width` and `allowNA` is a logical value which determines whether `NA` be returned for invalid multibyte strings or "bytes"-encoded strings rather than throwing an error.

Example Program

```
x <- c("red","green","blue","")
x
nchar(x)
nzchar(x)
```

Output

```
[1] "red" "green" "blue"  ""
[1] 3 5 4 0
[1] TRUE TRUE TRUE FALSE
```

10. **`noquote()`** – This function prints out strings without quotes. The syntax is `noquote(x)` where `x` is a character vector.

Example Program

```
letters
noquote(letters)
```

Output

```
[1] "a" "b" "c" "d" "e" "f" "g" "h" "i" "j" "k" "l" "m" "n" "o" "p"
"q" "r" "s"
[20] "t" "u" "v" "w" "x" "y" "z"
[1] a b c d e f g h i j k l m n o p q r s t u v w x y z
```

11. **`paste()`** – Strings in R are combined using the `paste() function.` It can take any number of string arguments to be combined together. The syntax for `paste()` function is as follows.

```
paste(..., sep = " ", collapse = NULL)
```

where ... represents any number of arguments to be combined, `sep` represents any separator between the arguments. It is optional. `collapse` is used to eliminate the space in between two strings but not the space within two words of one string.

Example Program

```
a <- "Hello,"
b <- 'Good Morning'
c <- "Everyone! "
print(paste(a,b,c))
print(paste(a,b,c, sep = "-"))
print(paste(a,b,c, sep = "", collapse = ""))
```

Output

```
[1] "Hello, Good Morning Everyone! "
[1] "Hello,-Good Morning-Everyone! "
[1] "Hello,Good MorningEveryone! "
```

12. **replace()** - This function replaces the values in `x` with indices given in `list` by those given in values. If necessary, the values in `values` are recycled. Following is the syntax for this function.

    `replace(x, list, values)`

    where `x` is a vector, `list` is the collection of indices and `values` are the replacement values.

Example Program

```
x <- c("green","red","yellow")
x
y <- replace(x,1,"black")
y
y <- replace(x,c(1,2),c("blue","white"))
y
```

Output

```
[1] "green"  "red"    "yellow"
[1] "black"  "red"    "yellow"
[1] "blue"   "white"  "yellow"
```

13. **sQuote()** - This function is used for putting single quote on a text. The syntax is `sQoute(x)` where `x` is the string.

Example Program

```
x <- "2013-06-12 19:18:05"
sQuote(x)
```

Output

```
[1] "'2013-06-12 19:18:05'"
```

14. **`strsplit()`** - This function splits the elements of a character vector x into substrings according to the matches to substring split within them. Following is the syntax of this function.

    `strsplit(x, split)`

    where `x` is a character vector, `split` is the separator.

Example Program

```
x <- "apples are red cherries are red"
strsplit(x," ")
y <- strsplit(x,"are")
y
```

Output

```
[[1]]
[1] "apples"   "are"      "red"      "cherries" "are"      "red"
[[1]]
[1] "apples "           " red cherries " " red"
```

15. **`substr()`** - This function extracts or replace substrings in a character vector. Following is the syntax for this function.

    `substr(x, start, stop)`

    `substr(x, start, stop) <- value`

    where `x` is the character vector, `start` is an integer which gives the index of the first element to be replaced, `stop` is an integer which gives the last element to be replaced and `value` is a character vector, recycled if necessary.

Example Program

```
substr("programming",2,3)
x=c("red","blue","green","yellow")
substr(x,2,3)
substr(x,2,3)<-"gh"
x
```

Output

```
[1] "ro"
[1] "ed" "lu" "re" "el"
[1] "rgh"    "bghe"   "gghen"   "yghlow"
```

16. **`tolower()`** - This function converts string to its lower case. Following is the syntax of this function.

    `tolower(x)` where `x` is a character vector.

Example Program

```
tolower("R PROGRAMMING")
```

```
x <- c("GREEN", "Red", "Black")
tolower(x)
```

Output

```
[1] "r programming"
[1] "green" "red"   "black"
```

17. **`toString()`** – This function produces a single character string describing an R object. The syntax is as follows.

```
toString(x)
toString(x, width = NULL)
```

where `x` is an R object and width is the suggestion for the maximum field width. Values of `NULL` or `0` indicate no maximum. The minimum value accepted is 6 and smaller values are taken as 6.

Example Program

```
x <- c("Green", "Red", "Black")
toString(x)
toString(x,width=5)
toString(x,width=12)
```

Output

```
[1] "Green, Red, Black"
[1] "Gr...."
[1] "Green, R...."
```

18. **`toupper()`** – This function converts string to its upper case. Following is the syntax of this function.

`toupper(x)` where `x` is a character vector.

Example Program

```
toupper("r programming")
x <- c("GREEN", "Red", "Black")
toupper(x)
```

Output

```
[1] "R PROGRAMMING"
[1] "GREEN" "RED" "BLACK"
```

4.3.3 Statistical Functions

Statistical analysis in R is performed by using many in-built functions. Most of these functions are part of the R base package. These functions take R vector as an input along with the arguments and give the result. We will discuss some of the basic and frequently used statistical functions here. Rest of the functions for distributions, regression and advanced statistics will be discussed in Chapter 6 and 7.

1. **`mean()`** -It is calculated by taking the sum of the values and dividing with the number of values in a data series. The function `mean()` is used to calculate average or mean in R. The syntax for calculating mean is `mean(x, trim = 0, na.rm = FALSE)` where x is the input vector, `trim` is used to drop some observations from both end of the sorted vector and `na.rm` is used to remove the missing values from the input vector.

   Example Program

   ```
   x<-c(10,2,30,4,5,6,70,8,9,10)
   y<-c(1,2,3,4,5,NA)
   #Mean of x
   mean(x)
   #Mean of x with trim attribute
   mean(x,trim=0.2)
   #Mean of y with na.rm attribute
   mean(y,na.rm=TRUE)
   ```

   Output

   ```
   #Mean of x
   [1] 15.4
   #Mean of x with trim attribute
   [1] 8
   #Mean of y with na.rm attribute
   [1] 3
   ```

   In the above example, when the `trim` attribute is given as 0.2, it will remove 2 elements from both ends and mean will be calculated using the rest of the elements. If there are missing values, then the mean function returns NA. To drop the missing values from the calculation, use `na.rm = TRUE` which remove the NA values.

2. **`median()`** -The middle most value in a data series is called the median. The `median()` function is used in R to calculate this value. The syntax for calculating median in R is `median(x, na.rm = FALSE)`, where x is the input vector, `na.rm` is used to remove the missing values from the input vector.

   Example Program

   ```
   x<-c(10,2,30,2,5,8,70,8,9,2)
   y<-c(3,2,3,4,5,NA)
   #Median of x
   median(x)
   ```

```
#Median of y with na.rm attribute
median(y,na.rm=TRUE)
```

Output

```
#Median of x
[1] 8
#Median of y with na.rm attribute
[1] 3
```

3. **var()** - The function `var()` returns the estimated variance of the population from which the numbers in vector x are sampled. The syntax for calculating variance in R is `var(x, na.rm = FALSE)`, where x is the input vector, `na.rm` is used to remove the missing values from the input vector.

   Example Program

```
x<-c(10,2,30,2,5,8,70,8,9,2)
y<-c(3,2,3,4,5,NA)
#Variance of x
var(x)
#Variance of y with na.rm attribute
var(y,na.rm=TRUE)
```

Output

```
#Variance of x
[1] 446.0444
#Variance of y with na.rm attribute
[1] 1.3
```

4. **sd()** - The function `sd()` returns the estimated standard deviation of the population from which the numbers in vector x are sampled. The syntax for calculating standard deviation in R is `sd(x, na.rm = FALSE)`, where x is the input vector, `na.rm` is used to remove the missing values from the input vector.

   Example Program

```
x<-c(10,2,30,2,5,8,70,8,9,2)
y<-c(3,2,3,4,5,NA)
#Standard Deviation of x
sd(x)
#Standard Deviation of y with na.rm attribute
sd(y,na.rm=TRUE)
```

Output

```
#Standard Deviation of x
```

```
[1] 21.11976
#Standard Deviation of y with na.rm attribute
[1] 1.140175
```

5. **`scale()`** – The function `scale(x,center=TRUE,scale=TRUE)` returns the standard scores (z-scores) for the numbers in vector `x`. This is used for standardizing a matrix.

Example Program

```
x<-matrix(1:9,3,3)
x
#scale(x)
scale(x)
```

Output

```
     [,1] [,2] [,3]
[1,]    1    4    7
[2,]    2    5    8
[3,]    3    6    9
#scale(x)
     [,1] [,2] [,3]
[1,]   -1   -1   -1
[2,]    0    0    0
[3,]    1    1    1
attr(,"scaled:center")
[1] 2 5 8
attr(,"scaled:scale")
[1] 1 1 1
```

6. **`sum()`** – This function adds up all elements of a vector. The syntax is `sum(x)`, where `x` is a numeric vector.

Example Program

```
sum(c(1:10))
sum(c(1,2,3,4,5))
```

Output

```
[1] 55
[1] 15
```

7. **`diff(x, lag=1)`** – This function returns suitably lagged and iterated differences. The syntax is `diff(x, lag, differences)` where `x` is a numeric vector or matrix containing the values to be differenced, `lag` is an integer indicating which lag to use and `differences` is an integer indicating the order of the difference. For example, if `lag = 2`, the differences between

the third and the first value, between the fourth and the second value, between the fifth and the third value etc. are calculated. The attribute differences returns the differences of differences.

Example Program

```
diff(c(5,20,14,4,2,10,19))
diff(c(5,20,14,4,2,10,19),lag=2)
diff(c(5,20,14,4,2,10,19),differences=2)
```

Output

```
[1] 15 -6 -10 -2 8 9
[1] 9 -16 -12 6 17
[1] -21 -4 8 10 1
```

8. **`range()`** - This function returns a vector of the minimum and maximum values. The syntax is `range(x, na.rm = FALSE, finite = FALSE)`, where `x` is a numeric vector, `na.rm` is the attribute to decide whether `NA` should be removed and `finite` determines whether non-finite elements should be omitted.

Example Program

```
x<-c(10,2,30,4,5,6,70,8,9,10)
y<-c(1,2,3,4,5,NA)
range(x)
range(y,na.rm=FALSE)
```

Output

```
[1] 2 70
[1] NA NA
```

9. **`quantile()`** - A quantile, or percentile, tells how much of our data lies below a certain value. The 50 percent quantile, for example, is the same as the median. The syntax for `quantile()` function is `quantile(x,probs)` where `x` is the numeric vector whose quantiles are desired and `probs` is a numeric vector with probabilities in range `[0,1]`.

Example Program

```
x<-c(1,2,3,4,5,6,7,8,9,10)
quantile(x,c(0.03,0.5))
```

Output

```
3% 50%
1.27 5.50
```

In the above example, we the third quartile and 50th quartile is calculated.

10. **`rank()`** - This function returns the ranks of the numbers (in increasing order) in vector `x`. The syntax of the function is `rank(x, na.last = TRUE, ties.method = c("average",`

"first", "last", "random", "max", "min")), where `x` is a numeric, complex, character or logical vector, `na.last` is for controlling the treatment of NAs. If `TRUE`, missing values in the data are put last; if `FALSE`, they are put first; if `NA`, they are removed; if "keep" they are kept with rank `NA`. The attribute `ties.method` is a character string specifying how ties are treated. If x is given as -x, the function returns the ranks of the numbers in decreasing order in vector x.

Example Program

```
x <- c(3, 1, 4, 1, 5, 9, 2, 6, 5, 3, 5)
x
#Rank in ascending order
rank(x)
#Rank in descending order
rank(-x)
#Tie is broken with average
rank(x,ties.method="average")
#Tie is broken with first element
rank(x,ties.method="first")
#Tie is broken with last element
rank(x,ties.method="last")
#Tie is broken with random element
rank(x,ties.method="random")
#Tie is broken with largest element
rank(x,ties.method="max")
#Tie is broken with smallest element
rank(x,ties.method="min")
```

Output

```
[1] 3 1 4 1 5 9 2 6 5 3 5
#Rank in ascending order
[1] 4.5 1.5 6.0 1.5 8.0 11.0 3.0 10.0 8.0 4.5 8.0
#Rank in descending order
[1] 7.5 10.5 6.0 10.5 4.0 1.0 9.0 2.0 4.0 7.5 4.0
#Tie is broken with average rank
[1] 4.5 1.5 6.0 1.5 8.0 11.0 3.0 10.0 8.0 4.5 8.0
#Tie is broken with rank of first element
[1] 4 1 6 2 7 11 3 10 8 5 9
#Tie is broken with rank of last element
[1] 5 2 6 1 9 11 3 10 8 4 7
```

```
#Tie is broken with rank of random element
[1] 5 1 6 2 8 11 3 10 7 4 9
#Tie is broken with rank of largest element
[1] 5 2 6 2 9 11 3 10 9 5 9
#Tie is broken with rank of smallest element
[1] 4 1 6 1 7 11 3 10 7 4 7
```

11. **`moment()`** -A central moment is a moment of a probability distribution of a random variable about the random variable's mean. It is the expected value of a specified integer power of the deviation of the random variable from the mean. The kth central moment (or moment about the mean) of a data population is:

$$\mu_k = \frac{1}{N}\sum_{i=1}^{N}(x_i - \mu)^k$$

Similarly, the kth central moment of a data sample is:

$$\mu_k = \frac{1}{n}\sum_{i=1}^{n}(x_i - \bar{x})^k$$

In particular, the second central moment of a population is its variance. The following program illustrates how to calculate the third central moment. The syntax of the `moment ()` function is as follows. `moment(x, order=value, center=TRUE)` where `x` is a vector, `order` gives which moment to be calculated and `center=TRUE` calculates the central moment. We apply the function `moment` from the `e1071` package. As it is not in the core R library, the package has to be installed and loaded into the R workspace.

Example Program

```
library(e1071)
x=c(24,30,27,24,39,45,42,51)
moment(x, order=3, center=TRUE)
```

Output

```
[1] 205.0312
```

12. **`skewness()`** - Skewness is asymmetry in a statistical distribution, in which the curve appears distorted or skewed either to the left or to the right. Skewness can be quantified to define the extent to which a distribution differs from a normal distribution. This situation is also called negative skewness. The skewness of a data population is defined by the following formula, where μ_2 and μ_3 are the second and third central moments.

$$\gamma_1 = \mu_3 / \mu_2^{3/2}$$

As a rule, negative skewness indicates that the mean of the data values is less than the median, and the data distribution is left-skewed. Positive skewness would indicate that the mean of the data values is larger than the median, and the data distribution is right-skewed.

The syntax of `skewness()` function is `skewness(x)` where `x` is a vector. We apply the function skewness from the `e1071` package. As the package is not in the core R library, it has to be installed and loaded into the R workspace. Following program illustrates this.

Example Program

```
library(e1071)
x=c(24,30,27,24,39,45,42,51)
skewness(x)
```

Output

```
[1] 0.1843205
```

13. **`kurtosis()`** - In probability theory and statistics, kurtosis is a measure of the "tailedness" of the probability distribution of a real-valued random variable. The kurtosis of a univariate population is defined by the following formula, where μ_2 and μ_4 are respectively the second and fourth central moments.

$$\gamma_2 = \mu_4 / \mu_2^2 - 3$$

The normal distribution has zero kurtosis and thus the standard tail shape. It is said to be mesokurtic. Negative kurtosis would indicate a thin-tailed data distribution, and is said to be platykurtic. Positive kurtosis would indicate a fat-tailed distribution, and is said to be leptokurtic.

The syntax of `kurtosis()` function is `kurtosis(x)` where `x` is a vector. We apply the function `kurtosis` from the `e1071` package. As the package is not in the core R library, it has to be installed and loaded into the R workspace.

Example Program

```
library(e1071)
x=c(24,30,27,24,39,45,42,51)
kurtosis(x)
```

Output

```
[1] -1.804028
```

Since the output is a negative value, it shows that the distribution is a thin-tailed data distribution, and is said to be platykurtic.

4.3.4 Date and Time Functions

R provides several options for dealing with date and date/time data. Three date/time classes commonly used in R are Date, POSIXct and POSIXlt.

1. **Date** - `date()` function returns a date without time as character string. `Sys.Date()` and `Sys.time()` returns the system's date and time.

Example

```
> date()
[1] "Wed Sep 06 09:57:55 2017"
> Sys.Date()
[1] "2017-09-06"
> Sys.time()
[1] "2017-09-06 10:01:00 IST"
```

We can create a date as follows.

```
>dt1 <- as.Date("2012-07-22")
>dt1
[1] "2012-07-22"
```

While creating a date, the non-standard formats must be specified. For example

```
>dt2 <- as.Date("04/20/2011", format = "%m/%d/%Y")
>dt2
[1] "2011-04-20"
>dt3 <- as.Date("October 6, 2010", format= "%B %d, %Y")
>dt3
[1] "2010-10-06"
```

Following Table 4.1 shows the formats and their description used in date and time of R.

Table 4.1 Formats and their description used in date and time of R

%a	Abbreviated weekday name in the current locale. (Also matches full name on input.)
%A	Full weekday name in the current locale. (Also matches abbreviated name on input.)
%b	Abbreviated month name in the current locale. (Also matches full name on input.)
%B	Full month name in the current locale. (Also matches abbreviated name on input.)
%c	Date and time. Locale-specific on output, "%a %b %e %H:%M:%S %Y" on input.
%d	Day of the month as decimal number (01-31).
%H	Hours as decimal number (00-23). As a special exception times such as 24:00:00 are accepted for input, since ISO 8601 allows these.
%I	Hours as decimal number (01-12).
%j	Day of year as decimal number (001-366).
%m	Month as decimal number (01-12).
%M	Minute as decimal number (00-59).
%p	AM/PM indicator in the locale. Used in conjunction with %I and not with %H. An empty string in some locales.

%S	Second as decimal number (00-61), allowing for up to two leap-seconds (but POSIX-compliant implementations will ignore leap seconds).
%U	Week of the year as decimal number (00-53) using Sunday as the first day 1 of the week (and typically with the first Sunday of the year as day 1 of week 1). The US convention.
%w	Weekday as decimal number (0-6, Sunday is 0).
%W	Week of the year as decimal number (00-53) using Monday as the first day of week (and typically with the first Monday of the year as day 1 of week 1). The UK convention.
%x	Date. Locale-specific on output, "%y/%m/%d" on input.
%X	Time. Locale-specific on output, "%H:%M:%S" on input.
%y	Year without century (00-99). On input, values 00 to 68 are prefixed by 20 and 69 to 99 by 19 - that is the behaviour specified by the 2004 and 2008 POSIX standards, but they do also say "it is expected that in a future version the default century inferred from a 2-digit year will change".
%Y	Year with century. Note that whereas there was no zero in the original Gregorian calendar, ISO 8601:2004 defines it to be valid (interpreted as 1BC): see http://en.wikipedia.org/wiki/0_(year). Note that the standard also says that years before 1582 in its calendar should only be used with agreement of the parties involved.
%z	Signed offset in hours and minutes from UTC, so -0800 is 8 hours behind UTC.
%Z	(output only.) Time zone as a character string (empty if not available). Where leading zeros are shown they will be used on output but are optional on input. Note that when %z or %Z is used for output with an object with an assigned timezone an attempt is made to use the values for that timezone, but it is not guaranteed to succeed.

Calculations with dates can be performed as follows.

To find the difference between two dates we can give as

```
>dt1 - dt2
Time difference of 459 days
>difftime(dt1, dt2, units = "weeks")
Time difference of 65.57 weeks
```

To add or subtract days we can give as

```
>dt2 + 10
[1] "2011-04-30"
>dt2 - 10
[1] "2011-04-10"
```

To create a vector of dates and find the intervals between them we can give as

```
>three.dates <- as.Date(c("2010-07-22", "2011-04-20", "2012-10-06"))
>three.dates
[1] "2010-07-22" "2011-04-20" "2012-10-06"
```

```
>diff(three.dates)
Time differences in days
[1] 272 535
```

To create a sequence of dates we can give as

```
>six.weeks <- seq(dt1, length = 6, by = "week")
>six.weeks
 [1] "2012-07-22" "2012-07-29" "2012-08-05" "2012-08-12" "2012-08-19"
 [6] "2012-08-26"
six.weeks <- seq(dt1, length = 6, by = 14)
six.weeks
[1] "2012-07-22" "2012-08-05" "2012-08-19" "2012-09-02" "2012-09-16"
[6] "2012-09-30"
>six.weeks <- seq(dt1, length = 6, by = "2 weeks")
>six.weeks
[1] "2012-07-22" "2012-08-05" "2012-08-19" "2012-09-02" "2012-09-16"
[6] "2012-09-30"
```

2. **POSIXct** - If we have times in your data, this is usually the best class to use. In POSIXct, "ct" stands for calender time. We can create some POSIXct objects as follows.

```
>tm1 <- as.POSIXct("2013-07-24 23:55:26")
>tm1
[1] "2013-07-24 23:55:26 PDT"
>tm2 <- as.POSIXct("25072013 08:32:07", format = "%d%m%Y %H:%M:%S")
>tm2
[1] "2013-07-25 08:32:07 PDT"
```

We can specify the time zone as follows.

```
>tm3 <- as.POSIXct("2010-12-01 11:42:03", tz = "GMT")
>tm3
[1] "2010-12-01 11:42:03 GMT"
```

We can perform the following calculations with times. Times can be compared as follows.

```
>tm2 > tm1
 [1] TRUE
```

We can add or subtract seconds as follows

```
>tm1 + 30
[1] "2013-07-24 23:55:56 PDT"
>tm1 - 30
[1] "2013-07-24 23:54:56 PDT"
```

We can find the difference between times as given below.

```
>tm2 - tm1
Time difference of 8.611 hours
```

We can automatically adjusts for daylight savings time as follows.

```
>as.POSIXct("2013-03-10 08:32:07") - as.POSIXct("2013-03-09 23:55:26")
Time difference of 7.611 hours
```

3. **POSIXlt** - This class enables easy extraction of specific components of a time. In POSIXlt, "lt" stands for local time. "lt" also helps one remember that POSIXlt objects are lists.

   We can create time using POSIXlt as follows.

```
>tm1.lt <- as.POSIXlt("2013-07-24 23:55:26")
>tm1.lt
[1] "2013-07-24 23:55:26"
```

   We can extract the components in time as follows.

```
>unlist(tm1.lt)
sec   min   hour   mday   mon   year   wday   yday   isdst
26    55    23     24     6     113    3      204    1
```

In the above example, `mday`, `wday` and `yday` stands for day of the month, day of the week and day of the year respectively. A particular component of a time can be extracted as follows.

```
>tm1.lt$sec
[1] 26
>tm1.lt$wday
[1] 3
```

   We can truncate or round off the time as given below.

```
trunc(tm1.lt, "days")
[1] "2013-07-24"
trunc(tm1.lt, "mins")
[1] "2013-07-24 23:55:00"
```

4.3.5 Other Functions

1. **seq(from,to,by)** - This function generates a sequence starting with `from`, ends with `to` and with a difference of `by`.

Example Program

```
seq(1,15,2)
```

Output

```
[1] 1 3 5 7 9 11 13 15
```

2. **rep(x, ntimes)** - This function repeats x n times.

Example Program

```
rep(1:3,4)
```

Output

```
[1] 1 2 3 1 2 3 1 2 3 1 2 3
```

3. **cut(x, n)** - This function divide continuous variable in factor with n levels.

Example Program

```
x<-c(1,2,3,1,2,3,1)
cut(x,2)
cut(rep(1,5), 4)
```

Output

```
[1] (0.998,2] (0.998,2] (2,3]    (0.998,2] (0.998,2] (2,3]    (0.998,2]
Levels: (0.998,2] (2,3]
[1] (0.9995,1] (0.9995,1] (0.9995,1] (0.9995,1] (0.9995,1]
Levels: (0.999,0.9995] (0.9995,1] (1,1.0005] (1.0005,1.001]
```

4. **which()** - This function gives the TRUE indices of a logical object, allowing for array indices. The syntax is which(x, arr.ind = FALSE, useNames = TRUE), where x is a logical vector or array. NAs are allowed and omitted (treated as if FALSE), arr.ind is a logical value which decides whether array indices be returned when x is an array.

Example Program

```
x <- matrix(1:9,3,3)
x
# array indices will be returned
which(x %% 3 == 0, arr.ind=TRUE)
# array indices will not be returned
which(x %% 3 == 0, arr.ind=FALSE)
```

Output

```
     [,1] [,2] [,3]
[1,]    1    4    7
[2,]    2    5    8
[3,]    3    6    9
# array indices will be returned
     row col
[1,]   3   1
[2,]   3   2
```

```
[3,]    3   3
# array indices will not be returned
[1] 3 6 9
```

5. **`table()`** - This function uses the cross-classifying factors to build a contingency table of the counts at each combination of factor levels. It simply creates tabular results of categorical variables. However, when combined with the powers of logical expressions in R, we can gain even more insights into our data, including identifying potential problems. For example, we use the built-in data set `mtcars`.

   Example Program

   ```
   table(mtcars$am)
   ```

   Output

   ```
   0   1
   19 13
   ```

   We can give logical conditions in this function. For example we want to find out how many cars have miles per gallon greater than 15 in `mtcars` dataset.

   Example Program

   ```
   table(mtcars$mpg>15)
   ```

   Output

   ```
   FALSE  TRUE
       6    26
   ```

4.4 Recursive Function

A function that calls itself is called a recursive function and this technique is known as recursion. This special programming technique can be used to solve problems by breaking them into smaller and simpler sub-problems. Let us take the example of finding the factorial of a number. Factorial of a positive integer number is defined as the product of all the integers from 1 to that number. For example, the factorial of 5 (denoted as 5!) will be

```
5! = 1*2*3*4*5 = 120
```

This problem of finding factorial of 5 can be broken down into a sub-problem of multiplying the factorial of 4 with 5.

```
5! = 5*4!
```

Or more generally, n! = n*(n-1)! Now we can continue this until we reach 0! which is 1. The implementation of this is provided below.

Example Program

```
# Recursive function to find factorial
recursive.factorial <- function(x) {
   if (x == 0)     return (1)
```

```
    else            return (x * recursive.factorial(x-1))
}
recursive.factorial(5)
```

Output

```
[1] 120
```

Here, we have a function which will call itself. Something like `recursive.factorial(5)` will turn into `5 * recursive.factorial(4)` until `x` becomes 0. When `x` becomes 0, we return 1 since the factorial of 0 is 1. This is the terminating condition and is very important. Without this the recursion will not end and continue indefinitely. The use of recursion often makes code shorter and looks clean. However, it is sometimes hard to follow through the code logic. It might be hard to think of a problem in a recursive way. Recursive functions are also memory intensive, since it can result into a lot of nested function calls. This must be kept in mind when using it for solving big problems.

Another problem which uses recursion to convert decimal number to binary is given below.

Example Program

```
convert_to_binary <- function(n) {
    if(n > 1) {
        convert_to_binary(as.integer(n/2))
    }
    cat(n %% 2)
}
convert_to_binary(5)
```

Output

```
[1] 101
```

4.5 Infix Operator

Most of the operators that we use in R are binary operators. Binary operators are operators having two operands. They are also called infix operators, used between the operands. Actually, these operators do a function call in the background. For example, the expression `a+b` is actually calling the function `` `+`() `` with the arguments `a` and `b`, as `` `+`(a,b) ``. The back tick (`) is important as the function name contains special symbols.

Following are some example expressions along with the actual functions that get called in the background.

```
> 5+3
[1] 8
> `+`(5,3)
[1] 8
> 5-3
```

```
[1] 2
>`-`(5,3)
[1] 2
> 5*3-1
[1] 14
> `-`(`*`(5,3),1)
[1] 14
```

It is possible to create user-defined infix operators in R. This is done by naming a function that starts and ends with %. Table 4.2 shows a list of predefined infix operators in R.

Table 4.2 Predefined infix operators in R

%%	Remainder operator
%/%	Integer division
%*%	Matrix multiplication
%o%	Outer product
%x%	Kronecker product
%in%	Matching operator

Following is an example of user-defined infix operator to see if a number is exactly divisible by another. This function can be used as infix operator a %divisible% b or as a function call `%divisible%`(a, b).

Example Program

```
`%divisible%` <- function(x,y)
{
  if (x%%y ==0) return (TRUE)
  else          return (FALSE)
}
#Function Call
9 %divisible% 3
10 %divisible% 3
`%divisible%`(10,5)
```

Output

```
[1] TRUE
[1] FALSE
[1] TRUE
```

4.6 Packages

R packages are a collection of R functions, complied code and sample data. They are stored under a directory called "library" in the R environment. By default, R installs a set of packages during installation. More packages are added later, when they are needed for some specific purpose. When we start the R console, only the default packages are available by default. Other packages which are already installed have to be loaded explicitly to be used by the R program that is going to use them. We can check the library locations containing R packages using the function as shown below.

```
>.libPaths()
```

When we execute the above code, it produces the following result. It may vary depending on the local settings of your computer.

```
[1] "C:/Users/USER/Documents/R/win-library/3.4"
[2] "C:/Program Files/R/R-3.4.0/library"
```

We will get the list of all packages installed using the following command.

```
>library()
```

For getting all the packages currently loaded in the R environment, we can use the following command.

```
>search()
```

The output obtained is as follows.

```
[1] ".GlobalEnv"        "package:stats"     "package:graphics"
[4] "package:grDevices" "package:utils"     "package:datasets"
[7] "package:methods"   "Autoloads"         "package:base"
```

Both the output of the functions `library()` and `search()` depends on the local settings of your computer.

4.6.1 Installing a Package

There are two ways to add new R packages. One is installing directly from the CRAN directory and another is downloading the package to your local system and installing it manually.

1. Install directly from CRAN

The following command gets the packages directly from CRAN webpage and installs the package in the R environment. You may be prompted to choose a nearest mirror. Choose the one appropriate to your location. The syntax is as follows.

```
install.packages("Package Name")
```

Example

```
# Install the package named "reshape".
 install.packages("reshape")
```

2. Install package manually

Go to the link R Packages to download the package needed. Save the package as a .zip file in a suitable location in the local system. Now we can run the following command to install this package in the R environment.

```
install.packages(file_name_with_path, repos = NULL, type = "source")
```

```
# Install the package named "reshape"
install.packages("E:/reshape_3.98-1.3.zip", repos = NULL, type = "source"
```

4.6.2 Loading a Package

Before a package can be used in the code, it must be loaded to the current R environment. We also need to load a package that is installed previously but not available in the current environment. A package is loaded using the following command.

```
library("package Name", lib.loc = "path to library")
```

4.7 Conclusion

This Chapter gives a very good idea about functions, how functions are defined, calling a function etc. Various types of functions like functions without arguments, named arguments and default arguments are discussed. A systematic explanation of various built-in functions including mathematical functions, character functions, statistical functions, date & time functions and other useful functions in R is given in this Chapter. How to create recursive functions are illustrated in this Chapter. Another important operator known as infix operator is also discussed. Finally a detailed explanation of packages, how to locate a package, how to install a package and loading a package are also well explained in this Chapter. All sections have ample number of examples and solved programs.

5 Charts and Graphs

5.1 Bar Charts

A bar chart represents data in rectangular bars with length of the bar proportional to the value of the variable. R uses the function `barplot()` to create bar charts. R can draw both vertical and horizontal bars in the bar chart. In bar chart, each of the bars can be given different colors. We can supply a vector or matrix to this function. If we supply a vector, the plot will have bars with their heights equal to the elements in the vector. Let us suppose, we have a vector of maximum temperatures (in degree Celsius) for seven days as follows. Now we can make a bar plot out of this data.

Example Program

```
> max.temp <- c(22, 27, 26, 24, 23, 26, 28)
> barplot(max.temp)
```

Output

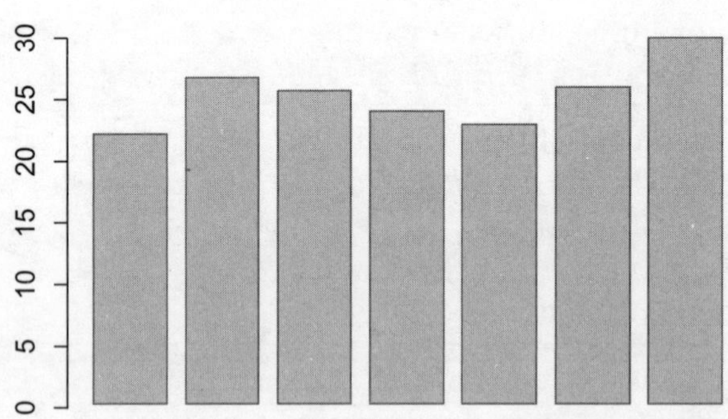

This function can take a lot of argument to control the way our data is plotted. The syntax for plotting a bar graph is as follows.

```
barplot(height, width = 1, space = NULL,
        names.arg = NULL, legend.text = NULL, beside = FALSE,
        horiz = FALSE, density = NULL, angle = 45,
        col = NULL, border = par("fg"),
```

```
main = NULL, sub = NULL, xlab = NULL, ylab = NULL,
xlim = NULL, ylim = NULL, xpd = TRUE, log = "",
axes = TRUE, axisnames = TRUE,
cex.axis = par("cex.axis"), cex.names = par("cex.axis"),
inside = TRUE, plot = TRUE, axis.lty = 0,  offset = 0,
add = FALSE, args.legend = NULL, ...)
```

Arguments

`height`	This is either a vector or matrix of values describing the bars which make up the plot. If `height` is a vector, the plot consists of a sequence of rectangular bars with heights given by the values in the vector. If `height` is a matrix and `beside` is `FALSE` then each bar of the plot corresponds to a column of `height`, with the values in the column giving the heights of stacked sub-bars making up the bar. If `height` is a matrix and `beside` is `TRUE`, then the values in each column are juxtaposed rather than stacked.
`width`	This is optional vector of bar widths. Re-cycled to length the number of bars drawn. Specifying a single value will have no visible effect unless `xlim` is specified.
`space`	This gives the amount of space (as a fraction of the average bar width) left before each bar. May be given as a single number or one number per bar. If `height` is a matrix and `beside` is `TRUE`, `space` may be specified by two numbers, where the first is the space between bars in the same group, and the second the space between the groups. If not given explicitly, it defaults to `c(0, 1)` if `height` is a matrix and `beside` is `TRUE`, and to 0.2 otherwise.
`names.arg`	This gives a vector of names to be plotted below each bar or group of bars. If this argument is omitted, then the names are taken from the `names` attribute of `height` if this is a vector, or the column names if it is a matrix.
`legend.text`	This is a vector of text used to construct a legend for the plot, or a logical indicating whether a legend should be included. This is only useful when `height` is a matrix. In that case given legend labels should correspond to the rows of `height`; if `legend.text` is true, the row names of `height` will be used as labels if they are non-null.
`beside`	This is a logical value. If `FALSE`, the columns of `height` are portrayed as stacked bars, and if `TRUE` the columns are portrayed as juxtaposed bars.
`horiz`	This is a logical value. If `FALSE`, the bars are drawn vertically with the first bar to the left. If `TRUE`, the bars are drawn horizontally with the first at the bottom.
`density`	This is a vector giving the density of shading lines, in lines per inch, for the bars or bar components. The default value of `NULL` means that no shading lines are drawn. Non-positive values of `density` also inhibit the drawing of shading lines.

`angle`	This is the slope of shading lines, given as an angle in degrees (counter-clockwise), for the bars or bar components.
`col`	This is a vector of colors for the bars or bar components. By default, grey is used if `height` is a vector, and a gamma-corrected grey palette if `height` is a matrix.
`border`	This is the color to be used for the border of the bars. Use `border = NA` to omit borders. If there are shading lines, `border = TRUE` means use the same color for the border as for the shading lines.
`main,sub`	This gives overall and sub title for the plot.
`xlab`	This is the label for the x axis.
`ylab`	This is the label for the y axis.
`xlim`	This gives limits for the x axis.
`ylim`	This gives limits for the y axis.
`xpd`	This is a logical value which decides whether bars be allowed to go outside region.
`log`	This is a string specifying if axis scales should be logarithmic.
`axes`	This is a logical value. If `TRUE`, a vertical (or horizontal, if `horiz` is true) axis is drawn.
`axisnames`	This is a logical value. If `TRUE`, and if there are `names.arg` (see above), the other axis is drawn (with `lty = 0`) and labeled.
`cex.axis`	This is the expansion factor for numeric axis labels.
`cex.names`	This is the expansion factor for axis names (bar labels).
`inside`	This is a logical value. If `TRUE`, the lines which divide adjacent (non-stacked!) bars will be drawn. Only applies when `space = 0` (which it partly is when `beside = TRUE`).
`plot`	This is logical value. If `FALSE`, nothing is plotted.
`axis.lty`	The graphics parameter `lty` applied to the axis and tick marks of the categorical (default horizontal) axis. Note that by default the axis is suppressed.
`offset`	This is a vector indicating how much the bars should be shifted relative to the x axis.
`add`	This is a logical value specifying if bars should be added to an already existing plot; default is `FALSE`.
`args.legend`	This is a list of additional arguments to pass to `legend()`; names of the list are used as argument names. Only used if `legend.text` is supplied.
`...`	arguments to be passed to/from other methods.

Saving Graphs

We can save the graph in a variety of formats from the menu File → Save As. We can also save the graph via code using one of the following functions given in Table 5.1.

Table 5.1: List of Functions and their Output for Graphs

Function	Output to
pdf("mygraph.pdf")	pdf file
win.metafile("mygraph.wmf")	windows metafile
png("mygraph.png")	png file
jpeg("mygraph.jpg")	jpeg file
bmp("mygraph.bmp")	bmp file
postscript("mygraph.ps")	postscript file

5.1.1 Plotting Bars Vertically

We have already seen a bar chart above which is drawn vertically. Now we will see a vertical bar chart with some more arguments. This bar chart will be saved as .png file in the current working directory. We can add values on top of each bar using the `text()` function. The `text()` function has the following syntax.

```
text (x, y = NULL, labels = seq_along(x$x), adj = NULL,
    pos = NULL, offset = 0.5, cex = 1, col = NULL, font = NULL, ...)
```

where `x`, `y` gives the numeric vectors of coordinates where the text `labels` should be written. All other parameters are same as that of the syntax for bar chart mentioned above.

Example Program

```
B <- c(3, 2, 25, 35, 22, 34, 19)
# Give the chart file a name.
png(file = "Mybarchart.png")
# Plot the graph
b=barplot(B, main="MY NEW BARPLOT", xlab="LETTERS", ylab="MY Y VALUES",
names.arg=c("A","B","C","D","E","F","G"),
col="yellow",border="red", density=c(90, 70, 50, 40, 30, 20, 10))
# adding vaues on top of each bar
text(b, B, label=B, cex=0.9, pos=3, col="black", xpd=TRUE)
# save the file.
dev.off()
```

In the above program, the `text()` function is used for adding values on top of each bar. In this function, the parameter `cex` is the number indicating the amount by which plotting text should be scaled relative to the default. The default is 1. The parameter `pos` is the position specifier with values as 1-below, 2-left, 3-above and 4-right.

Output

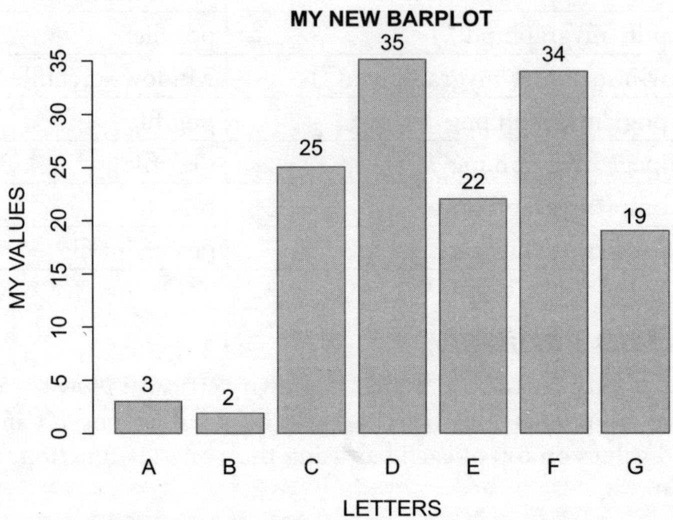

5.1.2 Plotting Bars Horizontally

We can also plot bars horizontally by providing the argument `horiz = TRUE`. The following program plots a horizontal bar chart with temperature in degree celsius on x axis and day on y axis.

Example Program

```
max.temp <- c(22, 27, 26, 24, 23, 26, 30)
barplot(max.temp,
  main = "Maximum Temperatures in a Week",
  xlab = "Degree Celsius",
  ylab = "Day",
  names.arg = c("Sun", "Mon", "Tue", "Wed", "Thu", "Fri", "Sat"),
  col = "lightgreen",
  horiz = TRUE)
```

Output

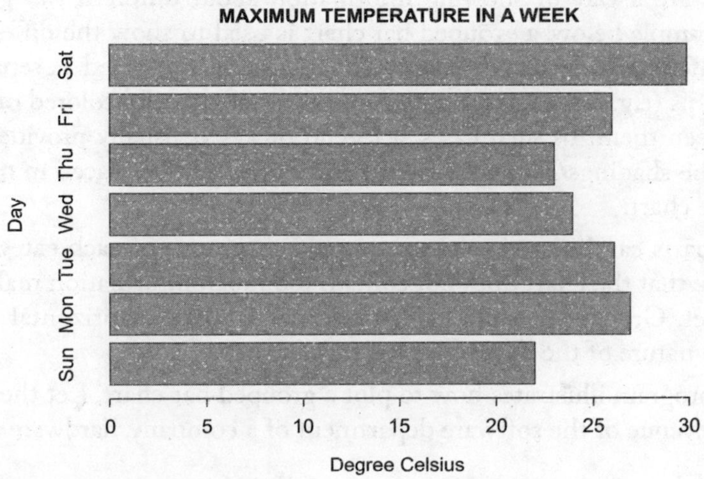

5.1.3 Plotting Categorical Data

Sometimes we have to plot the count of each item as bar plots from categorical data. For example, here is a vector of age of 10 students.

```
age <- c(17,18,18,17,18,19,18,16,18,18)
```

Simply calling `barplot(age)` will not give us the required plot. It will plot 10 bars with height equal to the student's age. But we want to know the number of students in each age category. This count can be quickly found using the `table()` function, as shown below.

Example Program

```
age <- c(17,18,18,17,18,19,18,16,18,18)
barplot(table(age),main="Age Count of 10 Students",
xlab="Age", ylab="Count", border="blue", col="orange" )
```

Output

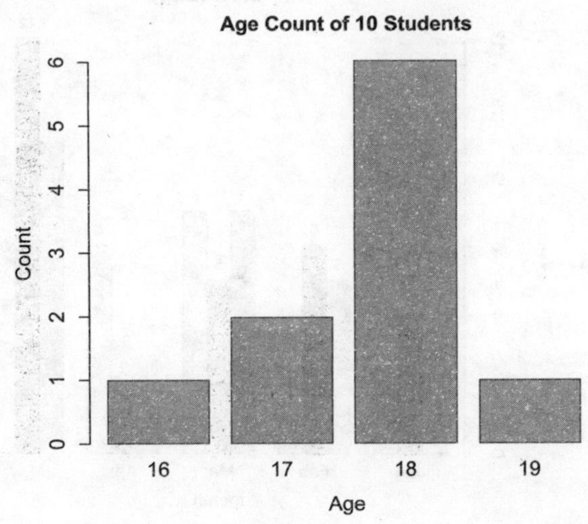

5.1.4 Grouped Bar Chart

Grouped bar charts are a way of showing information about different sub-groups of the main categories. In the example below, a grouped bar chart is used to show the different schemes (sub-groups) by which different categories of household materials are recycled. A separate bar represents each of the sub-groups (e.g. civic amenity sites) and these are usually colored or shaded differently to distinguish between them. In such cases, a legend or key is usually provided to indicate what sub-group each of the shadings/colors represent. The legend can be placed in the plot area or may be located below the chart.

Grouped bar charts can be used to show several sub-groups of each category but care needs to be taken to ensure that the chart does not contain too much information making it complicated to read and interpret. Grouped bar charts can be drawn as both horizontal and vertical charts depending upon the nature of the data to be presented.

The following program illustrates how to plot a grouped bar chart. Let the bar chart be about the comparison of revenue of the software department of a company, hardware and services.

Example Program

```
A<-matrix(c(3,5,7,1,9,4,6,5,2,12,2,1,7,6,8),nrow=3,ncol=5,byrow=TRUE)
#Plot the graph
b=barplot(A,main="Total Revenue",
beside=TRUE, names.arg=c("Jan","Feb","Mar","Apr","May"),
xlab="month",ylab="revenue",col=c("tan2","blue","darkslategray3"))
#Add the legend to the chart
legend(x=1,y=11,c("software","hardware","service"),cex=.8,
col=c("tan2","blue","darkslategray3"),pch=c(1))
#Adding values on top of each bar
text(b,A[,],labels=A[,],pos=3,cex=0.8,xpd=TRUE)
```

Output

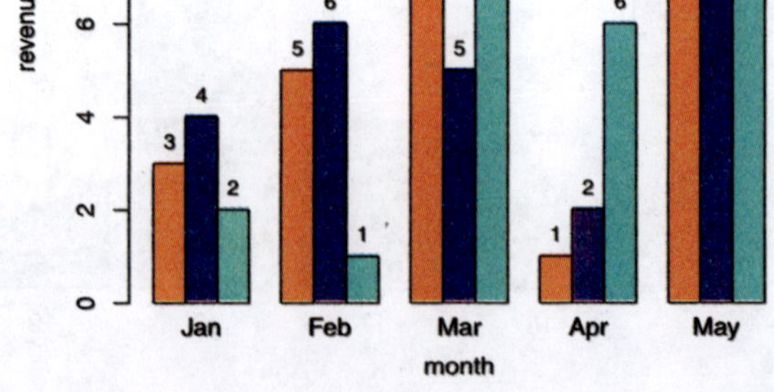

In the above program, pch in legend stands for the plotting character. The number 1 stands for rhombus, 2 stands for triangle and so on. In the above example, 22 represents for square.

5.1.5 Stacked Bar Chart

Stacked bar charts are similar to grouped bar charts in that they are used to display information about the sub-groups that make up the different categories. In stacked bar charts the bars representing the sub-groups are placed on top of each other to make a single column, or side by side to make a single bar. The overall height or length of the bar shows the total size of the category whilst different colors or shadings are used to indicate the relative contribution of the different sub-groups.

Stacked bar charts can also be used to show the percentage contribution which different sub-groups contribute to each separate category. In this case the bars representing the individual categories are all the same size. The information could also be presented in a series of pie charts.

The same example discussed for drawing a grouped bar chart is redrawn using a stacked bar chart.

Example Program

```
A=matrix(c(3,5,7,1,9,4,6,5,2,12,2,1,7,6,8),nrow=3,ncol=5,byrow=TRUE)
b=barplot(A,main="Total Revenue",
names.arg=c("Jan","Feb","Mar","Apr","May"),xlab="Month",
ylab="Revenue", col=c("red","green","yellow"))
legend(x=0,y=20,c("software","hardware","service"), cex=0.8,
col=c("red","green","yellow"), pch=c(10))
text(b,A[1,]-2,labels=A[1,],pos=3,cex=0.8,xpd=TRUE)
text(b,A[1,]+A[2,]-2,labels=A[2,],pos=3,cex=0.8,xpd=TRUE)
text(b,colSums(A)-2,labels=A[3,],pos=3,cex=0.8,xpd=TRUE)
```

Output

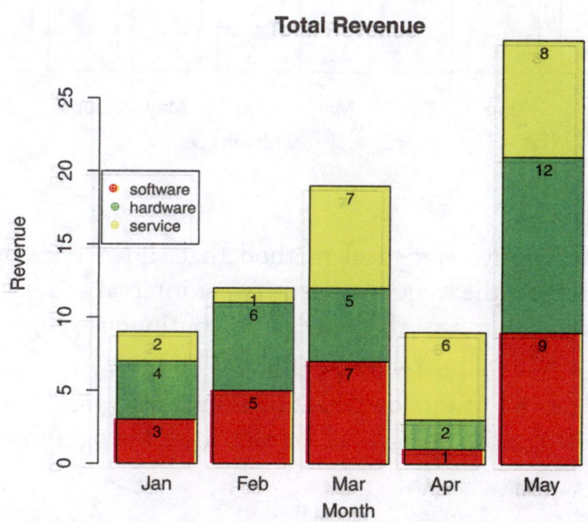

It is also possible to add values to a bar chart. The following program illustrates this.

Example Program

```
A <- matrix(c(3,5,7,1,9,4,6,5,2,12,1,7,6,8),nrow=2,ncol=7,byrow=TRUE)
#Plot the graph
bb<-barplot(A,main="total revenue",names.arg=c("Jan","Feb","Mar","Apr","
May","June","July"),
 xlab="Month",ylab="revenue",col=c("green","yellow"))
#Add the legend to the chart
legend(x=0.2,y=18,c("software","hardware"),cex=.8,
col=c("green","yellow"),pch=c(2))
text(bb,A[1,]-0.5,labels=A[1,],cex=.8)
text(bb,colSums(A)-0.5,labels=A[2,],cex=0.8)
```

Output

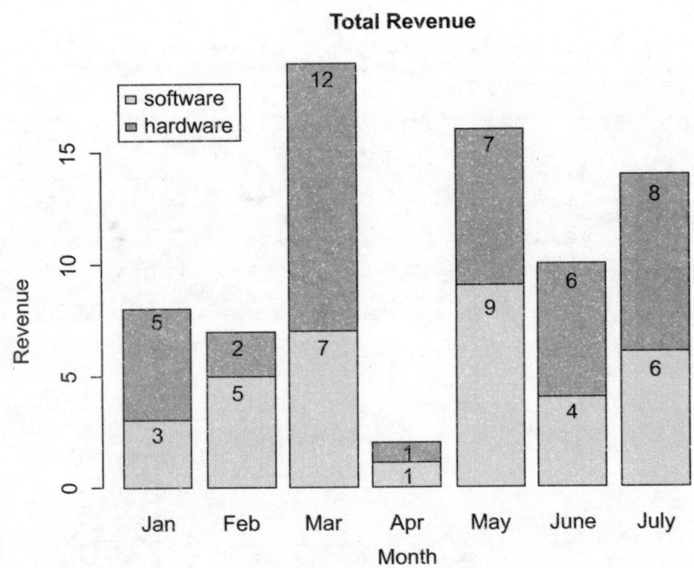

5.2 Histogram

Histogram is a popular descriptive statistical method that shows data by dividing the range of values into intervals and plotting the frequency/density per interval as a bar. Histogram is similar to bar chart but the difference is, it groups the values into continuous ranges. Each bar in histogram represents the height of the number of values present in that range.

R creates histogram using `hist()` function. This function takes a vector as an input and uses some more parameters to plot histograms. The syntax for plotting a histogram is as follows.

```
hist(x, breaks = "Sturges",
     freq = NULL, probability = !freq,
     include.lowest = TRUE, right = TRUE,
```

```
density = NULL, angle = 45, col = NULL, border = NULL,
main = paste("Histogram of" , xname),
xlim = range(breaks), ylim = NULL,
xlab = xname, ylab,
axes = TRUE, plot = TRUE, labels = FALSE,
nclass = NULL, warn.unused = TRUE, ...)
```

Arguments

`x`	This shows a vector of values for which the histogram is desired.
`breaks`	It can be any one of the following. • a vector giving the breakpoints between histogram cells. • a function to compute the vector of breakpoints. • a single number giving the number of cells for the histogram. • a character string naming an algorithm to compute the number of cells. • a function to compute the number of cells. In the last three cases the number is a suggestion only; the breakpoints will be set to pretty values. If `breaks` is a function, the `x` vector is supplied to it as the only argument.
`freq`	This is a logical value; if `TRUE`, the histogram graphic is a representation of frequencies, the `counts` component of the result; if `FALSE`, probability densities, component `density`, are plotted (so that the histogram has a total area of one). Defaults to `TRUE` *if and only if* `breaks` are equidistant (and `probability` is not specified).
`probability`	This is an *alias* for `freq`, for S compatibility.
`include.lowest`	This is a logical value; if `TRUE`, an `x[i]` equal to the `breaks` value will be included in the first (or last, for `right = FALSE`) bar. This will be ignored (with a warning) unless `breaks` is a vector.
`right`	This is a logical value; if `TRUE`, the histogram cells are right-closed (left open) intervals.
`density`	This gives the density of shading lines, in lines per inch. The default value of `NULL` means that no shading lines are drawn. Non-positive values of `density` also inhibit the drawing of shading lines.
`angle`	This gives the slope of shading lines, given as an angle in degrees (counter-clockwise).
`col`	This is the color to be used to fill the bars. The default of `NULL` yields unfilled bars.

border	This gives the color of the border around the bars. The default is to use the standard foreground color.
main, xlab, ylab	These are arguments to `title`, label of the x-axis and y-axis .
xlim, ylim	This gives the range of x and y values with sensible defaults. Note that `xlim` is *not* used to define the histogram (breaks), but only for plotting (when `plot = TRUE`).
axes	This is a logical value. If `TRUE` (default), axes are drawn if the plot is drawn.
plot	This is a logical value. If `TRUE` (default), a histogram is plotted, otherwise a list of breaks and counts is returned. In the latter case, a warning is used if (typically graphical) arguments are specified that only apply to the `plot = TRUE` case.
labels	This is logical or character string. Additionally draw labels on top of bars, if not `FALSE`;
nclass	This is a numeric (integer). For S(-PLUS) compatibility only, `nclass` is equivalent to `breaks` for a scalar or character argument.
warn.unused	This is a logical value. If `plot = FALSE` and `warn.unused = TRUE`, a warning will be issued when graphical parameters are passed to `hist.default()`.
...	further arguments and graphical parameters passed to `plot.histogram` and hence to `title` and `axis` (if `plot = TRUE`).

5.2.1 A Simple Histogram

Consider the following example to plot a histogram with daily wages of workers and their frequencies. If we want probability distribution instead of frequency, set the argument `freq=FALSE`.

Example Program

```
wages=c(400, 700, 200, 700, 400, 600, 500, 400, 500, 600, 700, 300, 600,
700, 400, 300)
hist(wages,main="Daily Wages", xlab="Wages in Rupees",ylab="frequency",
 xlim=c(200, 700),col="pink",freq=TRUE)
```

Output

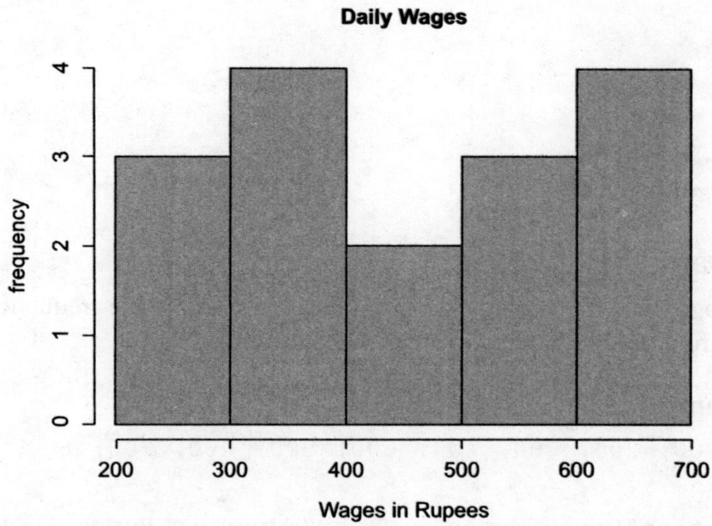

Consider the following example. Let us see what all are the attributes returned by `hist()` function.

Example Program

```
wages=c(400, 700, 200, 700, 400, 600, 500, 400, 500, 600, 700, 300, 600,
700, 400, 300)
h<-hist(wages)
h
```

Output

```
# Shows in which all points the graph is broken
$breaks
[1] 200 300 400 500 600 700
# Gives the count for each value
$counts
[1] 3 4 2 3 4
# Gives the density for each count
$density
[1] 0.001875 0.002500 0.001250 0.001875 0.002500
# Gives the mid position for each range
$mids
[1] 250 350 450 550 650
# Gives the name of the vector used
$xname
```

```
[1] "wages"
# Specifies whether all the bars are at equidistance
$equidist
[1] TRUE
# Gives the class
attr(,"class")
[1] "histogram"
```

5.2.2 Histogram with Labels

We can draw histograms with frequencies specified on each bar. The frequencies can be specified using the `text()` function. Following program illustrates this.

Example Program

```
wages=c(400, 700, 200, 700, 400, 600, 500, 400, 500, 600, 700, 300, 600,
700, 400, 300)
h=hist(wages,main="Daily Wages", xlab="Wages in Rupees", ylab="
frequency",
xlim=c(200, 700),col="pink",freq=TRUE)
text(h$mids,h$counts,labels=h$counts, adj=c(0.5, -0.5))
```

Output

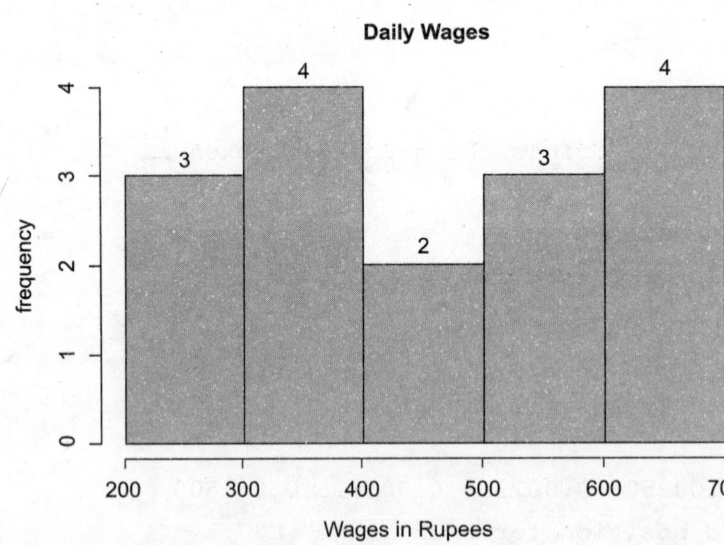

In the above `text()` function `mids` and `counts` are already explained and `adj` stands for adjustment for each string in reading direction. For strings parallel to the axes, `adj = 0` means left or bottom alignment, and `adj = 1` means right or top alignment. If `adj` is not a finite value (the default), the values in vector determines the adjustment.

5.2.3 Histogram with Breaks

With the breaks argument we can specify the number of cells we want in the histogram. However, this number is just a suggestion. R calculates the best number of cells, keeping this suggestion in mind. Following are two histograms on the same data with different number of cells. In the below figure we see that the actual number of cells plotted is greater than we had specified. We can also define breakpoints between the cells as a vector. This makes it possible to plot a histogram with unequal intervals. In such case, the area of the cell is proportional to the number of observations falling inside that cell.

Example Program

```
wages=c(400, 450, 250, 650, 650, 360, 270, 490, 580, 480, 520, 410,
390, 480, 210, 360, 540, 640, 760, 620, 700, 200, 700, 400, 600, 500,
290, 480, 440, 680, 660, 400, 500, 600, 700, 300, 600, 700, 400, 300)
hist(wages, breaks=10,  main="With breaks=10")
hist(wages, breaks=40,  main="With breaks=40")
```

Output

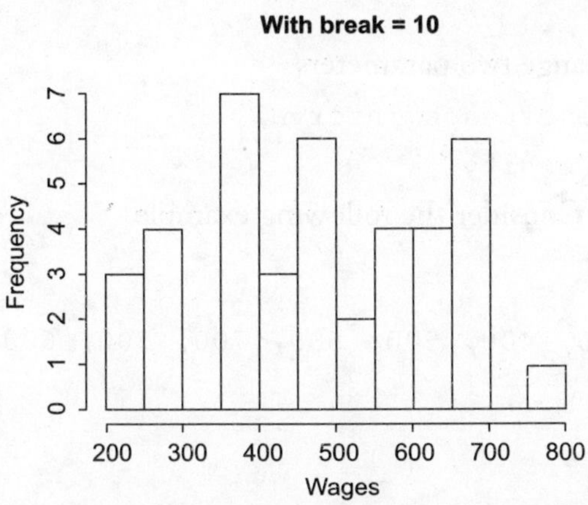

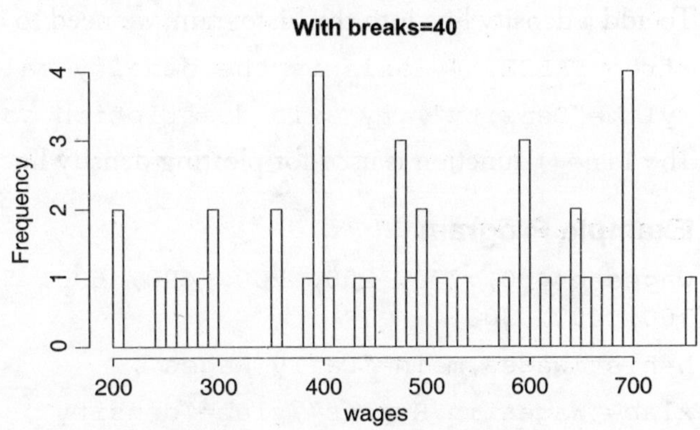

We can also draw a histogram with manual breaks. Following program illustrates this.

Example Program

```
wages=c(400, 700, 200, 700, 400, 600, 500, 400, 500, 600, 700, 300, 600,
700, 400, 300)
h=hist(wages,breaks=c(200, 350, 450, 550, 650, 780),main="Daily Wages",
xlab="Wages in Rupees",ylab="frequency",
xlim=c(200, 700),col="pink",freq=TRUE)
```

Output

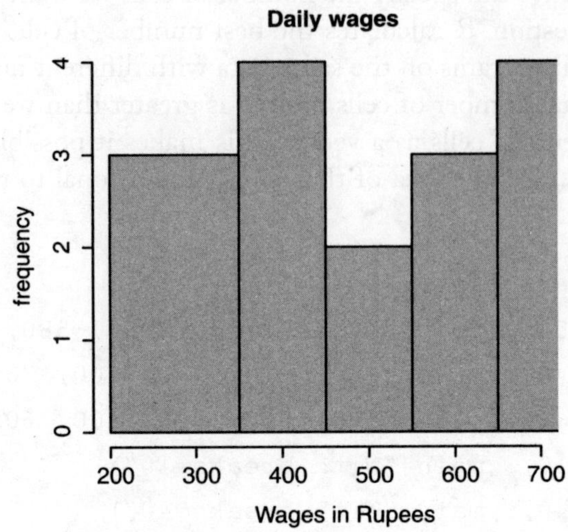

The histogram is broken at points which we have specified in `breaks` attribute.

5.2.4 Histogram with Density Lines

To add a density line into the histogram, we need to change two parameters.

- `freq=FALSE, #y axis is the density value of each interval`
- `ylab="Density", #y axis description as Density`

The `line()` function is used for plotting density lines. Consider the following example.

Example Program

```
wages=c(400, 700, 200, 700, 400, 600, 500, 400, 500, 600, 700, 300, 600,
700, 400, 300)
h=hist(wages,main="Daily Wages",
xlab="Wages in Rupees",ylab="density",
xlim=c(200, 700),col="yellow",freq=FALSE)
lines(density(wages),col="red")
```

Output

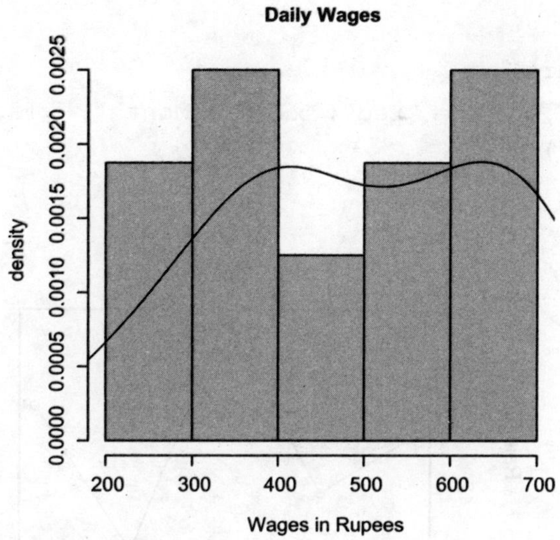

5.3 Line Graph

A line chart is a graph that connects a series of points by drawing line segments between them. These points are ordered in one of their coordinate usually the x-coordinate value. Line charts are usually used in identifying the trends in data.

5.3.1 A Simple Line Graph

The `plot()` function in R is used to create the line graph. The syntax of `plot()` function is as follows.

```
plot(x, y, type=,col, main, sub, xlab, ylab, asp ...)
```

Arguments

x	The x coordinates of points in the plot. Alternatively, a single plotting structure, function or any R object with a `plot` method can be provided.
y	The y coordinates of points in the plot, *optional* if x is an appropriate structure.
type	Arguments to be passed to methods, such as what type of plot should be drawn. Possible types are "p" for **p**oints, "l" for **l**ines, "b" for **b**oth, "c" for the lines part alone of "b", "o" for both '**o**verplotted', "h" for '**h**istogram' like (or 'high-density') vertical lines, "s" for stair **s**teps, "S" for other **s**teps, "n" for no plotting.
col	The color for the line graph
main	an overall title for the plot
sub	a sub title for the plot
xlab	a title for the x axis
ylab	a title for the y axis
asp	the *y/x* aspect ratio

Example Program

```
y=c(14,12,18,10, 15)
x=c(1,2,3,4,5)
# Plot the line chart.
plot(x,y,type = "o", col = "red", xlab ="Month", ylab = "Rain fall",main
= "Rain fall chart")
```

Output

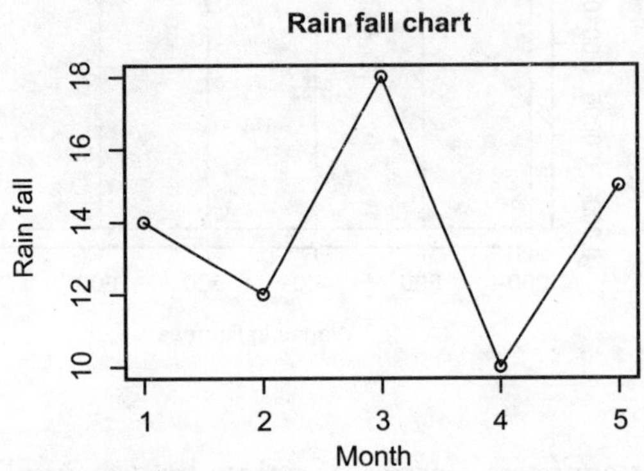

5.3.2 Graphs with Multiple Lines

For drawing line graphs with multiple lines, we can use the function `lines(x, y, type=)` where `x` and `y` are numeric vectors of `(x,y)` points to connect. `type=` can take the following values.

Type	Description
p	points
l	lines
o	overplotted points and lines
b, c	points (empty if "c") joined by lines
s, S	stair steps
h	histogram-like vertical lines
n	does not produce any points or lines

The following example illustrates how to draw line charts for comparing rainfall in three states.

Example Program

```
y=c(14,12,13,10, 15)
k=c(15,10, 11,15,12)
z=c(10, 13,11,12,14)
x=c(1,2,3,4,5)
```

```
# Plot the line chart.
plot(x,y,type="o",col="red",xlab="Month",ylab="Rain    fall",main="Rain
fall chart")
lines(x,k,type="o",col="blue")
lines(x,z,type="o",col="green")
legend("top", legend = c("Rainfall in Kerala","Rainfall in Goa","Rainfall
in Assam"), col=1:3, pch=1)
```

Output

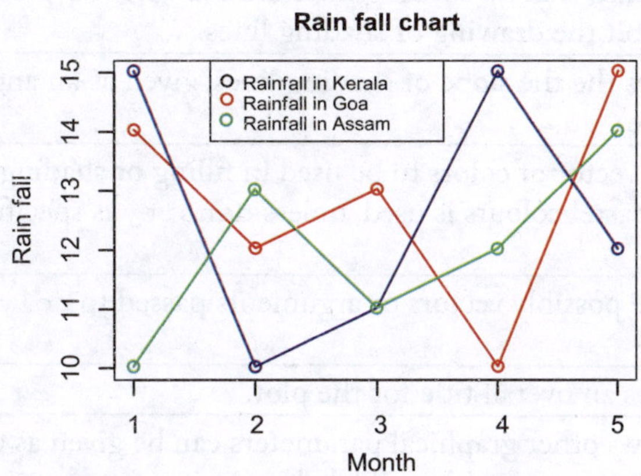

5.4 Pie Charts

A pie chart is a representation of values as slices of a circle with different colors. The slices are labeled and the numbers corresponding to each slice is also represented in the chart. In R, the pie chart is created using the `pie()` function which takes positive numbers as a vector input. The additional parameters are used to control labels, color, title etc. The basic syntax for drawing a pie chart is as follows.

```
pie(x, labels = names(x), edges = 200,  radius = 0.8,
    clockwise = FALSE, init.angle = if(clockwise) 90 else 0,
    density = NULL, angle = 45, col = NULL, border = NULL,
    lty = NULL, main = NULL, ...)
```

Arguments

`x`	This is a vector of non-negative numerical quantities. The values in x are displayed as the areas of pie slices.
`labels`	This gives one or more expressions or character strings giving names for the slices.
`edges`	This is the circular outline of the pie and is approximated by a polygon with this many edges.

`radius`	The pie is drawn centered in a square box whose sides range from *-1* to *1*. If the character strings labeling the slices are long, it may be necessary to use a smaller radius.
`clockwise`	This is a logical value indicating if slices are drawn clockwise or counter clockwise (i.e., mathematically positive direction), the latter is default.
`init.angle`	This is a number specifying the *starting angle* (in degrees) for the slices. Defaults to 0 (i.e., '3 o'clock') unless `clockwise` is true where `init.angle` defaults to 90 (degrees), (i.e., '12 o'clock').
`density`	This gives the density of shading lines, in lines per inch. The default value of `NULL` means that no shading lines are drawn. Non-positive values of `density` also inhibit the drawing of shading lines.
`angle`	This gives the the slope of shading lines, given as an angle in degrees (counter-clockwise).
`col`	This is a vector of colors to be used in filling or shading the slices. If missing, a set of 6 pastel colours is used, unless `density` is specified when `par("fg")` is used.
`border`, `lty`	These are possibly vectors or arguments passed to `polygon` which draws each slice.
`main`	This gives an overall title for the plot.
`...`	This shows other graphical parameters can be given as arguments to `pie`. They will affect the main title and labels only.

5.4.1 A Simple Pie Chart

Consider the below data represents the monthly expenditure breakdown of an individual.

```
Housing    Food    Clothing   Entertainment    Other
  600      300     150        100              200
```

We can draw a pie chart for the above information.

Example Program

```
expenditure=c(600, 300, 150, 100, 200)
pie(expenditure,
 labels=c("Housing","Food","Clothing","Entertainment","Other"),
 main="Monthly Expenditure Breakdown",
 col=c("red","orange","yellow","blue","green"), border="brown",
 clockwise=TRUE)
```

Output

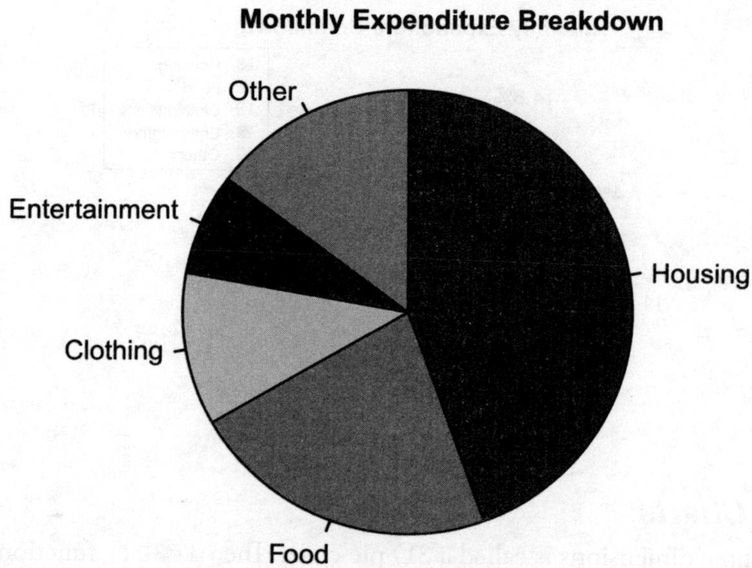

As seen in the above figure, we have used the labels to represent each slice. Also, the chart is drawn in clockwise fashion. Since the human eye is relatively bad at judging angles, other types of charts are appropriate than pie charts.

5.4.2 Pie Chart with Slice Percentages

In the above example, pie chart is drawn with the actual value for each slice. We can add slice percentage and a chart legend by creating additional chart variables.

Example Program

```
expenditure=c(600, 300, 150, 100, 200)
#Calculating the percentage
piepercent<- round(100*expenditure/sum(expenditure),1)
#Adding percentage Symbol to each value
piepercent <- paste(piepercent,"%",sep="")
#Plotting the Pie Graph
pie(expenditure, labels=piepercent, main="Monthly Expenditure Breakdown",
 col=c("red","orange","yellow","blue","green"), border="brown",
 clockwise=TRUE)
#Legend for the Pie Graph
legend("topright",c("Housing","Food","Clothing","Entertainment","Oth
er"),
 cex = 0.8, fill=c("red","orange","yellow","blue","green"))
```

Output

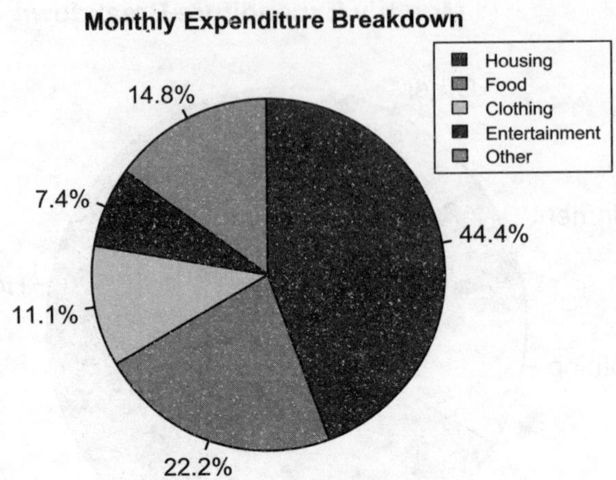

5.4.3 3D Pie Charts

A pie chart with three dimensions is called a 3D pie chart. The `pie3D()` function in the `plotrix` package provides 3D exploded pie charts. Following program shows how to draw a 3D pie chart. The syntax of the `pie3D()` function is as follows.

```
pie3D(x,edges=NA,radius=1,height=0.1,theta=pi/6,start=0,
border=par("fg"), col=NULL,labels=NULL,labelpos=NULL,labelcol=par("fg"),
labelcex=1.5, sector.order=NULL,explode=0, shade=0.8,mar=c(4,4,4,4),pty=
"s",...)
```

Arguments

`x`	A numeric vector for which each value will be a sector.
`edges`	The number of lines forming an ellipse.
`radius`	The radius of the pie in user units.
`height`	The height of the pie in user units.
`theta`	The angle of viewing in radians.
`start`	The angle at which to start drawing sectors.
`border`	The color of the sector border lines.
`col`	The colors of the sectors.
`labels`	Optional labels for each sector.
`labelpos`	Optional positions for the labels.
`labelcol`	The color of the labels.
`labelcex`	The character expansion factor for the labels.
`sector.order`	Allows the operator to specify the order in which the sectors are drawn.

explode	The amount to "explode" the pie in user units.
shade	If > 0 and < 1, the proportion to reduce the brightness of the sector color to get a better 3D effect.
mar	Margins around the pie.
pty	Whether to force a square plot region or not.
...	Graphical parameters passed to plot.

Example Program

```
#Include the library
library(plotrix)
expenditure=c(600, 300, 150, 100, 200)
#Calculating the percentage
piepercent<- round(100*expenditure/sum(expenditure),1)
#Adding percentage Symbol to each value
piepercent <- paste(piepercent,"%",sep="")
#Plotting the 3D Pie Graph
pie3D(expenditure, labels=piepercent, explode=0.1,
main="Monthly Expenditure Breakdown",
col=c("red","orange","yellow","blue","green"),
border="brown", clockwise=TRUE)
#Legend for the Pie Graph
legend("topright",c("Housing","Food","Clothing","Entertainment","Oth
er"),
 cex = 0.8, fill=c("red","orange","yellow","blue","green"))
```

Output

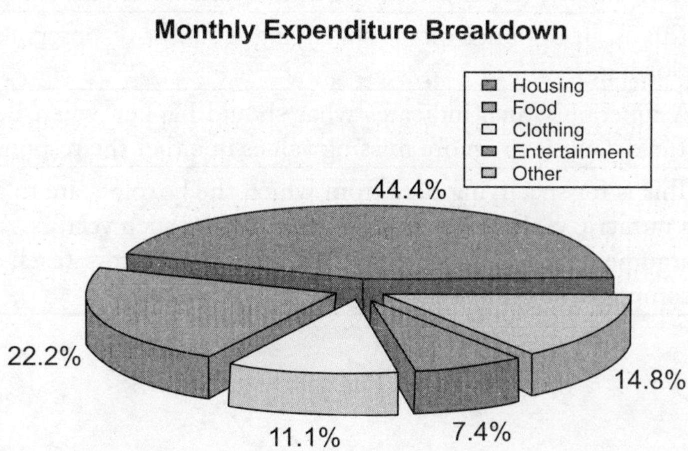

5.5 Boxplots

Boxplots are a measure of how well distributed is the data in a data set. It divides the data set into three quartiles. This graph represents the minimum, maximum, median, first quartile and third quartile in the data set. It is also useful in comparing the distribution of data across data sets by drawing boxplots for each of them.

In descriptive statistics, a box plot or boxplot is a method for graphically depicting groups of numerical data through their quartiles. Boxplots may also have lines extending vertically from the boxes (whiskers) indicating variability outside the upper and lower quartiles, hence the terms box-and-whisker plot and box-and-whisker diagram. Outliers may be plotted as individual points. Boxplots are non-parametric. They display variation in samples of a statistical population without making any assumptions of the underlying statistical distribution. The spacing between the different parts of the box indicates the degree of dispersion (spread) and skewness in the data, and show outliers. Boxplots received their name from the box in the middle.

Boxplots are created in R by using the `boxplot()` function. This function takes in any number of numeric vectors, drawing a boxplot for each vector. We can also pass in a list (or data frame) with numeric vectors as its components. The syntax for `boxplot()` function is as follows.

```
boxplot(formula, data = NULL, ..., subset, na.action = NULL)
```

or

```
boxplot(x, ..., range = 1.5, width = NULL, varwidth = FALSE,
        notch = FALSE, outline = TRUE, names, plot = TRUE,
        border = par("fg"), col = NULL, log = "",
        pars = list(boxwex = 0.8, staplewex = 0.5, outwex = 0.5),
        horizontal = FALSE, add = FALSE, at = NULL)
```

Arguments

`formula`	A formula, such as `y ~ grp`, where `y` is a numeric vector of data values to be split into groups according to the grouping variable `grp` (usually a factor).
`data`	A data.frame (or list) from which the variables in `formula` should be taken.
`subset`	This is an optional vector specifying a subset of observations to be used for plotting.
`na.action`	A function which indicates what should happen when the data contain `NA`s. The default is to ignore missing values in either the response or the group.
`x`	This is for specifying data from which the boxplots are to be produced. Either a numeric vector, or a single list containing such vectors. Additional unnamed arguments specify further data as separate vectors (each corresponding to a component boxplot). `NA`s are allowed in the data.

...	For the `formula` method, named arguments to be passed to the default method. For the default method, unnamed arguments are additional data vectors (unless `x` is a list when they are ignored), and named arguments are arguments and graphical parameters to be passed to `bxp` in addition to the ones given by argument `pars` (and override those in `pars`). Note that `bxp` may or may not make use of graphical parameters it is passed.
range	This determines how far the plot whiskers extend out from the box. If `range` is positive, the whiskers extend to the most extreme data point which is no more than `range` times the interquartile range from the box. A value of zero causes the whiskers to extend to the data extremes.
width	This is a vector giving the relative widths of the boxes making up the plot.
varwidth	If `varwidth` is `TRUE`, the boxes are drawn with widths proportional to the square-roots of the number of observations in the groups.
notch	If `notch` is `TRUE`, a notch is drawn in each side of the boxes. If the notches of two plots do not overlap this is 'strong evidence' that the two medians differ
outline	If `outline` is not true, the outliers are not drawn (as points whereas S+ uses lines).
names	These are group labels which will be printed under each boxplot. Can be a character vector or an expression.
boxwex	This is a scale factor to be applied to all boxes. When there are only a few groups, the appearance of the plot can be improved by making the boxes narrower.
staplewex	This is a staple line width expansion, proportional to box width.
outwex	This is an outlier line width expansion, proportional to box width.
plot	If `TRUE` (the default) then a boxplot is produced. If not, the summaries which the boxplots are based on are returned.
border	This is an optional vector of colors for the outlines of the boxplots. The values in `border` are recycled if the length of `border` is less than the number of plots.
col	If `col` is non-null it is assumed to contain colors to be used to colour the bodies of the box plots. By default they are in the background colour.
log	This is a character indicating if x or y or both coordinates should be plotted in log scale.
pars	This is a list of (potentially many) more graphical parameters, e.g., `boxwex` or `outpch`; these are passed to `bxp` (if `plot` is true.
horizontal	This is a logical value indicating if the boxplots should be horizontal; default `FALSE` means vertical boxes.
add	This is a logical value, if true *add* boxplot to current plot.
at	This is a numeric vector giving the locations where the boxplots should be drawn, particularly when `add = TRUE`; defaults to `1:n` where `n` is the number of boxes.

5.5.1 A Simple Boxplot

Let us use the built-in dataset `airquality` which has "Daily air quality measurements in New York, May to September 1973" for creating the boxplot. Let us make a boxplot for the ozone readings in `airquality`.

Example Program

```
boxplot(airquality$Ozone)
```

Output

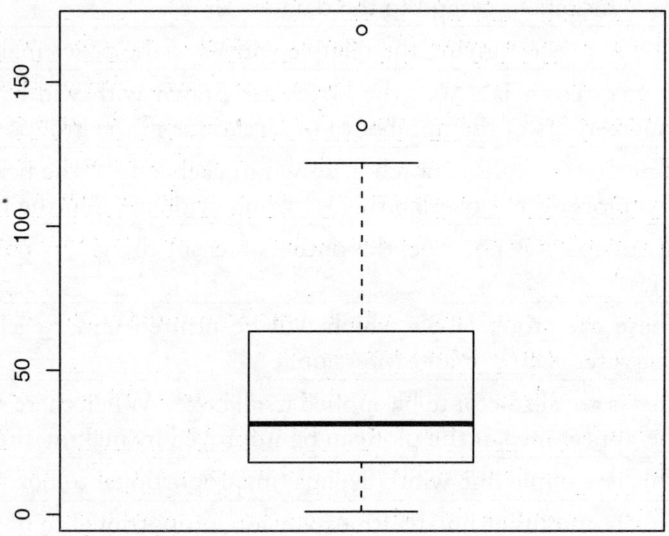

We can see that data above the median is more dispersed. We can also notice two outliers at the higher extreme. We can pass in additional parameters to control the way our plot looks.

5.5.2 Boxplot with Notch

We can have boxplots with a notch. The following program illustrates this. The boxplot can be drawn horizontally by making the argument `horizontal=TRUE`.

Example Program

```
boxplot(airquality$Ozone,
  main = "Mean ozone in parts per billion",
  xlab = "Parts Per Billion",
  ylab = "Ozone",
  col = "yellow",
  border = "red",
   notch = TRUE
)
```

Output

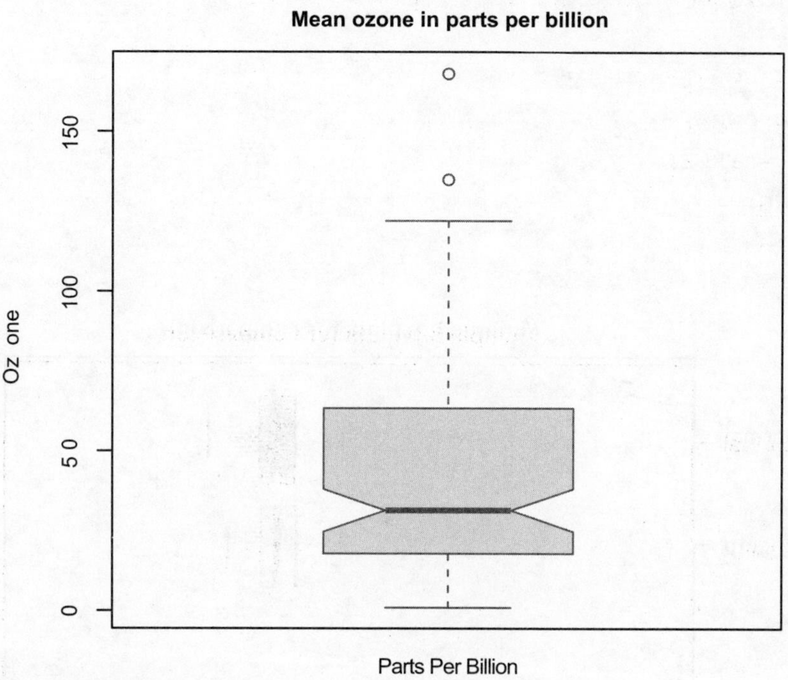

5.5.3 Multiple Boxplots

We can draw multiple boxplots in a single plot, by passing in a list, data frame or multiple vectors. Let us consider the `Ozone` and `Temp` field of `airquality` dataset. Let us also generate normal distribution with the same mean and standard deviation and plot them side by side for comparison. Now let us make 4 boxplots with this data. We use the arguments `at` and `names` to denote the place and label. Normal distribution will be discussed in detail in the coming Chapter.

Example Program

```
# prepare the data
ozone <- airquality$Ozone
temp <- airquality$Temp
# gererate normal distribution with same mean and sd
ozone_norm <- rnorm(200, mean=mean(ozone, na.rm=TRUE), sd=sd(ozone, na.rm=TRUE))
temp_norm <- rnorm(200, mean=mean(temp, na.rm=TRUE), sd=sd(temp, na.rm=TRUE))
# Plotting multiple box plots
boxplot(ozone, ozone_norm, temp, temp_norm,
  main = "Multiple boxplots for comparision",
```

```
at = c(1,2,4,5),
names = c("ozone", "normal", "temp", "normal"),
las = 2,
col = c("orange","red"),
border = "brown",
horizontal = TRUE,
notch = TRUE)
```

Output

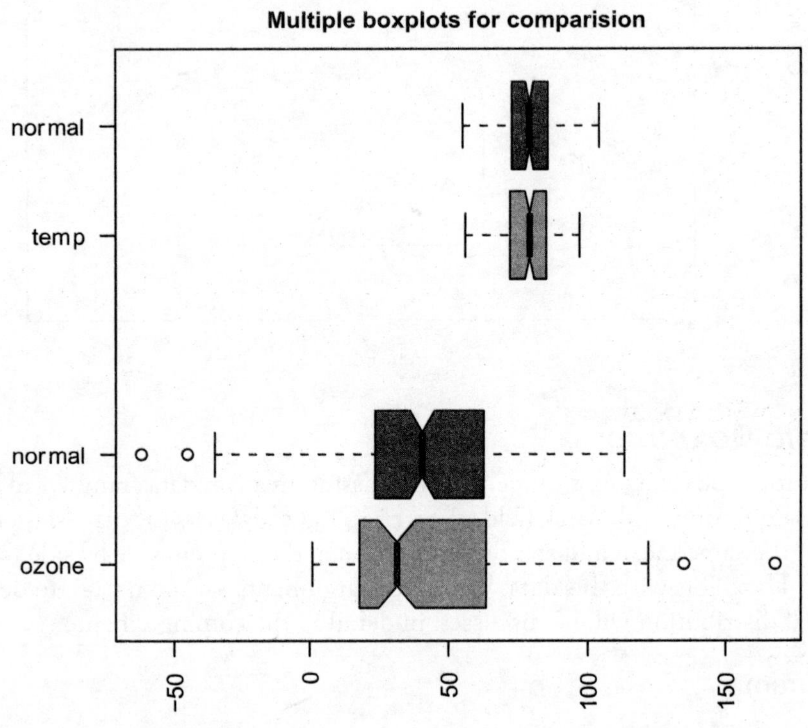

5.5.4 Boxplots using Formula

The function `boxplot()` can also take in formulas of the form `y~x` where, `y` is a numeric vector which is grouped according to the value of `x`. For example, in our dataset `airquality`, the `Temp` can be our numeric vector. `Month` can be our grouping variable, so that we get the boxplot for each month separately. In our dataset, month is in the form of number (1=January, 2-Febuary and so on).

Example Program

```
boxplot(Temp~Month,data=airquality,
main="Different boxplots for each month",xlab="Month Number",
ylab="Degree Fahrenheit",col="yellow",border="black")
```

Output

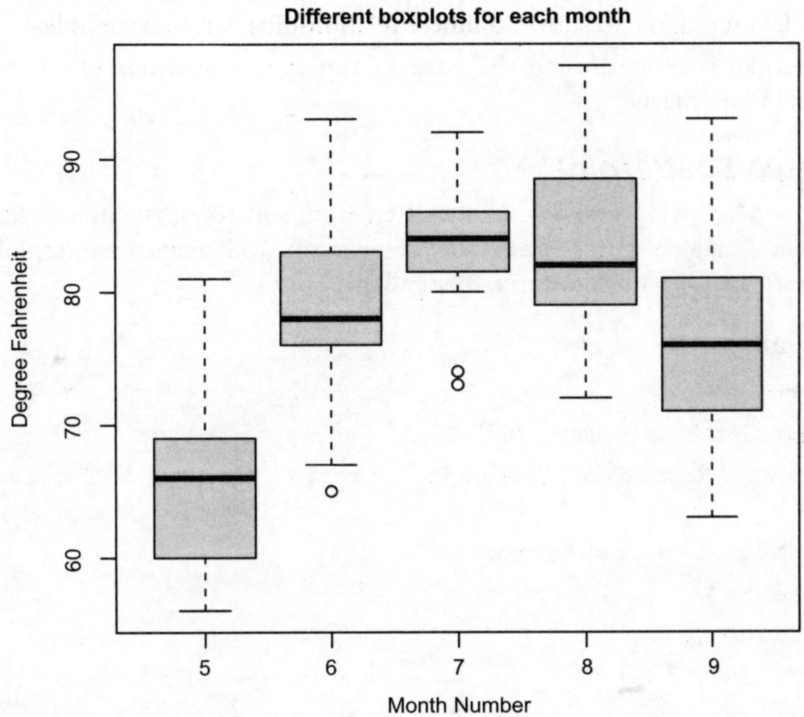

5.6 Scatterplots

A scatter plot (also called a scatter graph, scatter chart, scattergram, or scatter diagram) is a type of plot or mathematical diagram using Cartesian coordinates to display values for typically two variables for a set of data. If the points are color-coded, one additional variable can be displayed. The data is displayed as a collection of points, each having the value of one variable determining the position on the horizontal axis and the value of the other variable determining the position on the vertical axis.

A scatter plot can be used either when one continuous variable that is under the control of the experimenter and the other depends on it or when both continuous variables are independent. If a parameter exists that is systematically incremented and/or decremented by the other, it is called the control parameter or independent variable and is customarily plotted along the horizontal axis. The measured or dependent variable is customarily plotted along the vertical axis. If no dependent variable exists, either type of variable can be plotted on either axis and a scatter plot will illustrate only the degree of correlation between two variables.

A scatter plot can suggest various kinds of correlations between variables with a certain confidence interval. For example, weight and height, weight would be on y axis and height would be on the x axis. Correlations may be positive (rising), negative (falling), or null (uncorrelated). If the pattern of dots slopes from lower left to upper right, it indicates a positive correlation between the variables being studied. If the pattern of dots slopes from upper left to lower right, it indicates a negative correlation. A line of best fit (alternatively called 'trendline') can be drawn in order to study the relationship between the variables. A scatter plot is also very useful when we wish to see how two comparable data sets agree to show nonlinear relationships between variables.

The simple scatterplot is created using the `plot()` function. The syntax of `plot()` function is already explained in line charts.

5.6.1 A Simple Scatterplot

We use the data set "`mtcars`" available in the R environment to create a basic scatterplot. Let's use the columns "`wt`" and "`mpg`" in `mtcars`. The below script will create a scatterplot graph for the relation between `wt`(weight) and `mpg`(miles per gallon).

Example Program

```
# Get the input values.
input <- mtcars[,c('wt','mpg')]
# Plot the chart for cars with weight between 2.5 to 5 and mileage between
15 and 30.
plot(x = input$wt,y = input$mpg,
   xlab = "Weight",
   ylab = "Milage",
   xlim = c(2.5,5),
   ylim = c(15,30),
   main = "Weight vs Milage"
)
```

Output

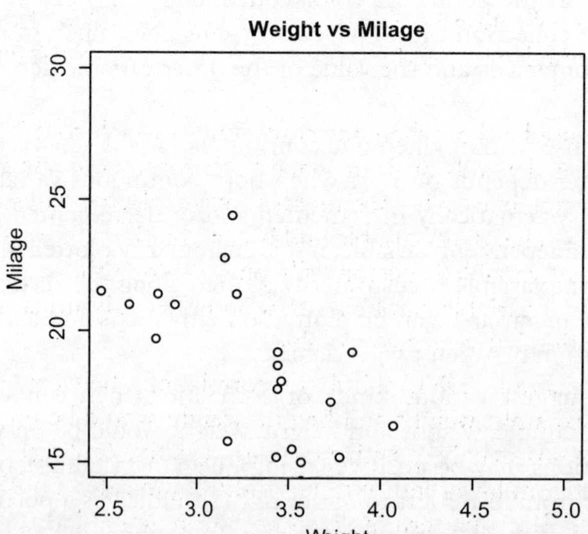

5.6.2 Scatterplot with Trendlines

It is also possible to add trendlines to a scatterplot. The function `abline()` can be used to add vertical, horizontal or regression lines to a graph. `lm()` is a linear model function, such like linear regression analysis. The syntax of `lm()` function is as follows.

`lm(formula, data, subset, weights, ...)` where `formula` is a model description, such as `x ~ y`, `data` is optional which gives variables in the model, `subset` is optional, a subset vector of observations to be used in the fitting process and `weights` is optional, a vector of weights to be used in the fitting process. Following program illustrates this.

Example Program

```
input <- mtcars[,c('wt','mpg')]
plot(x = input$wt,y = input$mpg,
   xlab = "Weight",
   ylab = "Milage",
   main = "Weight vs Milage")
abline(lm(input$mpg~ input$wt),col="blue")
```

Output

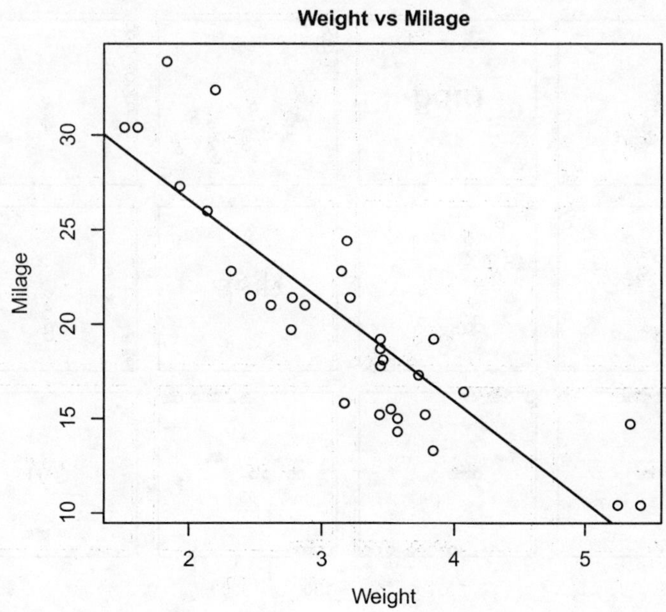

5.6.3 Scatterplot Matrices

When we have more than two variables and we want to find the correlation between one variable versus the remaining ones we use scatterplot matrix. We use `pairs()` function to create matrices of scatterplots. The basic syntax for creating scatterplot matrices in R is as follows.

`pairs(formula, data)` where `formula` represents the series of variables used in pairs and `data` represents the data set from which the variables will be taken. Each variable is paired up with each of the remaining variable. A scatterplot is plotted for each pair.

Example Program

```
# Plot the matrices between 4 variables giving 12 plots.
# One variable with 3 others and total 4 variables.
pairs(~wt+mpg+disp+cyl,data = mtcars,
   main = "Scatterplot Matrix")
```

Output

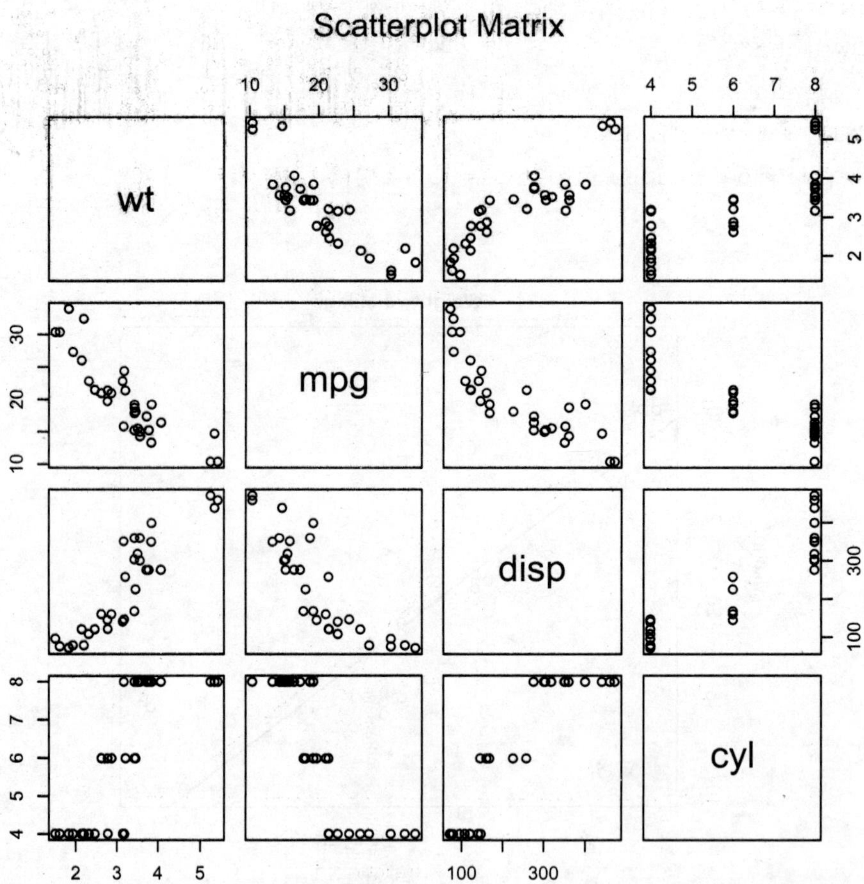

5.6.4 3D Scatterplot

To draw 3D scatterplots, we need to install the package `"scatterplot3d"`. We can draw scatterplots in three dimensions using the `scatterplot3d` package. Let us draw a 3D scatterplot with three parameters weight, milage and displacement of `mtcars` dataset available in R.

Example Program

```
attach(mtcars)
scatterplot3d(wt,disp,mpg, main="3D Scatterplot")
```

Output

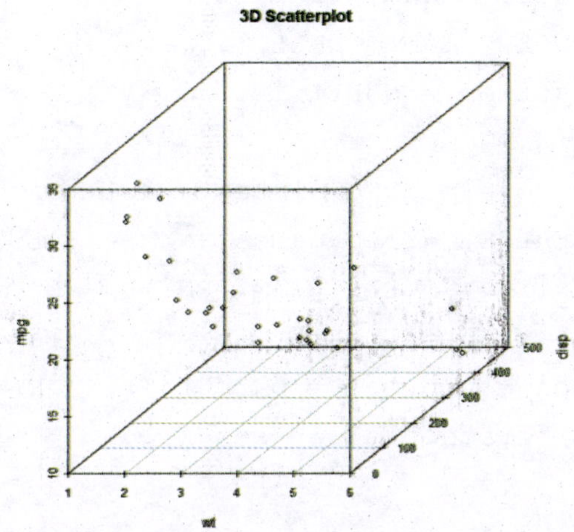

We can also draw 3D scatterplots with colors and vertical drop lines. Following program illustrates this.

Example Program

```
# 3D Scatterplot with Coloring and Vertical Drop Lines
attach(mtcars)
scatterplot3d(wt,disp,mpg, pch=16, highlight.3d=TRUE,
  type="h", main="3D Scatterplot")
```

Output

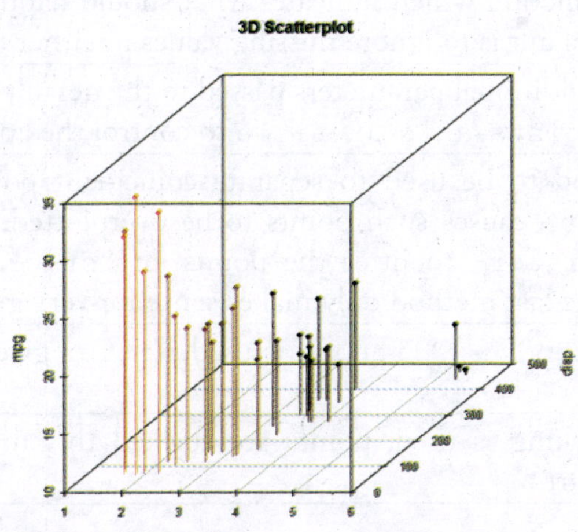

5.7 Strip Charts

A strip chart is the most basic type of plot available. It plots the data in order along a line with each data point represented as a box. These plots are a good alternative to boxplots when sample sizes are small. Strip charts can be created using the `stripchart()` function in R programming language. This function takes in a numeric vector or a list of numeric vectors, drawing a strip chart for each vector. The syntax for `stripchart()` function is as follows.

```
stripchart(x, data = NULL, dlab = NULL, ...,
           subset, na.action = NULL)
```

OR

```
stripchart(x, method = "overplot", jitter = 0.1, offset = 1/3,
           vertical = FALSE, group.names, add = FALSE,
           at = NULL, xlim = NULL, ylim = NULL,
           ylab = NULL, xlab = NULL, dlab = "", glab = "",
           log = "", pch = 0,  col = par("fg"), cex = par("cex"),
           axes = TRUE, frame.plot = axes, ...)
```

Arguments

`x`	The data from which the plots are to be produced. In the default method the data can be specified as a single numeric vector, or as list of numeric vectors, each corresponding to a component plot. In the `formula` method, a symbolic specification of the form `y ~ g` can be given, indicating the observations in the vector `y` are to be grouped according to the levels of the factor `g`. `NA`s are allowed in the data.
`data`	This is a data.frame (or list) from which the variables in `x` should be taken.
`subset`	This is an optional vector specifying a subset of observations to be used for plotting.
`na.action`	This is a function which indicates what should happen when the data contain `NA`s. The default is to ignore missing values in either the response or the group.
`...`	These are additional parameters passed to the default method or by it to `plot.window`, `points`, `axis` and `title` to control the appearance of the plot.
`method`	The method to be used to separate coincident points. The default method `"overplot"` causes such points to be overplotted, but it is also possible to specify `"jitter"` to jitter the points, or `"stack"` have coincident points stacked. The last method only makes sense for very granular data.
`jitter`	When `method = "jitter"` is used, `jitter` gives the amount of jittering applied.
`offset`	When stacking is used, points are stacked this many line-heights (symbol widths) apart.

`vertical`	When vertical is `TRUE` the plots are drawn vertically rather than the default horizontal.
`group.names`	The group labels which will be printed alongside (or underneath) each plot.
`add`	This is a logical value, if true *add* the chart to the current plot.
`at`	This is a numeric vector giving the locations where the charts should be drawn, particularly when `add = TRUE`; defaults to `1:n` where `n` is the number of boxes.
`ylab, xlab`	Labels for x-axis and y-axis.
`dlab, glab`	An alternate way to specify axis labels.
`xlim, ylim`	Plot limits for x-axis and y-axis.
`log`	Specifies on which axes to use a log scale.
`pch, col, cex`	Graphical parameters.
`axes, frame.plot`	Axis control.

5.7.1 A Simple Strip Chart

Let us use the built-in dataset `airquality` which has "Daily air quality measurements in New York, May to September 1973" for creating a strip chart. Let us make a strip chart for the ozone readings.

Example Program

```
stripchart(airquality$Ozone)
```

Output

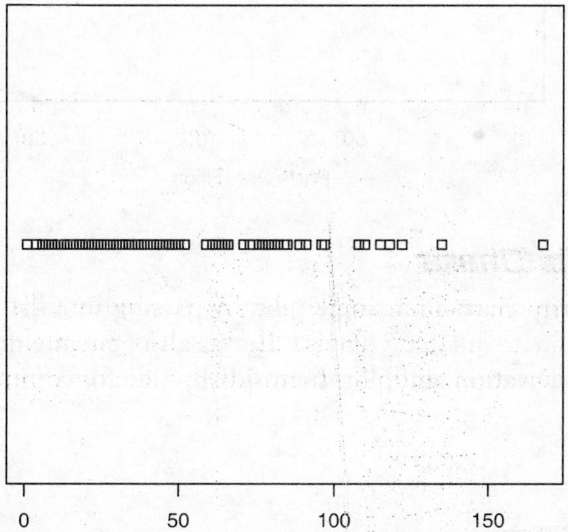

We can see that the data is mostly cluttered below 50 with one falling outside 150. We can pass in additional parameters to control the way our plot looks. Some of the frequently used ones are, `main`-to give the `title`, `xlab` and `ylab`-to provide labels for the axes, `method`-to specify the way coincident points are plotted like `stacked` or `jitter`, `col`-to define color etc. Additionally, with the argument `vertical=TRUE` we can plot it vertically and with `pch` we can specify the plotting character (square by default). Some values of `pch` are 0 for square, 1 for circle, 2 for triangle etc.

Example Program

```
stripchart(airquality$Ozone,
 main="Mean ozone in parts per billion", xlab="Parts Per Billion",
 ylab="Ozone", method="jitter", col="red", pch=1)
```

Output

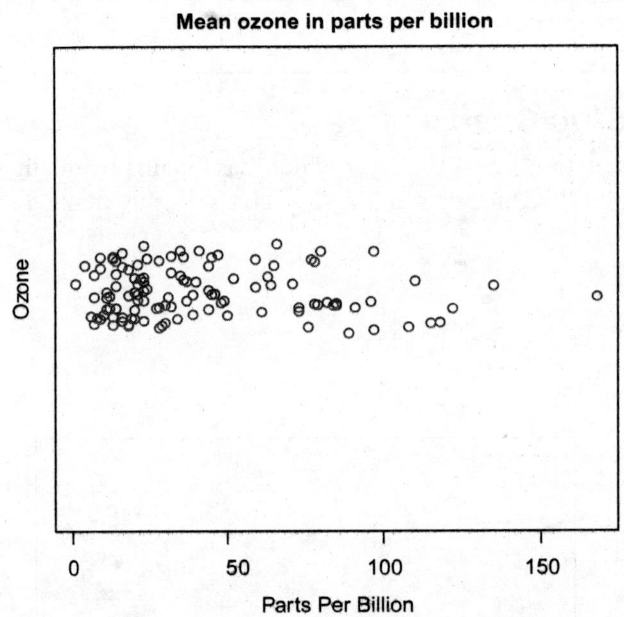

5.7.2 Multiple Strip Charts

We can draw multiple strip charts in a single plot, by passing in a list of numeric vectors. Let us consider the `Temp` field of `airquality` dataset. Let us also generate normal distribution with the same mean and standard deviation and plot them side by side for comparison.

Example Program

```
# prepare the data
temp <- airquality$Temp
# gererate normal distribution with same mean and sd
```

```
tempNorm <- rnorm(200, mean=mean(temp, na.rm=TRUE), sd = sd(temp,
na.rm=TRUE))
# make a list
x <- list("temp"=temp, "norm"=tempNorm)
stripchart(x, main="Multiple stripchart for comparision",
 xlab="Degree Fahrenheit", ylab="Temperature",
 method="jitter", col=c("green","red"), pch=16)
```

Output

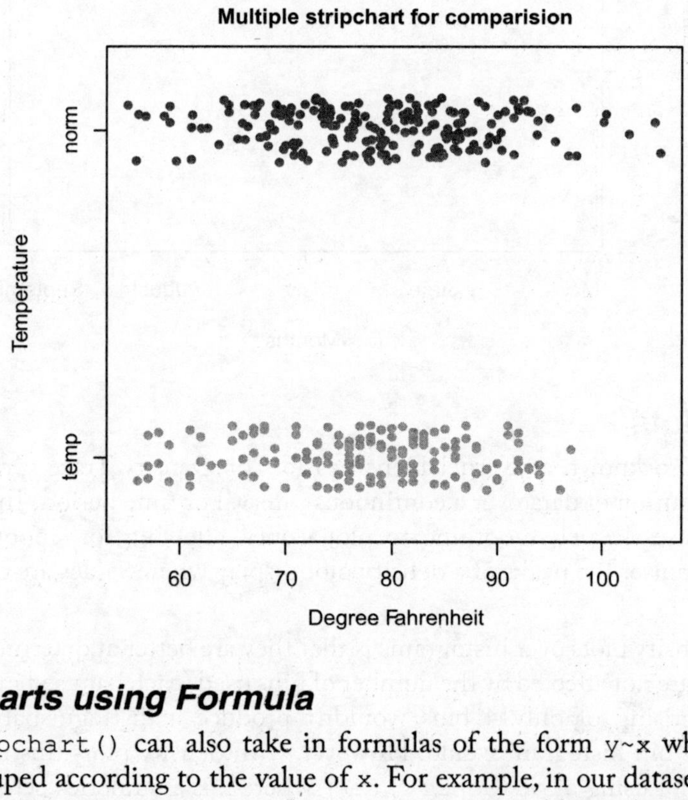

5.7.3 Strip Charts using Formula

The function `stripchart()` can also take in formulas of the form `y~x` where, `y` is a numeric vector which is grouped according to the value of `x`. For example, in our dataset `airquality`, the `Temp` can be our numeric vector. `Month` can be our grouping variable, so that we get the strip chart for each month separately. In our dataset, `month` is in the form of number (1=January, 2-Febuary and so on). Following program illustrates how strip charts can be created using formula.

Example Program

```
stripchart(Temp~Month,
 data=airquality, main="Different strip chart for each month",
 xlab="Months", ylab="Temperature", col="green",
 group.names=c("May","June","July","August","September"),
 vertical=TRUE,pch=16)
```

Output

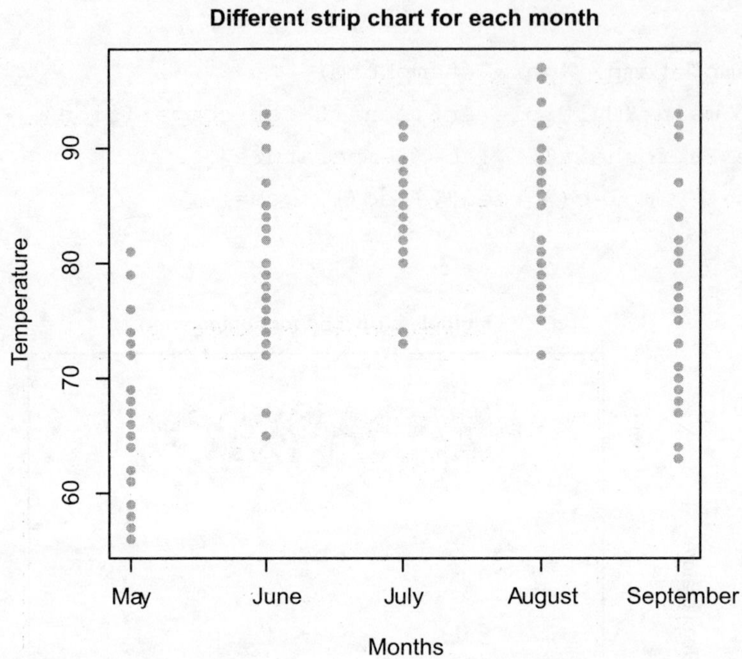

5.8 Density Plots

Density plots are also known as Kernel Density Plots or Density Trace Graph. A Density Plot visualizes the distribution of data over a continuous interval or time period. This chart is a variation of histogram that uses kernel smoothing to plot values, allowing for smoother distributions by smoothing out the noise. The peaks of a density plot display where values are concentrated over the interval.

An advantage of density plots over histograms is that they are better at determining the distribution shape because they are not affected by the number of bins used (each bar used in a typical histogram). A histogram comprising of only 4 bins wouldn't produce a distinguishable enough shape of distribution as a 20-bin histogram would. However, with density plots this isn't an issue. We can create the density plot using `plot(density(x))` where `x` is a numeric vector. For illustrating the density plot, we are using the built-in `mtcars` dataset. Following program illustrates how to draw a density plot.

Example Program

```
d <- density(mtcars$mpg) # returns the density data
plot(d) # plots the results
```

Output

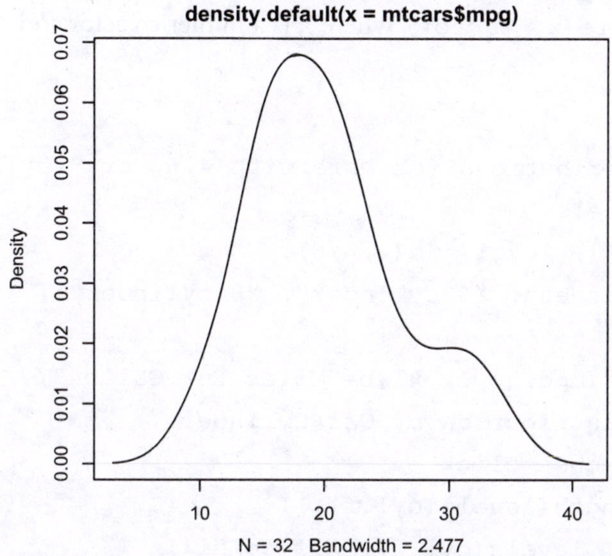

Density plots can be filled with colors. Following program illustrates this.

Example Program

```
# Filled Density Plot
d <- density(mtcars$mpg)
plot(d, main="Kernel Density of Miles Per Gallon")
polygon(d, col="blue", border="yellow")
```

Output

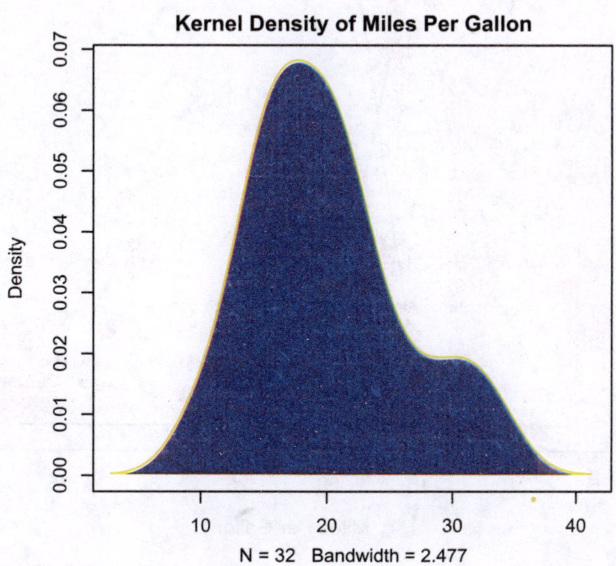

It is possible to compare two or more density plots. The `sm.density.compare( )` function in the `sm` package allows us to superimpose the kernal density plots of two or more groups. The format is `sm.density.compare(x, factor)` where x is a numeric vector and `factor` is the grouping variable.

Example Program

```
# Compare MPG distributions for cars with 4,6, or 8 cylinders
# create value labels
cyl.f <- factor(cyl, levels= c(4,6,8),
labels = c("4 cylinder", "6 cylinder", "8 cylinder"))
# plot densities
sm.density.compare(mpg, cyl, xlab="Miles Per Gallon")
title(main="MPG Distribution by Car Cylinders")
# add legend via mouse click
colfill<-c(2:(2+length(levels(cyl.f))))
legend(locator(1), levels(cyl.f), fill=colfill)
```

Output

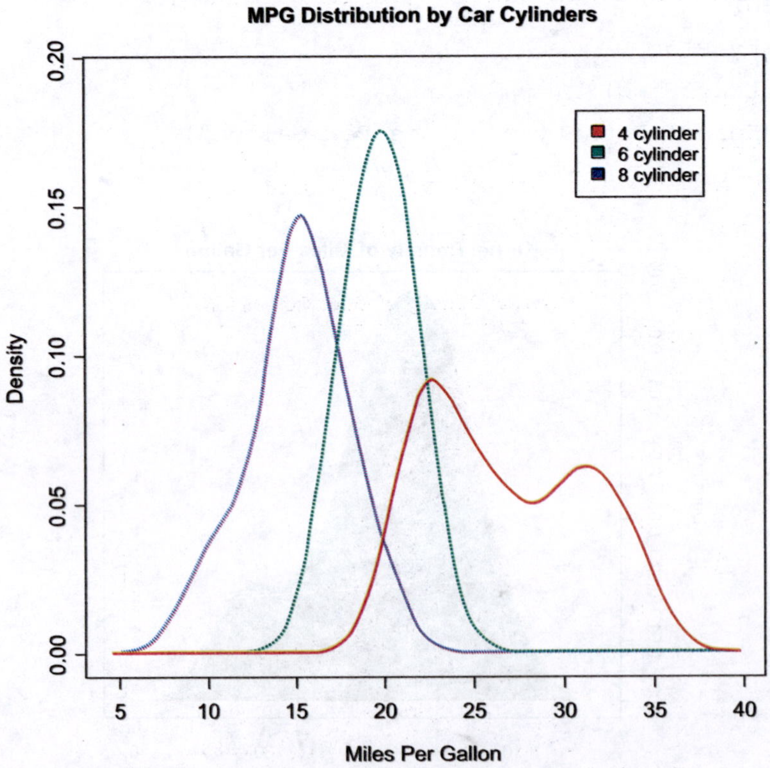

5.9 Dot Plots

A dot chart or dot plot is a statistical chart consisting of data points plotted on a fairly simple scale, typically using filled in circles. There are two common, yet very different, versions of the dot chart. The first has been used in hand-drawn (pre-computer era) graphs to depict distributions. The other version is described by William S. Cleveland as an alternative to the bar chart, in which dots are used to depict the quantitative values (e.g. counts) associated with categorical variables.

The dot plot as a representation of a distribution consists of group of data points plotted on a simple scale. Dot plots are used for continuous, quantitative, univariate data. Data points may be labelled if there are few of them. Dot plots are one of the simplest statistical plots, and are suitable for small to moderate sized data sets. They are useful for highlighting clusters and gaps, as well as outliers. Their other advantage is the conservation of numerical information. When dealing with larger data sets (around 20–30 or more data points) the related stemplot, box plot or histogram may be more efficient, as dot plots may become too cluttered after this point. Dot plots may be distinguished from histograms in that dots are not spaced uniformly along the horizontal axis.

Dot plot may also refer to plots of points that each belong to one of several categories. They are an alternative to bar charts or pie charts, and look somewhat like a horizontal bar chart where the bars are replaced by dots at the values associated with each category. Compared to (vertical) bar charts and pie charts, dot plots allow more accurate interpretation of the graph by readers by making the labels easier to read, reducing graph clutter and supporting table look-up.

We can create dotplots with the `dotchart(x, labels=)` function, where `x` is a numeric vector and `labels` is a vector of labels for each point. We can add a `groups=` option to designate a factor specifying how the elements of `x` are grouped. If so, the option `gcolor=` controls the color of the groups label. `cex` controls the size of the labels. Following program illustrates how to draw a dot plot. For this the built-in data set `mtcars` is used.

Example Program

```
# Simple Dotplot
dotchart(mtcars$mpg,labels=row.names(mtcars),cex=.7,main="Gas Milage for
Car Models",
xlab="Miles Per Gallon")
```

Output

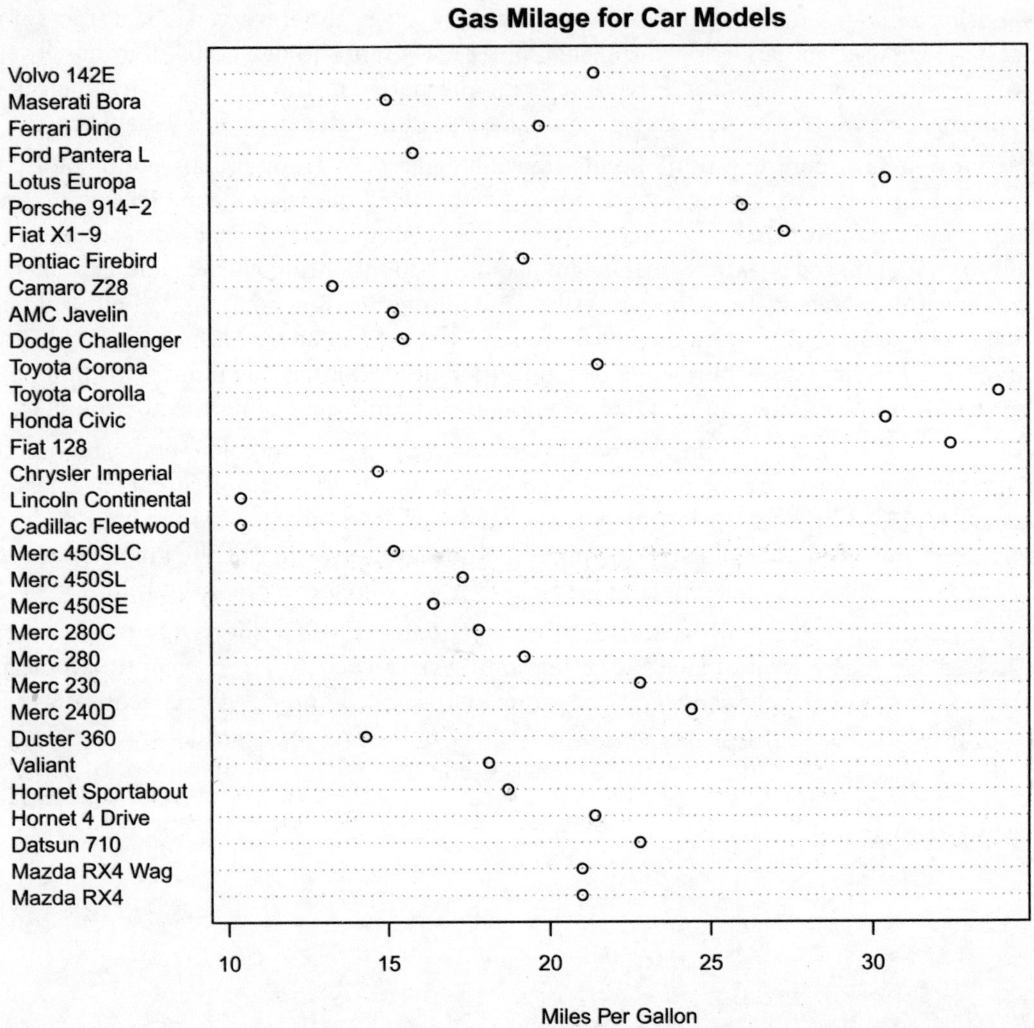

We can also have grouped and sorted dot plots with additional parameters. Following program illustrates how to draw grouped and sorted dot plots. For this the built-in data set `mtcars` is used. The cars are sorted based on mileage and grouped on the number of cylinders.

Example Program

```
#Dotplot: Grouped Sorted and Colored.Sort by mpg, group and color by cylinder
x <- mtcars[order(mtcars$mpg),] # sort by mpg
x$cyl <- factor(x$cyl) # it must be a factor
x$color[x$cyl==4] <- "red"
```

```
x$color[x$cyl==6] <- “blue”
x$color[x$cyl==8] <- “darkgreen”
dotchart(x$mpg,labels=row.names(x),cex=.7,groups=      x$cyl,main=”Gas
Milage for Car Models\ngrouped by cylinder”,xlab=”Miles Per Gallon”,
gcolor=”black”, color=x$color)
```

Output

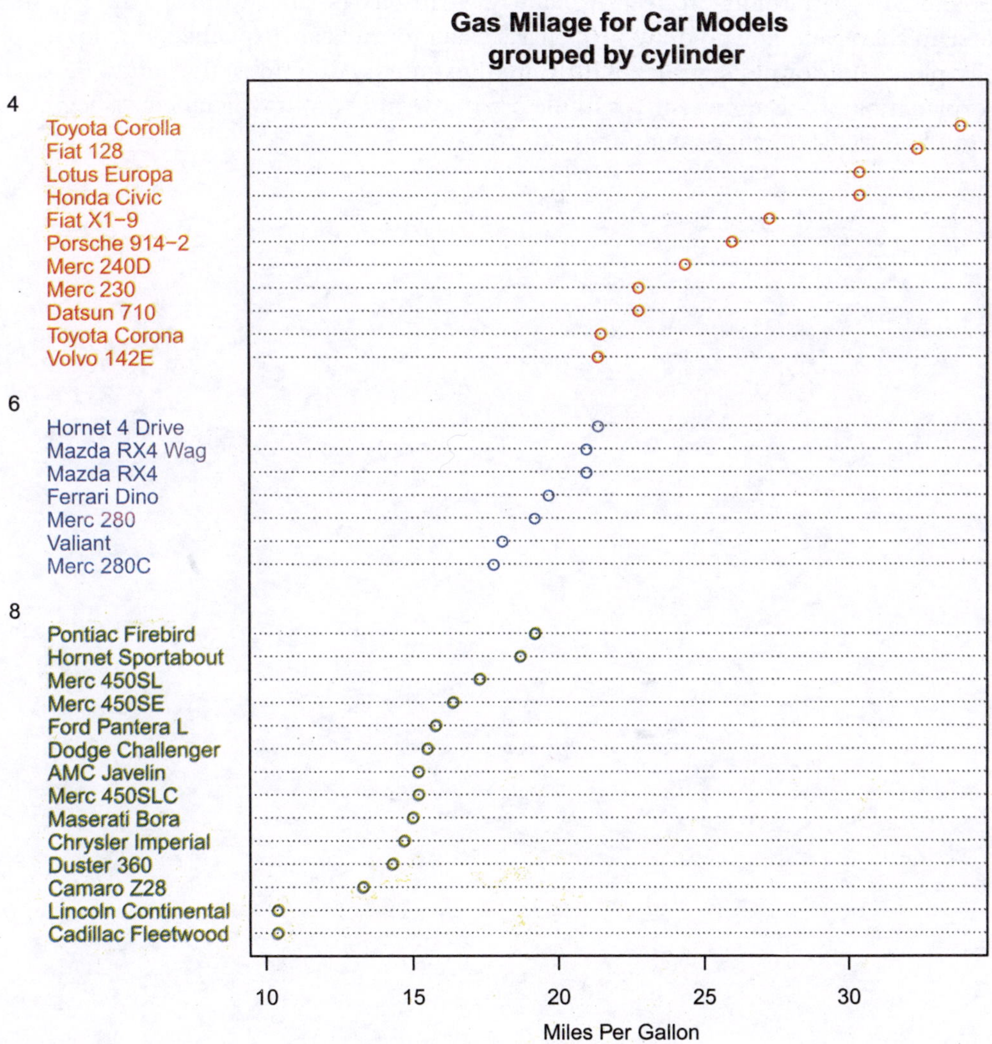

5.10 Conclusion

This Chapter gives a detailed description of a variety of charts and graphs available in R. The Chapter begins with bar charts, how to plot bar charts vertically, how to plot bar charts horizontally, plotting categorical data using bar charts, grouped bar charts and stacked bar charts. Another type of charts called histogram, how to plot a simple histogram, plotting histogram with labels, plotting histogram with breaks and plotting histogram with density lines are clearly illustrated. The line graph, how to draw a simple line graph and line graph with multiple lines are also explained. Coming to pie charts, how to draw a simple pie chart, pie chart with slice percentages and 3D pie charts are also described in detail. Another important plot known as boxplots, how to draw a simple boxplot, boxplot with notch, multiple boxplots and how to draw boxplots using formula are also explained. Scatterplots, how to draw a simple scatterplot, scatterplot with trendlines, scatterplot matrices and 3D scatterplots are well explained. Strip charts, how to plot a simple strip chart, multiple strip charts and how to draw strip charts using formula are explained. Finally various kinds of density plots and dot plots available in R are illustrated. All graphs are simply illustrated with syntax, explanation of the arguments, example programs and output which helps a beginner to gain an in depth knowledge in charts and graphs of R.

6 Connecting R to External Interfaces

In R, there may be situations where we need to read data from files stored outside the R environment. We can also write data into files which will be stored and accessed by the operating system. R can read and write into various file formats like csv, xlsx, xml etc. R can also read and write binary files. Similarly R is capable of reading and writing JSON files. We can read data from or write data to any database from R. Likewise many of the data published by international organizations are available through their web site. R is also capable of reading web data from html pages which makes R a powerful programming language. We will see how R deals with each of them one by one.

6.1 CSV Files

In this section we will learn to read data from a `csv` file and then write data into a `csv` file. The `csv` file is a text file in which the values in the columns are separated by a comma. CSV stands for "comma-separated values". The file should be present in current working directory so that R can read it. We can also set the directory from which files are to be read or written. Following program illustrates this.

Example Program

```
# Get and print current working directory.
getwd()
# Set current working directory.
setwd("D:/R Programs")
# Get and print current working directory.
getwd()
```

Output

```
# Get and print current working directory.
[1] "C:/Users/USER/Documents"
# Get and print current working directory.
[1] "D:/R Programs"
```

Before reading from a `csv` file, we need to create it first. We can create a `csv` file either using notepad or Microsoft Excel. Type the following data in a notepad and save as "**Employee.csv**".

```
empno,empname,dept,dob,salary
10,Jack,Sales,1970-09-01,40000
11,Jill,Marketing,1972-05-28,50000
15,Smith,HR,1977-04-08,45000
16,Joe,Sales,1990-07-21,25000
18,John,HR,1991-01-26,35000
20,Adam,Sales,1985-03-22,32000
22,Bob,Finance,1980-05-12,42000
23,Sam,HR,1973-06-09,60000
24,Dawn,Marketing,1988-12-13,50000
25,Solomon,Sales,1978-11-27,60000
```

6.1.1 Reading from a csv File

We can read from a csv file using the function `read.csv()`. The output will be a data frame. We can check for the type, number of rows and columns in the data frame. Following program illustrates this.

Example Program

```
data <- read.csv("Employee.csv")
# data frame
data
# check whether data is of type data frame
is.data.frame(data)
# prints the number of columns in data
ncol(data)
# prints the number of rows in data
nrow(data)
```

Output

```
# data frame
   empno empname      dept        dob salary
1     10    Jack     Sales 1970-09-01  40000
2     11    Jill Marketing 1972-05-28  50000
3     15   Smith        HR 1977-04-08  45000
4     16     Joe     Sales 1990-07-21  25000
5     18    John        HR 1991-01-26  35000
6     20    Adam     Sales 1985-03-22  32000
7     22     Bob   Finance 1980-05-12  42000
```

```
8      23      Sam          HR 1973-06-09  60000
9      24     Dawn Marketing 1988-12-13  50000
10     25 Solomon      Sales 1978-11-27  60000
# check whether data is of type data frame
[1] TRUE
# prints the number of columns in data
[1] 5
# prints the number of rows in data
[1] 10
```

Once the data is available in the data frame we can apply the functions to the data frame to process the data and get the desired results. Following program illustrates this.

Example Program

```
data <- read.csv("Employee.csv")
# data frame
data
# Get the max salary from data frame.
sal <- max(data$salary)
sal
# Get the details of person having max salary.
detail <- subset(data, salary == max(salary))
detail
# Get the min salary in each dept.
minsal <- aggregate(data$salary,list(m=data$dept),min)
minsal
# Get the details of people in HR dept
retval <- subset( data, dept == "HR")
retval
# Get the details of people with salary>25000 in Sales dept.
info <- subset(data, salary > 25000 & dept == "Sales")
info
# Get the details of people who born on or before 1980
bornval <- subset(data, as.Date(dob) > as.Date("1980-01-01"))
bornval
```

Output

```
# data frame
   empno empname      dept         dob salary
```

```
1     10    Jack     Sales 1970-09-01  40000
2     11    Jill Marketing 1972-05-28  50000
3     15   Smith        HR 1977-04-08  45000
4     16     Joe     Sales 1990-07-21  25000
5     18    John        HR 1991-01-26  35000
6     20    Adam     Sales 1985-03-22  32000
7     22     Bob   Finance 1980-05-12  42000
8     23     Sam        HR 1973-06-09  60000
9     24    Dawn Marketing 1988-12-13  50000
10    25 Solomon     Sales 1978-11-27  60000
# Get the max salary from data frame.
 [1] 60000
# Get the details of person having max salary.
   empno empname  dept        dob salary
8     23     Sam    HR 1973-06-09  60000
10    25 Solomon Sales 1978-11-27  60000
# Get the min salary in each dept.
          m     x
1   Finance 42000
2        HR 35000
3 Marketing 50000
4     Sales 25000
# Get the details of people in HR dept
  empno empname dept        dob salary
3    15   Smith   HR 1977-04-08  45000
5    18    John   HR 1991-01-26  35000
8    23     Sam   HR 1973-06-09  60000
# Get the details of people with salary>25000 in Sales dept.
   empno empname  dept        dob salary
1     10    Jack Sales 1970-09-01  40000
6     20    Adam Sales 1985-03-22  32000
10    25 Solomon Sales 1978-11-27  60000
# Get the details of people who born on or before 1980
  empno empname      dept        dob salary
4    16     Joe     Sales 1990-07-21  25000
5    18    John        HR 1991-01-26  35000
```

```
6     20     Adam      Sales 1985-03-22  32000
7     22      Bob    Finance 1980-05-12  42000
9     24     Dawn Marketing 1988-12-13  50000
```

6.1.2 Writing to a csv File

We can create csv file from existing data frame in R. The write.csv() function is used to create the csv file. This file gets created in the working directory. Following program illustrates this.

Example Program

```
data <- read.csv("Employee.csv")
# Get the details of people in HR dept
hr <- subset( data, dept == "HR")
# Write filtered data into a new file.
write.csv(hr,"hr.csv")
hrdata <- read.csv("hr.csv")
# Details of people in HR dept from hr.csv file
hrdata
```

Output

```
# Details of people in HR dept from hr.csv file
  X empno empname dept        dob salary
1 3    15    Smith   HR 1977-04-08  45000
2 5    18     John   HR 1991-01-26  35000
3 8    23      Sam   HR 1973-06-09  60000
```

Here we can see additional column X comes from the data set while writing to the file. This can be dropped using additional parameters while writing the file as follows.

```
write.csv(hr,"hr.csv",row.names=FALSE)
```

This will produce the output as follows

```
  empno empname dept        dob salary
1    15    Smith   HR 1977-04-08  45000
2    18     John   HR 1991-01-26  35000
3    23      Sam   HR 1973-06-09  60000
```

6.2 Microsoft Excel

Microsoft Excel is the most widely used spreadsheet program. We need to read from excel files and write into excel files from R. The excel files will be in the format .xls or .xlsx. R needs excel specific packages to read from Microsoft Excel. Some of the packages are XLConnect, xlsx, gdata etc. We will be using xlsx package in this Chapter. Before using this package, we need to install this package. It may ask to install some additional packages on which this package is dependent. Open a Microsoft Excel file. We can create an `xlsx` file by typing the same values given in "`Employee.csv`" given above and save it as "`Employee.xlsx`".

6.2.1 Reading from `xlsx` File

We can read from a `xlsx` file using the function `read.xlsx()`. The output will be a data frame. Following program illustrates this.

Example Program

```
d <- read.xlsx("Employee.xlsx", sheetIndex = 1)
d
```

Output

```
   empno empname      dept        dob salary
1     10    Jack     Sales 1970-09-01  40000
2     11    Jill Marketing 1972-05-28  50000
3     15   Smith        HR 1977-04-08  45000
4     16     Joe     Sales 1990-07-21  25000
5     18    John        HR 1991-01-26  35000
6     20    Adam     Sales 1985-03-22  32000
7     22     Bob   Finance 1980-05-12  42000
8     23     Sam        HR 1973-06-09  60000
9     24    Dawn Marketing 1988-12-13  50000
10    25 Solomon     Sales 1978-11-27  60000
```

Once the data is read into a data frame we can apply all the functions supported by data frame as in the case of `csv` files.

6.2.2 Writing to `xlsx` File

We can write data from R to an excel file. For this we can use `write.xlsx()` function. The syntax is as follows.

```
write.xlsx(x, file, sheetName = "Sheet1",
  col.names = TRUE, row.names = TRUE, append = FALSE)
```

where `x` is a data frame to be written into the workbook, `file` is the path to the output file, `sheetName` is a character string to use for the sheet name, `col.names`, `row.names` is a logical value specifying whether the column names/row names of `x` are to be written to the file, `append` is a logical value indicating if `x` should be appended to an existing file.

Following program illustrates how to write to an excel file.

Example Program

```
data <- read.xlsx("Employee.xlsx")
```

```
# Get the details of people in HR dept
hr <- subset( data, dept == "HR")
# Write filtered data into a new file.
write.xlsx(hr, "hrEmployees.xlsx", sheetName = "Sheet1",
  col.names = FALSE, row.names = FALSE, append = FALSE)
hrdata <- read.xlsx("hrEmployees.xlsx")
# Details of people in HR dept from hr.xlsx file
hrdata
```

Output

```
  empno empname dept        dob salary
1    15   Smith   HR 1977-04-08  45000
2    18    John   HR 1991-01-26  35000
3    23     Sam   HR 1973-06-09  60000
```

6.3 Databases

R can connect easily to many relational databases like MySQL, Oracle, Sql server etc. and fetch records from them as a data frame. Once the data is available in the R environment, it becomes a normal R data set and can be manipulated or analyzed using all the powerful packages and functions. In this Chapter we will be using MySQL database for connecting to R. R has a built-in package named "RMySQL" which provides native connectivity between R and MySQL database. We need to install this package before dealing with databases.

6.3.1 Connecting R to MySQL

Once the package is installed, we create a connection object in R to connect to the database. It takes the username, password, database name and host name as input. Following program illustrates this.

Example Program

```
# Create a connection Object to MySQL database.
# Connect to the sample database named "mysql" that comes with MySql
installation.
mysqlconnection = dbConnect(MySQL(), user = "Jeeva", password = "Jose",
dbname = "mysql", host = "localhost")
# List the tables available in this database.
 dbListTables(mysqlconnection)
```

Output

```
[1] "columns_priv"                 "db"
[3] "dept"                         "event"
```

```
 [5] "func"                          "general_log"
 [7] "help_category"                 "help_keyword"
 [9] "help_relation"                 "help_topic"
[11] "innodb_index_stats"            "innodb_table_stats"
[13] "ndb_binlog_index"              "plugin"
[15] "proc"                          "procs_priv"
[17] "proxies_priv"                  "sailor"
[19] "servers"                       "slave_master_info"
[21] "slave_relay_log_info"          "slave_worker_info"
[23] "slow_log"                      "tables_priv"
[25] "time_zone"                     "time_zone_leap_second"
[27] "time_zone_name"                "time_zone_transition"
[29] "time_zone_transition_type" "user"
```

6.3.2 Creating Tables

We can create tables in MySQL using the function `dbWriteTable()`. It overwrites the table if it already exists and takes a data frame as input. For creating the table, we are taking input from "Employee.csv" file. After executing the above code we can see the table created in MySQL environment. Following program illustrates this.

Example Program

```
# Reading data from Employee.csv file to the data frame data
data <- read.csv("Employee.csv")
# Create the connection object to the database where we want to create the table.
mysqlconnection = dbConnect(MySQL(), user ="Jeeva", password = "Jose", dbname = 'mysql',
  host = 'localhost')
# Use the R data frame data to create the table EMP in MySQL.
# All the rows of data frame data are taken into MySQL.
dbWriteTable(mysqlconnection, "EMP", data, overwrite = TRUE)
```

6.3.3 Inserting Rows

We can insert records into the newly created table `EMP` using the `dbSendQuery()` function. Following program illustrates how to insert records into `EMP`. After executing the below code we can see the row inserted into `EMP` in MySQL environment. The connection is detached using the method `dbDisconnect()`.

Example Program

```
mysqlconnection = dbConnect(MySQL(), user = "Jeeva", password = "Jose",
dbname = "mysql",host = "localhost")
query="insert      into      emp(row_names,empno,empname,dept,dob,salary)
values(11,30, 'Tom', 'Sales','1985-01-10',54000)"
dbSendQuery(mysqlconnection,query)
dbDisconnect(mysqlconnection)
```

6.3.4 Updating Rows

We can update the rows in a database by using the function `dbSendQuery()`. Following program illustrates how to update records into EMP. After executing the below code we can see the corresponding row is updated with new values in MySQL environment.

Example Program

```
mysqlconnection = dbConnect(MySQL(), user = "Jeeva", password = "Jose",
dbname = "mysql",host = "localhost")
query="update EMP set salary=90000 where empno=25"
query
dbSendQuery(mysqlconnection,query)
dbDisconnect(mysqlconnection)
```

6.3.5 Deleting Rows

Like inserting and updating records, we can delete unwanted rows from a table using the function `dbSendQuery()`. Following program illustrates this.

Example Program

```
mysqlconnection = dbConnect(MySQL(), user = "Jeeva", password = "Jose",
dbname = "mysql",host = "localhost")
query="delete from EMP where empno =30"
query
dbSendQuery(mysqlconnection,query)
dbDisconnect(mysqlconnection)
```

6.3.6 Querying Tables

We can query the database tables in MySQL using the function `dbSendQuery()`. The query gets executed in MySQl and the result set is returned using the R `dbFetch()` function. Finally it is stored as a data frame in R. The function `dbClearResult()` clears the result set.

Example Program

```
mysqlconnection = dbConnect(MySQL(), user = "Jeeva", password = "Jose",
```

```
dbname = "mysql",host = "localhost")
query="select * from EMP"
result=dbSendQuery(mysqlconnection,query)
d=dbFetch(result)
d
dbClearResult(result)
dbDisconnect(mysqlconnection)
```

Output

```
   row_names empno empname      dept        dob salary
1          1    10    Jack     Sales   9/1/1970  40000
2          2    11    Jill Marketing  5/28/1972  50000
3          3    15   Smith        HR   4/8/1977  45000
4          4    16     Joe     Sales  7/21/1990  25000
5          5    18    John        HR  1/26/1991  44000
6          6    20    Adam     Sales  3/22/1985  32000
7          7    22     Bob   Finance  5/12/1980  42000
8          8    23     Sam        HR   6/9/1973  60000
9          9    24    Dawn Marketing 12/13/1988  50000
10        10    25 Solomon     Sales 11/27/1978  90000
```

6.3.7 Dropping Tables

We can drop the tables in MySQL database by passing the drop table statement into the `dbSendQuery()` in the same way we used it for querying data from tables. After executing the above code we can see the table is dropped from the MySQL environment.

Example Program

```
mysqlconnection = dbConnect(MySQL(), user = "Jeeva", password = "Jose",
dbname = "mysql",host = "localhost")
query="drop table if exists emp1"
result=dbSendQuery(mysqlconnection,query)
dbDisconnect(mysqlconnection)
```

6.4 XML Files

XML is a file format which shares both the file format and the data on the World Wide Web, intranets and elsewhere using standard ASCII text. It stands for Extensible Markup Language (XML). Similar to HTML it contains markup tags. But unlike HTML where the markup tag describes structure of the page, in XML the markup tags describe the meaning of the data contained in the file. For reading an XML file in R, we need to install the `"XML"` package.

6.4.1 Reading from XML Files

Create an XML file by copying the below data into a text editor like notepad. Save the file with a `.xml` extension.

```
<RECORDS>
   <EMPLOYEE>
      <EMPNO>1</EMPNO>
      <EMPNAME>SAM</EMPNAME>
      <DEPT>SALES</DEPT>
      <DOB>20/1/1980</DOB>
      <SALARY>27000</SALARY>
   </EMPLOYEE>
   <EMPLOYEE>
      <EMPNO>2</EMPNO>
      <EMPNAME>JOHN</EMPNAME>
      <DEPT>MARKETING</DEPT>
      <DOB>8/9/1978</DOB>
      <SALARY>70000</SALARY>
   </EMPLOYEE>
   <EMPLOYEE>
      <EMPNO>3</EMPNO>
      <EMPNAME>ADAMS</EMPNAME>
      <DEPT>HR</DEPT>
      <DOB>1/1/1973</DOB>
      <SALARY>65000</SALARY>
   </EMPLOYEE>
   <EMPLOYEE>
      <EMPNO>4</EMPNO>
      <EMPNAME>ROGER</EMPNAME>
      <DEPT>HR</DEPT>
      <DOB>13/10/1977</DOB>
      <SALARY>47000</SALARY>
   </EMPLOYEE>
   <EMPLOYEE>
      <EMPNO>5</EMPNO>
      <EMPNAME>BOB</EMPNAME>
      <DEPT>SALES</DEPT>
```

```
    <DOB>14/1/1979</DOB>
    <SALARY>67000</SALARY>
  </EMPLOYEE>
  <EMPLOYEE>
    <EMPNO>6</EMPNO>
    <EMPNAME>HORATIO</EMPNAME>
    <DEPT>MARKETING</DEPT>
    <DOB>5/5/1982</DOB>
    <SALARY>56000</SALARY>
  </EMPLOYEE>
  <EMPLOYEE>
    <EMPNO>7</EMPNO>
    <EMPNAME>HOPKINS</EMPNAME>
    <DEPT>MARKETING</DEPT>
    <DOB>10/7/1987</DOB>
    <SALARY>58000</SALARY>
  </EMPLOYEE>
  <EMPLOYEE>
    <EMPNO>8</EMPNO>
    <EMPNAME>CLARK</EMPNAME>
    <DEPT>HR</DEPT>
    <DOB>10/9/1980</DOB>
    <SALARY>39000</SALARY>
  </EMPLOYEE>
  <EMPLOYEE>
    <EMPNO>9</EMPNO>
    <EMPNAME>JIM</EMPNAME>
    <DEPT>HR</DEPT>
    <DOB>3/9/1982</DOB>
    <SALARY>49000</SALARY>
  </EMPLOYEE>
  <EMPLOYEE>
    <EMPNO>10</EMPNO>
    <EMPNAME>CLARANS</EMPNAME>
    <DEPT>SALES</DEPT>
    <DOB>8/9/1983</DOB>
```

```
    <SALARY>32000</SALARY>
  </EMPLOYEE>
</RECORDS>
```

The `xml` file is read by R and converted to data frames using the function `xmlToDataFrame()`. The result is stored as a list in R. Following program illustrates how to read from `.xml` files.

Example Program

```
library("XML")
library("methods")
result <- xmlToDataFrame("XMLREAD.xml")
# print the result.
Result
```

Output

```
   EMPNO EMPNAME      DEPT        DOB SALARY
1      1     SAM     SALES  20/1/1980  27000
2      2    JOHN MARKETING   8/9/1978  70000
3      3   ADAMS        HR   1/1/1973  65000
4      4   ROGER        HR 13/10/1977  47000
5      5     BOB     SALES  14/1/1979  67000
6      6 HORATIO MARKETING   5/5/1982  56000
7      7 HOPKINS MARKETING  10/7/1987  58000
8      8   CLARK        HR  10/9/1980  39000
9      9     JIM        HR   3/9/1982  49000
10    10 CLARANS     SALES   8/9/1983  32000
```

Since the file is read to a data frame, all the functions supported by data frames can be applied for processing the data.

6.5 JSON Files

JSON, or JavaScript Object Notation, is a minimal, readable format for structuring data. It is used primarily to transmit data between a server and web application, as an alternative to XML. The JSON format is often used for serializing and transmitting structured data over a network connection. For reading a JSON file, we need to install `rjsonlite` package. We need to create a JSON file before reading from it. Type the following data into a text editor like notepad. Save the file with a `.json` extension.

```
{
"Empno":["1","2","3","4","5","6","7","8","9","10"],
"Name":["SAM","JOHN","ADAMS","ROGER","BOB","HORATIO","HOPKINS","CLARK",
"JIM","CLARANS"],
```

```
"Dept":["SALES","MARKETING","HR","HR","SALES","MARKETING","MARKETING","
HR","HR","SALES"],
"DOB":[ "8/9/1978","20/1/1980 ","8/9/1978","1/1/1973","13/10/1977",
        "14/1/1979","5/5/1982","10/7/1987","10/9/1980","3/9/1982"],
"Salary":["27000","70000","65000","47000","67000","56000",
"58000","39000","49000","32000"]
}
```

6.5.1 Reading from JSON Files

We can read from a `.json` file using the function `fromJSON()`. The function `fromJSON()` will return as a list. Following program illustrates this.

Example Program

```
# Load the package required to read JSON files.
library("jsonlite")
# Give the input file name to the function.
jsonresult <- fromJSON("Emp.json")
jsonresult
```

Output

```
$Empno
 [1] "1"  "2"  "3"  "4"  "5"  "6"  "7"  "8"  "9"  "10"
$Name
 [1] "SAM"     "JOHN"    "ADAMS"   "ROGER"   "BOB"     "HORATIO" "HOPKINS"
 [8] "CLARK"   "JIM"     "CLARANS"
$Dept
 [1] "SALES"     "MARKETING" "HR"        "HR"        "SALES"     "MARKETING"
 [7] "MARKETING" "HR"        "HR"        "SALES"
$DOB
 [1] "8/9/1978"   "20/1/1980 " "8/9/1978"   "1/1/1973"   "13/10/1977"
 [6] "14/1/1979"  "5/5/1982"   "10/7/1987"  "10/9/1980"  "3/9/1982"
$Salary
  [1] "27000" "70000" "65000" "47000" "67000" "56000" "58000" "39000"
"49000"
[10] "32000"
```

We can convert the above result into a data frame using the function `as.data.frame()`. Once the data frame is obtained we can apply all the functions supported by data frames to process the data. Below is the program to convert the list to a data frame.

Example Program

```
# Convert JSON file to a data frame.
json_data_frame <- as.data.frame(jsonresult)
json_data_frame
```

Output

```
   Empno     Name      Dept        DOB Salary
1      1      SAM     SALES   8/9/1978  27000
2      2     JOHN MARKETING  20/1/1980  70000
3      3    ADAMS        HR   8/9/1978  65000
4      4    ROGER        HR   1/1/1973  47000
5      5      BOB     SALES 13/10/1977  67000
6      6  HORATIO MARKETING  14/1/1979  56000
7      7  HOPKINS MARKETING   5/5/1982  58000
8      8    CLARK        HR  10/7/1987  39000
9      9      JIM        HR  10/9/1980  49000
10    10  CLARANS     SALES   3/9/1982  32000
```

6.6 Binary Files

A binary file is a file that contains information stored only in form of bits and bytes.(0's and 1's). They are not human readable as the bytes in it translate to characters and symbols which contain many other non-printable characters. Attempting to read a binary file using any text editor will show characters like Ø and ð. The binary file has to be read by specific programs to be usable. For example, the binary file of a Microsoft Word program can be read to a human readable form only by the Word program. This means that, besides the human readable text, there is a lot more information like formatting of characters and page numbers etc., which are also stored along with alphanumeric characters. And finally a binary file is a continuous sequence of bytes. The line break we see in a text file is a character joining first line to the next.

Sometimes, the data generated by other programs are required to be processed by R as a binary file. Also R is required to create binary files which can be shared with other programs.

6.6.1 Writing to Binary Files

We can write to binary files from R using the function `writeBin()`. The syntax of `writeBin()` function is `writeBin(object, con)`, where `object` is the binary file to be written and `con` is the connection object to write the binary file. The binary file is opened in `"wb"` mode. In `"wb"` mode, if the file exists, its contents are overwritten. If the file does not exist, it will be created.

Example Program

```
# Read from a csv file to a data frame
empdata <- read.csv("Empinfo.csv")
```

```
# Create a connection object to write the binary file using mode "wb".
write.filename = file("Emp.dat", "wb")
# Write the column names of the data frame to the connection object.
writeBin(colnames(empdata), write.filename)
# Write the records in each of the column to the file.
writeBin(c(empdata$empno,empdata$height,
empdata$weight), write.filename)
# Close the file for writing so that it can be read by other program.
close(write.filename)
```

6.6.2 Reading from Binary Files

We can read from binary files using the function `readBin()`. The syntax of `readBin()` function is `readBin(con,what,n)`, where `con` is the connection object to read from the binary file, `what` is the mode like character, integer etc. representing the bytes to be read and `n` is the number of bytes to read from the binary file. Following program illustrates this.

Example Program

```
# Create a connection object to read the file in binary mode using "rb".
read.filename <- file("Emp.dat", "rb")
# First read the column names. n = 3 as we have 3 columns.
column.names <- readBin(read.filename, character(),  n =3)
# Next read the column values. n = 3 as we have 3 column names and 5
values.
read.filename <- file("Emp.dat", "rb")
bindata <- readBin(read.filename, integer(),  n = 30)
# Print the data.
print(bindata)
# Read the values from 6th byte to 10th byte which represents "empno".
empnodata = bindata[6:10]
print(empnodata)
# Read the values from 11th byte to 15th byte which represents "height".
heightdata = bindata[11:15]
print(heightdata)
# Read the values form 16th byte to 20th byte which represents "weight".
weightdata = bindata[16:20]
print(weightdata)
# Combine all the read values to a data frame.
```

```
fdata = cbind(empnodata,heightdata,weightdata)
colnames(fdata) = column.names
print(fdata)
```

Output

```
# Print the data.
 [1] 1852861797 1701314671 1952999273 1768257280    7628903         10
 [7]         11         12         13         14        160        172
[13]        165        160        167         70         75         68
[19]         65         70
# Read the values from 6th byte to 10th byte which represents "empno".
 [1] 10 11 12 13 14
# Read the values from 11th byte to 15th byte which represents "height".
 [1] 160 172 165 160 167
# # Read the values form 16th byte to 20th byte which represents "weight".
 [1] 70 75 68 65 70
# Combine all the read values to a data frame.
     empno height weight
[1,]    10    160     70
[2,]    11    172     75
[3,]    12    165     68
[4,]    13    160     65
[5,]    14    167     70
```

6.7 Conclusion

This Chapter explains how to connect R to external interfaces like csv files, Microsoft Excel files, MySQL database, XML files, JSON files and binary files. For connecting R with these external interfaces, the corresponding packages need to be installed. In most of the cases, data is read and stored into a data frame so that many built-in functions available in R for data frames can be used for processing and manipulating the data. In case of MySQL, this Chapter explains how to establish the connection to a database, create tables, insert records to the table, update table, delete rows, query the tables using select statement and drop tables. Connecting R to external interfaces is one of the most flexible and powerful feature of R that the user need not worry about the data storage. The data can be imported from and exported to external interfaces using R.

7 Elementary Statistics

7.1 Introduction

We have already discussed about the built-in functions available for mean, median, variance, standard deviation and quantiles in Chapter 4. In this Chapter, we will discuss about probability distributions, sampling methods & distributions, one sample Z-test, two sample Z-test, Fisher Test(F-test) and Student's t-test.

Probability is defined as the chance to occur an event. Many of the real-time events are subject to probability. Whether it is the events which occur in day-to-day life of people or business, one can visualize many examples of probability. Sometimes the probabilistic events of people may have direct or indirect impact on the performance of business establishments. Some examples for probability are getting a head while tossing a coin, getting a 6 while rolling a dice, getting a rainfall on a particular day, achieving 10% more profit than last year etc. The study of probability and related aspects are highly essential for effective use of necessary tools for data analysis.

To understand the concept of probability, we need to understand the terms `experiment, sample space` and `event`. Tossing a coin is an example of `experiment` which has the following attributes.

- There will be two or more outcomes of an experiment.
- The list of all outcomes can be specified in advance
- Actual occurrence of the outcomes cannot be predicted in advance.

`Sample space` is the list of all possible outcomes of an experiment. In tossing a coin, the possible outcomes are 'head' or 'tail'. So the `sample space` of this experiment consists of head and tail.

`Event` is the occurrence of a particular outcome or a combination of outcomes. The `events` of tossing a coin are '`head`' or '`tail`'.

7.2 Probability Distributions

In most of the researches, after data collection, the next stage is to present the data in the form of probability distributions. This will facilitate further analysis of data in more meaningful ways. The probability distributions can be classified into **discrete probability distribution** and **continous probability distribution**.

Some examples of discrete probability distributions are binomial distribution, poisson distribution etc. Examples of continous probability distributions are exponential distribution, normal distribution, t-distribution etc. A probability distribution describes how the values of a random variable are distributed. For example, the collection of all possible outcomes of a sequence of coin tossing is known to follow the binomial distribution while the means of sufficiently large samples of a data population are known to resemble the normal distribution. Since the characteristics of these theoretical distributions are well understood, they can be used to make statistical inferences on the entire data population as a whole.

7.2.1 Binomial Distribution

The binomial distribution model deals with finding the probability of success of an event which has only two possible outcomes in a series of experiments. For example, tossing of a coin always gives a head or a tail. The probability of finding exactly 3 heads in tossing a coin repeatedly for 10 times is estimated during the binomial distribution. The binomial distribution is a discrete probability distribution. It describes the outcome of `n` independent trials in an experiment. Each trial is assumed to have only two outcomes, either success or failure. If the probability of a successful trial is `p`, then the probability of having `x` successful outcomes in an experiment of `n` independent trials is as follows.

$$f(x) = \left(\frac{n}{x}\right) p^x (1-p)^{(n-x)} \qquad \text{where } x = 0,1,2,\ldots,n$$

R has four in-built functions to generate binomial distribution. They are as follows.

```
dbinom(x, size, prob, log = FALSE)
pbinom(q, size, prob, lower.tail = TRUE, log.p = FALSE)
qbinom(p, size, prob, lower.tail = TRUE, log.p = FALSE)
rbinom(n, size, prob)
```

where `x, q` - vector of quantiles.

`p` - vector of probabilities.

`n` - number of observations. If `length(n) > 1`, the length is taken to be the number required.

`size` - number of trials (zero or more).

`prob` - probability of success on each trial.

`log, log.p` – This is a logical value; if `TRUE`, probabilities `p` are given as `log(p)`.

`lower.tail` – This is a logical value; if `TRUE` (default), probabilities are `P[X ≤ x]`, otherwise, `P[X > x]`.

`dbinom()` - This function gives the probability density distribution at each point.

Example Program

```
# Create a sample of 50 numbers which are incremented by 1.
x <- seq(0,100,by = 1)
# Create the binomial distribution.
y <- dbinom(x,100,0.5)
```

```
# Plot the graph for this sample.
plot(x,y)
```

Output

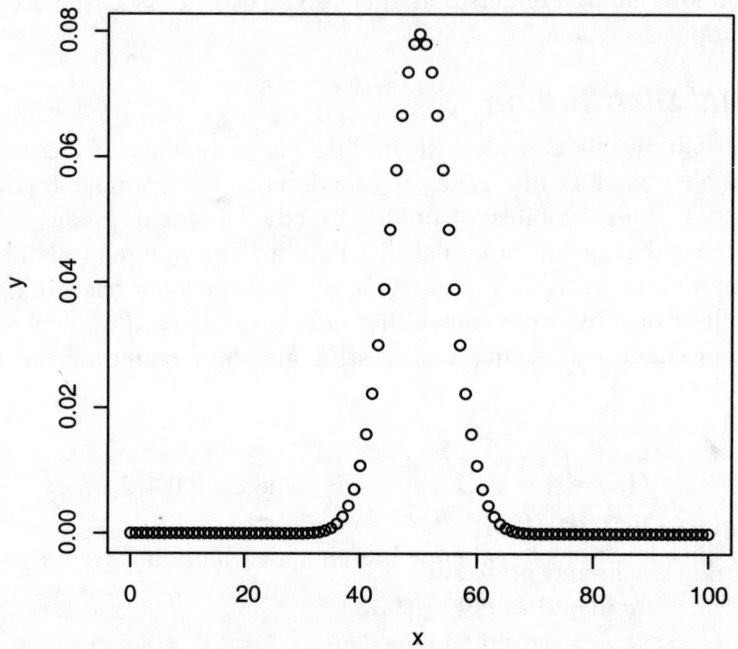

pbinom() - This function gives the cumulative probability of an event. It is a single value representing the probability.

Example Program

```
# Probability of getting 25 or less tails from a 50 tosses of a coin.
x <- pbinom(25,50,0.5)
print(x)
```

Output

```
[1] 0.5561376
```

qbinom() - This function takes the probability value and gives a number whose cumulative value matches the probability value.

Example Program

```
# How many tails will have a probability of 0.75 will come out
# when a coin is tossed 25 times.
x <- qbinom(0.75,25,1/2)
print(x)
```

Output

```
[1] 14
```

`rbinom()` - This function generates required number of random values of given probability from a given sample.

Example Program

```
# Find 4 random values from a sample of 100 with probability of 0.25.
x <- rbinom(4,100,.25)
print(x)
```

Output

```
[1] 18 26 24 27
```

Negative binomial distribution represents the number of failures which occur in a sequence of trials before a target number of successes is reached. For negative binomial distribution, we can use the following functions `dnbinom()`, `pnbinom()`, `qnbinom()` and `rnbinom()`. The parameters passed are same as those passed to positive binomial distribution functions `dnbinom()`, `pnbinom()`, `qnbinom()` and `rnbinom()`.

7.2.2 Poisson Distribution

Poisson distribution is a discrete probability distribution. This is usually used to represent the number of occurrence of an event in one unit of time. The Poisson distribution is the probability distribution of independent event occurrences in an interval. If λ is the mean occurrence per interval, then the probability of having x occurrences within a given interval is as follows.

$$f(x) = \frac{\lambda^x e^{-\lambda}}{x!} \qquad \text{where } x = 0, 1, 2, 3, \ldots$$

In this distribution, the probability of occurrence for the smaller values of the random variable `x` is relatively higher and it goes on increasing up to a point and then it decreases. R has 4 built-in functions to generate Poisson distribution. They are as follows.

`dpois(x, lambda, log = FALSE)` - This function gives the (log) density.

`ppois(q, lambda, lower.tail = TRUE, log.p = FALSE)` - This function gives the (log) distribution function.

`qpois(p, lambda, lower.tail = TRUE, log.p = FALSE)` - This gives the quantile function.

`rpois(n, lambda)` - This function generates the random deviates.

where `x` - vector of (non-negative integer) quantiles.

`q` - vector of quantiles.

`p` - vector of probabilities.

`n` - number of random values to return.

`lambda` - vector of (non-negative) means.

`log, log.p` – This is a logical value. If `TRUE`, probabilities p are given as log(p).

`lower.tail` – This is a logical value. If `TRUE` (default), probabilities are `P[X ≤ x]`, otherwise, `P[X > x]`.

Example Program

```
lower<-qpois(0.001, lambda=2.5)
upper<-qpois(0.999, lambda=2,5)
n<-seq(lower,upper,1)
q<-seq(0.001,0.999,0.001)
dPoisson25 <- data.frame(N=n,
                  Density=dpois(n, lambda=2.5),
                  Distribution=ppois(n, lambda=2.5))
dPoisson25
qPoisson25 <- data.frame(Q=q, Quantile=qpois(q, lambda=2.5))
tail(qPoisson25)
```

Output

```
  N     Density Distribution
1 0 0.082084999    0.0820850
2 1 0.205212497    0.2872975
3 2 0.256515621    0.5438131
4 3 0.213763017    0.7575761
5 4 0.133601886    0.8911780
6 5 0.066800943    0.9579790
7 6 0.027833726    0.9858127
8 7 0.009940617    0.9957533
9 8 0.003106443    0.9988597
        Q Quantile
994 0.994        7
995 0.995        7
996 0.996        8
997 0.997        8
998 0.998        8
999 0.999        9
```

7.2.3 Normal Distribution

This is a continuous probability distribution. In a random collection of data from independent sources, it is generally observed that the distribution of data is normal. On plotting a graph with the value of the variable in the horizontal axis and the count of the values in the vertical axis we get a bell shape curve. The center of the curve represents the mean of the data set. In the graph, fifty percent of values lie to the left of the mean and the other fifty percent lie to the right of the graph. This is referred as normal distribution. The normal distribution is defined by the following probability density function, where μ is the population mean and σ^2 is the variance.

$$f(x) = \frac{1}{\sigma\sqrt{2\pi}} e^{-(x-\mu)2/2\sigma^2}$$

If a random variable X follows the normal distribution, then we write $X \sim N(\mu, \sigma^2)$

In particular, the normal distribution with $\mu = 0$ and $\sigma = 1$ is called the standard normal distribution, and is denoted as N(0,1). The normal distribution is important because of the Central Limit Theorem, which states that the population of all possible samples of size n from a population with mean μ and variance σ^2 approaches a normal distribution with mean μ and σ^2/n when n approaches infinity. Following are the built-in functions to generate normal distribution.

`dnorm(x, mean = 0, sd = 1, log = FALSE)` - This function gives height of the probability distribution at each point for a given mean and standard deviation.

`pnorm(q, mean = 0, sd = 1, lower.tail = TRUE, log.p = FALSE)` - This function gives the probability of a normally distributed random number to be less than the value of a given number. It is also called "Cumulative Distribution Function".

`qnorm(p, mean = 0, sd = 1, lower.tail = TRUE, log.p = FALSE)` - This function takes the probability value and gives a number whose cumulative value matches the probability value.

`rnorm(n, mean = 0, sd = 1)` - This function is used to generate random numbers whose distribution is normal. It takes the sample size as input and generates that many random numbers.

where `x, q` - vector of quantiles.

`p` - vector of probabilities.

`n` - number of observations. If `length(n) > 1,` the length is taken to be the number required.

`mean` - vector of means.

`sd` - vector of standard deviations.

`log, log.p` - This is a logical value. If `TRUE,` probabilities p are given as log(p).

`lower.tail` -This is a logical value. If `TRUE` (default), probabilities are `P[X ≤ x]` otherwise, `P[X > x]`.

Example Program

```
z<-seq(-3.5,3.5,0.1)  # 71 points from -3.5 to 3.5 in 0.1 steps
q<-seq(0.001,0.999,0.001)  # 1999 points from 0.1% to 99.9% on 0.1% steps
dStandardNormal <- data.frame(Z=z,
                              Density=dnorm(z, mean=0, sd=1),
                              Distribution=pnorm(z, mean=0, sd=1))
```

```
head(dStandardNormal)
qStandardNormal <- data.frame(Q=q,Quantile=qnorm(q, mean=0, sd=1))
head(qStandardNormal)
```

Output

```
     Z       Density Distribution
1 -3.5 0.0008726827 0.0002326291
2 -3.4 0.0012322192 0.0003369293
3 -3.3 0.0017225689 0.0004834241
4 -3.2 0.0023840882 0.0006871379
5 -3.1 0.0032668191 0.0009676032
6 -3.0 0.0044318484 0.0013498980
      Q  Quantile
1 0.001 -3.090232
2 0.002 -2.878162
3 0.003 -2.747781
4 0.004 -2.652070
5 0.005 -2.575829
6 0.006 -2.512144
```

7.2.4 Exponential Distribution

The exponential distribution is used to model the time interval between successive random events. The exponential distribution describes the arrival time of a randomly recurring independent event sequence. If μ is the mean waiting time for the next event recurrence, its probability density function is as follows.

$$f(x) = \begin{cases} \frac{1}{\mu} e^{-x/\mu} & \text{when } x \geq 0 \\ 0 & \text{when } x < 0 \end{cases}$$

R has 4 functions for exponential distribution.

```
dexp(x, rate = 1, log = FALSE)
pexp(q, rate = 1, lower.tail = TRUE, log.p = FALSE)
qexp(p, rate = 1, lower.tail = TRUE, log.p = FALSE)
rexp(n, rate = 1)
```

where `x, q` - vector of quantiles.

`p` - vector of probabilities.

`n` - number of observations. If `length(n) > 1`, the length is taken to be the number required.

`rate` - vector of rates.

`log, log.p` – This is a logical value. If `TRUE`, probabilities `p` are given as `log(p)`.

`lower.tail` - This is a logical value. If `TRUE` (default), probabilities are `P[X ≤ x]`, otherwise, `P[X > x]`.

Example Program

```
lower <- floor(qexp(0.001, rate=0.2))
  upper <- ceiling(qexp(0.999, rate=0.2))
  t <- seq(lower,upper,0.1)
  q <- seq(0.001,0.999,0.001)
  dexp02 <- data.frame(T=t,
                       Density=dexp(t, rate=0.2),
                       Distribution=pexp(t, rate=0.2))
  head(dexp02)
  qexp02 <- data.frame(Q=q, Quantile=qexp(q, rate=0.2))
  head(qexp02)
```

Output

```
    T   Density Distribution
1 0.0 0.2000000   0.00000000
2 0.1 0.1960397   0.01980133
3 0.2 0.1921579   0.03921056
4 0.3 0.1883529   0.05823547
5 0.4 0.1846233   0.07688365
6 0.5 0.1809675   0.09516258
      Q    Quantile
1 0.001 0.005002502
2 0.002 0.010010013
3 0.003 0.015022545
4 0.004 0.020040107
5 0.005 0.025062709
6 0.006 0.030090362
```

7.2.5 Chi-Squared Distribution

The chi-squared distribution (also chi-square or χ^2-distribution) with k degrees of freedom is the distribution of sum of the squares of k independent standard normal random variables. The chi-square distribution is one of the most widely used probability distributions in inferential statistics. If $X_1, X_2, \ldots, X_m$ are m independent random variables having the standard normal distribution, then the following quantity follows a chi-squared distribution with m degrees of freedom. Its mean is m, and its variance is 2m.

$$V = X_1^2 + X_2^2 + \ldots + X_m^2 \sim X_{(m)}^2$$

R has 4 built-in functions for chi-square distribution.

```
dchisq(x, df, ncp = 0, log = FALSE)
pchisq(q, df, ncp = 0, lower.tail = TRUE, log.p = FALSE)
qchisq(p, df, ncp = 0, lower.tail = TRUE, log.p = FALSE)
rchisq(n, df, ncp = 0)
```

where `x, q` - vector of quantiles.

`p` - vector of probabilities.

`n` - number of observations. If `length(n) > 1`, the length is taken to be the number required.

`df` - degrees of freedom.

`ncp` - non-centrality parameter (non-negative).

`log, log.p` –This is a logical value. If `TRUE`, probabilities `p` are given as `log(p)`.

`lower.tail` – This is a logical value. If `TRUE` (default), probabilities are `P[X ≤ x]`, otherwise, `P[X > x]`.

Example Program

```
lower <- floor(qchisq(0.001, df=10))
  upper <- ceiling(qchisq(0.999, df=10))
  x <- seq(lower,upper,0.1)
  q <- seq(0.001,0.999,0.001)
  dchisq10 <- data.frame(X=x,
                         Density=dchisq(x, df=10),
                         Distribution=pchisq(x, df=10))
 head(dchisq10)
qchisq10 <- data.frame(Q=q, Quantile=qchisq(q, df=10))
  head(qchisq10)
```

Output

```
    X      Density Distribution
1 1.0 0.0007897535 0.0001721156
2 1.1 0.0010998857 0.0002660262
3 1.2 0.0014817914 0.0003944860
4 1.3 0.0019414257 0.0005649763
5 1.4 0.0024839611 0.0007855354
```

```
6 1.5 0.0031137444 0.0010646778
      Q Quantile
1 0.001 1.478743
2 0.002 1.734460
3 0.003 1.907676
4 0.004 2.042980
5 0.005 2.155856
6 0.006 2.253695
```

7.2.6 Student's t–Distribution

In probability and statistics, Student's t-distribution (or simply the t-distribution) is any member of a family of continuous probability distributions that arises when estimating the mean of a normally distributed population in situations where the sample size is small and population of standard deviation is unknown. Assume that a random variable `Z` has the standard normal distribution, and another random variable `V` has the chi-squared distribution with m degrees of freedom. Assume further that `Z` and `V` are independent, then the following quantity follows a Student's t distribution with `m` degrees of freedom.

$$t = \frac{z}{\sqrt{V / m}} \sim t_{(m)}$$

R has 4 built-in functions for Student's t distribution as follows.

```
dt(x, df, ncp, log = FALSE)
pt(q, df, ncp, lower.tail = TRUE, log.p = FALSE)
qt(p, df, ncp, lower.tail = TRUE, log.p = FALSE)
rt(n, df, ncp)
```

where `x, q` - vector of quantiles.

`p` - vector of probabilities.

`n` - number of observations. If `length(n) > 1`, the length is taken to be the number required.

`df` - degrees of freedom . `df = Inf` is allowed.

`ncp` - non-centrality parameter delta. If omitted, use the central t distribution.

`log, log.p` – This is a logical value. If `TRUE`, probabilities `p` are given as `log(p)`.

`lower.tail` –This is a logical value. If `TRUE` (default), probabilities are `P[X ≤ x]`, otherwise, `P[X > x]`.

Example Program

```
lower <- floor(qt(0.001, df=10))
  upper <- ceiling(qt(0.999, df=10))
  x <- seq(lower,upper,0.1)
```

```
q <- seq(0.001,0.999,0.001)
dstudent <- data.frame(X=x,
                       Density=dt(x, df=10),
                       Distribution=pt(x, df=10))
head(dstudent)
qstudent <- data.frame(Q=q, Quantile=qt(q, df=10))
head(qstudent)
```

Output

```
     X      Density Distribution
1 -5.0 0.0003960011 0.0002686668
2 -4.9 0.0004636968 0.0003115579
3 -4.8 0.0005436888 0.0003618156
4 -4.7 0.0006383181 0.0004207831
5 -4.6 0.0007503858 0.0004900599
6 -4.5 0.0008832446 0.0005715525
      Q  Quantile
1 0.001 -4.143700
2 0.002 -3.716236
3 0.003 -3.472098
4 0.004 -3.300998
5 0.005 -3.169273
6 0.006 -3.062169
```

7.2.7 F Distribution

The F distribution is a right-skewed distribution used most commonly in analysis of variance. When referencing the F distribution, the numerator degrees of freedom are always given first, as switching the order of degrees of freedom changes the distribution. If `V1` and `V2` are two independent random variables having the chi-squared distribution with `m1` and `m2` degrees of freedom respectively, then the following quantity follows an F distribution with `m1` numerator degrees of freedom and `m2` denominator degrees of freedom, i.e., `(m1,m2)` degrees of freedom.

$$F = \frac{V_1 / m_1}{V_2 / m_2} \sim F_{(m_1, m_2)}$$

R has 4 built-in functions for F distribution as follows.

```
df(x, df1, df2, ncp, log = FALSE)
pf(q, df1, df2, ncp, lower.tail = TRUE, log.p = FALSE)
qf(p, df1, df2, ncp, lower.tail = TRUE, log.p = FALSE)
```

```
rf(n, df1, df2, ncp)
```

where `x, q` - vector of quantiles.

`p` - vector of probabilities.

`n` - number of observations. If `length(n) > 1`, the length is taken to be the number required.

`df1, df2` - degrees of freedom. `Inf` is allowed.

`ncp` - non-centrality parameter. If omitted the central F is assumed.

`log, log.p` – This is a logical value. If `TRUE`, probabilities `p` are given as `log(p)`.

`lower.tail` – This is a logical value. If `TRUE` (default), probabilities are `P[X ≤ x]`, otherwise, `P[X > x]`

Example Program

```
lower <- floor(qf(0.001, df1=5,df2=10))
  upper <- ceiling(qf(0.999, df1=5,df2=10))
  x <- seq(lower,upper,0.1)
  q <- seq(0.001,0.999,0.001)
  dfunc <- data.frame(X=x,
                      Density=df(x, df1=5,df2=10),
                      Distribution=pf(x, df1=5,df2=10))
 head(dfunc)
 qfunc <- data.frame(Q=q, Quantile=qf(q,df1=5,df2=10))
 head(qfunc)
```

Output

```
    X   Density Distribution
1 0.0 0.0000000   0.00000000
2 0.1 0.2274001   0.01011509
3 0.2 0.4537433   0.04480823
4 0.3 0.5972532   0.09804202
5 0.4 0.6682532   0.16183474
6 0.5 0.6876070   0.22997512
      Q   Quantile
1 0.001 0.03715184
2 0.002 0.04966613
3 0.003 0.05897744
4 0.004 0.06669865
5 0.005 0.07343125
6 0.006 0.07947607
```

7.2.8 Uniform Distribution

A uniform distribution, sometimes also known as a rectangular distribution, is a distribution that has constant probability. The continuous uniform distribution is the probability distribution of random number selection from the continuous interval between a and b. The continuous uniform distribution or rectangular distribution is a family of symmetric probability distributions such that for each member of the family, all intervals of the same length on the distribution's support are equally probable. The support is defined by the two parameters, a and b, which are its minimum and maximum values. The distribution is often abbreviated U(a,b). Its density function is defined by the following.

$$f(x) = \begin{cases} \frac{1}{b-a} & when\ a \leq x \leq b \\ 0 & when\ x < a\ or\ x > b \end{cases}$$

R has 4 built-in functions for continuous uniform distribution as follows.

```
dunif(x, min = 0, max = 1, log = FALSE)
punif(q, min = 0, max = 1, lower.tail = TRUE, log.p = FALSE)
qunif(p, min = 0, max = 1, lower.tail = TRUE, log.p = FALSE)
runif(n, min = 0, max = 1)
```

where x, q - vector of quantiles.

p - vector of probabilities.

n - number of observations. If length(n) > 1, the length is taken to be the number required.

min, max - lower and upper limits of the distribution. It must be finite.

log, log.p – This is a logical value. If TRUE, probabilities p are given as log(p).

lower.tail – This is a logical value. If TRUE (default), probabilities are P[X ≤ x], otherwise, P[X > x].

Example Program

```
z<-seq(230,450,10)
q<-seq(0.001,0.999,0.001)
duniform <- data.frame(Z=z,
                       Density=dunif(z, min=230, max=450),
                       Distribution=punif(z, min=230, max=450))

head(duniform)
```

Output

```
    Z     Density Distribution
1 230 0.004545455   0.00000000
2 240 0.004545455   0.04545455
3 250 0.004545455   0.09090909
```

```
4 260 0.004545455    0.13636364
5 270 0.004545455    0.18181818
6 280 0.004545455    0.22727273
```

7.3 Z-Test

An Z-test is a statistical test used to determine whether two population means are different when the variances are known and the sample size is large. The test statistic is assumed to have a normal distribution, and nuisance parameters such as standard deviation should be known for an accurate Z-test to be performed.

7.3.1 One Sample Z-Test

Suppose that 10 volunteers have done an intelligence test and following are the results obtained. The mean obtained at the same test, from the entire population is 75. We want to check if there is a statistically significant difference (with a significance level of 95%) between the means of the sample and the population, assuming that the sample variance is known and equal to 18.

$$65, 78, 88, 55, 48, 95, 66, 57, 79, 81$$

To solve this problem it is necessary to develop a one sample Z-test. In R there isn't a similar function, so we can create our function. Recalling the formula for calculating the value of z, we will write this function as

```
z.test = function(a, mu, var){
   zeta = (mean(a) - mu) / (sqrt(var / length(a)))
   return(zeta)
}
```

We have built the function `z.test`. It receives in input a vector of values `a`, the mean of the population to perform the comparison `mu`, the population variance `var` and returns the value of zeta. Following program apply the function to our problem.

Example Program

```
a = c(65, 78, 88, 55, 48, 95, 66, 57, 79, 81)
z.test(a, 75, 18)
```

Output

```
[1] -2.832353
```

The value of zeta is equal to -2.83, which is higher than the critical value Zcv = 1.96, with alpha = 0.05. We therefore conclude that the mean of our sample is significantly different from the mean of the population.

7.3.2 Two Sample Z-Test

Two sample Z-test is used for comparison of the means of two independent groups of samples, taken from two populations with known variance.

The first group (A) consists of individuals of Indian nationality (the variance of the Indian population is 5); the second group is taken from individuals of American nationality (the variance of American population variance is 8.5). The data is given below:

```
A: 175, 168, 168, 190, 156, 181, 182, 175, 174, 179
B: 185, 169, 173, 173, 188, 186, 175, 174, 179, 180
```

Since we have the variance of the population, we must proceed with a two sample Z-test. Even in this case a built-in function is not available in R, we need to write a function as follows to solve the problem.

```
z.test2sam = function(a, b, var.a, var.b){
   n.a = length(a)
   n.b = length(b)
   zeta = (mean(a) - mean(b)) / (sqrt(var.a/n.a + var.b/n.b))
   return(zeta)
}
```

The function `z.test2sam` provides output of zeta, after receiving two input vectors (a and b), the variance of the first population `(var.a)` and the variance of the second population `(var.b)`. Using this function we can perform the two sampled Z-test.

Example Program

```
a = c(175, 168, 168, 190, 156, 181, 182, 175, 174, 179)
b = c(185, 169, 173, 173, 188, 186, 175, 174, 179, 180)
z.test2sam(a, b, 5, 8.5)
```

Output

```
[1] -2.926254
```

The value of zeta is greater than the value of the critical value zeta tabulated for alpha equal to `0.05` (z-tabulated = 1.96 for a two-tailed test). Hence we reject the null hypothesis in favor of the alternative hypothesis. We conclude that the two means are significantly different.

7.4 F-Test

An F-test is any statistical test in which the test statistic has an F-distribution under the null hypothesis. It is most often used when comparing statistical models that have been fitted to a data set, in order to identify the model that best fits the population from which the data were sampled. F-Test is used for comparison of the means of two independent groups, extracted from two populations at variance unknown. The sample variances are not homogeneous.

We want to compare the heights in inches of two groups of individuals. Following are the measurements.

```
A: 175, 168, 168, 190, 156, 181, 182, 175, 174, 179
B: 120, 180, 125, 188, 130, 190, 110, 185, 112, 188
```

We can perform the F-test as follows.

Example Program

```
a = c(175, 168, 168, 190, 156, 181, 182, 175, 174, 179)
b = c(120, 180, 125, 188, 130, 190, 110, 185, 112, 188)
var.test(b,a)
```

Output

```
        F test to compare two variances
data:  b and a
F = 14.643, num df = 9, denom df = 9, p-value = 0.0004636
alternative hypothesis: true ratio of variances is not equal to 1
95 percent confidence interval:
  3.637133 58.952936
sample estimates:
ratio of variances
          14.64308
```

We obtained `p-value 0.0004636` which is less than `0.05`, then the two variances are not homogeneous. Indeed we can compare the value of F computed with the tabulated value of F for alpha = `0.05`, degrees of freedom at numerator = 9, and degrees of freedom of denominator = 9, using the function `qf(p, df.num, df.den)`.

Example Program

```
qf(0.95, 9, 9)
```

Output

```
[1] 3.178893
```

F-computed is greater than F-tabulated, so we can reject the null hypothesis H_0 of homogeneity of variances.

7.5 Student's t-Test

A t-test is an analysis of two population means through the use of statistical examination. A t-test with two samples is commonly used with small sample sizes, testing the difference between the samples when the variances of two normal distributions are not known.

Student's t-test is used to compare the means of two groups under the assumption that both samples are random, independent, and come from normally distributed population with unknown but equal variances. Here we will use the same data seen in F-test. The data are given below.

```
A: 175, 168, 168, 190, 156, 181, 182, 175, 174, 179
B: 185, 169, 173, 173, 188, 186, 175, 174, 179, 180
```

To solve this problem we must use a Student's t-test with two samples, assuming that the two samples are taken from populations that follow a Gaussian distribution. Before proceeding with the t-test, it is necessary to evaluate the sample variances of the two groups, using a Fisher's F-test to verify the homogeneity of variances. In R we can do this as seen in the example program given in F-test.

The F distribution has only one tail, so with a confidence level of 95%, p = `0.95`. Conversely, the t-distribution has two tails and in the R's function `qt(p, df)` we insert a value p = `0.0975` when we are testing a two-tailed alternative hypothesis.

Then call the function `t.test` for homogeneous variances (`var.equal = TRUE`) and independent samples (`paired = FALSE`: we can omit this because the function works on independent samples by default) in this way.

Example Program

```
a = c(175, 168, 168, 190, 156, 181, 182, 175, 174, 179)
b = c(120, 180, 125, 188, 130, 190, 110, 185, 112, 188)
t.test(a,b, var.equal=TRUE, paired=FALSE)
```

Output

```
data:  a and b
t = 1.8827, df = 18, p-value = 0.07601
alternative hypothesis: true difference in means is not equal to 0
95 percent confidence interval:
 -2.549943 46.549943
sample estimates:
mean of x mean of y
    174.8     152.8
```

We obtained p-value greater than `0.05`, then we can conclude that the averages of two groups are significantly similar. Indeed the value of t-computed is less than the tabulated t-value for 18 degrees of freedom, which in R we can calculate as follows.

Example Program

```
qt(0.975, 18)
```

Output

```
[1] 2.100922
```

This confirms that we can accept the null hypothesis H_0 of equality of the means.

7.6 Conclusion

This Chapter gives a detailed description of the most commonly used probability distribution functions available which includes binomial distribution, poisson distribution, normal distribution, exponential distribution, chi-squared distribution, Student's t distribution, F distribution and uniform distribution. Parametric tests like Z-test, F-test and Student's t-Test are also well explained. All sections are illustrated with example programs.

8 Tests of Hypotheses

8.1 Introduction

Hypothesis testing is a useful statistical tool that can be used to draw a conclusion about the population from a sample. For instance, we are interested in knowing if the average value of a certain parameter differs significantly from a given value within a well defined confidence level. We would probably set up our test like this.

$$\begin{cases} H_0 : \mu = \mu_0 \\ H_1 : \mu \neq \mu_0 \end{cases}$$

The two hypotheses above are mutually exclusive. Now what can we do to check which one is more probable?

First, we should check what kind of distribution our data follows. If the number of samples is > 30 we can plot a histogram to get a visual grasp of the distribution and then run a few simple functions, to assess the skewness and kurtosis of the distribution. If these parameters are close to those of a normal distribution, then we could assume that the data comes from a normal distribution. This assumption is not 100% sure but it is reasonable if the above parameters are close to those of a normal distribution. If we are not sure, the other option is to run some normality tests or gather more data. Now that we are confident that our data is normally distributed and hopefully the samples are independent and identically distributed, we can estimate the sample mean and as far as the variance is concerned.

If the population variance is known, we can use the normal distribution in R. If the population variance is unknown, then we should use a t-distribution with n-1 degrees of freedom (n is the number of observations). As n tends to infinity t-distribution tends to normal, therefore if n is sufficiently large (say > 60) we could approximate the t-distribution with a normal one. Now, by fixing a certain alpha (confidence level), we decide to reject the null hypothesis (H_0) if

$$\left| \frac{\bar{x} - \mu}{\sigma / \sqrt{n}} \right| \geq z_1 - \alpha/2$$

where $\bar{x}$ is the sample mean, σ the standard deviation and z the percentile of the normal (or

Student's t-distribution. The idea behind the test is that we should reject the null hypothesis if the data shows that it is highly unlikely H_0 to be true.

Type I error

A type I error is the mishap of falsely rejecting a null hypothesis when the null hypothesis is true. The probability of committing a type I error is called the significance level of the hypothesis testing, and is denoted by the Greek letter α.

8.2 Population Mean with Known Variance

In the following examples, we demonstrate the procedure of hypothesis testing in R first with the intuitive critical value approach. Then we discuss the popular p-value approach as alternative. We will see lower tail test, upper tail test and two tailed test of population mean with known variance in this section.

8.2.1 Lower Tail Test

The null hypothesis of the lower tail test of the population mean can be expressed as follows.

$$\mu \geq \mu_0$$

where μ_0 is a hypothesized lower bound of the true population mean μ. Let us define the test statistic z in terms of the sample mean, the sample size *n* and the population standard deviation σ.

$$z = \frac{\bar{x} - \mu_0}{\sigma / \sqrt{n}}$$

Then the null hypothesis of the lower tail test is to be rejected if $z \leq -z_\alpha$, where z_α is the $100(1 - \alpha)$ percentile of the standard normal distribution. Let us see a problem to illustrate how lower tail test can be performed.

Problem

Suppose the manufacturer claims that the mean lifetime of a light bulb is more than 10,000 hours. In a sample of 30 light bulbs, it was found that they only last 9,900 hours on average. Assume the population standard deviation is 120 hours. Can we reject the claim by the manufacturer at significance level 0.05?

The null hypothesis is that $\mu \geq 10000$. We begin with computing the test statistic. Following program illustrates this.

Program

```
xbar = 9900                  # sample mean
mu0 = 10000                  # hypothesized value
sigma = 120                  # population standard deviation
n = 30                       # sample size
z = (xbar-mu0)/(sigma/sqrt(n))
z                            # test statistic
```

Output

```
[1] -4.564355
```

We then compute the critical value at significance level `0.05` to decide whether to accept or reject the hypothesis.

Program

```
alpha = .05
z.alpha = qnorm(1-alpha)
-z.alpha                      # critical value
```

Output

```
[1] -1.644854
```

The test statistic `-4.564355` is less than the critical value of `-1.644854`. Hence, at significance level `0.05`, we reject the claim that, mean lifetime of a light bulb is above 10,000 hours.

An alternate solution instead of using the critical value is by using p-value. We apply the `pnorm` function to compute the lower tail p-value of the test statistic.

Program

```
pval = pnorm(z)
pval                          # lower tail p-value
```

Output

```
[1] 2.505166e-06
```

Since the p-value `pval` is less than the significance level `0.05`, we reject the null hypothesis that $\mu \geq 10000$.

8.2.2 Upper Tail Test

The null hypothesis of the upper tail test of the population mean can be expressed as follows.

$$\mu \leq \mu_0$$

where μ_0 is a hypothesized upper bound of the true population mean μ. Let us define the test statistic z in terms of the sample mean, the sample size n and the population standard deviation σ.

$$z = \frac{\bar{x} - \mu_0}{\sigma / \sqrt{n}}$$

Then the null hypothesis of the upper tail test is to be rejected if $z \geq z_\alpha$, where z_α is the 100 $(1 - \alpha)$ percentile of the standard normal distribution. Let us see a problem which illustrates the upper tail test.

Problem

Suppose the food label on a cookie bag states that there is at most 2 grams of saturated fat in a single cookie. In a sample of 35 cookies, it is found that the mean amount of saturated fat per cookie is 2.1 grams. Assume that the population standard deviation is 0.25 grams. Can we reject the claim on food label at significance level 0.05?

The null hypothesis is that $\mu \le 2$. We begin with computing the test statistic. Following program illustrates this.

Program

```
xbar = 2.1                    # sample mean
mu0 = 2                       # hypothesized value
sigma = 0.25                  # population standard deviation
n = 35                        # sample size
z = (xbar-mu0)/(sigma/sqrt(n))
z                             # test statistic
```

Output

```
[1] 2.366432
```

We then compute the critical value at significance level `0.05`.

Program

```
alpha = .05
z.alpha = qnorm(1-alpha)
z.alpha                       # critical value
```

Output

```
[1] 1.644854
```

The test statistic `2.366432` is greater than the critical value of `1.644854`. Hence, at significance level `0.05`, we reject the claim that there is atmost 2 grams of saturated fat in a cookie.

An alternate solution instead of using the critical value is by using p-value. We apply the `pnorm` function to compute the upper tail p-value of the test statistic.

Program

```
pval = pnorm(z, lower.tail=FALSE)
pval                          # upper tail p-value
```

Output

```
[1] 0.008980239
```

Since the `pval` is less than the `0.05` significance level, we reject the null hypothesis that $\mu \le 2$.

8.2.3 Two-Tailed Test

The null hypothesis of the two-tailed test of the population mean can be expressed as follows.

$$\mu = \mu_0$$

where μ_0 is a hypothesized value of the true population mean μ. Let us define the test statistic z in terms of the sample mean, the sample size *n* and the population standard deviation σ.

$$z = \frac{\bar{x} - \mu_0}{\sigma / \sqrt{n}}$$

Then the null hypothesis of the two-tailed test is to be rejected if $z \le -z_{\alpha/2}$ or $z \ge z_{\alpha/2}$, where $z_{\alpha/2}$ is the 100(1 - α/2) percentile of the standard normal distribution. We will see a problem that illustrates two-tailed test.

Problem

Suppose the mean weight of King Penguins found in an Antarctic colony last year was 15.4 kg. In a sample of 35 penguins same time this year in the same colony, the mean penguin weight is 14.6 kg. Assume the population standard deviation is 2.5 kg. Can we reject the null hypothesis that the mean penguin weight does not differ from last year at significance level 0.05?

The null hypothesis is that μ = 15.4. We begin with computing the test statistic. Following program illustrates this.

Program

```
xbar = 14.6                # sample mean
mu0 = 15.4                 # hypothesized value
sigma = 2.5                # population standard deviation
n = 35                     # sample size
z = (xbar-mu0)/(sigma/sqrt(n))
z                          # test statistic
```

Output

```
[1] -1.893146
```

We then compute the critical values at significance level `0.05`.

Program

```
alpha = .05
z.half.alpha = qnorm(1-alpha/2)
c(-z.half.alpha, z.half.alpha)
```

Output

```
[1] -1.959964  1.959964
```

The test statistic `-1.893146` lies between the critical values `-1.959964` and `1.959964`. Hence, at significance level `0.05`, we accept the null hypothesis that the mean penguin weight does not differ from last year.

Instead of using the critical value, we apply the pnorm function to compute the two-tailed p-value of the test statistic. It doubles the lower tail p-value as the sample mean is less than the hypothesized value.

Program

```
pval = 2 * pnorm(z)      # lower tail
pval                     # two-tailed p-value
```

Output

```
[1] 0.05833852
```

Since it turns out to be greater than the 0.05 significance level, we accept the null hypothesis that $\mu = 15.4$.

8.3 Population Mean with Unknown Variance

We have seen the lower tail, upper tail and two tailed test of the population mean when variance is known to us. Now we will see how to perform lower tail, upper tail and two tailed test of the population mean when variance of the population is unknown.

8.3.1 Lower Tail Test

The null hypothesis of the lower tail test of the population mean can be expressed as follows.

$$\mu \geq \mu_0$$

where μ_0 is a hypothesized lower bound of the true population mean μ. Let us define the test statistic t in terms of the sample mean, the sample size n and the sample standard deviation s.

$$t = \frac{\bar{x} - \mu_0}{s / \sqrt{n}}$$

Then the null hypothesis of the lower tail test is to be rejected if $t \leq -t_\alpha$, where t_α is the 100 $(1 - \alpha)$ percentile of the Student's t distribution with n – 1 degrees of freedom.

Let us see a problem that illustrates the lower tail test when the variance of the population is unknown.

Problem

Suppose the manufacturer claims that the mean lifetime of a light bulb is more than 10,000 hours. In a sample of 30 light bulbs, it was found that they only last 9,900 hours on average. Assume the sample standard deviation is 125 hours. Can we reject the claim by the manufacturer at significance level 0.05?

The null hypothesis is that $\mu \geq 10000$. We begin with computing the test statistic. Following program illustrates this.

Program

```
xbar = 9900                    # sample mean
mu0 = 10000                    # hypothesized value
s = 125                        # sample standard deviation
n = 30                         # sample size
t = (xbar-mu0)/(s/sqrt(n))
t                              # test statistic
```

Output

```
[1] -4.38178
```

We then compute the critical value at significance level `0.05`.

Program

```
alpha = .05
t.alpha = qt(1-alpha, df=n-1)
-t.alpha                       # critical value
```

Output

```
[1] -1.699127
```

The test statistic `-4.38178` is less than the critical value of `-1.699127`. Hence, at significance level `0.05`, we can reject the claim that, mean lifetime of a light bulb is above 10,000 hours.

Instead of using the critical value, we apply the `pt` function to compute the lower tail p-value of the test statistic.

Program

```
pval = pt(t, df=n-1)
pval                           # lower tail p-value
```

Output

```
[1] 7.035026e-05
```

Since `7.035026e-05` is less than the significance level `0.05`, we reject the null hypothesis that $\mu \geq 10000$.

8.3.2 Upper Tail Test

The null hypothesis of the upper tail test of the population mean can be expressed as follows.

$$\mu \leq \mu_0$$

where μ_0 is a hypothesized upper bound of the true population mean μ. Let us define the test statistic t in terms of the sample mean, the sample size *n* and the sample standard deviation s.

$$t = \frac{\overline{x} - \mu_0}{s / \sqrt{n}}$$

Then the null hypothesis of the upper tail test is to be rejected if $t \geq t_\alpha$, where t_α is the 100(1 – α) percentile of the Student's t distribution with n – 1 degrees of freedom. Following problem illustrates how to use upper tail test to test the mean of the population when variance is unknown.

Suppose the food label on a cookie bag states that there is at most 2 grams of saturated fat in a single cookie. In a sample of 35 cookies, it is found that the mean amount of saturated fat per cookie is 2.1 grams. Assume that the sample standard deviation is 0.3 gram. Can we reject the claim on food label at significance level 0.05?

The null hypothesis is that $\mu \leq 2$. We begin with computing the test statistic. Following program illustrates this.

Program

```
xbar = 2.1                  # sample mean
mu0 = 2                     # hypothesized value
s = 0.3                     # sample standard deviation
n = 35                      # sample size
t = (xbar-mu0)/(s/sqrt(n))
t                           # test statistic
```

Output

```
[1] 1.972027
```

We then compute the critical value at significance level `0.05`.

Program

```
alpha = .05
t.alpha = qt(1-alpha, df=n-1)
t.alpha                     # critical value
```

Output

```
[1] 1.690924
```

The test statistic `1.97207` is greater than the critical value of `1.690924`. Hence, at significance level `0.05`, we can reject the claim that there is at most 2 grams of saturated fat in a cookie.

Instead of using the critical value, we apply the `pt` function to compute the upper tail p-value of the test statistic.

Program

```
pval = pt(t, df=n-1, lower.tail=FALSE)
pval                        # upper tail p-value
```

Output

```
[1] 0.02839295
```

Since the p-value `0.02839295` is less than the significance level `0.05`, we reject the null hypothesis that $\mu \leq 2$.

8.3.3 Two-Tailed Test

The null hypothesis of the two-tailed test of the population mean can be expressed as follows.

$$\mu = \mu_0$$

where μ_0 is a hypothesized value of the true population mean μ. Let us define the test statistic t in terms of the sample mean, the sample size *n* and the sample standard deviation s.

$$t = \frac{\bar{x} - \mu_0}{s / \sqrt{n}}$$

Then the null hypothesis of the two-tailed test is to be rejected if $t \leq -t_{\alpha 2}$ or $t \geq t_{\alpha 2}$, where $t_{\alpha 2}$ is the $100(1 - \alpha)$ percentile of the Student t distribution with $n - 1$ degrees of freedom. The following problem illustrates the two-tailed test.

Problem

Suppose the mean weight of King Penguins found in an Antarctic colony last year was 15.4 kg. In a sample of 35 penguins same time this year in the same colony, the mean penguin weight is 14.6 kg. Assume the sample standard deviation is 2.5 kg. Can we reject the null hypothesis that the mean penguin weight does not differ from last year at significance level 0.05?

The null hypothesis is that $\mu = 15.4$. We begin with computing the test statistic. Following program illustrates this.

Program

```
xbar = 14.6                # sample mean
mu0 = 15.4                 # hypothesized value
s = 2.5                    # sample standard deviation
n = 35                     # sample size
t = (xbar-mu0)/(s/sqrt(n))
t                          # test statistic
```

Output

```
[1] -1.893146
```

We then compute the critical values at significance level `0.05`.

Program

```
alpha = .05
t.half.alpha = qt(1-alpha/2, df=n-1)
c(-t.half.alpha, t.half.alpha)
```

Output

```
[1] -2.032245  2.032245
```

The test statistic `-1.893146` lies between the critical values `-2.032245`, and `2.032245`. Hence, at significance level `0.05`, we accept the null hypothesis that the mean penguin weight does not differ from last year.

Instead of using the critical value, we apply the `pt` function to compute the two-tailed p-value of the test statistic. It doubles the lower tail p-value as the sample mean is less than the hypothesized value.

Program

```
pval = 2 * pt(t, df=n-1)   # lower tail
pval                       # two-tailed p-value
```

Output

```
[1] 0.066876
```

Since the p-value is greater than the significance level `0.05`, we accept the null hypothesis that $\mu = 15.4$.

8.4 Population Proportion

A population proportion, generally denoted by P is a parameter that describes a percentage value associated with a population. A population proportion is usually estimated through an unbiased sample statistic obtained from an observational study or experiment. For example, the National Technological Literacy Conference conducted a national survey of 2,000 adults to determine the percentage of adults who are economically illiterate. The study showed that 72% of the 2,000 adults sampled did not understand what a gross domestic product is. The value of 72% is a sample proportion. In this section we will see the lower tail test, upper tail test and two-tailed test of population proportion.

8.4.1 Lower Tail Test

The null hypothesis of the lower tail test about population proportion can be expressed as follows.

$$p \geq p_0$$

where p_0 is a hypothesized lower bound of the true population proportion p. Let us define the test statistic z in terms of the sample proportion and the sample size.

$$z = \frac{\bar{p} - p_0}{\sqrt{p_0(1-p_0)/n}}$$

Then the null hypothesis of the lower tail test is to be rejected if $z \leq -z_\alpha$, where z_α is the 100 $(1 - \alpha)$ percentile of the standard normal distribution. The following problem illustrates how to perform lower tail test on population proportion.

Problem

Suppose 60% of citizens voted in last election. 85 out of 148 people in a telephone survey said that they voted in current election. Can we reject the null hypothesis that the proportion of voters in the population is above 60% this year at a significance level 0.5?

The null hypothesis is that p ≥ 0.6. We begin with computing the test statistic. Following program illustrates this.

Program

```
pbar = 85/148                  # sample proportion
p0 = .6                        # hypothesized value
n = 148                        # sample size
z = (pbar-p0)/sqrt(p0*(1-p0)/n)
z                              # test statistic
```

Output

```
[1] -0.6375983
```

We then compute the critical value at significance level `0.05`.

Program

```
alpha = .05
z.alpha = qnorm(1-alpha)
-z.alpha                       # critical value
```

Output

```
[1] -1.644854
```

The test statistic `-0.6375983` is not less than the critical value of `-1.644854`. Hence, at significance level `0.05`, we do not reject the null hypothesis that the proportion of voters in the population is above 60% this year.

Instead of using the critical value, we apply the `pnorm` function to compute the lower tail p-value of the test statistic as follows.

Program

```
pval = pnorm(z)
pval                           # lower tail p-value
```

Output

```
[1] 0.2618676
```

Since `0.2618676` is greater than the significance level `0.05`, we do not reject the null hypothesis that p ≥ 0.6.

8.4.2 Upper Tail Test

The null hypothesis of the upper tail test about population proportion can be expressed as follows.

$$p \le p_0$$

where p_0 is a hypothesized upper bound of the true population proportion p. Let us define the test statistic z in terms of the sample proportion and the sample size.

$$z = \frac{\bar{p} - p_0}{\sqrt{p_0(1 - p_0)/n}}$$

Then the null hypothesis of the upper tail test is to be rejected if $z \geq z_\alpha$, where z_α is the 100(1 - α) percentile of the standard normal distribution. Following problem illustrates how to perform upper tail test of population proportion.

Problem

Suppose that 12% of apples harvested in an orchard last year were rotten. 30 out of 214 apples in a harvest sample this year turns out to be rotten. Can we reject the null hypothesis that the proportion of rotten apples in harvest stays below 12% this year at significance level 0.05?

The null hypothesis is that $p \leq 0.12$. We begin with computing the test statistic. Following program illustrates this.

Program

```
pbar = 30/214                # sample proportion
p0 = .12                     # hypothesized value
n = 214                      # sample size
z = (pbar-p0)/sqrt(p0*(1-p0)/n)
z                            # test statistic
```

Output

```
[1] 0.908751
```

We then compute the critical value at significance level `0.05`.

Program

```
alpha = .05
z.alpha = qnorm(1-alpha)
z.alpha                      # critical value
```

Output

```
[1] 1.644854
```

The test statistic `0.908751` is not greater than the critical value of `1.644854`. Hence, at significance level `0.05`, we do not reject the null hypothesis that the proportion of rotten apples in harvest stays below 12% this year.

Instead of using the critical value, we apply the `pnorm` function to compute the upper tail p-value of the test statistic.

Program

```
pval = pnorm(z, lower.tail=FALSE)
pval                          # upper tail p-value
```

Output

```
[1] 0.1817408
```

Since the p-value 0.1817408 is greater than the significance level 0.05, we do not reject the null hypothesis that $p \le 0.12$.

8.4.3 Two-Tailed Test

The null hypothesis of the two-tailed test about population proportion can be expressed as follows.

$$p = p_0$$

where p_0 is a hypothesized value of the true population proportion p. Let us define the test statistic z in terms of the sample proportion and the sample size.

$$z = \frac{\bar{p} - p_0}{\sqrt{p_0(1 - p_0)/n}}$$

Then the null hypothesis of the two-tailed test is to be rejected if $z \le -z_{\alpha/2}$ or $z \ge z_{\alpha/2}$, where $z_{\alpha/2}$ is the $100(1 - \alpha)$ percentile of the standard normal distribution. Following problem illustrates how to perform two-tailed test of population proportion.

Problem

Suppose a coin toss turns up 12 heads out of 20 trials. Can one reject the null hypothesis that the coin toss is fair at significance level 0.05?

The null hypothesis is that p = 0.5. We begin with computing the test statistic. Following program illustrates this.

Program

```
pbar = 12/20                  # sample proportion
p0 = .5                       # hypothesized value
n = 20                        # sample size
z = (pbar-p0)/sqrt(p0*(1-p0)/n)
z                             # test statistic
```

Output

```
[1] 0.8944272
```

We then compute the critical values at significance level 0.05.

Program

```
alpha = .05
```

```
z.half.alpha = qnorm(1-alpha/2)
c(-z.half.alpha, z.half.alpha)
```

Output

```
[1] -1.959964  1.959964
```

The test statistic `0.8944272` lies between the critical values `-1.999964` and `1.959964`. Hence, at significance level `0.05`, we do not reject the null hypothesis that the coin toss is fair.

Instead of using the critical value, we apply the `pnorm` function to compute the two-tailed p-value of the test statistic. It doubles the upper tail p-value as the sample proportion is greater than the hypothesized value.

Program

```
pval = 2 * pnorm(z, lower.tail=FALSE)   # upper tail
pval                          # two-tailed p-value
```

Output

```
[1] 0.3710934
```

Since the p-value `0.3710934` turns out to be greater than the significance level `0.05`, we do not reject the null hypothesis that p = `0.5`.

8.5 Type II Error

A type II error is a statistical term used within the context of hypothesis testing that describes the error that occurs when one accepts a null hypothesis that is actually false. The error rejects the alternative hypothesis, even though it does not occur due to chance.

8.5.1 Population Mean with Known Variance

8.5.1.1 Lower Tail Test

In a lower tail test of the population mean, the null hypothesis claims that the true population mean μ is greater than a given hypothetical value μ_0.

$$\mu \geq \mu_0$$

A type II error occurs if the hypothesis test based on a random sample fails to reject the null hypothesis even when the true population mean μ is in fact less than μ_0. Assume that the population has a known variance σ^2. By the Central Limit Theorem, the population of all possible means of samples of sufficiently large size n approximately follows the normal distribution. Hence we can compute the range of sample means for which the null hypothesis will not be rejected, and then obtain an estimate of the probability of type II error.

Consider the following problem.

Problem

Suppose the manufacturer claims that the mean lifetime of a light bulb is more than 10,000 hours. Assume actual mean light bulb lifetime is 9,950 hours and the population standard deviation is 120 hours. At 0.05 significance level, what is the probability of having type II error for a sample size of 30 light bulb?

We will begin with computing the standard deviation of the mean, sem. Following program illustrates this.

Program

```
n = 30                          # sample size
sigma = 120                     # population standard deviation
sem = sigma/sqrt(n); sem    # standard error
```

Output

```
[1] 21.909
```

We next compute the lower bound of sample means for which the null hypothesis μ ≥ 10000 would not be rejected.

Program

```
alpha = .05                     # significance level
mu0 = 10000                     # hypothetical lower bound
q = qnorm(alpha, mean=mu0, sd=sem)
q
```

Output

```
[1] 9963.963
```

When rounded to the nearest integer, q becomes 9964. Therefore, so long as the sample mean is greater than 9964 in a hypothesis test, the null hypothesis will not be rejected. Since we assume that the actual population mean is 9950, we can compute the probability of the sample mean above 9964, and thus found the probability of type II error.

Program

```
mu = 9950                       # assumed actual mean
pnorm(q, mean=mu, sd=sem, lower.tail=FALSE)
```

Output

```
[1] 0.261957
```

If the light bulbs sample size is 30, the actual mean light bulb lifetime is 9,950 hours and the population standard deviation is 120 hours, then the probability of type II error for testing the null hypothesis μ ≥ 10000 at significance level 0.05 is 26.2%, and the power of the hypothesis test is 73.8%.

8.5.1.2 Upper Tail Test

In an upper tail test of the population mean, the null hypothesis claims that the true population mean μ is less than a given hypothetical value μ_0.

$$\mu \leq \mu_0$$

A type II error occurs if the hypothesis test based on a random sample fails to reject the null hypothesis even when the true population mean μ is infact greater than μ_0. Assume that the population has a known variance σ^2. By the Central Limit Theorem, the population of all possible means of samples of sufficiently large size n approximately follows the normal distribution. Hence we can compute the range of sample means for which the null hypothesis will not be rejected, and then obtain an estimate of the probability of type II error.Consider the following problem.

Problem

Suppose the food label on a cookie bag states that there is at most 2 grams of saturated fat in a single cookie. Assume the actual mean amount of saturated fat per cookie is 2.09 grams, and the population standard deviation is 0.25 grams. At significance level 0.05, what is the probability of having type II error for a sample size of 35 cookies?

We begin with computing the standard deviation of the mean, `sem`. Following program illustrates this.

Program

```
n = 35                    # sample size
sigma = 0.25              # population standard deviation
sem = sigma/sqrt(n); sem     # standard error
```

Output

```
[1] 0.04225771
```

We next compute the upper bound of sample means for which the null hypothesis $\mu \leq 2$ would not be rejected.

Program

```
alpha = .05               # significance level
mu0 = 2                   # hypothetical upper bound
q = qnorm(alpha, mean=mu0, sd=sem, lower.tail=FALSE)
q
```

Output

```
[1] 2.069508
```

Therefore, so long as the sample mean is less than `2.069508` in a hypothesis test, the null hypothesis will not be rejected. Since we assume that the actual population mean is `2.09`, we can compute the probability of the sample mean below `2.069508`, and thus found the probability of type II error.

Program

```
mu = 2.09                 # assumed actual mean
pnorm(q, mean=mu, sd=sem)
```

Output

```
[1] 0.3138612
```

If the cookies sample size is 35, the actual mean amount of saturated fat per cookie is 2.09 grams and the population standard deviation is 0.25 grams, then the probability of type II error for testing the null hypothesis $\mu \le 2$ at significance level 0.05 is 31.4%, and the power of the hypothesis test is 68.6%.

8.5.1.3 Two-Tailed Test

In a two-tailed test of the population mean, the null hypothesis claims that the true population mean μ is equal to a given hypothetical value μ_0.

$$\mu = \mu_0$$

A type II error occurs if the hypothesis test based on a random sample fails to reject the null hypothesis even when the true population mean μ is in fact different from μ_0.

Assume that the population has a known variance σ^2. By the Central Limit Theorem, the population of all possible means of samples of sufficiently large size n approximately follows the normal distribution. Hence we can compute the range of sample means for which the null hypothesis will not be rejected, and then obtain an estimate of the probability of type II error. Consider the following problem.

Suppose the mean weight of King Penguins found in an Antarctic colony last year was 15.4 kg. Assume the actual mean population weight is 15.1 kg, and the population standard deviation is 2.5 kg. At significance level 0.05, what is the probability of having type II error for a sample size of 35 penguins?

We begin with computing the standard deviation of the mean, `sem`.

Program

```
n = 35                      # sample size
sigma = 2.5                 # population standard deviation
sem = sigma/sqrt(n); sem    # standard error
```

Output

```
[1] 0.4225771
```

We next compute the lower and upper bounds of sample means for which the null hypothesis μ = `15.4` would not be rejected.

Program

```
alpha = .05                 # significance level
mu0 = 15.4                  # hypothetical mean
I = c(alpha/2, 1-alpha/2)
q = qnorm(I, mean=mu0, sd=sem); q
```

Output

```
[1] 14.57176 16.22824
```

Therefore, so long as the sample mean is between `14.57176` and `16.22824` in a hypothesis test, the null hypothesis will not be rejected. Since we assume that the actual population mean is `15.1`, we can compute the lower tail probabilities of both end points.

Program

```
mu = 15.1                  # assumed actual mean
p = pnorm(q, mean=mu, sd=sem); p
```

Output

```
[1] 0.1056435 0.9962062
```

Finally, the probability of type II error is the probability between the two end points. The difference between the end points is `0.8905627(0.9962062-0.1056435)`. If the penguin sample size is 35, the actual mean population weight is 15.1 kg and the population standard deviation is 2.5 kg, then the probability of type II error for testing the null hypothesis μ = `15.4` at `0.05` significance level is 89.1%, and the power of the hypothesis test is 10.9%.

8.5.2 Population Mean with Unknown Variance

8.5.2.1 Lower Tail Test

In a lower tail test of the population mean, the null hypothesis claims that the true population mean μ is greater than a given hypothetical value μ_0.

$$\mu \geq \mu_0$$

A type II error occurs if the hypothesis test based on a random sample fails to reject the null hypothesis even when the true population mean μ is in fact less than μ_0. Let s^2 be the sample variance. For sufficiently large n, the population of the following statistics of all possible samples of size n is approximately a Student's t distribution with degrees of freedom (n-1).

$$\frac{\bar{x} - \mu}{s / \sqrt{n}}$$

This allows us to compute the range of sample means for which the null hypothesis will not be rejected, and to obtain the probability of type II error. Consider the following problem.

Suppose the manufacturer claims that the mean lifetime of a light bulb is more than 10,000 hours. Assume in a random sample of 30 light bulbs, the standard deviation of the lifetime is 125 hours. If actual mean light bulb lifetime is 9,950 hours, what is the probability of type II error for a hypothesis test at significance level 0.05?

We begin with computing the standard error estimate, `SE`.

Program

```
n = 30                     # sample size
```

```
s = 125                       # sample standard deviation
SE = s/sqrt(n); SE            # standard error estimate
```

Output

```
[1] 22.82177
```

We next compute the lower bound of sample means for which the null hypothesis $\mu \geq 10000$ would not be rejected.

Program

```
alpha = .05                   # significance level
mu0 = 10000                   # hypothetical lower bound
q = mu0 + qt(alpha, df=n-1) * SE; q
```

Output

```
[1] 9961.223
```

Therefore, so long as the sample mean is greater than `9961.223` in a hypothesis test, the null hypothesis will not be rejected. Since we assume that the actual population mean is 9950, we can compute the probability of the sample mean above `9961.223`, and thus found the probability of type II error.

Program

```
mu = 9950                     # assumed actual mean
pt((q - mu)/SE, df=n-1, lower.tail=FALSE)
```

Output

```
[1] 0.3132943
```

If the light bulbs sample size is 30, the sample standard variance is 125 hours and the actual mean light bulb lifetime is 9,950 hours, then the probability of type II error for testing the null hypothesis $\mu \geq 10000$ at significance level `0.05` is 31.3%, and the power of the hypothesis test is 68.7%.

8.5.2.2 Upper Tail Test

In an upper tail test of the population mean, the null hypothesis claims that the true population mean μ is less than a given hypothetical value μ_0.

$$\mu \leq \mu_0$$

A type II error occurs if the hypothesis test based on a random sample fails to reject the null hypothesis even when the true population mean μ is in fact greater than μ_0. Let s^2 be the sample variance. For sufficiently large n, the population of the following statistics of all possible samples of size n is approximately a Student's t distribution with degrees of freedom (n-1).

$$\frac{\bar{x} - \mu}{s / \sqrt{n}}$$

This allows us to compute the range of sample means for which the null hypothesis will not be rejected, and to obtain the probability of type II error. Consider the following problem.

Problem

Suppose the food label on a cookie bag states that there is at most 2 grams of saturated fat in a single cookie. Assume in a random sample of 35 cookies, the standard deviation of saturated fat is 0.3 grams. If actual mean amount of saturated fat per cookie is 2.09 grams, what is the probability of type II error for a hypothesis test at significance level 0.05?

We begin with computing the standard error estimate, `SE`.

Program

```
n = 35                  # sample size
s = 0.3                 # sample standard deviation
SE = s/sqrt(n); SE      # standard error estimate
```

Output

```
[1] 0.05070926
```

We next compute the upper bound of sample means for which the null hypothesis $\mu \le 2$ would not be rejected.

Program

```
alpha = .05             # significance level
mu0 = 2                 # hypothetical upper bound
q = mu0 + qt(alpha, df=n-1, lower.tail=FALSE) * SE; q
```

Output

```
[1] 2.085746
```

Therefore, so long as the sample mean is less than `2.085746` in a hypothesis test, the null hypothesis will not be rejected. Since we assume that the actual population mean is `2.09`, we can compute the probability of the sample mean below `2.085746`, and thus found the probability of type II error.

Program

```
mu = 2.09               # assumed actual mean
pt((q - mu)/SE, df=n-1)
```

Output

```
[1] 0.4668141
```

If the cookies sample size is 35, the sample standard deviation of saturated fat per cookie is 0.3 grams and the actual mean amount of saturated fat per cookie is 2.09 grams, then the probability of type II error for testing the null hypothesis $\mu \le 2$ at .05 significance level is 46.7%, and the power of the hypothesis test is 53.3%.

8.5.2.3 Two-Tailed Test

In a two-tailed test of the population mean, the null hypothesis claims that the true population mean μ is equal to a given hypothetical value μ_0.

$$\mu = \mu_0$$

A type II error occurs if the hypothesis test based on a random sample fails to reject the null hypothesis even when the true population mean μ is in fact different from μ_0. Let s^2 be the sample variance. For sufficiently large n, the population of the following statistics of all possible samples of size n is approximately a Student t distribution with degrees of freedom (n – 1).

$$\frac{\bar{x} - \mu}{s / \sqrt{n}}$$

This allows us to compute the range of sample means for which the null hypothesis will not be rejected, and to obtain the probability of type II error. Consider the following problem.

Problem

Suppose the mean weight of King Penguins found in an Antarctic colony last year was 15.4 kg. Assume in a random sample 35 penguins, the standard deviation of the weight is 2.5 kg. If actual mean penguin weight is 15.1 kg, what is the probability of type II error for a hypothesis test at significance level 0.05?

We begin with computing the standard error estimate, `SE`.

Program

```
n = 35                    # sample size
s = 2.5                   # sample standard deviation
SE = s/sqrt(n); SE        # standard error estimate
```

Output

```
[1] 0.4225771
```

We next compute the lower and upper bounds of sample means for which the null hypothesis μ = `15.4` would not be rejected.

Program

```
alpha = .05               # significance level
mu0 = 15.4                # hypothetical mean
I = c(alpha/2, 1-alpha/2)
q = mu0 + qt(I, df=n-1) * SE; q
```

Output

```
[1] 14.54122 16.25878
```

Therefore, so long as the sample mean is between `14.54122` and `16.25878` in a hypothesis test, the null hypothesis will not be rejected. Since we assume that the actual population mean is `15.1`, we can compute the lower tail probabilities of both end points.

Program

```
mu = 15.1                    # assumed actual mean
p = pt((q - mu)/SE, df=n-1); p
```

Output

```
[1] 0.09744507 0.99516802
```

Finally, the probability of type II error is the probability between the two end points. The difference between the end points is `0.89772295(0.99516802-0.09744507)`. If the penguin sample size is 35, the sample standard deviation of penguin weight is 2.5 kg and the actual mean population weight is 15.1 kg, then the probability of type II error for testing the null hypothesis μ = 15.4 at .05 significance level is 89.8%, and the power of the hypothesis test is 10.2%.

8.6 Inference about Two Populations

It is often necessary to draw conclusion on the difference between two populations by their data samples. In the following section, we discuss how to estimate the difference of means and proportions between two normally distributed data populations.

8.6.1 Population Mean between Two Matched Samples

Two data samples are matched if they come from repeated observations of the same subject. Here, we assume that the data populations follow the normal distribution. Using the paired t-test, we can obtain an interval estimate of the difference of the population means.

Problem

In the built-in data set named `immer`, the barley yield in years 1931 and 1932 of the same field are recorded. The yield data are presented in the data frame columns Y1 and Y2. Assuming that the data in `immer` follows the normal distribution, find the 95% confidence interval estimate of the difference between the mean barley yields between years 1931 and 1932.

Program

```
library(MASS)
t.test(immer$Y1, immer$Y2, paired=TRUE)
```

Output

```
        Paired t-test
data:  immer$Y1 and immer$Y2
t = 3.324, df = 29, p-value = 0.002413
alternative hypothesis: true difference in means is not equal to 0
95 percent confidence interval:
  6.121954 25.704713
```

```
sample estimates:
mean of the differences
               15.91333
```

In the above program, we have applied the `t.test` function to compute the difference in means of the matched samples. As it is a paired test, we set the "paired" argument as `TRUE`. Between years 1931 and 1932 in the data set `immer`, the 95% confidence interval of the difference in means of the barley yields is the interval between `6.122` and `25.705`.

8.6.2 Population Mean between Two Independent Samples

Two data samples are independent if they come from unrelated populations and the samples do not affect each other. Here, we assume that the data populations follow the normal distribution. Using the unpaired t-test, we can obtain an interval estimate of the difference between two population means.

Problem

In the data frame column `mpg` of the data set `mtcars`, there are gas mileage data of various 1974 U.S. automobiles. Meanwhile, another data column in `mtcars`, named `am`, indicates the transmission type of the automobile model (0 = automatic, 1 = manual). In particular, the gas mileages for manual and automatic transmissions are two independent data populations. Assuming that the data in `mtcars` follows the normal distribution, find the 95% confidence interval estimate of the difference between the mean gas mileage of manual and automatic transmissions.

Program

```
L = mtcars$am == 0
mpg.auto = mtcars[L,]$mpg
mpg.auto                    # automatic transmission mileage
mpg.manual = mtcars[!L,]$mpg
mpg.manual                  # manual transmission mileage
t.test(mpg.auto, mpg.manual)
```

Output

```
# automatic transmission mileage
[1] 21.4 18.7 18.1 14.3 24.4 22.8 19.2 17.8 16.4 17.3 15.2 10.4 10.4 14.7
21.5
[16] 15.5 15.2 13.3 19.2
# manual transmission mileage
[1] 21.0 21.0 22.8 32.4 30.4 33.9 27.3 26.0 30.4 15.8 19.7 15.0 21.4

        Welch Two Sample t-test

data:  mpg.auto and mpg.manual
t = -3.7671, df = 18.332, p-value = 0.001374
```

```
alternative hypothesis: true difference in means is not equal to 0
95 percent confidence interval:
 -11.280194  -3.209684
sample estimates:
mean of x mean of y
 17.14737  24.39231
```

In the above program, we have applied the `t.test` function to compute the difference in means of the two sample data. In `mtcars`, the mean mileage of automatic transmission is `17.14737` mpg and the manual transmission is `24.39231` mpg. The 95% confidence interval of the difference in mean gas mileage is between `3.2097` and `11.2802` mpg.

8.6.3 Comparison of Two Population Proportions

A survey conducted in two distinct populations will produce different results. It is often necessary to compare the survey response proportion between the two populations. Here, we assume that the data populations follow the normal distribution.

In the built-in data set named `quine`, children from an Australian town is classified by ethnic background, gender, age, learning status and the number of days absent from school. The data frame column `Eth` indicates whether the student is Aboriginal or Not ("A" or "N"), and the column Sex indicates Male or Female ("M" or "F"). In R, we can tally the student ethnicity against the gender with the `table()` function.

Program

```
library(MASS)
table(quine$Eth, quine$Sex)
```

Output

```
    F  M
  A 38 31
  N 42 35
```

From the result we can see that, within the Aboriginal student population, 38 students are female where as within the Non-Aboriginal student population, 42 are female.

Problem

Assuming that the data in `quine` follows the normal distribution, find the 95% confidence interval estimate of the difference between the female proportion of Aboriginal students and the female proportion of Non-Aboriginal students, each within their own ethnic group.

Program

```
prop.test(table(quine$Eth, quine$Sex), correct=FALSE)
```

Output

```
      2-sample test for equality of proportions without continuity
        correction
```

```
data:  table(quine$Eth, quine$Sex)
X-squared = 0.0040803, df = 1, p-value = 0.9491
alternative hypothesis: two.sided
95 percent confidence interval:
 -0.1564218  0.1669620
sample estimates:
   prop 1     prop 2
0.5507246 0.5454545
```

In the above program, we have applied the `prop.test` function to compute the difference in female proportions. The 95% confidence interval estimate of the difference between the female proportion of Aboriginal students and the female proportion of Non-Aboriginal students is between -15.6% and 16.7%.

8.7 Goodness of Fit

The goodness of fit of a statistical model describes how well it fits a set of observations. Measures of goodness of fit typically summarize the discrepancy between observed values and the values expected under the model in question. Many statistical quantities derived from data samples are found to follow the chi-squared distribution. Hence we can use it to test whether a population fits a particular theoretical probability distribution.

8.7.1 Multinomial Goodness of Fit

A population is called multinomial if its data is categorical and belongs to a collection of discrete non-overlapping classes. The null hypothesis for goodness of fit test for multinomial distribution is that the observed frequency f_i is equal to an expected count e_i in each category. It is to be rejected if the p-value of the following chi-squared test statistics is less than a given significance level α.

$$x^2 = \sum_i \frac{(f_i - e_i)^2}{e_i}$$

Consider the built-in data set `survey`, the `Smoke` column records the survey response about the student's smoking habit. There are exactly four proper response in the survey: "`Heavy`", "`Regul`" (regularly), "`Occas`" (occasionally) and "`Never`". Hence the `Smoke` data is multinomial. It can be confirmed with the levels function in R.

We can find the responses using the `levels` function and frequency distribution of qualitative data, with the `table` function. Following program illustrates this.

Program

```
library(MASS)          # load the MASS package
levels(survey$Smoke) # responses
smoke.freq = table(survey$Smoke)#frequency
smoke.freq
```

Output

```
# responses
[1] "Heavy" "Never" "Occas" "Regul"
#frequency
Heavy Never Occas Regul
   11   189    19    17
```

Problem

Suppose the campus smoking statistics is as below. Determine whether the sample data in survey supports it at significance level 0.05.

```
Heavy   Never   Occas   Regul
 4.5%   79.5%    8.5%    7.5%
```

Program

```
smoke.prob = c(.045, .795, .085, .075)
chisq.test(smoke.freq, p=smoke.prob)
```

Output

```
Chi-squared test for given probabilities
data:   smoke.freq
X-squared = 0.10744, df = 3, p-value = 0.9909
```

In the above program, we have saved the campus smoking statistics in a variable named `smoke.prob`. Then we apply the `chisq.test` function and perform the chi-squared test. As the p-value `0.9909` is greater than the significance level `0.05`, we do not reject the null hypothesis that the sample data in survey supports the campus-wide smoking statistics.

8.7.2 Chi-Square Test

Two random variables `x` and `y` are called independent if the probability distribution of one variable is not affected by the presence of another. Assume f_{ij} is the observed frequency count of events belonging to both i-th category of `x` and j-th category of `y`. Also assume e_{ij} to be the corresponding expected count if `x` and `y` are independent. The null hypothesis of the independence assumption is to be rejected if the p-value of the following chi-squared test statistics is less than a given significance level α.

$$x^2 = \sum_{i,j} \frac{\left(f_{ij} - e_{ij}\right)^2}{e_{ij}}$$

In the built-in data set `survey`, the `Smoke` column records the students smoking habit, while the `Exer` column records their exercise level. The allowed values in Smoke are `"Heavy"`, `"Regul"` (regularly), `"Occas"` (occasionally) and `"Never"`. For `Exer`, they are `"Freq"` (frequently), `"Some"` and "None". We can tally the students smoking habit against the exercise level with the table function in R. The result is called the contingency table of the two variables.

Program

```
library(MASS)        # load the MASS package
tbl = table(survey$Smoke, survey$Exer)
tbl # the contingency table
```

Output

```
       Freq None Some
  Heavy    7    1    3
  Never   87   18   84
  Occas   12    3    4
  Regul    9    1    7
```

Problem

Test the hypothesis whether the students smoking habit is independent of their exercise level at significance level 0.05.

Program

```
chisq.test(tbl)
```

Output

```
        Pearson's Chi-squared test
data:  tbl
X-squared = 5.4885, df = 6, p-value = 0.4828
Warning message:
In chisq.test(tbl) : Chi-squared approximation may be incorrect
```

We have applied the `chisq.test` function to the contingency table `tbl` and found the p-value to be 0.4828. As the p-value 0.4828 is greater than the 0.05 significance level, we do not reject the null hypothesis that the smoking habit is independent of the exercise level of the students.

The warning message found in the solution above is due to the small cell values in the contingency table. To avoid such warning, we combine the second and third columns of `tbl` and save it in a new table named `ctbl`. For this we are combining the columns of "None" and "Some". Then we apply the `chisq.test` function against `ctbl` instead.

Program

```
ctbl = cbind(tbl[,"Freq"], tbl[,"None"] + tbl[,"Some"])
ctbl
chisq.test(ctbl)
```

Output

```
       [,1] [,2]
Heavy    7    4
Never   87  102
Occas   12    7
Regul    9    8
Pearson's Chi-squared test
 data:  ctbl
X-squared = 3.2328, df = 3, p-value = 0.3571
```

8.8 Conclusion

This Chapter gives a very good idea about tests of hypotheses. The Chapter begins with lower tail test for population mean with known variance, upper tail test for population mean with known variance and two-tailed test for population mean with known variance. Followed by this the lower tail test for population mean with unknown variance, upper tail test for population mean with unknown variance and two-tailed test for population mean with unknown variance is explained in this Chapter. The lower tail test, upper tail test and two-tailed test of population proportion are also explained.

The Type II error for lower tail test, upper tail test and two-tailed test for population mean with known variance and unknown variance are explained. Inference about two populations which includes population mean between two matched samples, population mean between two independent samples and comparison of two population proportions are also explained. Finally the goodness of fit which includes multinomial goodness of fit and chi-square test are well explained in this Chapter. All sections are well illustrated with examples, solved problems and programs.

9 Non Parametric Tests

9.1 Introduction

In practical data used, there is a general assumption that data follows normal distribution. When data follows normal distribution, it is easy to calculate parameters such as mean, variance etc. and use the standard tests known as tests of hypotheses which are presented in Chapter 8. These types of tests are known as parametric tests. But there are situations where the practical data may be non-normal or/and it may not be able to estimate the parameters of the data. The tests which are used for such situations are called non-parametric tests. These tests are free from distributions and parameters. The non-parametric tests can be even used for nominal, ordinal and ranked data. Inference about the population can be made by the non parametric tests when the assumptions of the standard methods cannot be satisfied.

9.2 One-Sample Test

One-Sample sign test is applied to a situation where a sample is taken from a population that is non-normal. The probability of having a sample value less than the mean as well as the probability of having a sample value more than the mean value `p` is ½ or 0.5. It is very difficult to verify the symmetry of the distribution when the sample size is small. Each sample will be classified into either plus (+) or minus (-) as follows. If the sample value is more than the mean value μ, then it is replaced by a '+'. If sample value is less than the mean value μ, then it is replaced by a '-'. If it is equal, 0 is used to replace the value. One-sample sign test can be classified as follows.

- Lower-tailed one sample sign test for small sample
- Upper-tailed one sample sign test for small sample
- Two-tailed one sample sign test for small sample
- Lower-tailed one sample sign test for large sample
- Upper-tailed one sample sign test for large sample
- Two-tailed one sample sign test for large sample

9.2.1 One-Sample Sign Test for Small Sample

A random sample of size `n` is taken and its null hypothesis is tested using binomial distribution with p=1/2. The value of `np` as well as `n(1-p)` should be less than 5.

9.2.1.1 Lower Tail Test

The hypothesis for the lower tailed test can be stated as follows.

H_0: `p=1/2` and H_1: `p<1/2`

The objective of this test is to check whether the population is to be accepted based on the value of the sample statistic by placing the significance level α, at the left tail of the distribution. If p-value is more than the significance level α then the binomial statistic falls in the acceptance region. Hence accept H_0; otherwise reject H_0.

Consider the following problem.

Problem

A salesman of a company visited 8 random cities and the number of sales obtained are 5,6,4,8,2,4,9,1. Check whether the number of orders obtained in each city is 7 as against the alternate hypothesis H_1: $\mu<7$ at a significance level 0.05.

The sample size n=8, p=0.5, number of successes or '+' sign=2. We can perform the test using binomial test. The syntax for binomial test is

```
binom.test(nsuccesses, ntrials, p,alternative)
```

where `nsuccesses` is the number of success or '+' signs, `ntrials` is the no: of samples, `p=0.5` and `alternative` can be `"less","greater"` or `"two.sided"`. For lower tailed test, `alternative` is `"less"`, for upper tailed test, `alternative` is `"greater"` and for two-tailed test `alternative` is `"two.sided"`.

Following program illustrates this.

Program

```
binom.test(2,8,0.5, alternative="less")
```

Output

```
        Exact binomial test
data:   2 and 8
number of successes = 2, number of trials = 8, p-value=0.1445
alternative hypothesis: true probability of success is less than 0.5
95 percent confidence interval:
 0.0000000 0.5996894
sample estimates:
probability of success
                  0.25
```

Since the p-value is greater than the given significance level `0.05`, the binomial statistic falls in the acceptance region and accept H_0. Hence the number of sales obtained from each city is not less than 7.

9.2.1.2 Upper Tail Test

The hypothesis for the upper tailed test can be stated as follows.

H_0: p=1/2 and H_1: p>1/2

The objective of this test is to check whether the population is to be accepted based on the value of the sample statistic by placing the significance level α at the right tail of the distribution. If p-value is more than the significance level α, then the binomial statistic falls in the acceptance region. Hence accept H_0; otherwise reject H_0.

The following problem illustrates upper tail test.

Problem

A medical representative visited randomly 9 clinics and found that the waiting time in minutes before doctors are 16,30,17,22,31,11,19,18 and 8. Check whether the meeting time is 15 minutes (H_0: μ=15) as against the alternate hypothesis H_1: μ>15 at a significance level of 0.05.

In the above problem n=9, p=0.5 and number of '+' signs (No: of successes =7)

Program

```
binom.test(7,9,0.5,alternative="greater")
```

Output

```
        Exact binomial test
data:  7 and 9
number of successes = 7, number of trials = 9, p-value = 0.08984
alternative hypothesis: true probability of success is greater than 0.5
95 percent confidence interval:
 0.4503584 1.0000000
sample estimates:
probability of success
            0.7777778
```

Here p-value 0.08984 is more than the significance level 0.05. Hence the binomial statistic falls in the acceptance region and therefore accepts H_0. So the waiting time at the clinics is not more than 15 minutes.

9.2.1.3 Two-Tailed Test

The hypothesis for the two-tailed test can be stated as follows.

H_0: p=1/2 and H_1: p≠1/2

The objective of this test is to check whether the population is to be accepted based on the value of the sample statistic by placing half of the significance level α/2 at both tails of the distribution. If p-value is more than the significance level α/2, then the binomial statistic falls in the acceptance region. Hence accept H_0; otherwise reject H_0. Consider the following problem.

Problem

The annual income in lakhs of rupees of 9 CEOs is 12, 16, 20, 15, 14, 8, 11, 17 and 13. Check whether the annual income of the CEOs is 10 lakhs (H_0:μ=10) as against the alternate hypothesis (H_1: $\mu \neq 10$) at a significance level α=0.1. ($\alpha/2$=0.05)

In this problem n=9, p=0.05 and no: of successes=8

Program

```
binom.test(8,9,0.05,alternative="two.sided")
```

Output

```
        Exact binomial test
data:   8 and 9
number of successes = 8, number of trials = 9, p-value = 3.359e-10
alternative hypothesis: true probability of success is not equal to 0.05
95 percent confidence interval:
 0.5175035 0.9971909
sample estimates:
probability of success
             0.8888889
```

Since the p-value is less than one half of the significance level `0.05`, the binomial static falls in the rejection region. Hence reject H_0. The annual income of the CEOs does not equal to Rs.10 lakhs.

9.2.2 One-Sample Sign Test for Large Sample

In one-sample sign test, a random sample of size `n`, where `np` as well as `n(1-p)` is at least 5 is taken and its null hypothesis is tested using normal approximation to the binomial distribution with `p=1/2`, where X is the random variable representing the number of plus(+) signs. If `X~B(X,n,p)` then for large value of `n(n>30)`, one can approximate the binomial distribution to normal distribution as follows.

$$X \sim N[np, np(1-p)]$$

where `np` is the mean and `np(1-p)` is the variance of the normal distribution. Z statistic can be calculated as follows.

$$Z = \frac{X - np}{\sqrt{np(1-p)}}$$

9.2.2.1 Lower Tail Test

Consider the one-sample sign test for large sample. Here

H_0: `p=1/2` and H_1: `p<1/2`

The objective of this test is to check whether the population is to be accepted based on the value of the sample statistic by placing the significance level α at the lower tail of the distribution. If the computed Z value is more than $-Z_\alpha$, then accept H_0, otherwise reject H_0.

Consider the following problem.

Problem

The performance index (0-10 scale) of employees of a firm follows non-normal distribution. The personnel manager feels that the performance index of the trainees is more than 8. For testing his intuition, he has selected a sample of 40 trainees whose performance indices are as follows.

5	6	9	4	2	5	5	7	7	9
6	9	5	2	4	5	8	6	10	7
7	10	8	7	9	3	6	7	6	9
2	9	9	8	5	4	7	9	8	10

In the above problem, n=40, significance level α=0.05. Let X be the random variable representing the number of + signs. In the above problem X=11.

Following program illustrates how to calculate Z statistic.

Program

```
x=11     # No: of + signs
np=20    # Mean
p=0.5
z=(x-np)/sqrt(np*(1-p)) # Z statistic
z
```

Output

```
[1] -2.84605
```

We then compute the critical value at significance level `0.05`.

Program

```
alpha = .05
z.alpha = qnorm(1-alpha)
-z.alpha                    # critical value
```

Output

```
[1] -1.644854
```

The value of the standard normal z-statistic $-Z_\alpha$ is `-1.644854`. Since the calculated Z value `-2.84605` is less than the value of $-Z_\alpha$, we reject the null hypothesis H_0. Therefore the performance index of the trainees is less than 8.

9.2.2.2 Upper Tail Test

Consider the one-sample sign test for large sample. Here

$$H_0\text{: p=1/2 and } H_1\text{: p>1/2}$$

The objective of this test is to check whether the population is to be accepted based on the value of the sample statistic by placing the significance level α at the upper tail of the distribution. If the computed Z value is more than Z_α then reject H_0, otherwise accept H_0.

Problem

The weight of a drug produced by a drug's manufacturing company follows normal distribution. The specified weight of a drug is 100 mg. Any excess weight of the drug will lead to side effects. The quality manager of the company claims that the weight of the drugs is not greater than the specified mean weight of the population. He has selected a random sample of 36 drugs and their weights as follows. Verify the claim of the quality manager at a significance level of 0.05.

101	102	95	103	96	103	101	103	105
99	100	99	102	104	102	108	102	101
91	95	98	101	109	103	102	109	106
92	97	99	108	105	104	103	99	108

In the above problem, n=36, significance level α=0.05. Let X be the random variable representing the number of + signs. In the above problem X=24.

Following program illustrates how to calculate Z statistic.

Program

```
x=24     # No: of + signs
np=18    # Mean
p=0.5
z=(x-np)/sqrt(np*(1-p)) # Z statistic
z
```

Output

```
[1] 2
```

We then compute the critical value at significance level `0.05`.

Program

```
alpha = .05
z.alpha = qnorm(1-alpha)
z.alpha                  # critical value
```

Output

```
[1] 1.644854
```

Since the calculated Z value is 2 which is greater than `z.alpha` which is `1.644854`, we reject the null hypothesis H_0. Hence the weight of the drug is more than 100 mg.

9.2.2.3 Two-Tailed Test

Consider the one-sample sign test for large sample. Here

$$H_0: \texttt{p=1/2} \text{ and } H_1: \texttt{p}\neq\texttt{1/2}$$

The objective of this test is to check whether the population is to be accepted based on the value of the sample statistic by placing one-half of the significance level ($\alpha/2$) at both tails of the distribution. If the absolute value of the Z computed $|Z|$ is more than $Z_{\alpha/2}$ then reject H_0, otherwise accept H_0. Consider the following problem

Problem

The production rate of spindles of a machine follows non-normal distribution. The production manager of a company feels that the production rate of the machine is not different from 75 spindles per hour. To test this intuition, he has selected a random sample of 36 different hourly productions. Check the intuition of the manager at a significance level α=0.05.

67	70	76	85	60	66	80	85	77
79	80	89	82	74	82	98	82	71
81	85	78	71	89	83	82	89	86
72	87	89	78	75	74	73	89	88

In the above problem, n=36, significance level α=0.05. Let X be the random variable representing the number of + signs. In the above problem X=25.

Following program illustrates how to calculate Z statistic.

Program

```
x=25     # No: of + signs
np=18    # Mean
p=0.5
z=(x-np)/sqrt(np*(1-p)) # Z statistic
z
```

Output

```
[1] 2.333333
```

We then compute the critical value at significance level `0.05`.

Program

```
alpha = .05
z.half.alpha = qnorm(1-alpha/2)
c(-z.half.alpha, z.half.alpha)
```

Output

```
[1] -1.959964  1.959964
```

The $Z_{\alpha/2}$ values lie between `-1.959964` and `1.959964`. Since the calculated Z value `2.333333` lies outside $Z_{\alpha/2,}$ we reject the null hypothesis. Thus the production rate of the machines is different from 75 per hour.

9.3 Two-Samples Test

There will be situations where we may take decisions based on two samples. Each of the two samples may represent a particular population. There are several two-sample non parametric tests which includes two-sample sign test, Wilcoxon Signed-Rank test, Mann-Whitney-Wilcoxon test and Kolmogorov-Smirnov test. We will see one by one. Two-sample sign test can be classified as

- Lower-tailed two-sample sign test with binomial distribution
- Upper-tailed two-sample sign test with binomial distribution
- Two-tailed two-sample sign test with binomial distribution
- Lower-tailed two-sample sign test with normal approximation
- Upper-tailed two-sample sign test with normal approximation
- Two-tailed two- sample sign test with normal approximation

9.3.1 Two-Sample Sign Test with Binomial Distribution

There may be situations where two samples are taken from two populations having continous symmetrical distributions which are non-normal. The probability of having the first sample value less than the corresponding second sample value as well as the probability of having the first sample value more than the corresponding second sample is ½. If the ith observation of the first sample is more than that of the second sample, then the ith combined observation is marked as '+'. If the ith observation of the first sample is less than that of the second sample, then the ith combined observation is '-'. If they are equal, then the ith combined version is treated as 0. Two random samples of size `n` where `np`, as well as `n(1-p)` is less than 5 are taken. The null hypothesis is tested using binomial distribution with p=1/2.

9.3.1.1 Lower Tail Test

The combination of hypothesis for lower tailed test concerning two-samples for small sample is as follows.

$$H_0: \mu_x = \mu_y \text{ or } p=1/2$$
$$H_1: \mu_x < \mu_y \text{ or } p<1/2$$

The objective of the test is to check whether the null hypothesis is to be accepted based on the value of the combined samples static by placing the significance level α at the left tail of the distribution. If the computed p-value is more than the significance level α, then accept H_0, otherwise reject H_0.

Problem

The monthly revenues (in lakhs) of a product in 13 randomly selected retail stores before and after introducing point of sales is given below.

Retail Store	1	2	3	4	5	6	7	8	9	10	11	12	13
Before	17	18	16	18	13	17	14	18	13	16	17	15	16
After	22	23	25	15	18	14	20	24	17	21	20	18	15

Check whether the monthly sales of the product in these retail stores have improved after introducing point of sales at a significance level of 0.01.

In the above problem, No: of '+' signs=3

No: of '-' signs =10

The sign test is to perform at the lower tail. Following program illustrates this.

Program

```
binom.test(3,13,0.5,alternative="less")
```

Output

```
Exact binomial test
data:  3 and 13
number of successes = 3, number of trials = 13, p-value = 0.04614
alternative hypothesis: true probability of success is less than 0.5
95 percent confidence interval:
 0.0000000 0.4946497
sample estimates:
probability of success
            0.2307692
```

The calculated p-value `0.04614` is greater than the significance level `0.01`. Hence accept H_0. The sales revenue has not increased with the introduction of point of sales.

9.3.1.2 Upper Tail Test

The combination of hypothesis for upper tailed test concerning two-samples for small sample is as follows.

$$H_0: \mu_x = \mu_y \text{ or } p=1/2$$
$$H_1: \mu_x > \mu_y \text{ or } p>1/2$$

The objective of the test is to check whether the null hypothesis is to be accepted based on the value of the combined samples static by placing the significance level α at the right tail of the distribution. If the computed p-value is more than the significance level α, then accept H_0, otherwise reject H_0.

Problem

The daily average number of outpatients treated in 9 hospitals in a district before and after providing health care awareness program is given below. Check whether the daily average inflow of the patients to the hospitals is decreased considerably at a significance level of 0.05.

Hospital	1	2	3	4	5	6	7	8	9
Before	400	300	600	100	200	150	175	275	420
After	350	250	620	90	220	100	50	200	500

In the above problem, No: of '+' signs=6

No: of '-' signs =3

The sign test is to perform at the upper tail. Following program illustrates this.

Program

```
binom.test(6,9,0.5,alternative="greater")
```

Output

```
        Exact binomial test
data:  6 and 9
number of successes = 6, number of trials = 9, p-value = 0.2539
alternative hypothesis: true probability of success is greater than 0.5
95 percent confidence interval:
 0.3449414 1.0000000
sample estimates:
probability of success
             0.6666667
```

In the above problem, the computed p-value 0.2539 is greater than the significance level 0.05. The binomial statistic falls in the acceptance region and hence accepts H_0. Hence the inflow of patients to the hospitals has not decreased considerably after introducing the health care awareness programme.

9.3.1.3 Two-Tailed Test

The combination of hypothesis for two-tailed test concerning two-samples for small sample is as follows.

$$H_0: \mu_x = \mu_y \text{ or } p=1/2$$

$$H_1: \mu_x \neq \mu_y \text{ or } p\neq 1/2$$

The objective of the test is to check whether the null hypothesis is to be accepted based on the value of the combined samples static by placing half of the significance level $\alpha/2$ at both the tails of the distribution. If the computed p-value is more than half of the significance level $\alpha/2$, then accept H_0, otherwise reject H_0.

Problem

The number of defects found in the hourly production of 8 different machines before and after maintenance is given below. Check whether the number of defects in the hourly production of items before and after is different at a significance level of 0.05.

Machine	1	2	3	4	5	6	7	8
Before	10	8	12	15	20	3	9	6
After	8	10	7	12	12	6	8	4

In the above problem , number of '+' signs = 6

Number of '-' signs = 2

The half of the significance level $\alpha/2$ is 0.025. Following program illustrates the two-tailed test for two samples.

Program

```
binom.test(6,8,0.5,alternative="two.sided")
```

Output

```
        Exact binomial test
data:   6 and 8
number of successes = 6, number of trials = 8, p-value = 0.2891
alternative hypothesis: true probability of success is not equal to 0.5
95 percent confidence interval:
 0.3491442 0.9681460
sample estimates:
probability of success
                  0.75
```

The calculated p-value `0.2891` is more than half of the significance level `0.025`, the calculated binomial statistic falls in the acceptance region. Hence accept H_0. Thus the number of defects found in the hourly production of the items before and after maintenance is not significantly different.

9.3.2 Two-Sample Sign Test with Normal Approximation

In two-sample sign test, a random sample of size `n`, where `np` as well as `n(1-p)` is at least 5 is taken and its null hypothesis is tested using normal approximation to the binomial distribution with `p=1/2`, where Q is the random variable representing the number of plus(+) signs. If `X~B(X,n,p)` then for large value of `n(n>30)`, one can approximate the binomial distribution to normal distribution as follows.

`Q~N[np,np(1-p)]`

where `np` is the mean and `np(1-p)` is the variance of the normal distribution. Z statistic can be calculated as follows.

$$Z = \frac{Q - np}{\sqrt{np(1-p)}}$$

9.3.2.1 Lower Tail Test

The combination of hypotheses for lower tailed test with normal approximation is as follows.

$$H_0: \mu_x = \mu_y \text{ or } p=1/2$$
$$H_1: \mu_x < \mu_y \text{ or } p<1/2$$

The objective of this test is to check whether the population is to be accepted based on the value of the sample statistic by placing the significance level α at the lower tail of the distribution. If the computed Z value is more than $-Z_\alpha$, then accept H_0, otherwise reject H_0.

Consider the following problem.

Problem

The weekly sales revenue (in lakhs) of a product in 14 stores before and after releasing a competing product is given below. Check whether the weekly sales revenue of the product has improved after introducing the price discount at a significance level of 0.05.

Retail Store	1	2	3	4	5	6	7	8	9	10	11	12	13	14
Before	7	8	6	8	3	7	4	8	3	6	7	5	6	5
After	9	9	8	7	6	6	8	9	6	9	9	8	4	4

In the above problem, n=14, significance level α=0.10. Let Q be the random variable representing the number of + signs. In the above problem Q=4.

Following program illustrates how to calculate Z statistic.

Program

```
#Upper Tail
x=4      # No: of + signs
np=7     # Mean
p=0.5
z=(x-np)/sqrt(np*(1-p)) # Z statistic
z
```

Output

```
[1] -1.603567
```

We then compute the critical value at significance level `0.10`.

Program

```
alpha = 0.10
z.alpha = qnorm(1-alpha)
-z.alpha               # critical value
```

Output

```
[1] -1.281552
```

The value of the standard normal z-statistic $-Z_\alpha$ is `-1.281552`. Since the calculated Z value `-1.603567` is less than the value of $-Z_\alpha$, we reject the null hypothesis H_0. Therefore the sales revenue of the product has improved after introducing the price discount.

9.3.2.2 Upper Tail Test

The combination of hypothesis for upper tailed test with normal approximation is as follows.

$$H_0: \mu_x = \mu_y \text{ or } p=1/2$$

$$H_1: \mu_x > \mu_y \text{ or } p>1/2$$

The objective of this test is to check whether the population is to be accepted based on the value of the sample statistic by placing the significance level α at the upper tail of the distribution. If the computed Z value is more than Z_α then reject H_0, otherwise accept H_0.

Problem

The weekly sales revenue (in lakhs) of a product in 14 stores before and after releasing a competing product is given below. Check whether the weekly sales revenue of the product has declined after releasing the competing product at a significance level of 0.05.

Retail Store	1	2	3	4	5	6	7	8	9	10	11	12	13	14
Before	8	9	6	9	4	8	5	9	2	8	9	10	12	7
After	7	8	8	7	3	5	4	8	4	7	8	7	9	9

In the above problem, n=14, significance level α=0.05. Let Q be the random variable representing the number of + signs. In the above problem Q=11.

Following program illustrates how to calculate Z statistic.

Program

```
#Upper Tail
x=11      # No: of + signs
np=7      # Mean
p=0.5
z=(x-np)/sqrt(np*(1-p)) # Z statistic
z
```

Output

```
[1] 2.13809
```

We then compute the critical value at significance level `0.05`.

Program

```
alpha = .05
z.alpha = qnorm(1-alpha)
z.alpha                    # critical value
```

Output

```
[1]1.644854
```

The value of the standard normal z-statistic Z_α is `1.644854.` Since the calculated Z value `2.13809` is less than the value of Z_α, we reject the null hypothesis H_0. Hence the weekly sales of the product have declined after releasing its competing product.

9.3.2.3 Two-Tailed Test

The combination of hypothesis for two-tailed test with normal approximation is as follows.

$$H_0: \mu_x = \mu_y \text{ or } p=1/2$$
$$H_1: \mu_{x\neq} \mu_y \text{ or } p\neq 1/2$$

The objective of this test is to check whether the population is to be accepted based on the value of the sample statistic by placing one-half of the significance level ($\alpha/2$) at both tails of the distribution. If the absolute value of the Z computed $|Z|$ is more than $Z_{\alpha/2}$ then reject H_0, otherwise accept H_0. Consider the following problem.

Problem

The performance indices of 20 randomly selected employees before and after attending a training program is given below. Check whether the performance indices of the employees before attending the training program are different from that of the employees after attending the training program at a significance level of 0.10.

Employee	1	2	3	4	5	6	7	8	9	10	11	12	13	14	15	16	17	18	19	20
Before	7	5	7	4	8	9	4	1	6	9	8	7	2	8	5	3	4	7	7	8
After	9	4	8	5	9	7	7	7	9	8	7	9	6	6	7	2	6	9	9	6

In the above problem, n=20, significance level α=0.10 (α/2=0.05). Let Q be the random variable representing the number of + signs. In the above problem Q=7.

Following program illustrates how to calculate Z statistic.

Program

```
x=7      # No: of + signs
np=10    # Mean
p=0.5
z=(x-np)/sqrt(np*(1-p)) # Z statistic
z
```

Output

```
[1] -1.341641
```

We then compute the critical value at significance level `0.05`.

Program

```
alpha = 0.10
```

```
z.half.alpha = qnorm(1-alpha/2)
c(-z.half.alpha, z.half.alpha)
```

Output

```
[1] -1.644854  1.644854
```

The $Z_{\alpha/2}$ values lie between -1.644854 and 1.644854. Since the calculated Z value -1.341641 lies inside $Z_{\alpha/2}$, we accept the null hypothesis. Thus the performance indices of the employees before attending the training programme are not different from that of the employees after attending the training programme.

9.3.3 Wilcoxon Signed-Rank Test

The Wilcoxon Signed-Rank test is a non-parametric statistical hypothesis test used when comparing two related samples, matched samples, or repeated measurements on a single sample to assess whether their population mean ranks differ (i.e. it is a paired difference test). It can be used as an alternative to the paired Student's t-test, t-test for matched pairs, or the Student's t-test for dependent samples when the population cannot be assumed to be normally distributed. A Wilcoxon Signed-Rank test is a nonparametric test that can be used to determine whether two dependent samples were selected from populations having the same distribution.

Two data samples are matched if they come from repeated observations of the same subject. Using the Wilcoxon Signed-Rank Test, we can decide whether the corresponding data population distributions are identical without assuming them to follow the normal distribution.

Problem

The weekly capacity utilization of two different machines during randomly selected weeks is given below. Check whether the two samples are drawn from identical populations against the alternate hypothesis that the populations are not identical at a significance level 0.10.

Week	1	2	3	4	5	6	7	8	9	10	11	12	13	14	15
Machine-1	94	77	64	88	65	55	75	93	62	68	83	73	90	60	63
Machine-2	78	95	54	71	91	56	82	92	97	84	53	61	98	87	87

H_0: Two samples are drawn from identical populations.
H_1: Two samples are not drawn from identical populations.

Program

```
#Wilcoxon signed rank test
x<-c(94,77,64,88,65,55,75,93,62,68,83,73,90,60,63)
y<-c(78,95,54,71,91,56,82,92,97,84,53,61,98,87,87)
wilcox.test(x,y,alpha=0.1,alternate="two.sided", paired=TRUE)
```

Output

```
Wilcoxon signed rank test with continuity correction
```

```
data:  x and y
V = 43, p-value = 0.3485
alternative hypothesis: true location shift is not equal to 0
Warning message:
In wilcox.test.default(x, y, alpha = 0.1, alternate = "two.sided",:
  cannot compute exact p-value with ties
```

For the paired test, we set the "paired" argument as `TRUE`. As the p-value turns out to be `0.3485`, and is greater than the `0.05` significance level($\alpha/2$), we accept the null hypothesis that the two samples are drawn from identical populations.

9.3.4 Mann-Whitney-Wilcoxon Test

In statistics, the Mann–Whitney-Wilcoxon test (also called the Mann–Whitney U test, Wilcoxon Rank-Sum test, or Wilcoxon–Mann–Whitney test) is a nonparametric test of the null hypothesis that it is equally likely that a randomly selected value from one sample will be less than or greater than a randomly selected value from a second sample. Unlike the t-test, it does not require the assumption of normal distributions. It is nearly as efficient as the t-test on normal distributions. This test can be used to determine whether two independent samples were selected from populations having the same distribution; a similar nonparametric test used on dependent samples is the Wilcoxon Signed-Rank test.

Problem

The performance indices of randomly selected programmers of two branches of a company are given below. Check whether the two samples are drawn from identical populations as against the alternate hypothesis that the first population is stochastically larger than the second population at a significance level of 0.05.

Branch-1	87	76	57	50	43	73	40	90	75	85	91	68	73	79	59	50	35	82	73	66
Branch-2	78	55	92	71	25	62	45	77	34	50	83	97	53	89	74	30	54	32	-	-

H_0: Two samples drawn from different populations having the same distribution

H1: The mean performance rating of the programmers from the population of Branch-1 is stochastically larger than that of the programmers from the population of Branch-2.

The upper-tailed test is done in this case.

Program

```
#Mann-Whitney-Wilcoxon test
x<-c(87,76,57,50,43,73,40,90,75,85,91,68,73,79,59,50,35,82,73,66)
y<-c(78,55,92,71,25,62,45,77,34,50,83,97,53,89,74,30,54,32)
wilcox.test(x,y,alternate="greater")
```

Output

```
Wilcoxon rank sum test with continuity correction
```

```
data:  x and y
W = 208, p-value = 0.4212
alternative hypothesis: true location shift is not equal to 0
Warning message:
In wilcox.test.default(x, y, alternate = "greater"):
  cannot compute exact p-value with ties
```

Here p-value `0.4212` is more than the significance level `0.05`. Hence the binomial statistic falls in the acceptance region and therefore accepts H_0. Thus two samples are drawn from populations having identical distribution.

9.3.5 Kolmogorov-Smirnov Test

Kolmogorov-Smirnov (K-S Test) is similar to the Chi-square test to do the goodness of fit of a given set of data to an assumed distribution. The combination of hypotheses used in this test is as follows.

H_0: The given set of observations follows the assumed distribution.

H_1: The given set of observations does not follow the assumed distribution.

K-S test can be used for one-sample as well as two-sample. In this section, we will see how K-S test can be applied to two sample. In K-S test, the values of the observed cumulative distribution of the random variable in a given situation are compared with the corresponding values of the theoretical cumulative distribution of the random variable and their absolute differences are calculated. The maximum of these absolute differences is considered as the calculated statistic of K-S test. This is a one-tailed test. Hence if the calculated value of the test statistic is more than the theoretical value for a given significance level α, then reject the null hypothesis, otherwise accept the null hypothesis.

The function for K-S test is as follows.

```
ks.test(x, y, ..., alternative = c("two.sided", "less", "greater"),
      exact = NULL)
```

where

`x` is a numeric vector of data values, `y` is either a numeric vector of data values, or a character string naming a distribution function, `...` is the parameters of the distribution specified (as a character string) by `y`, `alternative` indicates the alternative hypothesis and must be one of `"two.sided" (default)`, `"less"`, or `"greater"` and `exact` is `NULL` or a logical value indicating whether an exact p-value should be computed. The argument `exact` is not used for the one-sided two-sample case.

Problem

The rating of two countries Italy and France are given as follows. Check whether the given data follow the same distribution using Kolmogorov-Smirnov test at a significance level of 0.10.

Italy	3	2	3	5	8	9	8	8
France	2	8	2	4	4	3	6	3

H_0: Both the countries follow the same distribution.

H_1: Both the countries do not follow the same distribution.

We are conducting a two-tailed test for the above data. Since the default is two-sided, the "alternative" parameter is not passed to the function. Following program illustrates this.

Program

```
a<-c(3,2,3,5,8,9,8,8)
b<-c(2,8,2,4,4,3,6,3)
ks.test(a,b)
```

Output

```
        Two-sample Kolmogorov-Smirnov test
data:  a and b
D = 0.375, p-value = 0.6272
alternative hypothesis: two-sided
Warning message:
In ks.test(a, b) : cannot compute exact p-value with ties
```

Since the p-value is greater than one half of the significance level `0.05`, the binomial static falls in the acceptance region. Hence accept H_0. Both the data set follows the same distribution.

9.4 K-Samples Test

There may be situations in which more than 2 samples (K samples) simultaneously to be checked whether they are from identical populations. Kruskal-Wallis test is one of the popularly used K-samples test.

9.4.1 Kruskal-Wallis Test

Kruskal-Wallis test is also known as H test. The objective of this test is to check whether the K independent samples are from K identical populations. A collection of data samples are independent if they come from unrelated populations and the samples do not affect each other. Using the Kruskal-Wallis test, we can decide whether the population distributions are identical without assuming them to follow the normal distribution. This is a non-parametric test which is an alternative to single factor ANOVA which will be discussed in the next Chapter. The combination of hypotheses for the H test is given below.

H_0: K independent samples are from K identical populations

H_1: K independent samples are not from K identical populations

H test follows chi-square distribution with K-1 degrees of freedom. The H statistic of Kruskal-Wallis test can be calculated as given below where K is the number of samples.

$$\frac{12}{N(N+1)}\sum_{j=1}^{K}\frac{Rj2}{nj}-3(N+1)$$

where R_j is the sum of the ranks of the sample j, n_j is the size of the sample j, j=1,2,3…K and N is the size of the pooled sample (n_1+n_2+…n_k). The calculated H value is compared against the chi-square value with (K-1) degrees of freedom at a given significance level α. If the p-value is more than α, then reject the null hypothesis, otherwise accept the null hypothesis.

In R, Kruskal-Wallis test is performed using the function `kruskal.test`. There are three constructors for `kruskal.test`.

```
kruskal.test(x,…)
kruskal.test(x,g,...)
kruskal.test(formula, data, subset, na.action, ...)
```

where `x` : a numeric vector of data values, or a list of numeric data vectors. Non-numeric elements of a list will be coerced, with a warning.

`g` : a vector or factor object giving the group for the corresponding elements of x. Ignored with a warning if x is a list.

`formula`: a formula of the form response ~ group where response gives the data values and group a vector or factor of the corresponding groups.

`data`: an optional matrix or data frame containing the variables in the formula. By default the variables are taken from formula.

`subset`: an optional vector specifying a subset of observations to be used.

`na.action` : a function which indicates what should happen when the data contain NAs.

… : further arguments to be passed to or from methods.

Problem

The production volume of units assembled by three different operators during 9 shifts is given below. Check whether there is significant difference between the production volumes of units assembled by the three operators using Kruskal-Wallis H test at a significance level of 0.05.

Shifts	1	2	3	4	5	6	7	8	9
Operator-1	29	34	34	20	32	45	42	24	35
Operator-2	30	21	23	25	44	37	34	19	38
Operator-3	26	36	41	48	27	39	28	46	15

The combination of hypotheses for the problem is as given below.

H_0: There is no significant difference between the production volumes of units assembled by three operators.

H_1: There is significant difference between the production volumes of units assembled by three operators.

For the solution of above problem, the first constructor is used. The program is given below.

Program

```
x<-c(29,34,34,20,32,45,42,24,35)
y<-c(30,21,23,25,44,37,34,19,38)
```

```
z<-c(26,36,41,48,27,39,28,46,15)
kruskal.test(x,y,z)
```

Output

```
        Kruskal-Wallis rank sum test
data:  x and y
Kruskal-Wallis chi-squared = 8, df = 8, p-value = 0.4335
```

Since the p-value `0.4335` is greater than the significance level `0.05`, we accept the null hypothesis. Thus there is no significant difference between the production volumes of units assembled by the three operators.

Consider another example for Kruskal-Wallis test. We want to see if alcohol or coffee affects driving reaction times. There were three different groups of participants containing 10 participants drinking water, 10 participants drinking beer containing two units of alcohol and 10 drinking coffee. Reaction time on a driving simulation was measured for each participant. We want to find out whether there is a significant difference between several groups of measurements.

On the left side of the ~ we always use the dependent variable that we want to compare and on the right side we always use the independent (categorical) variable. The combination of hypotheses for the problem is as given below.

H_0: There is no significant difference between the groups of measurements.

H_1: There is significant difference between the groups of measurements.

For the solution of above problem, the third constructor is used. The program is given below.

Program

```
#Kurskal-Wallis Test
data=read.csv("Drink.csv", header=TRUE)
data
kruskal.test(data$Reactiontime~data$Drink)
```

Output

```
   Id Reactiontime   Drink Rank
1   1         0.37   Water  1.0
2   2         0.38   Water  2.0
3   3         0.61   Water  3.0
4   4         0.78   Water  4.0
5   5         0.83   Water  5.0
6   6         0.86   Water  6.0
7   7         0.97   Water  7.0
8   8         0.95   Water  8.0
9  11         0.98  Coffee  9.0
```

```
10 12          1.11  Coffee 10.0
11 13          1.27  Coffee 11.0
12 14          1.32  Coffee 12.0
13 15          1.44  Coffee 13.0
14 16          1.45  Coffee 14.0
15 17          1.46  Coffee 15.0
16  9          1.63   Water 16.0
17 21          1.69 Alcohol 17.0
18 22          1.71 Alcohol 18.0
19 23          1.75 Alcohol 19.0
20 18          1.76  Coffee 20.0
21 24          1.83 Alcohol 21.0
22 10          1.97   Water 22.5
23 25          1.97 Alcohol 22.5
24 26          2.53 Alcohol 24.0
25 19          2.56  Coffee 25.0
26 27          2.66 Alcohol 26.0
27 28          2.91 Alcohol 27.0
28 20          3.07  Coffee 28.0
29 29          3.28 Alcohol 29.0
30 30          3.47 Alcohol 30.0

        Kruskal-Wallis rank sum test
data:  data$Reactiontime by data$Drink
Kruskal-Wallis chi-squared = 16.322, df = 2, p-value = 0.0002856
```

Since the p-value `0.0002856` is less than `0.0001` we reject the null hypothesis. There is a significant difference between at least one pair of measurements.

9.5 Conclusion

This Chapter gives detailed information of various non-parametric tests. Various non-parametric tests on one-sample, two-samples and K-samples are discussed. One-sample test includes one-sample sign test for small sample and one-sample sign test for large sample. In both case, the lower-tail, upper-tail and two-tailed tests are performed. Two-samples test includes two-sample sign test with binomial distribution, two-sample sign test with normal approximation, Wilcoxon signed-rank test, Mann-Whitney-Wilcoxon test and Kolmogorov-Smirnov test. For two-sample sign test with binomial distribution and two-sample sign test with normal approximation, lower-tailed, upper-tailed and two-tailed tests are explained. Finally for larger number of samples, K-samples test is discussed. The most popular Kruskal-Wallis test is illustrated in detail. All sections have examples and solved problems using R.

10 Analysis of Variance

10.1 Introduction

ANOVA is a statistical technique that assesses potential differences in a scale-level dependent variable by a nominal-level variable having 2 or more categories. The ANOVA, developed by Ronald Fisher in 1918, extends the t and the z test which have the problem of only allowing the nominal level variable to have two categories. This test is also called the Fisher analysis of variance. Researchers and students use ANOVA in many ways. The use of ANOVA depends on the research design. Commonly, ANOVAs are used in three ways: one-way ANOVA, two-way ANOVA, and N-way ANOVA.

One-Way ANOVA

A one-way ANOVA has just one independent variable. For example, difference in IQ can be assessed by Country, and Country can have 2, 20, or more different categories to compare.

Two-Way ANOVA

A two-way ANOVA refers to an ANOVA using two independent variables. Expanding the example above, a 2-way ANOVA can examine differences in IQ scores (the dependent variable) by Country (independent variable 1) and Gender (independent variable 2). Two-way ANOVA can be used to examine the interaction between the two independent variables. Interactions indicate that differences are not uniform across all categories of the independent variables. For example, females may have higher IQ scores overall compared to males, but this difference could be greater (or less) in European countries compared to North American countries. Two-way ANOVAs are also called factorial ANOVAs.

M-Way ANOVA

A researcher can also use more than two independent variables, and this is an m-way ANOVA (with n being the number of independent variables we have). For example, potential differences in IQ scores can be examined by Country, Gender, Age group, Ethnicity, etc, simultaneously.

The null hypothesis for an ANOVA is that there is no significant difference among the groups. The alternative hypothesis assumes that there is atleast one significant difference among the groups. After cleaning the data, the researcher must test the assumptions of ANOVA. They must then calculate the F-ratio and the associated probability value (p-value). In general, if the p-value associated with the F is smaller than .05, then the null hypothesis is rejected and the alternative hypothesis is supported. If the null hypothesis is rejected, one concludes that the means of all the groups are not equal.

When we conduct an ANOVA, we are attempting to determine if there is a statistically significant difference among the groups.

10.2 Assumptions for ANOVA

The level of measurement of the variables and assumptions of the test play an important role in ANOVA. In ANOVA, the dependent variable must be a continuous (interval or ratio) level of measurement. The independent variables in ANOVA must be categorical (nominal or ordinal) variables. Like the Student's t-test, ANOVA is also a parametric test and has some assumptions. ANOVA assumes that the data is normally distributed. ANOVA also assumes homogeneity of variance, which means that the variance among the groups should be approximately equal and the observations are independent of each other. Researchers should keep in mind when planning any study to look out for extraneous or confounding variables. ANOVA has methods (i.e., ANCOVA) to control for confounding variables which will be discussed in Chapter 11.

Testing of the Assumptions

1. The population from which samples are drawn should be normally distributed.
2. Independence of cases: the sample cases should be independent of each other.
3. Homogeneity of variance: Homogeneity means that the variance among the groups should be approximately equal.

The assumption of independence can be determined from the design of the study. It is important to note that ANOVA is not robust to violations to the assumption of independence. This is to say, that even if we violate the assumptions of homogeneity or normality, we can conduct the test and basically trust the findings. However, the results of the ANOVA are invalid if the independence assumption is violated. In general, with violations of homogeneity the analysis is considered robust if we have equal sized groups. With violations of normality, continuing with the ANOVA generally creates no problem if we have a large sample size.

10.3 Factors in ANOVA

A factor which has the effect on response variable of an experiment can be classified into fixed factor or random factor.

10.3.1 Fixed Factor

In an experiment, if a specific set of treatments of a factor is selected with certainty, then that factor is called fixed factor. In this situation, the inference of the analysis of the experiment is applied to only the treatments of that factor. For example, we might be studying the effects of tea on weight loss and form three groups: green tea, black tea, and no tea. Then the inference of the analysis is applied to only these three groups. The effect of the treatments of fixed factor A on the response variable is given by the following formula.

$$A = \frac{\sum_{j=1}^{n} Aj}{a-1}$$

where (a-1) is the degrees of freedom of the factor A, and A_j is the effect of the jth treatment of the factor A.

10.3.2 Random Factor

In an experiment, if a set of treatments of a factor is selected randomly from among the available treatments, then the factor is termed as a random factor. In this, the inference of the analysis can be generalized to all the treatments of that factor. For example, if green tea, black coffee, coffee with milk and no tea are selected randomly from a set of beverages for studying their effects on weight loss, then the inference of the analysis of the experiment can be generalized to all beverages. The effect of the treatments of the random factor A on the response variable is given by the following formula

$$A = \sigma_A^2$$

where σ^2_A is the variance of the random factor A

Total sum of squares = Sum of squares of treatment + Sum of squares of error

$$SS_{total} = SS_A + SS_{error}$$

The generalized results for single factor ANOVA is given in Table 10.1

Table 10.1: Generalized Results for Single Factor ANOVA

Source of Variation	Degrees of Freedom	Sum of Squares	Mean Sum of Squares (MSS)	F Ratio
Between Treatments	a-1	$SS_{treatments}$	$SS_{treatments}/(a-1)$	$MSS_{treatments} / MSS_{error}$
Within Treatments	a(n-1)	SS_{error}	$SS_{error}/[a(n-1)]$	$SS_{error}/[a(n-1)]$
Total	N-1	SS_{total}		

There are different designs for ANOVA. It includes various techniques like Completely Randomized Design, Randomized Complete Block Design, Latin Square Design, Factorial Design etc. We will see each design in the coming sections.

10.4 Completely Randomized Design

In the design of experiments, completely randomized designs are for studying the effects of one primary factor without the need to take other variables into account. The experiment compares the values of a response variable based on the different levels of that primary factor. The concept and application of completely randomized design is demonstrated using the following example. The generalized result of completely randomized design is given in Table 10.2.

Table 10.2: Generalized Results for Completely Randomized Design

Source of Variation	Degrees of Freedom	Sum of Squares	Mean Sum of Squares (MSS)	F Ratio
Between Treatments	a-1	$SS_{treatments}$	$SS_{treatments}/(a-1)$	$SS_{treatments} / MSS_{error}$
Within Treatments	N-a	SS_{error}	$SS_{error}/(N-a)$	
Total	N-1	SS_{total}		

Problem

An organization has deputed four different batches of its employees to four different training organizations A, B, C and D for the same training programme which aims to improve their reasoning skills. Each batch consists of five employees with similar academic qualification and job experience. The percentage score of the employees in a test conducted after the training programme is summarized and given below. Perform ANOVA to check whether there is a significant difference between the training organizations in terms of reasoning skills of the employees by assuming a significance level of 0.05.

A	B	C	D
80	70	65	90
90	60	50	89
96	55	58	85
85	85	55	95
70	90	40	80

Solution

We assume the hypothesis as follows.

H_0: Treatment means are equal.

H_1: Treatment means are not equal for at least one pair of the treatment means.

The solution consists of the following steps:

1. Copy and paste the above values in a comma separated format and save it as "`Organization.csv`" with a text editor like notepad.
2. Load the file into a data frame named `df1` with the `read.csv` function. As the first line in the file contains the column names, we set the header argument as `TRUE`. The `read.csv` function is already discussed in Chapter 6.

Program

```
df1=read.csv("Organization.csv", header=TRUE)
df1
```

Output

```
   A  B  C  D
1 80 70 65 90
2 90 60 50 89
3 96 55 58 85
4 85 85 55 95
5 70 90 40 80
```

1. Concatenate the data rows of `df1` into a single vector `r`.

   Program

   ```
   r = c(t(as.matrix(df1))) # response data
   r
   ```

   Output

   ```
   [1] 80 70 65 90 90 60 50 89 96 55 58 85 85 85 55 95 70 90 40 80
   ```

2. Assign new variables for the treatment levels and number of observations.

   Program

   ```
   f = c("A","B","C","D") # treatment levels
   k = 4                   # number of treatment levels
   n = 5                   # observations per treatment
   ```

3. Create a vector of treatment factors that corresponds to each element of `r` in step 3 with the `gl` function. The `gl` function is explained in Chapter 2.

   Program

   ```
   tm = gl(k, 1, n*k, factor(f))    # matching treatments
   ```

4. Apply the function `aov` to a formula that describes the response `r` by the treatment factor `tm`.

   Program

   ```
   av = aov(r ~ tm)
   ```

5. We can print the ANOVA table with the `summary` function.

   Program

   ```
   summary(av)
   ```

   Output

   ```
             Df  Sum  Sq Mean Sq F value   Pr(>F)
   tm         3  3570  1190.0   10.59     0.000444
   Residuals  16  1799  112.4
   ```

Since the p-value `0.000444` is less than the significance level `0.05`, we reject the null hypothesis. This means that there is a significant difference in terms of percentage scores between the batches trained by different training organizations.

10.5 Randomized Complete Block Design

For randomized complete block designs, there is one factor or variable that is of primary interest. However, there are also several other factors. Other factors are those that may affect the measured result, but are not of primary interest. In a randomized complete block design, there is only one primary factor under consideration in the experiment. Similar test subjects are grouped into blocks. Each block is tested against all treatment levels of the primary factor at random order. This is intended to eliminate possible influence by other extraneous factors. The concept and application of completely randomized block design is demonstrated using the following problem. The generalized result of randomized complete block design is given in Table 10.3.

Table 10.3: Generalized Results for Randomized Complete Block Design

Source of Variation	Degrees of Freedom	Sum of Squares	Mean Sum of Squares (MSS)	F Ratio
Between Treatments	a-1	$SS_{treatments}$	$SS_{treatments}/(a-1)$	$MSS_{treatments} / MSS_{error}$
Within Treatments	b-1	SS_{blocks}	$SS_{blocks}/(b-1)$	$MSS_{blocks} / MSS_{error}$
Error	N-a-b+1	SS_{error}	$SS_{error}/(N-a-b-+1)$	
Total	N-1	SS_{total}		

Problem

An IT Fest was conducted in a college in which students from 15 different colleges participated in the IT Fest. Five different teams (T_1, T_2, T_3, T_4 and T_5) have been formed from these 15 schools to participate in various events. Each team consisted of a team leader (L_1, L_2, L_3, L_4 and L_5) and 4 members. The points earned after the IT Fest are summarized and given in the table below.

	L_1	L_2	L_3	L_4	L_5
T_1	40	30	55	25	35
T_2	45	60	10	22	33
T_3	38	55	40	55	28
T_4	30	27	32	56	17
T_5	45	34	20	34	37

Perform the randomized complete block design to check whether there is a significant difference between the team leaders (L_1, L_2, L_3, L_4, L_5) as well as between different teams (T_1, T_2, T_3, T_4 and T_5) in terms of the points scored by assuming a significance level 0.05.

Solution

We assume the hypothesis with respect to treatment (team leader) as follows.

H_0: Treatment means are equal.

H_1: Treatment means are not equal for at least one pair of the treatment means.

We assume the hypothesis with respect to block (team) as follows.

H_0: Block means are equal.

H_1: Block means are not equal for at least one pair of block means.

The solution consists of the following steps:

1. Copy and paste the above values in a comma separated format and save it as "ITFEST.csv" with a text editor like notepad.
2. Load the file into a data frame named `df1` with the `read.csv` function. As the first line in the file contains the column names, we set the header argument as `TRUE`.

   Program

   ```
   df1=read.csv("ITFEST.csv", header=TRUE)
   df1
   ```

   Output

   ```
      L1 L2 L3 L4 L5
    1 40 30 55 25 35
    2 45 60 10 22 33
    3 38 55 40 55 28
    4 30 27 32 56 17
    5 45 34 20 34 37
   ```

3. Concatenate the data rows of `df1` into a single vector `r`.

   Program

   ```
   r = c(t(as.matrix(df1))) # response data
   r
   ```

   Output

   ```
   [1] 40 30 55 25 35 45 60 10 22 33 38 55 40 55 28 30 27 32 56 17 45 34
   20 34
   [25] 37
   ```

4. Assign new variables for the treatment levels and number of observations.

   Program

   ```
   f = c("L1","L2","L3","L4","L5") # treatment levels
   k = 5                          # number of treatment levels
   n = 5                          # number of control blocks
   ```

5. Create a vector of treatment factors that corresponds to each element of `r` in step 3 with the `gl` function.

   Program

   ```
   tm = gl(k, 1, n*k, factor(f))    # matching treatments
   ```

6. Similarly, create a vector of blocking factors for each element in the response data `r`.

   Program

```
blk = gl(n, k, k*n)                # blocking factor
blk
```

   Output

```
[1] 1 1 1 1 1 2 2 2 2 2 3 3 3 3 3 4 4 4 4 4 5 5 5 5 5
Levels: 1 2 3 4 5
```

7. Apply the function `aov` to a formula that describes the response `r` by the treatment factor `tm`.

   Program

```
av = aov(r ~ tm+blk)
```

8. We can print the ANOVA table with the `summary` function.

   Program

```
summary(av)
```

   Output

```
            Df Sum Sq Mean Sq F value Pr(>F)
tm           4    514  128.56   0.636  0.644
blk          4    369   92.16   0.456  0.767
Residuals   16   3236  202.24
```

Since the p-value `0.644` is greater than the significance level `0.05`, we accept the null hypothesis. This means that there is no significant difference in terms of points scored between the team leaders. Similarly the p-value `0.767` is greater than the significance level `0.05`, we accept the null hypothesis. This means that there is no significant difference in terms of points scored between different teams.

10.6 Latin Square Design

This design is an improvement over the randomized complete block design. This function calculates ANOVA for a special three factor design known as Latin squares. The Latin square design applies when there are repeated exposures/treatments and two other factors. This design avoids the excessive numbers required for full three-way ANOVA. Rows and columns can be any two sources of variation in an experiment. In this sense a Latin square is a generalization of a randomized block design with two different blocking systems. The Latin square design is used where the researcher desires to control the variation in an experiment that is related to rows and columns in the field.

- Treatments are assigned at random within rows and columns, with each treatment once per row and once per column.
- There are equal numbers of rows, columns, and treatments.
- Useful where the experimenter desires to control variation in two different directions.

The generalized result of Latin square design is given in Table 10.4.

Table 10.4: Generalized Results for Latin Square Design

Source of Variation	Degrees of Freedom	Sum of Squares	Mean Sum of Squares (MSS)	F Ratio
Between Treatments	a-1	$SS_{treatments}$	$SS_{treatments}/(a-1)$	$MSS_{treatments} / MSS_{error}$
Between Rows	b-1	SS_{rows}	$SS_{rows}/(b-1)$	MSS_{rows} / MSS_{error}
Between Columns	c-1	$SS_{columns}$	$SS_{blocks}/(c-1)$	$MSS_{columns} / MSS_{error}$
Error	N-a-b-c+2	SS_{error}	$SS_{error}/(N-a-b-c+2)$	
Total	N-1	SS_{total}		

The following problem illustrates the use of Latin square design in ANOVA.

Problem

The production manager of a company has recorded the hourly production volume of a product. He feels that operators (A, B, C, D and E), machines (M1, M2, M3, M4 and M5) and suppliers (S1, S2, S3, S4 and S5) will affect the production volume of the product. The data is provided in a Latin square design as follows.

	S1	S2	S3	S4	S5
M1	12(A)	8(B)	9(C)	15(D)	18(E)
M2	14(B)	7(C)	13(D)	10(E)	12(A)
M3	7(C)	15(D)	12(E)	8(A)	6(B)
M4	16(D)	17(E)	13(A)	11(B)	12(C)
M5	9(E)	14(A)	8(B)	10(C)	8(D)

Perform ANOVA to test the following at a significance level `0.05`.

(a) Whether there is a significant difference between operators in terms of production volume.

(b) Whether there is a significant difference between machines in terms of production volume.

(c) Whether there is a significant difference between suppliers in terms of production volume.

Solution

We assume the hypothesis as follows.

Hypothesis with respect to treatment (operator):

H_0: Treatment means are equal

H_1: Treatment means are not equal for at least one pair of treatment means.

Hypothesis with respect to rows (machine):

H_0: Row means are equal

H_1: Row means are not equal for at least one pair of row means.

Hypothesis with respect to columns (supplier):

H_0: Column means are equal

H_1: Column means are not equal for at least one pair of column means.

The solution consists of the following steps:

1. Prepare a csv file in a comma separated format and save it as "`HourlyProduction.csv`" with a text editor like notepad with column headings `machine`, `supplier`, `operator` and `volume`. There will be 25 values altogether (5 machines, 5 supplier and 5 operators).
2. Load the file into a data frame named `df1` with the `read.csv` function. As the first line in the file contains the column names, we set the header argument as `TRUE`.

Program

```
df1=read.csv("HourlyProduction.csv", header=TRUE)
df1
```

Output

```
   machine supplier operator volume
1       M1       S1        A     12
2       M1       S2        B      8
3       M1       S3        C      9
4       M1       S4        D     15
5       M1       S5        E     18
6       M2       S1        B     14
7       M2       S2        C      7
8       M2       S3        D     13
9       M2       S4        E     10
10      M2       S5        A     12
11      M3       S1        C      7
12      M3       S2        D     15
13      M3       S3        E     12
14      M3       S4        A      8
15      M3       S5        B      6
16      M4       S1        D     16
17      M4       S2        E     17
18      M4       S3        A     13
19      M4       S4        B     11
20      M4       S5        C     12
21      M5       S1        E      9
22      M5       S2        A     14
23      M5       S3        B      8
24      M5       S4        C     10
25      M5       S5        D      8
```

3. Apply the function `aov` to a formula that describes the response `df1$volume` by the three treatment factors `df1$machine, df1$supplier` and `df1$operator.`

   Program

```
av = aov(df1$volume ~ df1$machine+df1$supplier+df1$operator,df1)
```

4. We can print the ANOVA table with the `summary` function.

   Program

```
summary(av)
```

   Output

```
               Df Sum Sq Mean Sq F value Pr(>F)
df1$machine     4  62.96   15.74   1.616  0.234
df1$supplier    4   6.16    1.54   0.158  0.956
df1$operator    4  85.76   21.44   2.201  0.130
Residuals      12 116.88    9.74
```

Component-treatment (operator):

The p-value `0.13` for operator is greater than the significance level `0.05`. Hence we accept the null hypothesis. This means that there is no significant difference between operators in terms of hourly production of volume.

Component-rows (machines):

The p-value `0.234` for machine is greater than the significance level `0.05`. Hence we accept the null hypothesis. This means that there is no significant difference between machines in terms of hourly production of volume.

Component-columns (supplier):

The p-value `0.956` for operator is greater than the significance level `0.05`. Hence we accept the null hypothesis. This means that there is no significant difference between suppliers in terms of hourly production of volume.

10.7 Factorial Design

Factorial ANOVA is used when we want to consider the effect of more than one factor on differences in the dependent variable. Factorial designs allow us to determine if there are interactions between the independent variables or factors considered. The generalized result of factorial design is given in Table 10.5.

Table 10.5: Generalized Results for Factorial Design

Source of Variation	Degrees of Freedom	Sum of Squares	Mean Sum of Squares (MSS)	F Ratio
Between Rows	a-1	SS_{rows}	$SS_{rows}/(a-1)$	MSS_{rows} / MSS_{error}
Between Columns	b-1	$SS_{columns}$	$SS_{blocks}/(b-1)$	$MSS_{columns} / MSS_{error}$

Between Rows x Columns	(a-1)(b-1)	$SS_{rows\ x\ columns}$	$SS_{rows\ x\ columns}$ / (a-1)(b-1)	$MSS_{rows\ x\ columns}$ / MSS_{error}
Error	ab(n-1)	SS_{error}	SS_{error}/ab(n-1)	
Total	abn-1	SS_{total}		

The concept and application of factorial design is demonstrated using the following problem.

Problem

The sales manager of a company wants to study the effect of sales regions as well as salesman on quarterly sales revenue. The factorial experiment involving two factors with two replications for each experimental combination is given below. As per the design, each salesman is assigned to each region for two different quarters. Perform ANOVA and check the following at a significance level of 0.05.

(a) Whether there is a significant difference in terms of sales revenue between sales regions.

(b) Whether there is a significant difference in terms of sales revenue between salesmen.

(c) Whether there is a significant difference in terms of sales revenue between different combinations of sales region and salesman.

Salesman(B) (Rupees in lakhs)					
Sales Region (A)	East	65	30	50	20
		70	35	65	40
	West	30	60	20	50
		35	55	25	40

Solution

The problem has two different factors namely sales region (A) and salesman (B). The number of treatments for the factor A is 2 (A1 and A2) and that of factor B is 4 (B1, B2, B3 and B4).

Hypothesis with respect to treatment of the factor A is as follows.

H_0: Treatment means of factor A are equal.

H_1: Treatment means are not equal for at least one pair of the treatment means of the factor A.

Hypothesis with respect to treatment of the factor B is as follows.

H_0: Treatment means of factor B are equal.

H_1: Treatment means are not equal for at least one pair of the treatment means of the factor B.

Hypothesis with respect to interaction component is as follows.

H_0: Interaction means of AB are equal.

H_1: Interaction means are not equal for at least one pair of the interaction means.

The solution consists of the following steps:

1. Copy and paste the above values in a comma separated format and save it as "`Sales.csv`" with a text editor like notepad.

2. Load the file into a data frame named `df1` with the `read.csv` function. As the first line in the file contains the column names, we set the header argument as `TRUE`.

   Program

```
df1=read.csv("Sales.csv", header=TRUE)
df1
```

   Output

```
   B1 B2 B3 B4
A1 65 30 50 20
A2 70 35 65 40
A3 30 60 20 50
A4 35 55 25 40
```

3. Concatenate the data rows of `df1` into a single vector `r`.

   Program

```
r = c(t(as.matrix(df1))) # response data
r
```

   Output

```
[1] 65 30 50 20 70 35 65 40 30 60 20 50 35 55 25 40
```

4. Assign new variables for the treatment levels and number of observations.

   Program

```
f1 = c("B1", "B2", "B3", "B4")        # 1st factor levels
f2 = c("East", "West")               # 2nd factor levels
k1 = length(f1)                 # number of 1st factors
k2 = length(f2)                 # number of 2nd factors
n = 2                           # observations per treatment
```

5. Create a vector that corresponds to the 1st treatment level of the response data `r` in step 3 element-by-element with the `gl` function.

   Program

```
tm1 = gl(k1, 1, n*k1*k2, factor(f1))
```

6. Similarly, create a vector that corresponds to the 2nd treatment level of the response data `r` in step 3.

   Program

```
tm2 = gl(k2, n*k1, n*k1*k2, factor(f2))
```

7. Apply the function `aov` to a formula that describes the response `r` by the two treatment factors `tm1` and `tm2` with interaction.

Program

```
av = aov(r ~ tm1*tm2)
```

8. We can print the ANOVA table with the `summary` function.

Program

```
summary(av)
```

Output

```
              Df Sum Sq Mean Sq F value   Pr(>F)
tm1            3  368.8   122.9   2.314 0.152507
tm2            1  225.0   225.0   4.235 0.073590
tm1:tm2        3 3075.0  1025.0  19.294 0.000508
Residuals      8  425.0    53.1
```

Component-factor A:

Since the p-value `0.152507` is greater than the significance level `0.05`, we accept the null hypothesis. This means that there is no significant difference in terms of quarterly sales between different sales regions.

Component-factor B:

Similarly the p-value `0.073590` is greater than the significance level `0.05`, we accept the null hypothesis. This means that there is no significant difference in terms of quarterly sales between different salesmen.

Component-interaction AxB:

The p-value `0.000508` is less than the significance level `0.05`, we reject the null hypothesis. This means that there is a significant difference in quarterly sales because of the interaction between the factor 'sales region' and the factor 'salesman'. This means that the interaction between 'sales region' and 'salesman' has significant effect on quarterly sales.

10.8 Conclusion

This Chapter explains in detail Analysis of Variance (ANOVA). Various assumptions for ANOVA, factors in ANOVA like fixed factor, random factor are discussed in this Chapter. The different design for ANOVA which includes completely randomized design, randomized complete block design, latin square design and factorial design are illustrated with example problem and solutions.

11 Basic Multivariate Analysis

11.1 Introduction

Multivariate Data Analysis refers to any statistical technique used to analyze data that arises from more than one variable. This essentially models reality where each situation, product, or decision involves more than a single variable. The information age has resulted in masses of data in every field. Despite the quantum of data available, the ability to obtain a clear picture of what is going on and make intelligent decisions is a challenge. When available information is stored in database tables containing rows and columns, Multivariate Analysis can be used to process the information in a meaningful fashion. Multivariate analysis methods are typically used for:

- Consumer and market research
- Quality control and quality assurance across a range of industries such as food and beverage, paint, pharmaceuticals, chemicals, energy, telecommunications, etc.
- Process optimization and process control
- Research and development

In this Chapter, the basic multivariate analysis techniques which includes correlation analysis, forecasting, linear regression, non-linear regression and time series analysis are explained. The advanced topics on multivariate analysis will be discussed in next Chapter.

11.2 Correlation Analysis

Correlation analysis consists of calculating the Karl Pearson's correlation coefficient or Spearman coefficient or Kendall coefficient, rank correlation and auto-correlation. The correlation coefficient of two variables in a data set equals to their covariance divided by the product of their individual standard deviations. It is a normalized measurement of how the two are linearly related. Formally, the sample correlation coefficient is defined by the following formula, where s_x and s_y are the sample standard deviations, and s_{xy} is the sample covariance.

$$r_{xy} = \frac{S_{xy}}{S_x S_y}$$

Similarly, the population correlation coefficient is defined as follows, where σ_x and σ_y are the population standard deviations, and σ_{xy} is the population covariance.

$$p_{xy} = \frac{\sigma_{xy}}{\sigma_x \sigma_y}$$

Correlation is the degree of association between two variables and it is represented in terms of a coefficient known as correlation coefficient. The range of correlation coefficient is between -1 and +1. If the correlation coefficient is close to +1, it would indicate that the variables are positively linearly related and the scatter plot falls almost along a straight line with positive slope. For -1, it indicates that the variables are negatively linearly related and the scatter plot almost falls along a straight line with negative slope. And for zero, it would indicate a weak linear relationship between the variables or there is no correlation. The correlation coefficient can be calculated using the function `cor()` in R. The syntax of `cor()` function is as follows.

```
cor(x, y = NULL, use = "everything", method = c("pearson", "kendall",
"spearman"))
```

where `x` is a numeric vector, matrix or data frame.

`y` – a vector, matrix or data frame with compatible dimensions to `x`. `NULL` is the default value. The default is equivalent to `y = x` (but more efficient).

`use` – an optional character string giving a method for computing covariances in the presence of missing values. This must be (an abbreviation of) one of the strings `"everything"`, `"all.obs"`, `"complete.obs"`, `"na.or.complete"`, or `"pairwise.complete.obs"`.

`method` – a character string indicating which correlation coefficient (or covariance) is to be computed. This can be one of `"pearson" (default)`, `"kendall"`, or `"spearman"`. This can be abbreviated.

If we use `"everything"`, `NA`s will propagate conceptually, i.e., a resulting value will be `NA` whenever one of its contributing observations is `NA`. If use is `"all.obs"`, then the presence of missing observations will produce an error. If use is `"complete.obs"` then missing values are handled by casewise deletion and if there are no complete cases, that gives an error. The use of `"na.or.complete"` is the same unless there are no complete cases that give `NA`. Finally, if use has the value `"pairwise.complete.obs"` then the correlation or covariance between each pair of variables is computed using all complete pairs of observations on those variables. Consider the following problem for correlation analysis.

Problem

The annual advertising expenditures (in lakhs of rupees) and the corresponding annual sales (in crores of rupees) for the past 10 years of a company is given below. Find the correlation coefficient between annual advertising expenditure and annual sales revenue.

Annual Advertising Expenditure	10	12	14	16	18	20	22	24	26	28
Annual Sales	20	30	37	50	56	78	89	100	120	110

We will solve the problem using Karl Pearson's correlation coefficient, Spearman correlation coefficient and finally using Kendall correlation coefficient.

Program for Karl Pearson's Correlation Coefficient

```
x=c(10,12,14,16,18,20,22,24,26,28)
y=c(20,30,37,50,56,78,89,100,120,110)
cor(x,y,method="pearson")
```

Output

```
[1] 0.9851764
```

The Karl Pearson's correlation coefficient `0.9851764` shows that there is a positive correlation between the variables `x` and `y`. This means that there is a positive correlation between annual advertising expenditure and annual sales.

The same problem given above is used for calculating the spearman correlation coefficient. The following program illustrates this.

Program for Spearman Correlation Coefficient

```
x=c(10,12,14,16,18,20,22,24,26,28)
y=c(20,30,37,50,56,78,89,100,120,110)
cor(x,y,method="spearman")
```

Output

```
[1] 0.9878788
```

Here also the Spearman correlation coefficient `0.9878788` shows a positive correlation. Now we will see the Kendall correlation coefficient for the same problem. Following program illustrates this.

Program for Kendall Correlation Coefficient

```
x=c(10,12,14,16,18,20,22,24,26,28)
y=c(20,30,37,50,56,78,89,100,120,110)
cor(x,y,method="kendall")
```

Output

```
[1] 0.9555556
```

The Kendall correlation coefficient also shows a value `0.9555556` which is near to 1. This means that there is a positive correlation between annual advertising expenditure and annual sales.

11.2.1 Co-variance

The covariance of two variables `x` and `y` in a data set measures how the two variables are linearly related. A positive covariance would indicate a positive linear relationship between the variables, and a negative covariance would indicate the opposite. The sample covariance is defined in terms of the sample means as:

$$s_{xy} = \frac{1}{n-1}\sum_{i=1}^{n}(x_i - \overline{x})(y_i - \overline{y})$$

Similarly, the population covariance is defined in terms of the population mean μ_x, μ_y as:

$$\sigma_{xy} = \frac{1}{N}\sum_{i=1}^{N}(x_i - \mu_x)(y_i - \mu_y)$$

The covariance can be found using `cov()` function. The syntax of `cov()` function is as follows.

```
cov(x, y = NULL, use = "everything",method = c("pearson", "kendall",
"spearman"))
```

The explanation of the attributes of `cov()` function is same as that of `cor()` function given above. Consider the following problem.

Problem

The preference ratings of 8 brands of soft drinks by two judges are given below. Find the covariance between the preference ratings assigned by the judges for the brands of soft drinks.

Brand	1	2	3	4	5	6	7	8
Rating by Judge -1	2	3	1	8	5	4	7	6
Rating by Judge-2	4	5	7	3	6	8	2	1

Program

```
x=c(2,3,1,8,5,4,7,6)
y=c(4,5,7,3,6,8,2,1)
cov(x,y)
```

Output

```
[1] -3.714286
```

The negative value for the covariance indicates that there is a negative linear relationship between the variables.

11.2.2 Rank Correlation

There may be situations where the data may be available in the forms of ranks of variables, X and Y. In such situation, the objective is to determine the coefficient of correlation between the ranks. Such coefficient of correlation can be found out using Spearman's rank correlation. The formula for calculating Spearman's rank correlation coefficient is as follows.

$$rs = 1 - \frac{6\sum_{i=1}^{n}(Xi - Yi)2}{n(n2-1)}$$

where X_i is the rank of the ith observation of the variable X, Y_i is the ith observation of the variable Y and n the number of pair of observations.

The Spearman's rank correlation coefficient can be calculated in R using `cor.test()` function. The syntax of `cor.test()` is as follows.

```
cor.test(x, y, alternative = c("two.sided", "less", "greater"),
        method = c("pearson", "kendall", "spearman"),
        exact = NULL, conf.level = 0.95, continuity = FALSE, ...)
```

where `x, y` – numeric vectors of data values. x and y must have the same length.

`alternative` – indicates the alternative hypothesis and must be one of "`two.sided`", "`greater`" or "`less`". We can specify just the initial letter. "`greater`" corresponds to positive association, "`less`" to negative association.

`method` – a character string indicating which correlation coefficient is to be used for the test. One of "`pearson`", "`kendall`", or "`spearman`", can be abbreviated.

`exact` – is a logical value indicating whether an exact p-value should be computed. Used for Kendall's τ and Spearman's ρ.

`conf.level` – confidence level for the returned confidence interval. Currently this is only used for the Pearson product moment correlation coefficient if there are at least 4 complete pairs of observations.

`continuity` – This is a logical value. If `TRUE`, a continuity correction is used for Kendall's τ and Spearman's ρ when not computed exactly.

The same method can be used for finding all the three rank correlation coefficient like Spearman's rank correlation coefficient ρ, Kendall's rank correlation co-efficient τ and Pearson's product moment correlation. We will see how to calculate all the three correlation coefficients in the below problem.

Problem

The preference ratings of 10 brands of washing machine by two customers are given below. Find the rank correlation between the preference ratings of the customers for different brands of washing machines. Test the significance of the coefficient at a significance level of 0.05.

Brand	1	2	3	4	5	6	7	8	9	10
Rating by customer-1	1	2	3	4	5	6	7	8	9	10
Rating by customer-2	2	4	5	1	3	6	7	9	10	8

For Spearman rank correlation coefficient, we assume the hypothesis as follows.

H_0: ρ is equal to 0

H_1: ρ is not equal to 0

Program for Spearman Rank Correlation Coefficient

```
#Spearman's rank correlation coefficient
x=c(1,2,3,4,5,6,7,8,9,10)
y=c(2,4,5,1,3,6,7,9,10,8)
cor.test(x,y,method="spearman")
```

Output

```
        Spearman's rank correlation rho
data:  x and y
S = 28, p-value = 0.005557
alternative hypothesis: true rho is not equal to 0
sample estimates:
    rho
0.830303
```

The correlation coefficient `rho` is `0.830303` which is fairly high. The p-value `0.005557` is less than the significance level `0.05`. Hence we reject the null hypothesis. This means that the rank correlation coefficient is significant. Now we will see how to find the Kendall rank correlation coefficient.

For Kendall rank correlation coefficient, we assume the hypothesis as follows.

H_0: τ is equal to 0

H_1: τ is not equal to 0

Program for Kendall Rank Correlation Coefficient

```
#Kendall's rank correlation coefficient
x=c(1,2,3,4,5,6,7,8,9,10)
y=c(2,4,5,1,3,6,7,9,10,8)
cor.test(x,y,method="kendall")
```

Output

```
        Kendall's rank correlation tau
data:  x and y
T = 38, p-value = 0.004687
alternative hypothesis: true tau is not equal to 0
sample estimates:
     tau
0.6888889
```

The correlation coefficient `tau` is `0.6888889` which is high. The p-value `0.004687` is less than the significance level `0.05`. Hence we reject the null hypothesis. This means that the Kendall rank correlation coefficient is significant. Now we will see how to find the Spearman product moment correlation coefficient. We assume the hypothesis as follows.

H_0: `cor` is equal to 0

H_1: `cor` is not equal to 0

Program for Pearson Product Moment Correlation Coefficient

```
x=c(1,2,3,4,5,6,7,8,9,10)
```

```
y=c(2,4,5,1,3,6,7,9,10,8)
cor.test(x,y,method="pearson")
```

Output

```
        Pearson's product-moment correlation
data:   x and y
t = 4.2139, df = 8, p-value = 0.00294
alternative hypothesis: true correlation is not equal to 0
95 percent confidence interval:
 0.4205125 0.9587260
sample estimates:
    cor
0.830303
```

The correlation coefficient `cor` is `0.830303` which is fairly high. The p-value `0.00294` is less than the significance level `0.05`. Hence we reject the null hypothesis. This means that the rank correlation coefficient is significant.

11.2.3 Auto-correlation

Autocorrelation is a characteristic of data in which the correlation between the values of the same variables is based on related objects. It violates the assumption of instance independence, which underlies most of the conventional models. It generally exists in those types of data-sets in which the data, instead of being randomly selected, is from the same source. In order to understand autocorrelation, we can discuss some instances that are based upon cross sectional and time series data. Suppose, if the change in the income of a person A, affects the savings of person B (a person other than person A), then autocorrelation is present. In the case of time series data, if the observations show inter-correlation, specifically in those cases where the time intervals are small, then these inter-correlations are given the term autocorrelation.

In time series data, autocorrelation is defined as the delayed correlation of a given series. Autocorrelation is a delayed correlation by itself, and is delayed by some specific number of time units. On the other hand, serial autocorrelation is that type which defines the lag correlation between the two series in time series data. Autocorrelation is a matter of degree, so it can be positive as well as negative. If the series (like an economic series) depicts an upward or downward pattern, then the series is considered to exhibit positive autocorrelation. If, on the other hand, the series depicts a constant upward and downward pattern, then the series is considered to exhibit negative autocorrelation.

Consider the values of X over three periods. Then one can find the correlation coefficient between X and Y_1 (or) X and Y_2 (or) X and Y_3, where Y_1 represents the values of X with 1 period lag, Y_2 represents the values of X with 2 periods lag, Y_3 represents values of X with 3 periods lag and so on. The auto-correlation coefficient (r_k) between the variable X and Y_k is given by the following formula.

$$rk = \frac{\sum_{t=1}^{n}(Xt - Xbar)(Xt + k - Xbar)}{\sum_{t=1}^{n}(Xt - Xbar)2}$$

where r_k is the auto-correlation co-efficient with k period lag, X_{bar} the mean of X, X_t the observation of the period t, X_{t+k} is the observation of X with *k* period lag and *n* is the number of observations of X.

Autocorrelation can be calculated in R using the function `acf()`. The syntax of `acf()` function is given below.

```
acf(x, lag.max = NULL, type = c("correlation", "covariance", "partial"),
  plot = TRUE, na.action = na.contiguous, demean = TRUE, ...)
```

where `x` – This will be a univariate or multivariate numeric time series object or a numeric vector or matrix.

`lag.max` – This gives the maximum lag at which to calculate the `acf`. Default is `10*log10(N/m)` where `N` is the number of observations and `m` the number of series. It will be automatically limited to one less than the number of observations in the series.

`type` – This is the character string giving the type of `acf` to be computed. Allowed values are `"correlation"` (the default), `"covariance"` or `"partial"`.

`plot` – This is a logical value. If `TRUE` (the default) the resulting `acf` is plotted.

`na.action` – This argument is to handle missing values. Default value is `na.contiguous`. Other useful alternatives are `na.pass` and `na.interp`. If we give `na.contiguous`, it finds the longest consecutive stretch of non-missing values in a time series object. The attribute `na.pass` returns the object unchanged and `na.interp` interpolates missing values in a time series.

`demean` – It is a logical value which decides whether covariances should be about the sample means.

... – shows the additional arguments passed to the plotting function.

The following problem illustrates how to find autocorrelation in R.

Problem

The demand values of a product over the past 10 years are given below. Find the autocorrelation coefficients and the ACF plot for the data given below.

Year	1	2	3	4	5	6	7	8	9	10
Demand	20	30	50	60	80	90	100	120	140	160

Program

```
#Autocorrelation
x=c(20,30,50,60,80,90,100,120,140,160)
```

```
acf.results<-acf(x,type="correlation", plot=TRUE)
plot(acf.results, main="Auto-correlation")
acf.results
```

Output

```
Autocorrelations of series 'x', by lag

     0      1      2      3      4      5      6      7      8      9
 1.000  0.682  0.377  0.134 -0.065 -0.214 -0.348 -0.412 -0.400 -0.253
```

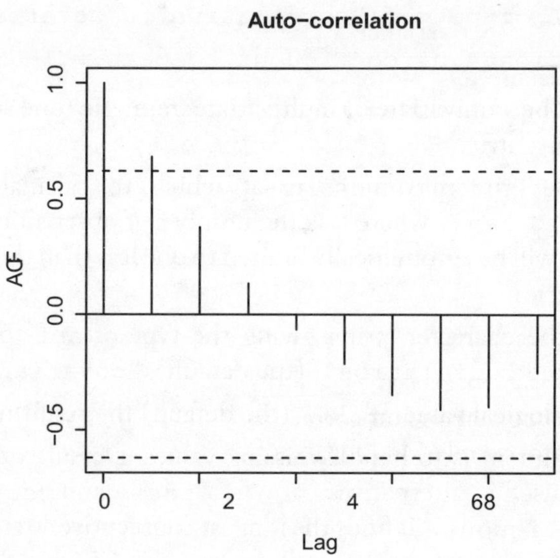

The output shows the autocorrelation coefficient of the series x at lag 0, lag 1, lag 2 …lag (n-1). The plot for autocorrelation is also shown in the output.

11.2.4 Partial Auto-correlation

The partial autocorrelation function (PACF) gives the partial correlation of a time series with its own lagged values, controlling for the values of the time series at all shorter lags. It contrasts with the autocorrelation function, which does not control for other lags.

In general, a partial correlation is a conditional correlation. It is the correlation between two variables under the assumption that we know and take into account the values of some other set of variables. For instance, consider a regression context in which y = response variable and x_1, x_2, and x_3 are predictor variables. The partial correlation between y and x_3 is the correlation between the variables determined taking into account how both y and x_3 are related to x_1 and x_2.

In regression, this partial correlation could be found by correlating the residuals from two different regressions: (1) regression in which we predict y from x_1 and x_2, (2) regression in which we predict x_3 from x_1 and x_2. Basically, we correlate the "parts" of y and x_3 that are not predicted by x_1 and x_2. More formally, we can define the partial correlation just described as

$$\frac{\text{Covariance}(y, x_3 \mid x_1, x_2)}{\sqrt{\text{Variance}(y \mid x_1, x_2)\text{Variance}(x_3 \mid x_1, x_2)}}$$

The 2nd order (lag) partial autocorrelation is

$$\frac{\text{Covariance}(x_t \mid x_{t-2} \mid x_{t-1})}{\sqrt{\text{Variance}(x_t \mid x_{t-1})\text{Variance}(x_{t-2} \mid x_{t-1})}}$$

The 3rd order (lag) partial autocorrelation is

$$\frac{\text{Covariance}(x_t, x_{t-3} \mid x_{t-1}, x_{t-2})}{\sqrt{\text{Variance}(x_t \mid x_{t-1}, x_{t-2})\text{Variance}(x_{t-3} \mid x_{t-1}, x_{t-2})}}$$

and so on for any lag.

Partial autocorrelation can be obtained in R using the function `pacf()`. The syntax of `pacf()` function is as follows.

```
pacf(x, lag.max = NULL, plot = TRUE, na.action = na.contiguous, demean
= TRUE, ...)
```

The meaning of the parameters of `pacf()` function is same as that of autocorrelation function `acf()`.

Consider the same problem given for autocorrelation. We will find out the partial autocorrelation coefficients and the partial auto-correlation plot for the data.

Program

```
#Partial Auto-correlation
x=c(20,30,50,60,80,90,100,120,140,160)
pacf.results<-pacf(x,type="c", plot=TRUE)
plot(pacf.results, main="Partial Auto-correlation")
pacf.results
```

Output

```
Partial autocorrelations of series 'x', by lag
    1      2      3      4      5      6      7      8      9
 0.682 -0.165 -0.102 -0.132 -0.123 -0.189 -0.110 -0.080  0.108
```

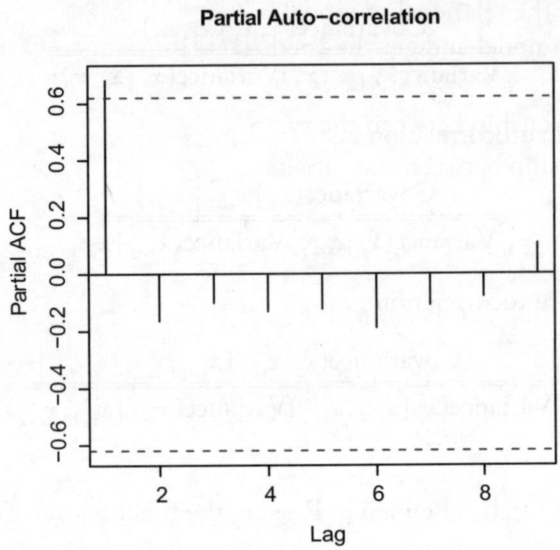

The output shows the partial autocorrelation coefficient of the series x at lag 0, lag 1, lag 2 … lag (n-1). The plot for partial autocorrelation is also shown in the output.

11.3 Regression

Regression is a statistical measure used in finance, investing and other disciplines that attempts to determine the strength of the relationship between one dependent variable (usually denoted by Y) and a series of other changing variables (known as independent variables). Regression analysis is a very widely used statistical tool to establish a relationship model between two variables. One of these variable is called predictor variable whose value is gathered through experiments. The other variable is called response variable whose value is derived from the predictor variable. There are different types of regression like simple linear regression, multiple linear regression, logistic regression, poisson regression etc. We will see each of them in detail.

11.3.1 Simple Linear Regression

The general mathematical equation for a linear regression is

$$y = ax + b$$

where y is the response variable, x is the predictor variable, a and b are constants which are called the coefficients. Simple linear regression can be illustrated with the following problem.

Problem

The demand values of a product in tons during the past 6 years are given below. Create the relationship model and get the coefficients. Perform the significance test for linear regression at a significance level 0.05.

Year	1997	1998	1999	2000	2001	2002
Demand	50	60	50	80	72	90

The function `lm()` creates the relationship model between the predictor and the response variable. We create the relationship model and get the coefficients as follows. We also assume the following hypothesis.

H_0: There is no linear relationship between the variables.

H_1: There is linear relationship between the variables.

Program

```
#Simple linear regression
x=c(1997,1998,1999,2000,2001,2002)
y=c(50,60,50,80,72,90)
r=lm(y~x)
summary(r)
```

Output

```
Call:
lm(formula = y ~ x)
Residuals:
    1     2     3     4     5     6
  2.0   4.4 -13.2   9.2  -6.4   4.0
Coefficients:
             Estimate Std. Error t value Pr(>|t|)
(Intercept) -15129.200   4401.498  -3.437   0.0264 *
x                7.600      2.201   3.453   0.0260 *
---
Signif. codes:  0 '***' 0.001 '**' 0.01 '*' 0.05 '.' 0.1 ' ' 1
Residual standard error: 9.209 on 4 degrees of freedom
Multiple R-squared:  0.7487,    Adjusted R-squared:  0.6859
F-statistic: 11.92 on 1 and 4 DF, p-value: 0.02599
```

From the above output, we can see the value of a is `-15129.200`, b is `7.600` and p-value is `0.02599`. We can construct the model for the linear regression as follows.

$$Y=-15129.200+7.6x$$

Since the p-value is greater than the significance level `0.05`, we accept the null hypothesis that there is no relationship between the variables. We can use the linear regression for prediction. This is done using the `predict()` function in R. The syntax of `predict()` function is as follows.

```
predict(object,newdata)
```

where `object` is the formula which is already created using the `lm()` function and `newdata` is the vector containing the new value for predictor variable. Consider the above problem. We want to predict the demand of the product for the year 2008. Following program illustrates this.

Program

```
a=data.frame(x=2008)
result=predict(r,a)
result
```

Output

```
     1
131.6
```

The output shows that the demand for the product for the year 2008 is `131.6`. We can also predict the values using linear regression equation `Y=-15129.200+7.6x`. Since `x=2008`, on substitution and simplification, we get `Y=131.6`.

The regression can be visualized graphically as shown below.

Program

```
plot(x,y,type = "o",xlab ="Year",ylab = "Demand in Tons",main = "Demand of a Product")
```

Output

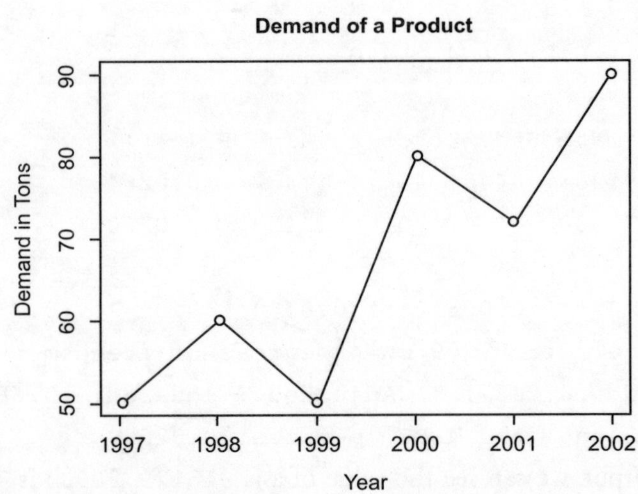

11.3.2 Multiple Linear Regression

Multiple linear regression is an extension of linear regression into relationship between more than two variables. In simple linear regression we have one predictor and one response variable, but in multiple linear regression we have more than one predictor variable and one response variable. The general mathematical equation for multiple regression is as follows.

$$y = a + b_1x_1 + b_2x_2 + \ldots b_nx_n$$

where `y` is the response variable, `a, b1, b2...bn` are the coefficients, `x1, x2, ...xn` are the predictor variables. Multiple linear regression can be illustrated using the following problem.

Problem

The annual sales revenue (in crores) of a product as a function of sales force and annual advertising expenditure (in lakhs) for the past 10 years is given below. Design a regression model to predict the annual sales revenue of the product. Predict the annual sales revenue when the sales force is 25 and annual advertising expenditure is 35.

Annual Sales Revenue	20	23	25	27	21	29	22	24	27	35
Sales Force	8	13	8	18	23	16	10	12	14	20
Annual Advertising Expenditure	28	23	38	16	20	28	23	30	26	32

Let the annual sales revenue be Y, sales force be X_1 and annual advertising expenditure be X_2.

Program

```
#Multiple linear regression
#Read the file to a dataframe
df1=read.csv("revenue.csv", header=TRUE)
df1
# Create the relationship model.
model <- lm(df1$revenue~df1$force+df1$expense, data = df1)
# Show the model.
model
summary(model)
```

Output

```
   revenue force expense
1       20     8      28
2       23    13      23
3       25     8      38
4       27    18      16
5       21    23      20
6       29    16      28
7       22    10      23
8       24    12      30
9       27    14      26
10      35    20      32
Call:
lm(formula = df1$revenue ~ df1$force + df1$expense, data = df1)
Coefficients:
```

```
(Intercept)     df1$force    df1$expense
     5.1483          0.6190          0.4304
Call:
lm(formula = df1$revenue ~ df1$force + df1$expense, data = df1)
Residuals:
    Min      1Q  Median      3Q     Max
-6.9928 -1.4793  0.3346  1.9713  3.8237
Coefficients:
            Estimate Std. Error t value Pr(>|t|)
(Intercept)   5.1483     8.3958   0.613   0.5591
df1$force     0.6190     0.2730   2.268   0.0577 .
df1$expense   0.4304     0.2191   1.964   0.0902 .
---
Signif. codes:  0 '***' 0.001 '**' 0.01 '*' 0.05 '.' 0.1 ' ' 1
Residual standard error: 3.671 on 7 degrees of freedom
Multiple R-squared:  0.4703,    Adjusted R-squared:  0.319
F-statistic: 3.108 on 2 and 7 DF, p-value: 0.1082
```

From the above output we can see the intercept value a as 5.1483, b1 as 0.6190 and b2 as 0.4304. We can construct the model as follows.

$$Y=5.1483+0.6190X_1+0.4304X_2$$

So we can make the prediction for the annual sales revenue when the sales force is 25 and annual advertising expenditure is 35.

```
Y=5.1483+0.6190*25+0.4304*35
Y=35.6873
```

The annual sales revenue will be 35.6873.

11.3.3 Logistic Regression

Logistic regression is a statistical method for analyzing a dataset in which there are one or more independent variables that determine an outcome. The outcome is measured with a dichotomous variable (in which there are only two possible outcomes). In logistic regression, the dependent variable is binary or dichotomous, i.e. it only contains data coded as 1 (TRUE, success, etc.) or 0 (FALSE, failure, etc.).

The goal of logistic regression is to find the best fitting model to describe the relationship between the dichotomous characteristic of interest (dependent variable = response or outcome variable) and a set of independent (predictor or explanatory) variables. Logistic regression generates the coefficients (and its standard errors and significance levels) of a formula to predict a logit transformation of the probability of presence of the characteristic of interest. The logistic regression equation is

$$logit(p) = b_0 + b_1X_1 + b_2X_2 + b_3X_3 + \ldots + b_kX_k$$

where p is the probability of presence of the characteristic of interest, $b_0, b_1, ..b_k$ are the coefficients which are numeric constants.

An independent variable with a regression coefficient not significantly different from 0 ($p>0.05$) can be removed from the regression model. If $p<0.05$ then the variable contributes significantly to the prediction of the outcome variable. The logistic regression coefficients show the change (increase when $b_i>0$, decrease when $b_i<0$) in the predicted logged odds of having the characteristic of interest for a one-unit change in the independent variables. When the independent variables X_1 and X_2 are dichotomous variables (e.g. smoking, sex) then the influence of these variables on the dependent variable can simply be compared by comparing their regression coefficients b_1 and b_2.

The function used to create the regression model is the `glm()` function. The basic syntax for `glm()` function in logistic regression is as follows.

```
glm(formula,data,family)
```

where `formula` is the symbol presenting the relationship between the variables, `data` is the data set giving the values of these variables and `family` is R object to specify the details of the model. It's value is `binomial` for logistic regression. Logistic regression can be illustrated with the following problem.

Problem

The age, height, weight and smoking status of 10 people are summarized in the table given below. Create a logistic regression model between smoking status and three other variables age, height and weight. In this problem, the dependent variable is smoking status and hence coded as 0 or 1.

Age	30	25	32	40	70	60	38	54	63	57
Height	165	180	172	150	169	175	179	168	171	185
Weight	68	80	76	54	71	78	84	73	79	90
Smoking Status	0	1	1	1	0	0	1	0	1	0

Program

```
#Logistic regression
#Read the file to a dataframe
df1=read.csv("Smoking.csv", header=TRUE)
df1
# Create the relationship model.
model <- glm(df1$Smoking~df1$Age+df1$Height+df1$Weight,family=binomial,
data = df1)
# Show the model.
model
summary(model
```

Output

```
   Age Height Weight Smoking
1  30   165    68     0
2  25   180    80     1
3  32   172    76     1
4  40   150    54     1
5  70   169    71     0
6  60   175    78     0
7  38   179    84     1
8  54   168    73     0
9  63   171    79     1
10 57   185    90     0
Call:  glm(formula = df1$Smoking ~ df1$Age + df1$Height + df1$Weight,
    family = binomial, data = df1)
Coefficients:
(Intercept)       df1$Age   df1$Height   df1$Weight
    95.2480       -0.1824      -0.9188       0.9338
Degrees of Freedom: 9 Total (i.e. Null); 6 Residual
Null Deviance:      13.86
Residual Deviance: 8.748        AIC: 16.75
Call:
glm(formula = df1$Smoking ~ df1$Age + df1$Height + df1$Weight,
    family = binomial, data = df1)
Deviance Residuals:
    Min       1Q   Median       3Q      Max
-1.9229  -0.6304   0.1857   0.8222   1.1715
Coefficients:
            Estimate Std. Error z value Pr(>|z|)
(Intercept)  95.2480    74.9908   1.270    0.204
df1$Age      -0.1824     0.1330  -1.372    0.170
df1$Height   -0.9188     0.7457  -1.232    0.218
df1$Weight    0.9338     0.7754   1.204    0.228
(Dispersion parameter for binomial family taken to be 1)
    Null deviance: 13.8629  on 9  degrees of freedom
Residual deviance:  8.7483  on 6  degrees of freedom
AIC: 16.748
Number of Fisher Scoring iterations: 6
```

In the summary as the p-value in the last column is more than `0.05` for the variables "`Age`", "`Height`" and "`Weight`", we consider them to be insignificant in contributing to the value of the variable "`Smoking`".

11.3.4 Poisson Regression

Poisson regression assumes the response variable Y has a Poisson distribution, and assumes the logarithm of its expected value can be modeled by a linear combination of unknown parameters. A Poisson regression model is sometimes known as a log-linear model, especially when used to model contingency tables. Poisson Regression involves regression models in which the response variable is in the form of counts and not fractional numbers. For example, the count of number of deaths, number of births, number of males in a ward etc. The values of the response variables should follow a Poisson distribution.

The general mathematical equation for Poisson regression is as follows.

$$\log(y) = a + b_1x_1 + b_2x_2 + b_nx_n \ldots.$$

where `y` is the response variable, `a` and `b` are the numeric coefficients and `x` is the predictor variable.

The function used to create the Poisson regression model is the `glm()` function which is already explained in logistic regression. The Poisson regression can be illustrated with the following problem.

Problem

The paper type, printing speed and number of defective papers are summarized as given below. There are two types of paper brown and white coded as B, W respectively. Similarly the printing speed is classified as Low, Medium and High and is coded as L, M and H respectively. Perform a Poisson regression to identify whether there is an impact on no: of defectives (response variable) with the two predictor variables paper type and speed.

Paper Type	B	W	B	W	W	B	W	W	B	W
Printing Speed	L	M	H	L	L	M	L	H	H	M
No: of defectives	15	18	22	13	15	21	16	17	19	16

Program

```
#Poisson regression
#Read the file to a dataframe
df1=read.csv("Paper.csv", header=TRUE)
df1
# Create the relationship model.
model <- glm(formula = df1$defective ~ df1$type+df1$speed,family =
poisson,data = df1)
# Show the model.
model
summary(model)
```

Output

```
  type speed defective
1   B    L      15
2   W    M      18
3   B    H      22
4   W    L      13
5   W    L      15
6   B    M      21
7   W    L      16
8   W    H      17
9   B    H      19
10  W    M      16
Call:
glm(formula = df1$defective ~ df1$type + df1$speed, family = poisson,
    data = df1)
Deviance Residuals:
     Min        1Q    Median        3Q       Max
-0.34998  -0.31198   0.00407   0.20565   0.46777
Coefficients:
             Estimate Std. Error z value Pr(>|z|)
(Intercept)  3.007490   0.140430  21.416   <2e-16 ***
df1$typeW   -0.143754   0.164771  -0.872    0.383
df1$speedL  -0.210415   0.197427  -1.066    0.287
df1$speedM  -0.005265   0.195990  -0.027    0.979
Signif. codes:  0 '***' 0.001 '**' 0.01 '*' 0.05 '.' 0.1 ' ' 1
(Dispersion parameter for poisson family taken to be 1)
    Null deviance: 4.11567  on 9  degrees of freedom
Residual deviance: 0.90918  on 6  degrees of freedom
AIC: 55.717
Number of Fisher Scoring iterations: 3
```

In the summary we look for the p-value in the last column to be less than `0.05` to consider an impact of the predictor variable on the response variable. Since all the p-values are greater than `0.05`, the paper type `"W"` and printing speed `"L"` and `"M"` doesn't have any impact on the number of defective papers.

11.4 Analysis of Co-variance

Analysis of covariance (ANCOVA) is a general linear model which blends ANOVA and regression.

Analysis of covariance (ANCOVA) allows comparing one variable in 2 or more groups taking into account variability of other variables, called covariates. Analysis of covariance combines one-way or two-way analysis of variance with linear regression. Regression analysis is used to create models which describe the effect of variation in predictor variables on the response variable. Sometimes, if we have a categorical variable with values like Yes/No or True/False etc. The simple regression analysis gives multiple results for each value of the categorical variable. In such situations, we can study the effect of the categorical variable by using it along with the predictor variable and comparing the regression lines for each level of the categorical variable using ANCOVA. This can be illustrated using the problem given below.

Problem

The shutter setting, height of water (meters) and volume of water discharged in litres per second of 10 similar dams are summarized and given in the table below. Study the effect of the value of "shuttersetting" on the regression between "volume" and "height".

Volume of water discharged (litres)/sec	1000	2225	3816	4123	1126	2307	2116	2114	3983	2102
Height of water (m)	53	65	76	86	55	80	64	70	81	74
Shutter Setting	0	1	1	1	0	0	1	0	1	0

Solution

This can be done by using the `aov()` function followed by the `anova()` function to compare the multiple regressions. Here we take "`volume`" as the response variable, "`height`" as the predictor variable and "`shuttersetting`" as the categorical variable. First we consider the model with interaction between categorical variable and predictor variable.

Program

```
#Analysis of Covariance
df1=read.csv("Dam.csv", header=TRUE)
df1
#create the regression model
result1 <- aov(volume~height*shuttersetting,data = df1)
summary(result1)
```

Output

```
  volume height shuttersetting
1   1000     53              0
2   2225     65              1
3   3816     76              1
4   4123     86              1
```

```
5    1126    55            0
6    2307    80            0
7    2116    64            1
8    2114    70            0
9    3983    81            1
10   2102    74            0
                            Df  Sum Sq Mean Sq F value   Pr(>F)
height                       1 8443610 8443610 156.000 1.61e-05 ***
shuttersetting               1 1979180 1979180  36.566 0.000926 ***
height:shuttersetting        1  522561  522561   9.655 0.020924 *
Residuals                    6  324754   54126
```

This result shows that both "height" and "shuttersetting" has significant effect on "volume" as the p-value in both cases is less than 0.05. But the interaction between these two variables is not significant as the p-value is more than 0.05.

Now we will see the model without interaction between categorical variable and predictor variable.

Program

```
#create the regression model
result2 <- aov(volume~height+shuttersetting,data = df1)
summary(result2)
```

Output

```
               Df  Sum Sq Mean Sq F value   Pr(>F)
height          1 8443610 8443610   69.76 6.92e-05 ***
shuttersetting  1 1979180 1979180   16.35  0.00491 **
Residuals       7  847315  121045
```

This result shows that both "height" and "shuttersetting" has significant effect on "volume" since the p-value in both cases is less than 0.05.

Now we can compare the two models to conclude if the interaction of the variables is truly insignificant. For this we use the anova() function.

Program

```
anova(result1,result2)
```

Output

```
Analysis of Variance Table
Model 1: volume ~ height * shuttersetting
Model 2: volume ~ height + shuttersetting
  Res.Df    RSS Df Sum of Sq      F  Pr(>F)
```

```
1       6 324754
2       7 847315 -1    -522561 9.6546 0.02092 *
```

Since the p-value is greater than `0.05` we conclude that the interaction between "`height`" and "`shuttersetting`" is not significant. So the "`volume`" will depend in a similar manner on the "`height`" for both "`shuttersetting`" 1 and 0.

11.5 Forecasting

Forecasting refers to the process of using statistical procedures to predict future values of a time series based on historical trends. Businesses utilize forecasting to determine how to allocate their budgets or plan for anticipated expenses for an upcoming period of time. This is typically based on the projected demand for the goods and services they offer. Forecasting is very useful in marketing, production, sales, finance and personnel. There are various forecasting techniques available like simple moving average, weighted moving average, single exponential smoothing, regression and time series analysis. We have already discussed various types of regression. Time series will be seen in the coming section.

11.5.1 Simple Moving Average

A simple moving average is a method of computing the average of a specified number of the most recent data values in a series. The formula for computing the simple moving average is as follows.

$$Mt = \frac{1}{n}[Dt-(n-1)+Dt-(n-2)+....Dt-2+Dt-1+Dt]$$

where `Mt` is the simple moving average at the end of period `t`, the actual demand in the period `t` and `n` is the number of periods included in each moving average. The syntax for calculating simple moving average in R is as follows.

`SMA(x, n = 10, ...)` where `x` is a vector or matrix or coercible to matrix, `n` is the number of periods to average over (must be between 1 and `nrow(x)`, inclusive) and ... shows any other pass through parameters. This function calculates the arithmetic mean of the series over the past `n` observations. This function `SMA()` is contained in the `TTR` package which does not come up with standard packages. Hence `TTR` package needs to be installed and loaded into the current R environment.

The simple moving average can be illustrated with the following problem.

Problem

The actual demand of a product for 8 months are summarized and given in the table below. Find the three months simple moving average.

Month	1	2	3	4	5	6	7	8
Demand	24	30	27	24	39	45	42	51

In the above problem n=3.

Program

```
library(TTR)
x=c(24,30,27,24,39,45,42,51)
x
n=3
y=SMA(x,n)#simple moving average
y
```

Output

```
[1] 24 30 27 24 39 45 42 51
#simple moving average
[1] NA NA 27 27 30 36 42 46
```

11.5.2 Weighted Moving Average

In simple moving average method, equal weights are assigned to the data of all periods while computing moving averages. But in practice, it may not be realistic to give equal such weight. Hence differential weights must be given to different periods which are used for computing the moving average such that the most recent piece of data has the highest weight and then it decreases for other preceding periods. This method is called weighted moving average method.

The formula to compute the weighted moving averages is

$$Wt.MAt = \frac{\sum_{i=1}^{n} WiDi}{\sum_{i=1}^{n} Wi}$$

where `Di` is the actual demand of the period `i`, n is the number of periods used for computing moving averages and W_i is the weight of the data of the time period `i` in the moving average. When `i` is equal to `n`, it corresponds to the oldest time period. The weighted moving average in R can be calculated using the function

```
WMA(x, n = 10, wts = 1:n, ...)
```

where `x` is a vector or matrix or coercible to matrix, `n` is the number of periods to average over (must be between 1 and `nrow(x)`, inclusive), `wts` is the vector of weights and ... shows any other pass through parameters. Length of `wts` vector must equal the length of `x`, or `n` (the default). This function `WMA()` is contained in the `TTR` package which does not come up with standard packages. Hence `TTR` package needs to be installed and loaded into the current R environment. The weighted moving average can be illustrated with the following problem.

Problem

Consider the same problem given above for simple moving average. Three weights `W1=0.2`,`W2=0.3` and `W3=0.5`.

Program

```
library(TTR)
x=c(24,30,27,24,39,45,42,51)
x
n=3
y=WMA(x,n,wts=c(0.2,0.3,0.5))#weighted moving average
y
```

Output

```
[1] 24 30 27 24 39 45 42 51
#weighted moving average
[1]NA NA 27.3 26.1 32.1 39.0 42.3 47.1
```

11.5.3 Single Exponential Smoothing

If we have a time series that can be described using an additive model with constant level and no seasonality, we can use simple exponential smoothing to make short-term forecasts. The simple exponential smoothing method provides a way of estimating the level at the current time point. Single exponential smoothing method is another form of weighted moving average. The forecast of the period t is computed by applying some correction over the forecast value of the immediate preceding period. The correction quantity is a portion α of the difference between the actual demand of the immediate preceding period and the forecast of the immediate preceding period. The formula to compute the exponential smoothed forecast is given below.

$$F_t=F_{t-1}+ \alpha (D_{t-1}-F_{t-1})$$

were F_t is the smoothed average forecast of the period t. F_{t-1} is the smoothed average forecast of the period t-1. D_{t-1} is the actual demand of the period t-1 and α is the smoothing constant ($0< \alpha<1$). If α is equal to 1, then the latest forecast would be equal to the previous period actual demand value. The preferred range for α is from 0.1 to 0.3.

In R, the single exponential smoothing method can be found out using the function `ses()`. The format of the `ses()` function is as follows.

```
ses(y, h = 10, level = c(80, 95), fan = FALSE, initial = c("optimal",
"simple"), alpha = NULL, lambda = NULL, biasadj = FALSE, x = y,...)
```

where `y` is a numeric vector or time series of class `ts`, `h` is the number of periods for forecasting, `level` is the confidence level for prediction intervals, `fan` is a logical value, (If `TRUE`, level is set to `seq(51,99,by=3)` and this is suitable for fan plots), `initial` is the method used for selecting initial state values, (If optimal, the initial values are optimized along with the smoothing parameters using `ets`. If simple, the initial values are set to values obtained using simple calculations on the first few observations) `alpha` is the value of smoothing parameter for the level. (If `NULL`, it will be estimated), `lambda` is the Box-Cox transformation parameter (ignored if `NULL`. Otherwise, data transformed before model is estimated. When `lambda=TRUE`, `additive.only` is set to `FALSE`), `biasadj` is to use adjusted back-transformed mean for Box-Cox transformations (if `TRUE`, point forecasts and fitted values are mean forecast. Otherwise, these points can be considered the median of the forecast densities), x is included for backwards compatibility and . . . shows other arguments passed to forecast.ets. For using ses() function, the library forecast should be installed and loaded into the current R envrionment.

Following problem illustrates single exponential smoothing method.

Problem

The volume of an item produced in a manufacturing company in tons from 1996 to 2007 is summarized below. Perform single exponential smoothing method at α =0.2.

Year	1996	1997	1998	1999	2000	2001	2002	2003	2004	2005	2006	2007
Volume	446.7	454.5	455.7	423.6	456.3	440.6	425.3	485.1	506	526.8	514.3	494.2

Program

```
library(forecast)
y=c(446.7,454.5,455.7,423.6,456.3,440.6,425.3,485.1,506,526.8,514.3,494
.2)
h=12
#single exponential smoothing method
s=ses(y,h,initial="simple",alpha=0.2)
summary(s)
```

Output

```
Forecast method: Simple exponential smoothing
Model Information:
Simple exponential smoothing
Call:
 ses(y = y, h = h, initial = "simple", alpha = 0.2)
  Smoothing parameters:
    alpha = 0.2
  Initial states:
    l = 446.7
  sigma:  32.1352
Error measures:
                   ME     RMSE      MAE      MPE     MAPE     MASE     ACF1
Training set 15.8755 32.13519 24.66592 3.006476 5.068924 1.135727 0.509897
Forecasts:
   Point Forecast    Lo 80    Hi 80    Lo 95    Hi 95
```

```
13          484.8012 443.6183 525.9841 421.8174 547.7850
14          484.8012 442.8027 526.7997 420.5701 549.0323
15          484.8012 442.0027 527.5997 419.3465 550.2559
16          484.8012 441.2173 528.3851 418.1454 551.4570
17          484.8012 440.4459 529.1565 416.9656 552.6369
18          484.8012 439.6876 529.9148 415.8059 553.7965
19          484.8012 438.9419 530.6605 414.6654 554.9370
20          484.8012 438.2081 531.3943 413.5431 556.0593
21          484.8012 437.4856 532.1168 412.4383 557.1641
22          484.8012 436.7741 532.8283 411.3501 558.2523
23          484.8012 436.0729 533.5295 410.2777 559.3247
24          484.8012 435.3817 534.2207 409.2206 560.3818
```

From the above output, the forecast value is `484.8012`. `Lo 80, Hi 80, Lo 95, Hi 95` gives the values for lower level and higher level value for prediction interval `80` and lower level and higher level prediction interval `95`. In addition, the summary also provides Mean Error `ME= 15.8755,` Root Mean Square Error `RMSE=32.13519,` Mean Absolute Error `MAE=24.66592,` Mean Forecast Error `MPE=3.006476,` Mean Absolute Forecast Error `MAPE=5.068924,` Mean Absolute Squared Error `MASE=1.135727` and Auto-correlation function `ACF1=0.509897.`

11.6 Time Series Analysis

A time series is a series of data points indexed (or listed or graphed) in time order. Most commonly, a time series is a sequence taken at successive equally spaced points in time. Thus it is a sequence of discrete-time data. Time series data have a natural temporal ordering. A simple example is the price of a stock in the stock market at different points of time on a given day. Another example is the amount of rainfall in a region at different months of the year or population of a region over 10 consecutive years. R language uses many functions to create, manipulate and plot the time series data. The data for the time series is stored in an R object called time-series object. It is also an R data object like a vector or data frame.

11.6.1 Creating Time Series

The time series object is created by using the `ts()` function. The syntax for `ts()` function in time series analysis is as follows.

```
timeseries.object.name <-ts(data, start, end, frequency)
```

where `data` is a vector or matrix containing the values used in the time series, `start` specifies the start time for the first observation in time series, `end` specifies the end time for the last observation in time series and `frequency` specifies the number of observations per unit time. All parameters except the parameter `data` are optional. The following problem illustrates the `ts()` function.

Problem

The birth rate of a state (in thousands) during 10 years starting from 2000 to 2010 is summarized and given below. Create an R time series object for a period of 10 years and plot it.

Year	2001	2002	2003	2004	2005	2006	2007	2008	2009	2010
Birth Rate (Thousands)	26	30	29	32	33	42	39	38	40	39

Program

```
x=c(2001,2002,2003,2004,2005,2006,2007,2008,2009,2010)
birthrate<- c(26,30,29,32,33,42,39,38,40,39)
# Convert it to a time series object.
birthrate.ts <- ts(birthrate,start = 2001,end=2010 frequency = 10)
# Print the timeseries data.
print(birthrate.ts)
# Plot a graph of the time series.
plot(x,birthrate.ts,type = "o",xlab ="Year",ylab = "Birth Rate in
Thousands",main = "Birth Rate of a State")
```

Output

```
Time Series:
Start = c(2001, 1)
End = c(2001, 10)
Frequency = 10
[1] 26 30 29 32 33 42 39 38 40 39
```

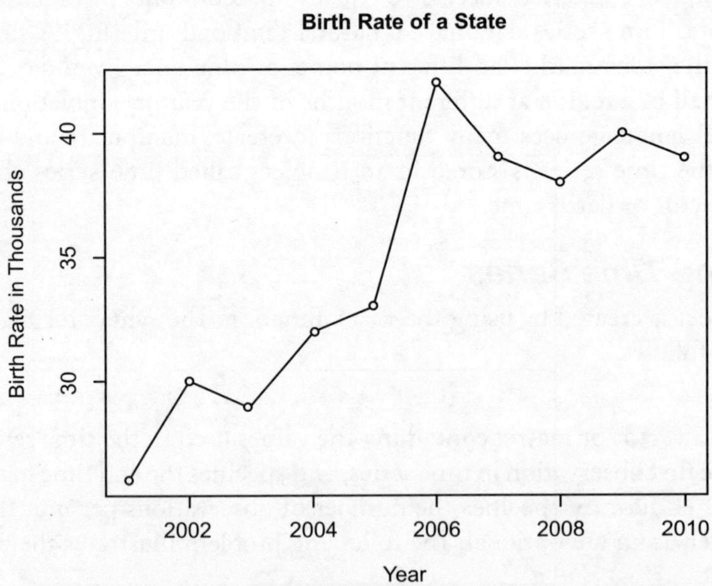

We can plot multiple time series in a single chart by combining both the time series into a matrix. The following problem illustrates this.

Problem

The birth rate of 2 states (in thousands) during 10 years starting from 2000 to 2010 is summarized and given below. Create an R time series object for a period of 10 years and plot it.

Year	2001	2002	2003	2004	2005	2006	2007	2008	2009	2010
Birth Rate (State 1)	26	30	29	32	33	42	39	38	40	39
Birth Rate (State 2)	20	25	22	30	32	29	28	30	31	28

Program

```
#Multiple Time Series
x=c(2001,2002,2003,2004,2005,2006,2007,2008,2009,2010)
birthrate1<- c(26,30,29,32,33,42,39,38,40,39)
birthrate2<- c(20,25,22,30,32,29,28,30,31,28)
# Convert them to a matrix.
birth.total <-  matrix(c(birthrate1,birthrate2),nrow = 10)
# Convert it to a time series object.
birthrate.ts <- ts(birth.total,start =c(2001,1),frequency = 10)
# Print the timeseries data.
print(birthrate.ts)
# Plot a graph of the time series.
plot(birthrate.ts, main="Multiple Time Series")
```

Output

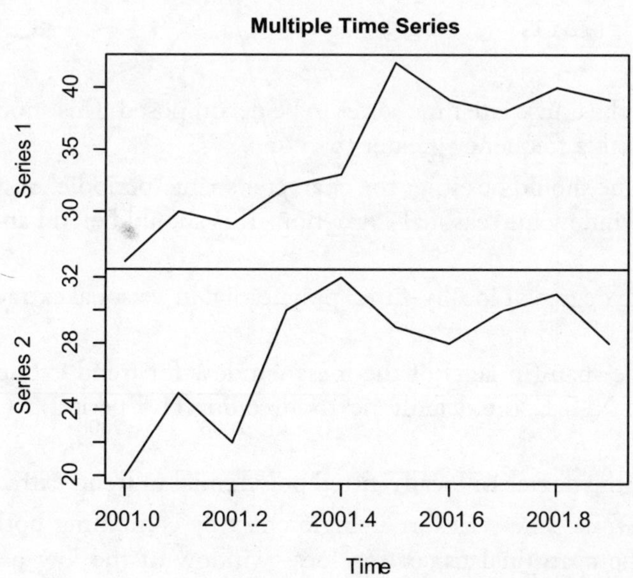

11.6.2 Seasonal Decomposition

The decomposition of time series is a statistical method that deconstructs a time series into several components, each representing one of the underlying categories of patterns.

For example, time series are usually decomposed into:

T_t, the trend component at time t that reflects the long-term progression of the series (secular variation). A trend exists when there is an increasing or decreasing direction in the data. The trend component does not have to be linear.

C_t, the cyclical component at time t, that describes repeated but non-periodic fluctuations. The duration of these fluctuations is usually of at least two years.

S_t, the seasonal component at time t, reflecting seasonality (seasonal variation). A seasonal pattern exists when a time series is influenced by seasonal factors. Seasonality is always of a fixed and known period (e.g., the quarter of the year, the month, or day of the week).

I_t, the irregular component (or "noise") at time t, that describes random, irregular influences. It represents the residuals or remainder of the time series after the other components has been removed.

A time series with additive trend, seasonal and irregular components can be decomposed using the Seasonal Decomposition of Time Series by Loess `stl()` function. Note that a series with multiplicative effects can often be transformed into series with additive effects through a log transformation. The syntax of the `stl()` function is as follows.

```
stl(x, s.window, s.degree = 0,t.window = NULL, t.degree = 1,
    l.window = nextodd(period), l.degree = t.degree,
    s.jump = ceiling(s.window/10),t.jump = ceiling(t.window/10),
    l.jump = ceiling(l.window/10),robust = FALSE,
    inner = if(robust)  1 else 2,outer = if(robust) 15 else 0,
    na.action = na.fail)
```

where

`x` – This is the univariate time series to be decomposed. This should be an object of class "`ts`" with a frequency greater than one.

`s.window` – The value should be either the character string "periodic" or the span (in lags) of the loess window for seasonal extraction. This should be odd and at least 7 and has no default.

`s.degree` – It is the degree of locally-fitted polynomial in seasonal extraction. It should be zero or one.

`t.window` – It is the span (in lags) of the loess window for trend extraction, which should be odd. If NULL, the default, nextodd(ceiling((1.5*period) / (1-(1.5/s.window)))), is taken.

`t.degree` – This is the degree of locally-fitted polynomial in trend extraction. It should be zero or one.

`l.window` – It is the span (in lags) of the loess window of the low-pass filter used for each subseries. The default is the smallest odd integer greater than or equal to frequency(x) which is recommended since it prevents competition between the trend and seasonal components. If not an odd integer's given value is increased to the next odd one.

`l.degree` – This gives the degree of locally-fitted polynomial for the subseries low-pass filter. It must be 0 or 1.

`s.jump, t.jump, l.jump` – These are integers at least one to increase speed of the respective smoother. Linear interpolation happens between every *.jumpth value.

`robust` – This is a logical value indicating if robust fitting be used in the loess procedure.

`inner` – This is an integer which is the number of 'inner' (backfitting) iterations. Usually very few (2) iterations will be enough.

`outer` – This is an integer which shows the number of 'outer' robustness iterations.

`na.action` – This indicates the action to be taken on missing values.

The use of the `stl()` function can be demonstrated using one of the data sets available within the base R installation. The well used `nottem` data set (Average Monthly Temperatures at Nottingham, 1920-1939) is used for this purpose. We can see the contents of `nottem` data set by simply typing

```
>nottem
      Jan  Feb  Mar  Apr  May  Jun  Jul  Aug  Sep  Oct  Nov  Dec
1920 40.6 40.8 44.4 46.7 54.1 58.5 57.7 56.4 54.3 50.5 42.9 39.8
1921 44.2 39.8 45.1 47.0 54.1 58.7 66.3 59.9 57.0 54.2 39.7 42.8
1922 37.5 38.7 39.5 42.1 55.7 57.8 56.8 54.3 54.3 47.1 41.8 41.7
1923 41.8 40.1 42.9 45.8 49.2 52.7 64.2 59.6 54.4 49.2 36.3 37.6
1924 39.3 37.5 38.3 45.5 53.2 57.7 60.8 58.2 56.4 49.8 44.4 43.6
1925 40.0 40.5 40.8 45.1 53.8 59.4 63.5 61.0 53.0 50.0 38.1 36.3
1926 39.2 43.4 43.4 48.9 50.6 56.8 62.5 62.0 57.5 46.7 41.6 39.8
1927 39.4 38.5 45.3 47.1 51.7 55.0 60.4 60.5 54.7 50.3 42.3 35.2
1928 40.8 41.1 42.8 47.3 50.9 56.4 62.2 60.5 55.4 50.2 43.0 37.3
1929 34.8 31.3 41.0 43.9 53.1 56.9 62.5 60.3 59.8 49.2 42.9 41.9
1930 41.6 37.1 41.2 46.9 51.2 60.4 60.1 61.6 57.0 50.9 43.0 38.8
1931 37.1 38.4 38.4 46.5 53.5 58.4 60.6 58.2 53.8 46.6 45.5 40.6
1932 42.4 38.4 40.3 44.6 50.9 57.0 62.1 63.5 56.3 47.3 43.6 41.8
1933 36.2 39.3 44.5 48.7 54.2 60.8 65.5 64.9 60.1 50.2 42.1 35.8
1934 39.4 38.2 40.4 46.9 53.4 59.6 66.5 60.4 59.2 51.2 42.8 45.8
1935 40.0 42.6 43.5 47.1 50.0 60.5 64.6 64.0 56.8 48.6 44.2 36.4
1936 37.3 35.0 44.0 43.9 52.7 58.6 60.0 61.1 58.1 49.6 41.6 41.3
1937 40.8 41.0 38.4 47.4 54.1 58.6 61.4 61.8 56.3 50.9 41.4 37.1
```

```
1938 42.1 41.2 47.3 46.6 52.4 59.0 59.6 60.4 57.0 50.7 47.8 39.2
1939 39.4 40.9 42.4 47.8 52.4 58.0 60.7 61.8 58.2 46.7 46.6 37.8
```

Following program illustrates the use of `stl()` function.

Program

```
# Seasonal Decomposition of Time Series by Loess
not.stl=stl(nottem,s.window="periodic")
plot(not.stl)
```

Output

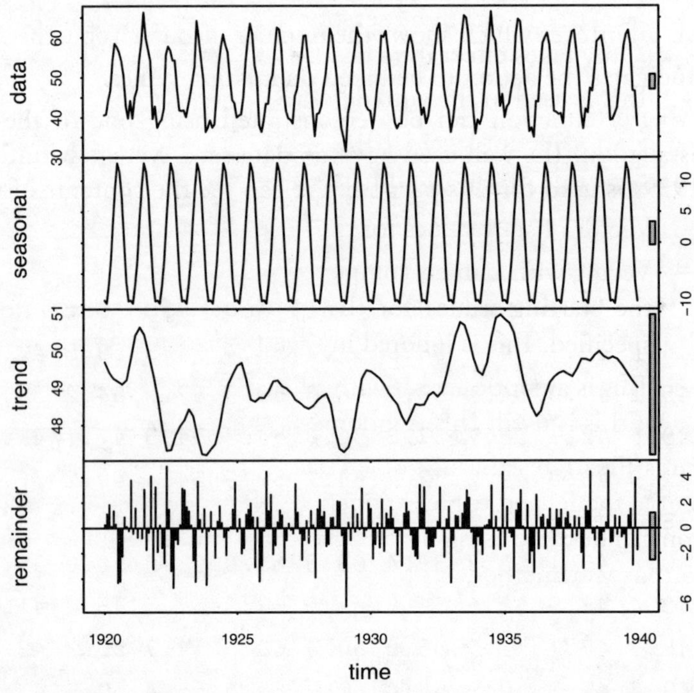

11.6.3 Exponential Models

We have already seen single exponential smoothing method. Both the `HoltWinters()` function in the base installation, and the `forecast()` function in the `forecast` package, can also be used to fit exponential models. The function `HoltWinters()` compute Holt-Winters filtering of a given time series. Unknown parameters are determined by minimizing the squared prediction error. The syntax of `HoltWinters()` function is as follows.

```
HoltWinters(x, alpha = NULL, beta = NULL, gamma = NULL,
            seasonal = c("additive", "multiplicative"),
            start.periods = 2, l.start = NULL, b.start = NULL,
            s.start = NULL,
```

```
            optim.start = c(alpha = 0.3, beta = 0.1, gamma = 0.1),
            optim.control = list())
```

where

`x`	–	is an object of class `ts`
`alpha`	–	is the alpha parameter of Holt-Winters Filter.
`beta`	–	gives the beta parameter of Holt-Winters Filter. If set to `FALSE`, the function will do exponential smoothing.
`gamma`	–	parameter is used for the seasonal component. If set to `FALSE`, a non-seasonal model is fitted.
`seasonal`	–	This is a character string to select an `"additive"` (the default) or `"multiplicative"` seasonal model. The first few characters are sufficient. (Only takes effect if `gamma` is non-zero).
`start.periods`	–	This is used in the auto detection of start values. It must be at least 2.
`l.start`	–	Start value for level (a[0]).
`b.start`	–	Start value for trend (b[0]).
`s.start`	–	Vector of start values for the seasonal component (s1[0]…sp[0])
`optim.start`	–	Vector with named components `alpha`, `beta`, and `gamma` containing the starting values for the optimizer. Only the values needed must be specified. This is ignored in the one-parameter case.
`optim.control`	–	This is an optional list with additional control parameters passed to `optim` if this is used. This is ignored in the one-parameter case.

Following programs illustrates the use of `HoltWinters()` function for single exponential model, double exponential model and triple exponential model. For this we use the built-in data set `nottem`. The prediction can be done using the `forecast()` method and accuracy of the model can be seen using the `accuracy()` method.

Program 1

```
library(forecast)
# simple exponential - models level
fit1 <- HoltWinters(nottem, beta=FALSE, gamma=FALSE)
fit1
# predict next three future values
f1=forecast(fit1,3)
f1
plot(forecast(f1))
#predictive accuracy
accuracy(f1)
```

Output 1

```
Holt-Winters exponential smoothing without trend and without seasonal
component.
Call:
HoltWinters(x = nottem, beta = FALSE, gamma = FALSE)
Smoothing parameters:
 alpha: 0.9999339
 beta : FALSE
 gamma: FALSE
Coefficients:
      [,1]
a 37.80058
# predict next three future values
         Point Forecast    Lo 80    Hi 80    Lo 95    Hi 95
Jan 1940       37.80058 31.07385 44.52731 27.51293 48.08823
Feb 1940       37.80058 28.28786 47.31330 23.25213 52.34903
Mar 1940       37.80058 26.15005 49.45111 19.98264 55.61853
#predictive accuracy
        ME      RMSE       MAE        MPE     MAPE     MASE
Training set -0.01171382 5.237918 4.319808 -0.6295348 8.997213 1.604098
                ACF1
Training set 0.4518389
```

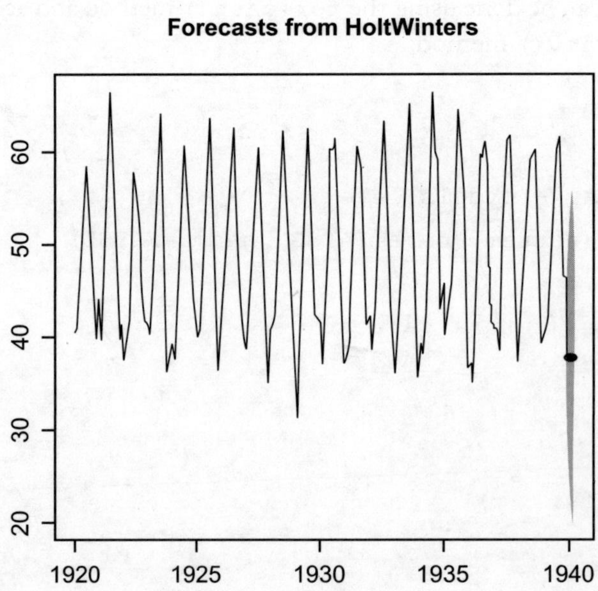

Program 2

```
# double exponential - models level and trend
fit2 <- HoltWinters(nottem, gamma=FALSE)
fit2
# predict next three future values
f2=forecast(fit2,3)
f2
plot(forecast(f2))
#predictive accuracy
accuracy(f2)
```

Output 2

```
Holt-Winters exponential smoothing with trend and without seasonal component.
Call:
HoltWinters(x = nottem, gamma = FALSE)
Smoothing parameters:
 alpha: 1
 beta : 0
 gamma: FALSE
Coefficients:
  [,1]
a 37.8
b 0.2
# predict next three future values
         Point Forecast     Lo 80    Hi 80    Lo 95    Hi 95
Jan 1940           38.0 31.25932 44.74068 27.69101 48.30899
Feb 1940           38.2 28.66723 47.73277 23.62089 52.77911
Mar 1940           38.4 26.72479 50.07521 20.54431 56.25569
#predictive accuracy
             ME      RMSE      MAE       MPE      MAPE     MASE     ACF1
Training set -0.212605 5.253026 4.335294 -1.054096 9.045732 1.609849
0.4516671
```

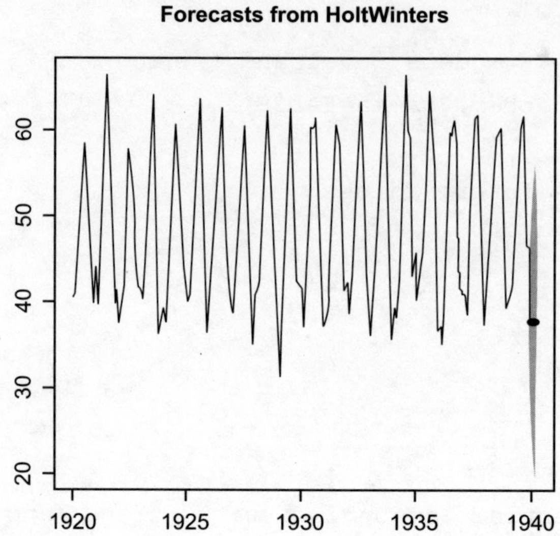

Program 3

```
# triple exponential - models level, trend, and seasonal components
fit3 <- HoltWinters(nottem)
fit3
# predict next three future values
f3=forecast(fit3,3)
f3
plot(forecast(f3))
# predictive accuracy
accuracy(f3)
```

Output 3

```
Holt-Winters exponential smoothing with trend and additive seasonal
component.
Call:
HoltWinters(x = nottem)

Smoothing parameters:
 alpha: 0.1383228
 beta : 0.02327472
 gamma: 0.2348744
Coefficients:
             [,1]
```

```
a     50.28764449
b     -0.00123644
s1  -10.52456577
s2  -10.63764008
s3   -7.72186809
s4   -3.71360349
s5    2.14676636
s6    8.32200567
s7   11.30166367
s8   11.28456696
s9    7.09287967
s10  -1.04659725
s11  -6.05060430
s12 -11.38814367
# predict next three future values
         Point Forecast     Lo 80     Hi 80     Lo 95     Hi 95
Jan 1940       39.76184 36.41232 43.11136 34.63919 44.88449
Feb 1940       39.64753 36.26462 43.03044 34.47382 44.82124
Mar 1940       42.56207 39.14459 45.97955 37.33548 47.78865
#predictive accuracy
                    ME     RMSE      MAE        MPE     MAPE     MASE
Training set -0.2369786 2.618653 2.028791 -0.9084845 4.437939 0.753362
                  ACF1
Training set 0.1731157
```

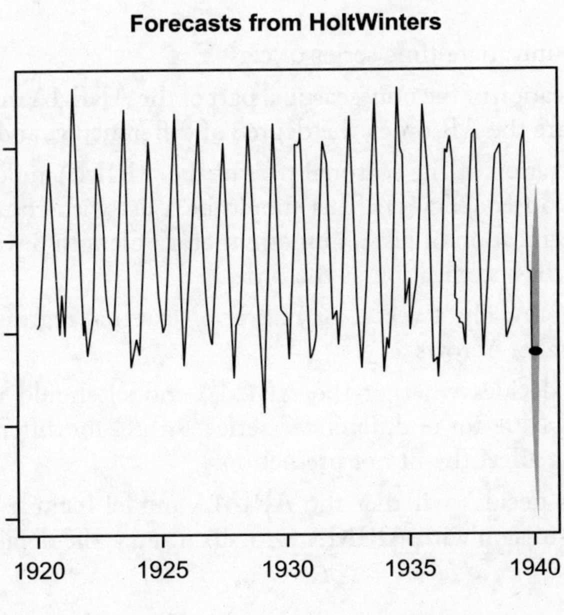

11.6.4 ARIMA Models

ARIMA stands for Autoregressive Integrated Moving Average models. Univariate (single vector) ARIMA is a forecasting technique that projects the future values of a series based entirely on its own inertia. Its main application is in the area of short term forecasting requiring at least 40 historical data points. Lags of the stationary series in the forecasting equation are called "autoregressive" terms, lags of the forecast errors are called "moving average" terms, and a time series which needs to be differenced to be made stationary is said to be an "integrated" version of a stationary series. Random-walk and random-trend models, autoregressive models, and exponential smoothing models are all special cases of ARIMA models. A non-seasonal ARIMA model is classified as an "`ARIMA(p,d,q)`" model, where:

`p` is the number of autoregressive terms,

`d` is the number of non-seasonal differences needed for stationarity, and

`q` is the number of lagged forecast errors in the prediction equation.

The forecasting equation is constructed as follows. First, let y denote the dth difference of Y, which means:

If d=0: $y_t = Y_t$

If d=1: $y_t = Y_t - Y_{t-1}$

If d=2: $y_t = (Y_t - Y_{t-1}) - (Y_{t-1} - Y_{t-2}) = Yt - 2Y_{t-1} + Y_{t-2}$

ARIMA models can be constructed in R using the function `Arima()`. The syntax of `Arima()` function is as follows.

```
Arima(y, order = c(0, 0, 0), seasonal = c(0, 0, 0), xreg = NULL,
      include.mean = TRUE, include.drift = FALSE, include.constant,
      lambda = model$lambda, biasadj = FALSE, method = c("CSS-ML", "ML",
      "CSS"), model = NULL, x = y, ...)
```

where

`y` – This is a univariate time series of class `ts`.

`order` – A specification of the non-seasonal part of the ARIMA model: the three components (p, d, q) are the AR order, the degree of differencing, and the MA order.

`seasonal` – A specification of the seasonal part of the ARIMA model, plus the period (which defaults to frequency(y)). This should be a list with components order and period, but a specification of just a numeric vector of length 3 will be turned into a suitable list with the specification as the order.

`xreg` – This is optionally, a vector or matrix of external regressors, which must have the same number of rows as `y`.

`include.mean` – This decides whether the ARIMA model should include a mean term. The default is `TRUE` for undifferenced series, `FALSE` for differenced ones (where a mean would not affect the fit nor predictions).

`include.drift` – This decides whether the ARIMA model include a linear drift term. (i.e., a linear regression with ARIMA errors is fitted.) The default is `FALSE`.

`include.constant` – If `TRUE`, then `include.mean` is set to be `TRUE` for undifferenced series and `include.drift` is set to be `TRUE` for differenced series. Note that if there is more than one difference taken, no constant is included regardless of the value of this argument. This is deliberate as otherwise quadratic and higher order polynomial trends would be induced.

`lambda` – Box-Cox transformation parameter. This is ignored if `NULL`. Otherwise, data transformed before model is estimated.

`biasadj` – Use adjusted back-transformed mean for Box-Cox transformations. If `TRUE`, point forecasts and fitted values are mean forecast. Otherwise, these points can be considered the median of the forecast densities.

`method` – Gives the fitting method: maximum likelihood or minimize conditional sum-of-squares. The default (unless there are missing values) is to use conditional-sum-of-squares to find starting values, then maximum likelihood.

`model` – Output from a previous call to `Arima`. If model is passed, this same model is fitted to y without re-estimating any parameters.

`x` – This is included for backwards compatibility.

... – Additional arguments to be passed to `Arima()`.

For forecasting stationary time series data we need to choose an optimal ARIMA model (p,d,q). For this we can use `auto.arima()` function which can choose optimal (p,d,q) value and return us. Following program illustrate the use of `auto.arima()` with built-in data set `nottem`. We can use the `forecast()` method to forecast the values.

Program

```
auto.arima(nottem)
#prediction by default for 2
x=forecast(auto.arima(nottem))
x
plot(forecast(x))
#predictive accuracy
accuracy(x)
```

Output

```
Series: nottem
ARIMA(1,0,3)(0,0,2)[12] with non-zero mean
Coefficients:
        ar1     ma1     ma2     ma3    sma1    sma2     mean
     0.4115  0.4790  0.4384  0.2412  0.1804  0.4761  48.9947
s.e. 0.1272  0.1284  0.1021  0.0757  0.0820  0.0629   1.2788
sigma^2 estimated as 11.84:  log likelihood=-637.36
```

```
AIC=1290.72   AICc=1291.34   BIC=1318.57
#prediction by default for 2
         Point Forecast    Lo 80    Hi 80    Lo 95    Hi 95
Jan 1940       41.53543 37.12550 45.94537 34.79102 48.27985
Feb 1940       43.69469 37.78968 49.59971 34.66375 52.72564
Mar 1940       45.90049 39.01077 52.79021 35.36357 56.43741
Apr 1940       47.48340 40.14575 54.82106 36.26143 58.70538
May 1940       49.24770 41.83686 56.65853 37.91380 60.58159
Jun 1940       52.83001 45.40685 60.25316 41.47726 64.18275
Jul 1940       53.51093 46.08569 60.93617 42.15500 64.86686
Aug 1940       53.34808 45.92248 60.77368 41.99161 64.70455
Sep 1940       52.05310 44.62745 59.47876 40.69654 63.40966
Oct 1940       48.89807 41.47241 56.32374 37.54150 60.25465
Nov 1940       50.17937 42.75370 57.60504 38.82279 61.53595
Dec 1940       45.09721 37.67155 52.52288 33.74063 56.45379
Jan 1941       44.80762 37.33937 52.27587 33.38591 56.22932
Feb 1941       45.83294 38.33113 53.33475 34.35992 57.30597
Mar 1941       47.18495 39.65586 54.71405 35.67019 58.69971
Apr 1941       48.17949 40.63663 55.72235 36.64368 59.71530
May 1941       49.21672 41.67153 56.76191 37.67734 60.75609
Jun 1941       51.35950 43.81392 58.90508 39.81953 62.89948
Jul 1941       52.17343 44.62778 59.71908 40.63335 63.71351
Aug 1941       52.91409 45.36843 60.45975 41.37399 64.45418
Sep 1941       51.79708 44.25141 59.34274 40.25698 63.33718
Oct 1941       47.12706 39.58139 54.67272 35.58696 58.66715
Nov 1941       48.99225 41.44658 56.53791 37.45215 60.53234
Dec 1941       45.72317 38.17751 53.26884 34.18308 57.26327
#predictive accuracy
                      ME     RMSE      MAE        MPE     MAPE      MASE
Training set 0.009365132 3.390536 2.686892 -0.6270266 5.727569 0.9977385
                    ACF1
Training set 0.01225898
```

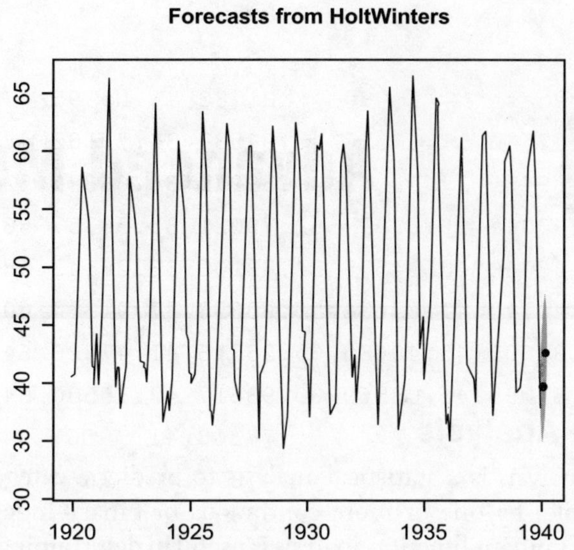

From the output, we can see that, the most suitable ARIMA model `ARIMA(1,0,3)(0,0,2)[12] with non-zero mean` for this series is called. Similarly when `forecast()` method is called, it automatically predict for the next 2 years.

11.7 Conclusion

In this Chapter, a detailed analysis of the basic multivariate analysis is performed. Correlation analysis, significance of co-variance, rank correlation, auto-correlation and partial auto-correlation is explained in detail. Various regression methods which include simple linear regression, multiple linear regression, logistic regression and Poisson regression is illustrated with examples. How to perform Analysis of Co-variance (ANCOVA) is also illustrated in this Chapter. Another important multivariate analysis is the forecasting techniques which include simple moving average, weighted moving average and simple exponential smoothing techniques is explained. Finally the time series analysis including how to create a time series, seasonal decomposition, exponential models and ARIMA models are covered in this Chapter. All sections have problems with solved programs written in R.

12 Advanced Multivariate Analysis

12.1 Discriminant Analysis

Discriminant function analysis is a statistical analysis to predict a categorical dependent variable (called a grouping variable) by one or more continuous or binary independent variables (called predictor variables). Discriminant function analysis is useful in determining whether a set of variables is effective in predicting category membership. Discriminant analysis is used when groups are known apriori (unlike in cluster analysis). Each case must have a score on one or more quantitative predictor measures, and a score on a group measure. In simple terms, discriminant function analysis is classification - the act of distributing things into groups, classes or categories of the same type.

In some situation, it may be essential to study the effect of two or more predictor variables on certain evaluation criterion as *good or bad*, *successful or unsuccessful*, *like or dislike*, *above expected level or below expected level.*

We need to check whether the predictor variables discriminate among the groups. More specifically, it is necessary to identify the predictor variable (independent variable) which is more important when compared to the other predictor variables. Such analysis is called discriminant analysis. The library MASS should be added to the R environment for performing discriminant analysis. The `lda()` function in this package is used for conducting discriminant analysis. The syntax of `lda()` function is as follows.

```
lda(formula, data)
```

where

`formula` is a formula describing the predictor and response variables.

`data` is the name of the data set used.

The following problem illustrates discriminant analysis.

Problem

The management of a school wants to do discriminant analysis concerning the effect of two factors namely the yearly spending in lakhs on infrastructure of the school (X1) and the yearly spending on interface events of the school (X2) on the grading of the school. The data of past 12 years is collected and is available in a file named "school.csv". Based on the data, the committee has awarded one of the following grades for each year which is also given in the same file.

Program

```
library(MASS)
df1=read.csv("school.csv",header=TRUE)
df1
fit <- lda(df1$grade ~ df1$infrastructure+df1$interface,data=df1)
fit
plot(fit)
```

Output

```
   year grade infrastructure interface
1     1 below              3         4
2     2 below              4         5
3     3 above             10         7
4     4 below              5         4
5     5 below              6         6
6     6 above             11         4
7     7 below              7         4
8     8 above             12         5
9     9 below              8         7
10   10 below              9         5
11   11 above             13         6
12   12 above             14         8
Call:
lda(df1$grade ~ df1$infrastructure + df1$interface, data = df1)
Prior probabilities of groups:
    above     below
0.4166667 0.5833333
Group means:
     df1$infrastructure df1$interface
above                12             6
below                 6             5
Coefficients of linear discriminants:
                          LD1
df1$infrastructure -0.5492406
df1$interface       0.1585437
```

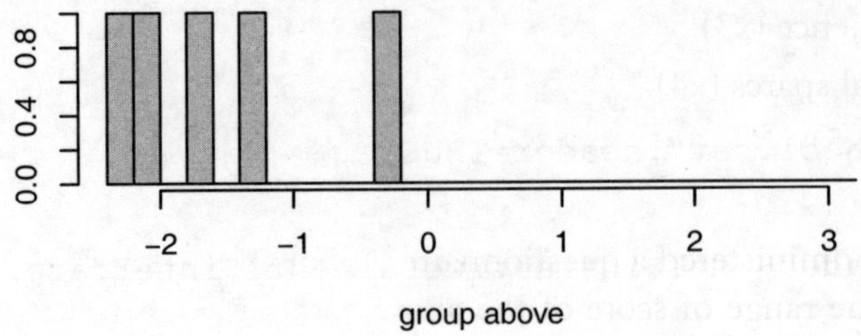

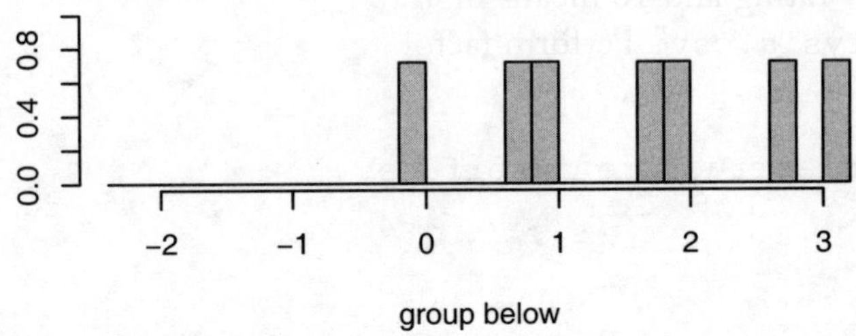

From the output, the negative value for infrastructure indicates that spending on infrastructure events is more important than spending on interface.

12.2 Exploratory Factor Analysis

Exploratory Factor Analysis (EFA) is a statistical technique that is used to identify the latent relational structure among a set of variables and narrow down to smaller number of variables. This essentially means that the variance of large number of variables can be described by few summary variables. EFA is often used to consolidate survey data by revealing the groupings (factors) that underlay individual questions. For performing factor analysis, we need to install `"psych"` package and loaded into the current R environment. The `fa()` function present in the `psych` package is used to perform factor analysis. Following problem illustrates factor analysis. The syntax of `fa()` function is as follows.

```
fa(r = corMat, nfactors = 2, rotate = "oblimin", fm = "pa")
```

where

`r:` the correlation matrix

`nfactors:` number of factors to be extracted (default = 1)

`rotate:` one of several matrix rotation methods, such as `"varimax"` or `"oblimin"`

`fm:` one of several factoring methods, such as `"pa" (principal axis)` or `"ml" (maximum likelihood)`

Problem

The marketing manager of a two-wheeler company designed a questionnaire to study the customer's feedback about its two-wheeler and in turn he is keen in identifying the factors of his study. He has identified six variables which are listed below.

1. Fuel efficiency (x1)
2. Life of the two-wheeler (x2)

3. Handling convenience (x3)
4. Quality of original spares (x4)
5. Breakdown rate (x5)
6. Price (x6)

So the company administered a questionnaire among 10 customers to obtain their opinion on the above variables. The range of score of the above variables is assumed to be between 0 and 10. The score 0 means low rating and 10 means high rating. The survey data is summarized and given in a file "`FactorAnalysis.csv`". Perform factor analysis.

Program

```
library(psych)
data=read.csv("FactorAnalysis.csv", header=TRUE)
data
#calculate the correlation matrix
corMat <- cor(data)
#display the correlation matrix
corMat
#use fa() to conduct an oblique principal-axis exploratory factor analysis
#save the solution to an R variable
solution <- fa(r = corMat, nfactors = 1, rotate = "oblimin", fm = "pa")
solution
```

Output

```
   respondent x1 x2 x3 x4 x5 x6
1           1  6  8  9  9  1  2
2           2  4  4  6  8  2  1
3           3  4  1  6  5  1  2
4           4  1  2  6  3  2  3
5           5  4  3  5  5  2  3
6           6  4  4  6  8  2  3
7           7  3  3  0  9  1  3
8           8  7  7  6  9  9  2
9           9  5  3  1  8  1  2
10         10  5  4  2  3  1  0
#calculate the correlation matrix
#display the correlation matrix
```

```
             respondent          x1          x2          x3          x4
respondent  1.00000000  0.2130532 -0.07746827 -0.75610457 -0.09729438
x1          0.21305322  1.0000000  0.74213984  0.16787327  0.49573077
x2         -0.07746827  0.7421398  1.00000000  0.42394078  0.56761122
x3         -0.75610457  0.1678733  0.42394078  1.00000000  0.05033894
x4         -0.09729438  0.4957308  0.56761122  0.05033894  1.00000000
x5          0.22557029  0.4841259  0.47414254  0.23818338  0.28969672
x6         -0.20297414 -0.4301669 -0.20441274  0.09208180  0.19596333
                   x5          x6
respondent 0.22557029 -0.20297414
x1         0.48412592 -0.43016693
x2         0.47414254 -0.20441274
x3         0.23818338  0.09208180
x4         0.28969672  0.19596333
x5         1.00000000  0.03662795
x6         0.03662795  1.00000000
Factor Analysis using method =  pa
Call: fa(r = corMat, nfactors = 2, rotate = "oblimin", fm = "pa")
Warning: A Heywood case was detected.
Standardized loadings (pattern matrix) based upon correlation matrix
             PA1   PA2    h2    u2 com
respondent -0.08  1.09 1.190 -0.19 1.0
x1          0.87  0.30 0.842  0.16 1.2
x2          0.93 -0.02 0.870  0.13 1.0
x3          0.42 -0.65 0.594  0.41 1.7
x4          0.53  0.00 0.277  0.72 1.0
x5          0.52  0.15 0.295  0.71 1.2
x6         -0.17 -0.24 0.085  0.92 1.8
                       PA1  PA2
SS loadings           2.38 1.77
Proportion Var        0.34 0.25
Cumulative Var        0.34 0.59
Proportion Explained  0.57 0.43
Cumulative Proportion 0.57 1.00
Mean item complexity =  1.3
Test of the hypothesis that 2 factors are sufficient.
```

```
The degrees of freedom for the null model are 21 and the objective
function was 4.7
The degrees of freedom for the model are 8 and the objective function was
1.82
The root mean square of the residuals (RMSR) is 0.1
The df corrected root mean square of the residuals is 0.17
Fit based upon off diagonal values = 0.92
```

Note that several rotation and factoring methods are available when conducting EFA. Rotation methods can be described as `orthogonal`, which do not allow the resulting factors to be correlated, and `oblique`, which do allow the resulting factors to be correlated. Factoring methods can be described as common, which are used when the goal is to better describe data, and component, which are used when the goal is to reduce the amount of data. The `fa()` function is used for common factoring. For component analysis, we can use `princomp()`. The best methods will vary by circumstance and it is therefore recommended that we should seek professional council in determining the optimal parameters for our future EFAs.

12.3 Cluster Analysis

Cluster analysis or clustering is the task of grouping a set of objects in such a way that objects in the same group (called a cluster) are more similar to each other than to those in other groups (clusters). There are various clustering approaches like partitioning methods, hierarchical methods and model based methods. We will see how to do each of these clustering methods in R.

12.3.1 Partitioning Methods

K-means clustering is the most popular partitioning method. K-means clustering is an unsupervised learning algorithm that tries to cluster data based on their similarity. Unsupervised learning means that there is no outcome to be predicted, and the algorithm just tries to find patterns in the data. In K-means clustering, we have to specify the number of clusters we want the data to be grouped into. The algorithm randomly assigns each observation to a cluster, and finds the centroid of each cluster. Then, the algorithm iterates through two steps:

- Reassign data points to the cluster whose centroid is closest.
- Calculate new centroid of each cluster.

These two steps are repeated till the within cluster variation cannot be reduced any further. The within cluster variation is calculated as the sum of the Euclidean distance between the data points and their respective cluster centroids.

The K-means algorithm is performed in R using the function `kmeans()`. The syntax of `kmeans()` function is as follows.

```
kmeans(x, centers, iter.max=10, num.seeds=10)
```

where

`x` – a numeric matrix of data, or an object that can be coerced to such a matrix (such as a numeric vector or a data frame with all numeric columns).

`centers` – The number of clusters in the solution.

`iter.max` – The maximum number of iterations allowed.

`num.seeds` – The number of different starting random seeds to use. Each random seed results in a different k-means solution.

For performing K-means in R, the built-in data set `iris` is used. Following program illustrates the `kmeans()` function.

Program

```
irisCluster <- kmeans(iris[, 1:4], 3, nstart = 20)
irisCluster
```

Output

```
K-means clustering with 3 clusters of sizes 38, 50, 62
Cluster means:
  Sepal.Length Sepal.Width Petal.Length Petal.Width
1     6.850000    3.073684     5.742105    2.071053
2     5.006000    3.428000     1.462000    0.246000
3     5.901613    2.748387     4.393548    1.433871
Clustering vector:
  [1] 2 2 2 2 2 2 2 2 2 2 2 2 2 2 2 2 2 2 2 2 2 2 2 2 2 2 2 2 2 2 2 2 2
2 2 2 2
 [38] 2 2 2 2 2 2 2 2 2 2 2 2 2 3 3 1 3 3 3 3 3 3 3 3 3 3 3 3 3 3 3 3 3
3 3 3 3
 [75] 3 3 3 1 3 3 3 3 3 3 3 3 3 3 3 3 3 3 3 3 3 3 3 3 3 1 3 1 1 1 1 3
1 1 1 1
[112] 1 1 3 3 1 1 1 1 3 1 3 1 3 1 1 3 3 1 1 1 1 1 3 1 1 1 1 3 1 1 1 3 1
1 1 3 1
[149] 1 3
Within cluster sum of squares by cluster:
[1] 23.87947 15.15100 39.82097
 (between_SS / total_SS =  88.4 %)
Available components:
[1] "cluster"      "centers"      "totss"      "withinss"      "tot.
withinss"
[6] "betweenss"    "size"      "iter"      "ifault"
```

Another important partitioning method is Partitioning Around Medoids (PAM). This algorithm is based on medoids and can be invoked by using `pam()`. The function `pamk()` in the `fpc` package is a wrapper for `pam()` that also prints the suggested number of clusters based on optimum average silhouette width. For illustrating PAM, the same dataset `iris` is used. The library `cluster` should be loaded in the current R environment for calling the `pam()` function.

Program

```
library(cluster)
irisCluster2 <- pam(iris[, 1:4], 3)
irisCluster2
```

Output

```
Medoids:
      ID Sepal.Length Sepal.Width Petal.Length Petal.Width
[1,]   8          5.0         3.4          1.5         0.2
[2,]  79          6.0         2.9          4.5         1.5
[3,] 113          6.8         3.0          5.5         2.1
Clustering vector:
  [1] 1 1 1 1 1 1 1 1 1 1 1 1 1 1 1 1 1 1 1 1 1 1 1 1 1 1 1 1 1 1 1 1 1
1 1 1 1
 [38] 1 1 1 1 1 1 1 1 1 1 1 1 1 2 2 3 2 2 2 2 2 2 2 2 2 2 2 2 2 2 2 2 2
2 2 2 2
 [75] 2 2 2 3 2 2 2 2 2 2 2 2 2 2 2 2 2 2 2 2 2 2 2 2 2 3 2 3 3 3 3 2
3 3 3 3
[112] 3 3 2 2 3 3 3 3 2 3 2 3 2 3 3 2 2 3 3 3 3 3 2 3 3 3 3 2 3 3 3 2 3
3 3 2 3
[149] 3 2
Objective function:
    build      swap
0.6709391 0.6542077
Available components:
 [1] "medoids"    "id.med"     "clustering" "objective"  "isolation"
 [6] "clusinfo"   "silinfo"    "diss"       "call"       "data"
```

12.3.2 Hierarchical Methods

Hierarchical method of clustering is a method of cluster analysis which seeks to build a hierarchy of clusters. Strategies for hierarchical clustering generally fall into two types.

- **Agglomerative**: This is a "bottom up" approach: each observation starts in its own cluster, and pairs of clusters are merged as one moves up the hierarchy.
- **Divisive**: This is a "top down" approach: all observations start in one cluster, and splits are performed recursively as one moves down the hierarchy.

Hierarchical clustering doesn't require specifying the number of clusters beforehand. The algorithm works as follows:

- Put each data point in its own cluster.
- Identify the closest two clusters and combine them into one cluster.
- Repeat the above step till all the data points are in a single cluster.

Once this is done, it is usually represented by a dendrogram like structure. There are a few ways to determine how close two clusters are:

1. Complete linkage clustering: Find the maximum possible distance between points belonging to two different clusters.
2. Single linkage clustering: Find the minimum possible distance between points belonging to two different clusters.
3. Mean linkage clustering: Find all possible pairwise distances for points belonging to two different clusters and then calculate the average.
4. Centroid linkage clustering: Find the centroid of each cluster and calculate the distance between centroids of two clusters.

Complete linkage and mean linkage clustering are the ones used most often. Let us see how well the hierarchical clustering algorithm can do. We can use `hclust()` function for this. The function `hclust()` requires us to provide the data in the form of a distance matrix. We can do this by using `dist()` method. The syntax of `hclust()` is as follows.

```
hclust(d, method = "complete", members = NULL)
```

where

`d` - a distance matrix.

`method` - the agglomeration method to be used.

`members` - `NULL` or a vector with length size of `d`

By default, the complete linkage method is used. For this the same built-in data set `iris` is used. The following program illustrates the hierarchical clustering.

Program

```
clusters <- hclust(dist(iris[, 3:4]))
clusters
plot(clusters)
```

Output

```
Call:
hclust(d = dist(iris[, 3:4]))
Cluster method   : complete
Distance         : euclidean
Number of objects: 150
```

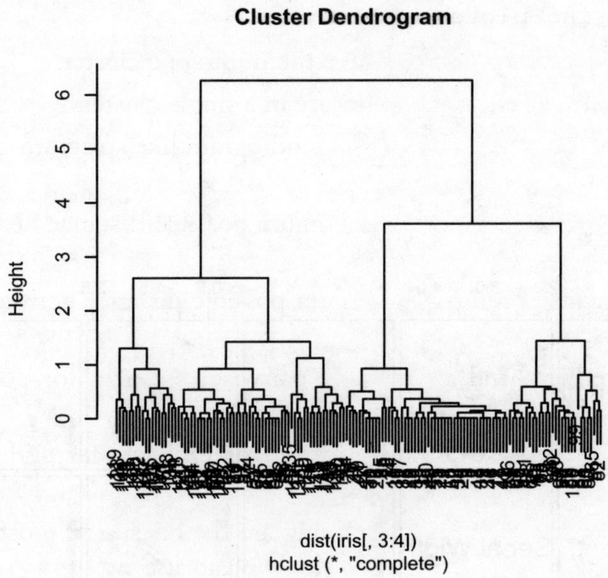

12.3.3 Model based Methods

Model based approaches assume a variety of data models and apply maximum likelihood estimation and Bayes criteria to identify the most likely model and number of clusters. Specifically, the `Mclust()` function in the `mclust` package selects the optimal model according to BIC (Bayesian Information Criterion) for EM (Expectation Maximization) initialized by hierarchical clustering for parameterized Gaussian mixture models. Following program illustrates the use of `mclust()` function.

Program

```
library(mclust)
fit <- Mclust(iris)
plot(fit) # plot results
summary(fit) # display the best model
```

Output

```
Model-based clustering plots:
1: BIC
2: classification
3: uncertainty
4: density
Selection: summary(fit) # display the best model
Enter an item from the menu, or 0 to exit
Selection: 4
```

```
Model-based clustering plots:
1: BIC
2: classification
3: uncertainty
4: density
Selection: 0
```

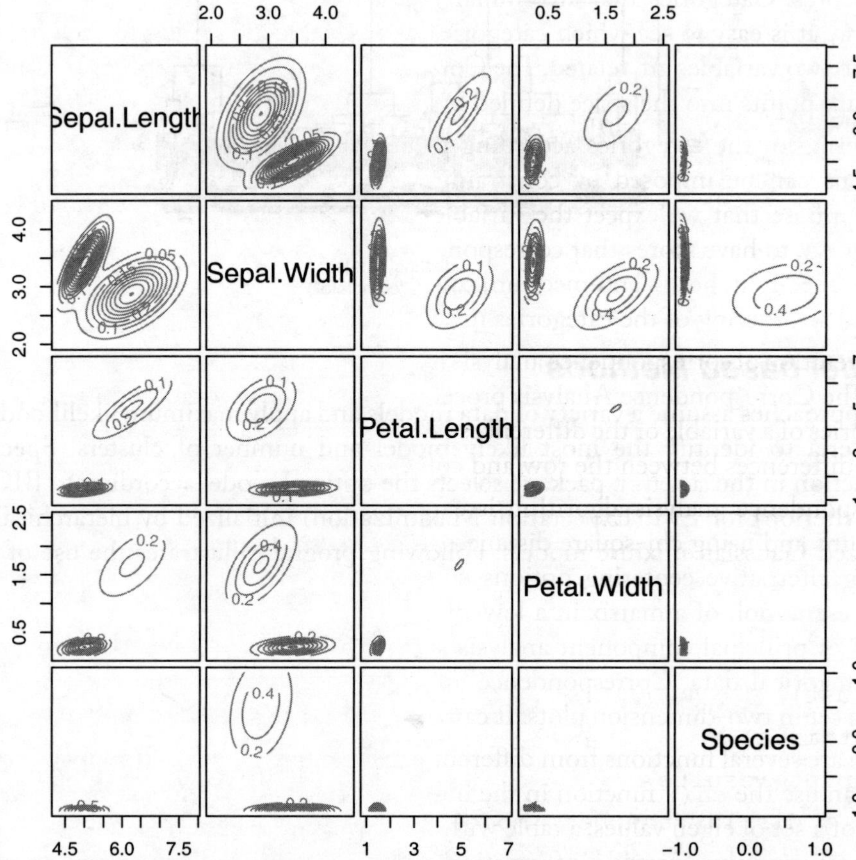

In the above example, we have chosen density based model for clustering.

12.4 Correspondence Analysis

A correspondence table is any two-way table whose cells contain some measurement of correspondence between the rows and the columns. The measure of correspondence can be any indication of the similarity, affinity, confusion, association, or interaction between the row and column variables. A very common type of correspondence table is a cross tabulation, where the cells contain frequency counts.

Such tables can be obtained easily with the crosstabs procedure. However, a cross tabulation does not always provide a clear picture of the nature of the relationship between the two variables.

This is particularly true if the variables of interest are nominal (with no inherent order or rank) and contain numerous categories. Cross tabulation may tell us that the observed cell frequencies differ significantly from the expected values in a 10x9 cross tabulation of occupation and breakfast cereal, but it may be difficult to discern which occupational groups have similar tastes or what those tastes are.

Correspondence Analysis allows us to examine the relationship between two nominal variables graphically in a multidimensional space. It computes row and column scores and produces plots based on the scores. Categories that are similar to each other appear close to each other in the plots. In this way, it is easy to see which categories of a variable are similar to each other or which categories of the two variables are related. The Correspondence Analysis procedure also allows us to fit supplementary points into the space defined by the active points.

If the ordering of the categories according to their scores is undesirable or counterintuitive, order restrictions can be imposed by constraining the scores for some categories to be equal. For example, suppose that we expect the variable smoking behavior, with categories none, light, medium, and heavy, to have scores that correspond to this ordering. However, if the analysis orders the categories none, light, heavy, and medium, constraining the scores for heavy and medium to be equal preserves the ordering of the categories in their scores.

The interpretation of correspondence analysis in terms of distances depends on the normalization method used. The Correspondence Analysis procedure can be used to analyze either the differences between categories of a variable or the differences between variables. With the default normalization, it analyzes the differences between the row and column variables.

The correspondence analysis algorithm is capable of many kinds of analyses. Centering the rows and columns and using chi-square distances correspond to standard correspondence analysis. However, using alternative centering options combined with Euclidean distances allows for an alternative representation of a matrix in a low-dimensional space. Correspondence Analysis (CA) is an extension of principal component analysis suited to explore relationships among qualitative variables or categorical data. Correspondence analysis provides a solution for summarizing and visualizing data set in two-dimension plots. It can be useful to discover structure in this type of data.

In R, there are several functions from different packages that allow us to apply Correspondence Analysis. We can use the `ca()` function in the library `ca` for Correspondence Analysis. The results should consist of a set of eigen values, a table with the row coordinates, and a table with the column coordinates. The eigen values provide information of the variability in the data. The row coordinates provide information about the structure of the rows in the analyzed table. The column coordinates provide information about the structure of the columns in the analyzed table.

We will use the dataset `author` that already comes with the R package `ca`. It is a data matrix containing the counts of the 26 letters of the alphabet (columns of matrix) for 12 different novels (rows of matrix). Each row contains letter counts in a sample of text from each work, excluding proper nouns. Following program illustrates this

Program

```
library(ca)
#data set author
```

```
author
#correspondence analysis
cal=ca(author)
cal
plot(cal)
```

Output

```
#data set author
                                  a   b   c   d    e   f
three daughters (buck)          550 116 147 374 1015 131
drifters (michener)             515 109 172 311  827 167
lost world (clark)              590 112 181 265  940 137
east wind (buck)                557 129 128 343  996 158
farewell to arms (hemingway)    589  72 129 339  866 108
sound and fury 7 (faulkner)     541 109 136 228  763 126
sound and fury 6 (faulkner)     517  96 127 356  771 115
profiles of future (clark)     592 151 251 238  985 168
islands (hemingway)             576 120 136 404  873 122
pendorric 3 (holt)              557  97 145 354  909  97
asia (michener)                 554 108 206 243  797 164
pendorric 2 (holt)              541  93 149 390  887 133
                                  g   h   i  j  k   l   m
three daughters (buck)          131 493 442  2 52 302 159
drifters (michener)             136 376 432  8 61 280 146
lost world (clark)              119 419 514  6 46 335 176
east wind (buck)                129 571 555  4 76 291 247
farewell to arms (hemingway)    159 449 472  7 59 264 158
sound and fury 7 (faulkner)     129 401 520  5 72 280 209
sound and fury 6 (faulkner)     189 478 558  6 80 322 163
profiles of future (clark)     152 381 544  7 39 416 236
islands (hemingway)             156 593 406  3 90 281 142
pendorric 3 (holt)              121 479 431 10 94 240 154
asia (michener)                 100 328 471  4 34 293 149
pendorric 2 (holt)              154 463 518  4 65 265 194
                                  n   o   p q   r   s   t
three daughters (buck)          534 516 115 4 409 467 632
```

```
drifters (michener)             470 561 140 4 368 387 632
lost world (clark)              403 505 147 8 395 464 670
east wind (buck)                479 509  92 3 413 533 632
farewell to arms (hemingway) 504 542  95 0 416 314 691
sound and fury 7 (faulkner)  471 589  84 2 324 454 672
sound and fury 6 (faulkner)  483 617  82 8 294 358 685
profiles of future (clark)   526 524 107 9 418 508 655
islands (hemingway)             516 488  91 3 339 349 640
pendorric 3 (holt)              417 477 100 3 305 415 597
asia (michener)                 482 532 145 8 361 402 630
pendorric 2 (holt)              484 545  70 4 299 423 644
                                  u   v   w  x   y  z
three daughters (buck)          174  66 155  5 150  3
drifters (michener)             195  60 156 14 137  5
lost world (clark)              224 113 146 13 162 10
east wind (buck)                181  68 187 10 184  4
farewell to arms (hemingway) 197  64 225  1 155  2
sound and fury 7 (faulkner)  247  71 160 11 280  1
sound and fury 6 (faulkner)  225  37 216 12 171  5
profiles of future (clark)   226  89 106 15 142 20
islands (hemingway)             194  40 250  3 104  5
pendorric 3 (holt)              237  64 194  9 140  4
asia (michener)                 196  66 149  2  80  6
pendorric 2 (holt)              193  66 218  2 127  2
Principal inertias (eigenvalues):
           1        2        3        4        5
Value      0.007664 0.003688 0.002411 0.001383 0.001002
Percentage 40.91%   19.69%   12.87%   7.38%    5.35%
           6        7        8        9        10
Value      0.000723 0.000659 0.000455 0.000374 0.000263
Percentage 3.86%    3.52%    2.43%    2%       1.4%
           11
Value      0.000113
Percentage 0.6%
 Rows:
       three daughters (buck) drifters (michener)
```

```
Mass                0.085407             0.079728
ChiDist             0.097831             0.094815
Inertia             0.000817             0.000717
Dim. 1             -0.095388             0.405697
Dim. 2             -0.794999            -0.405560
       lost world (clark) east wind (buck)
Mass             0.084881         0.089411
ChiDist          0.128432         0.118655
Inertia          0.001400         0.001259
Dim. 1           1.157803        -0.173901
Dim. 2          -0.023114         0.434443
       farewell to arms (hemingway)
Mass                       0.082215
ChiDist                    0.122889
Inertia                    0.001242
Dim. 1                    -0.831886
Dim. 2                    -0.136485
       sound and fury 7 (faulkner)
Mass                      0.082310
ChiDist                   0.172918
Inertia                   0.002461
Dim. 1                    0.302025
Dim. 2                    2.707599
       sound and fury 6 (faulkner)
Mass                      0.083338
ChiDist                   0.141937
Inertia                   0.001679
Dim. 1                   -0.925572
Dim. 2                    0.966944
       profiles of future (clark) islands (hemingway)
Mass                     0.089722                  0.082776
ChiDist                  0.187358                  0.165529
Inertia                  0.003150                  0.002268
Dim. 1                   1.924060                 -1.566481
Dim. 2                  -0.249310                 -1.185338
       pendorric 3 (holt) asia (michener)
```

```
Mass             0.079501          0.077827
ChiDist          0.113174          0.155115
Inertia          0.001018          0.001873
Dim. 1          -0.724758          1.179548
Dim. 2          -0.106349         -1.186934
        pendorric 2 (holt)
Mass             0.082884
ChiDist          0.101369
Inertia          0.000852
Dim. 1          -0.764937
Dim. 2          -0.091188
```

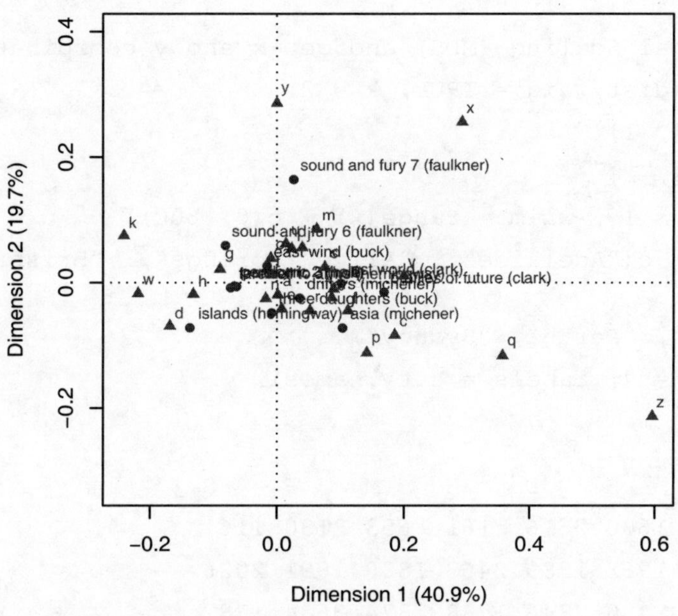

Row points (column points) that are closer together have more similar column profiles (row profiles). Keep in mind that we cannot interpret the distance between row and column points directly.

12.5 Multidimensional Scaling

Multidimensional scaling (MDS) is a means of visualizing the level of similarity of individual cases of a dataset. It refers to a set of related ordination techniques used in information visualization, in particular to display the information contained in a distance matrix. It is a form of non-linear dimensionality reduction. An MDS algorithm aims to place each object in N-dimensional space such that the distances between the objects are preserved as well as possible. Each object is then assigned coordinates in each of the N dimensions. The number of dimensions of an MDS plot

N can exceed 2 and is specified apriori. Choosing N=2 optimizes the object locations for a two-dimensional scatter plot. In R, we can perform a classical MDS using the `cmdscale( )` function. For illustrating MDS, an example of automatic layout of Australian cities based on distances between them is chosen. The layout obtained with MDS is very close to their locations on a map. Following program illustrates this.

Program

```
dist<-read.csv("Austcities.csv", header=T)
dist
#Remove the first column,acronyms of cities and set them to row names.
row.names(dist) <- dist[, 1]
dist <- dist[, -1]
dist
#Multidimensional Scaling (MDS) and get x and y coordinates.
fit <- cmdscale(dist, eig = TRUE, k = 2)
x <- fit$points[, 1]
y <- fit$points[, 2]
plot(x, y, pch = 19, xlim = range(x) + c(0, 600))
city.names  <-  c("Adelaide",  "Alice  Springs",  "Brisbane",  "Darwin",
"Hobart",
    "Melbourne", "Perth", "Sydney")
text(x, y, pos = 4, labels = city.names)
```

Output

```
   X    A   AS    B    D    H    M    P    S
1  A    0 1328 1600 2616 1161  653 2130 1161
2 AS 1328    0 1962 1289 2463 1889 1991 2026
3  B 1600 1962    0 2846 1788 1374 3604  732
4  D 2616 1289 2846    0 3734 3146 2652 3146
5  H 1161 2463 1788 3734    0  598 3008 1057
6  M  653 1889 1374 3146  598    0 2720  713
7  P 2130 1991 3604 2652 3008 2720    0 3288
8  S 1161 2026  732 3146 1057  713 3288    0
#Remove the first column,acronyms of cities and set them to row names.
      A   AS    B    D    H    M    P    S
A     0 1328 1600 2616 1161  653 2130 1161
AS 1328    0 1962 1289 2463 1889 1991 2026
B  1600 1962    0 2846 1788 1374 3604  732
```

```
D 2616 1289 2846    0 3734 3146 2652 3146
H 1161 2463 1788 3734    0  598 3008 1057
M  653 1889 1374 3146  598    0 2720  713
P 2130 1991 3604 2652 3008 2720    0 3288
S 1161 2026  732 3146 1057  713 3288    0
```

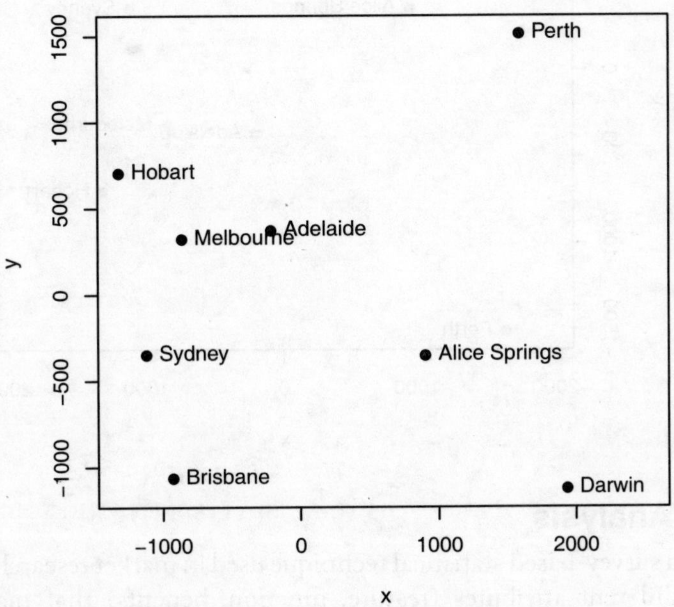

By flipping both x- and y-axis, Darwin and Brisbane are moved to the top (north), which makes it easier to compare with a map.

Program

```
x <- 0 - x
y <- 0 - y
plot(x, y, pch = 19, xlim = range(x) + c(0, 600))
text(x, y, pos = 4, labels = city.names)
```

Output

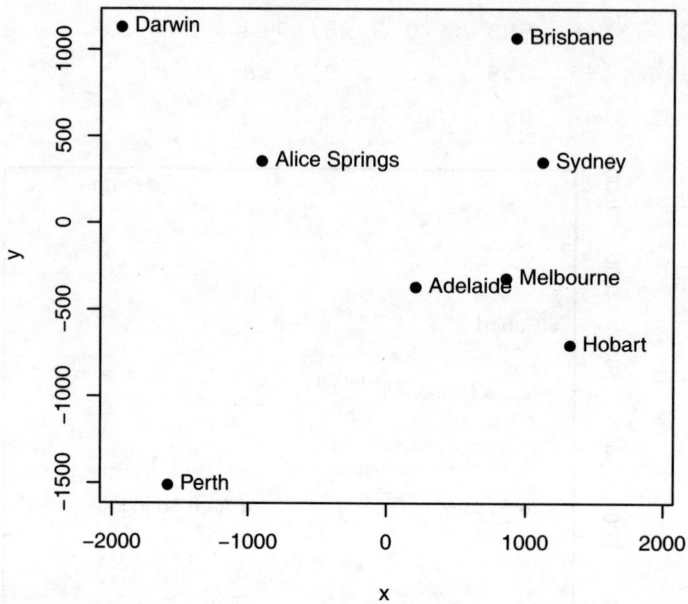

12.6 Conjoint Analysis

Conjoint analysis is a survey-based statistical technique used in market research that helps determine how people value different attributes (feature, function, benefits) that make up an individual product or service. The objective of conjoint analysis is to determine what combination of a limited number of attributes is most influential on respondent choice or decision making. A controlled set of potential products or services is shown to survey respondents and by analyzing how they make preferences between these products, the implicit valuation of the individual elements making up the product or service can be determined. These implicit valuations can be used to create market models that estimate market share, revenue and even profitability of new designs.

Conjoint Analysis in R can be performed by using the function `Conjoint()` in the `conjoint` package. The syntax of `Conjoint()` function is as follows.

```
Conjoint(y, x, z)
```

where

`y` - matrix of preferences

`x` - matrix of profiles

`z` - matrix of level names

For performing conjoint analysis, the built-in dataset `herbata` is used.

Program

```
library(conjoint)
data(herbata)
```

```
#preferences
head(hpref)
#profiles
print(hprof)
#level names
print(hlevn)
Conjoint(hpref,hprof,hlevn)
```

Output

```
#preferences
  Y
1 8
2 1
3 1
4 3
5 9
6 2
#profiles
   cena gatunek rodzaj aromat
1   3      1      1      1
2   1      2      1      1
3   2      2      2      1
4   2      1      3      1
5   3      3      3      1
6   2      1      1      2
7   3      2      1      2
8   2      3      1      2
9   3      1      2      2
10  1      3      2      2
11  1      1      3      2
12  2      2      3      2
13  3      2      3      2
#level names
        levels
1        niska
2      srednia
```

```
3       wysoka
4       czarna
5      zielona
6     czerwona
7   ekspresowa
8  granulowana
9    lisciasta
10         tak
11         nie
Call:
lm(formula = frml)
Residuals:
    Min      1Q  Median      3Q     Max
-5,1888 -2,3761 -0,7512  2,2128  7,5134
Coefficients:
                     Estimate Std. Error t value Pr(>|t|)
(Intercept)           3,55336    0,09068  39,184  < 2e-16 ***
factor(x$cena)1       0,24023    0,13245   1,814    0,070 .
factor(x$cena)2      -0,14311    0,11485  -1,246    0,213
factor(x$gatunek)1    0,61489    0,11485   5,354 1,02e-07 ***
factor(x$gatunek)2    0,03489    0,11485   0,304    0,761
factor(x$rodzaj)1     0,13689    0,11485   1,192    0,234
factor(x$rodzaj)2    -0,88977    0,13245  -6,718 2,76e-11 ***
factor(x$aromat)1     0,41078    0,08492   4,837 1,48e-06 ***
---
Signif. codes:  0 '***' 0,001 '**' 0,01 '*' 0,05 '.' 0,1 ' ' 1
Residual standard error: 2,967 on 1292 degrees of freedom
Multiple R-squared:  0,09003,   Adjusted R-squared:  0,0851
F-statistic: 18,26 on 7 and 1292 DF,  p-value: < 2,2e-16
[1] "Part worths (utilities) of levels (model parameters for whole sample):"
     levnms    utls
1  intercept  3,5534
2      niska  0,2402
3    srednia -0,1431
4     wysoka -0,0971
```

```
5       czarna  0,6149
6      zielona  0,0349
7     czerwona -0,6498
8   ekspresowa  0,1369
9  granulowana -0,8898
10   lisciasta  0,7529
11         tak  0,4108
12         nie -0,4108
[1] "Average importance of factors (attributes):"
[1] 24,76 32,22 27,15 15,88
[1] Sum of average importance:  100,01
[1] "Chart of average factors importance"
```

12.7 Decision Tree

A decision tree is an algorithm that builds a flowchart like graph to illustrate the possible outcomes of a decision. To build the tree, the algorithm first finds the variable that does the best job of separating the data into two groups. Then, it repeats the above step with the other variables. This results in a tree graph, where each split represents a decision. The algorithm chooses the splits such that the maximum number of observations is classified correctly. The biggest advantage of a decision tree is that it is really intuitive and can be understood even by people with no experience in the field.

Decision tree is a graph to represent choices and their results in form of a tree. The nodes in the graph represent an event or choice and the edges of the graph represent the decision rules or conditions. It is mostly used in Machine Learning and Data Mining applications using R. Examples of use of decision trees are - predicting whether a person buys computer or not, an email as spam or not spam, or predicting a loan as a good or bad credit risk based on the factors in each of these. Generally, a model is created with observed data also called training data. Then a set of validation data is used to verify and improve the model. R has packages which are used to create and visualize decision trees. For new set of predictor variable, we use this model to arrive at a decision on the category (Yes/No, spam/not spam) of the data. Figure shows a decision tree for predicting whether a person buys computer based on age, whether he /she is a student and credit rating.

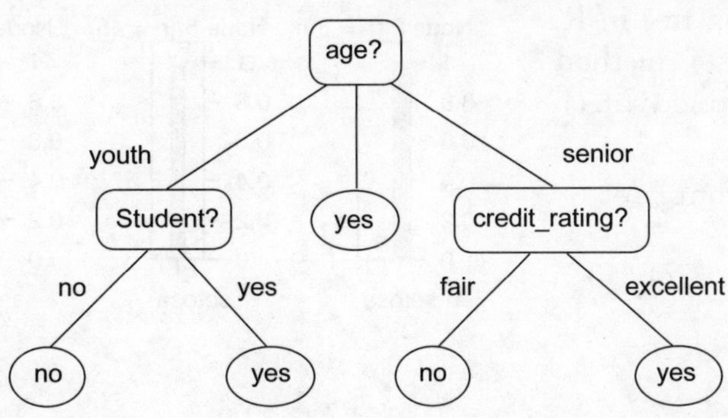

The R package `party` is used to create decision trees. The package `party` has the function `ctree()` which is used to create and analyze decision tree. Before using the `ctree()` function, we should install the `party` package and loaded into the current R environment. The basic syntax for creating a decision tree in R is as follows.

```
ctree(formula, data)
```

where `formula` is a formula describing the predictor and response variables and `data` is the name of the data set used. The decision tree can be illustrated using the built-in data set `iris`.

The data set `iris` contains the fields `Species, Sepal.Length, Sepal.Width, Petal.Length` and `Petal.Width`.

Program

```
library(party)
# Create the tree.
  Output.tree <- ctree(Species ~ Sepal.Length + Sepal.Width + Petal.
Length + Petal.Width,
  data = iris)
summary(Output.tree)
# Plot the tree.
plot(Output.tree)
```

Output

```
Length     Class       Mode
   1 BinaryTree          S4
```

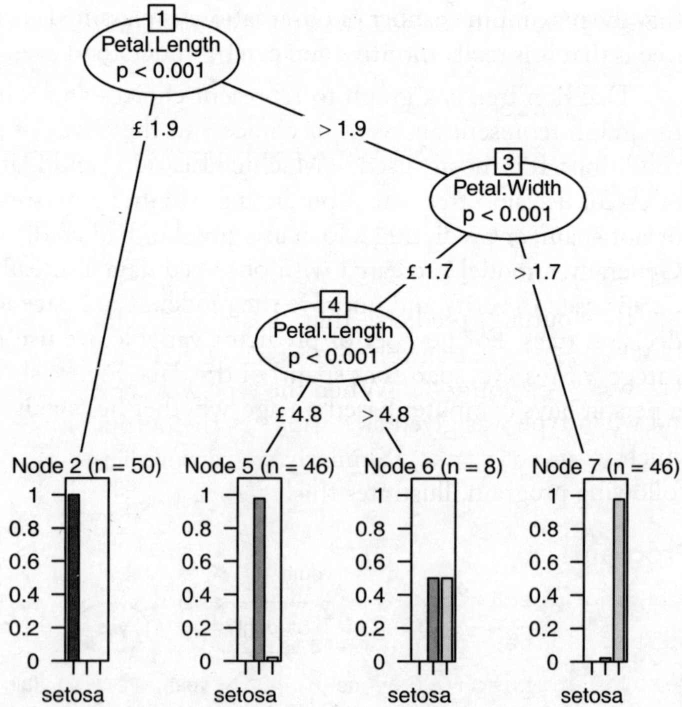

From the output we can conclude that if `Petal.Length>1.9` and `Petal.Width>1.7` then the `Species` will be `virginica`.

We can predict the species using the above decision tree in R. For this the `predict()` method is used. The syntax of `predict()` method is as follows.

```
  predict(decisiontree,
inputdata, type=c
("response, node, prob"))
```

where

`decisiontree`	–	the decision tree constructed using the training set.
`inputdata`	–	the data given as predictor variables.
`type`	–	`response` gives the response variable, `node` gives the value for the node and `prob` gives the probability.

Following program predicts the species of the flower for a single row of data.

Program

```
#Making predictions for single row of data
newdata<-data.frame(Sepal.Length=7,Sepal.Width=4,Petal.Length=6,Petal.
Width=2)
newdata
# perform prediction
predict(Output.tree, newdata,type="response")
predict(Output.tree, newdata,type="prob")
predict(Output.tree, newdata,type="node")
```

Output

```
  Sepal.Length Sepal.Width Petal.Length Petal.Width
1            7           4            6           2
[1] virginica
Levels: setosa versicolor virginica
[[1]]
[1] 0.00000000 0.02173913 0.97826087
[1] 7
```

The output predicts that a flower with the attributes `Sepal.Length=7,Sepal.Width=4,Petal.Length=6,Petal.Width=2` belongs to the `Species virginica` when the type was `"response"`. When the type was `"prob"` the highest probability is for `virginica` and when type was given as `"node"`, the output shows that the input data belongs to `node 7` which is `virginica`. Similarly we can predict the species for the multiple rows of input data. Following program illustrates this.

Program

```
#Making predictions for multiple row of data
multipledata<-data.frame(Sepal.Length=c(7,8,6,5),Sepal.Width=c(4,3,2,4),
Petal.Length=c(6,3.4,5.6,6.3),Petal.Width=c(2,3,4,2.3))
multipledata
# perform prediction
predict(Output.tree, multipledata,type="response")
```

Output

```
  Sepal.Length Sepal.Width Petal.Length Petal.Width
1            7           4          6.0         2.0
2            8           3          3.4         3.0
3            6           2          5.6         4.0
4            5           4          6.3         2.3
[1] virginica virginica virginica virginica
Levels: setosa versicolor virginica
```

The output shows that all the 4 input data set belongs to the species `virginica`.

12.8 Random Forest

Random forests or random decision forests are an ensemble learning method for classification, regression and other tasks that operate by constructing a multitude of decision trees at training time and outputting the class. This is the model of the classes (classification) or mean prediction (regression) of the individual trees. Decision trees have a problem of overfitting to their training set. But random forests eliminate this overfitting. In the random forest approach, a large number of decision trees are created. Every observation is fed into every decision tree. The most common outcome for each observation is used as the final output. A new observation is fed into all the trees and taking a majority vote for each classification model. An error estimate is made for the cases which were not used while building the tree. That is called an OOB (Out-of-bag) error estimate which is mentioned as a percentage.

For generating random forest in R, we need to install and load the package `randomForest` in the current R environment. Similarly the `party` package should also be loaded into the current R environment. The package `randomForest` has the function `randomForest()` which is used to create and analyze random forests. The syntax of `randomForest()` function is as follows.

```
randomForest(formula, data)
```

where

`formula` is a formula describing the predictor and response variables.

`data` is the name of the data set used.

The random forest can be illustrated using the built-in data set `iris` which was used for creating decision trees.

Program

```
library(randomForest)
library(party)
# Create the forest.
  Output.forest <- randomForest(Species ~ Sepal.Length + Sepal.Width +
Petal.Length + Petal.Width, data = iris)
Output.forest
```

Output

```
Call:
 randomForest(formula = Species ~ Sepal.Length + Sepal.Width +      Petal.
Length + Petal.Width, data = iris)
                 Type of random forest: classification
                       Number of trees: 500
No. of variables tried at each split: 2
         OOB estimate of error rate: 4.67%
Confusion matrix:
          setosa versicolor virginica class.error
setosa        50          0         0        0.00
versicolor     0         47         3        0.06
virginica      0          4        46        0.08
```

The output shows that `setosa` has been correctly classified while for `versicolor` 3 was wrongly classified and for `virginica` 4 was wrongly classified. The error rate for `setosa` was `0` while error rates for `versicolor` and `virginica` are `0.06` and `0.04` respectively. The model has `4.67%` error which means we can predict with `95.33%` accuracy.

We can also plot the output of the random forest as follows.

Program

```
# Plot the forest
plot(Output.forest)
```

Output

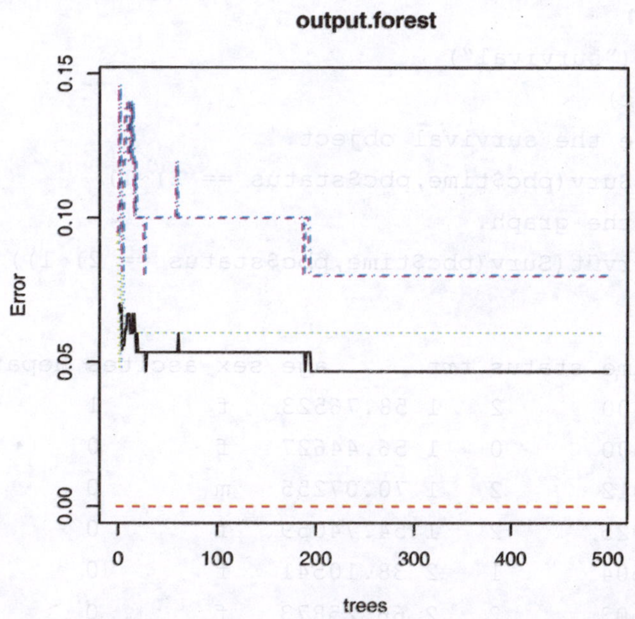

From the output we can see that as the number of trees increases, the error rate decreases and after 200 trees, the error rate is steady for both species `versicolor` and `virginica`.

12.9 Survival Analysis

Survival analysis is a branch of statistics for analyzing the expected duration of time until one or more events happen, such as death in biological organisms and failure in mechanical systems. This topic is called reliability theory or reliability analysis in engineering, duration analysis or duration modeling in economics, and event history analysis in sociology. For example predicting the number of days a person with cancer will survive or predicting the time when a mechanical system is going to fail.

The R has a package named `survival` to carry out survival analysis. This package contains the function `Surv()` which takes the input data as a R formula and creates a survival object among the chosen variables for analysis. Then we use the function `survfit()` to create a plot for the analysis. The syntax of `Surv()` function and `survfit()` function is as follows.

```
Surv(time,event)
survfit(formula)
```

where `time` is the follow up time until the event occurs, `event` gives the status of occurrence of the expected event and `formula` is the relationship between the predictor variables.

We will consider the data set named `pbc` present in the `survival` packages installed above. It describes the survival data points about people affected with primary biliary cirrhosis (PBC) of the liver. Among the many columns present in the data set we are primarily concerned with the fields `time` and `status`. `Time` represents the number of days between registration of the patient and earlier of the event between the patient receiving a liver transplant or death of the patient. Following program illustrates the survival analysis.

Program

```
library("survival")
head(pbc)
# Create the survival object.
survfit(Surv(pbc$time,pbc$status == 2)~1)
# Plot the graph.
plot(survfit(Surv(pbc$time,pbc$status == 2)~1))
```

Output

```
  id time status trt      age sex ascites hepato spiders edema
1  1  400      2   1 58.76523   f       1      1       1   1.0
2  2 4500      0   1 56.44627   f       0      1       1   0.0
3  3 1012      2   1 70.07255   m       0      0       0   0.5
4  4 1925      2   1 54.74059   f       0      1       1   0.5
5  5 1504      1   2 38.10541   f       0      1       1   0.0
6  6 2503      2   2 66.25873   f       0      1       0   0.0
```

```
  bili chol albumin copper alk.phos    ast trig platelet protime
1 14.5  261    2.60    156   1718.0 137.95  172      190    12.2
2  1.1  302    4.14     54   7394.8 113.52   88      221    10.6
3  1.4  176    3.48    210    516.0  96.10   55      151    12.0
4  1.8  244    2.54     64   6121.8  60.63   92      183    10.3
5  3.4  279    3.53    143    671.0 113.15   72      136    10.9
6  0.8  248    3.98     50    944.0  93.00   63       NA    11.0
  stage
1     4
2     3
3     4
4     4
5     3
6     3
Call: survfit(formula = Surv(pbc$time, pbc$status == 2) ~ 1)
      n  events  median 0.95LCL 0.95UCL
    418     161    3395    3090    3853
```

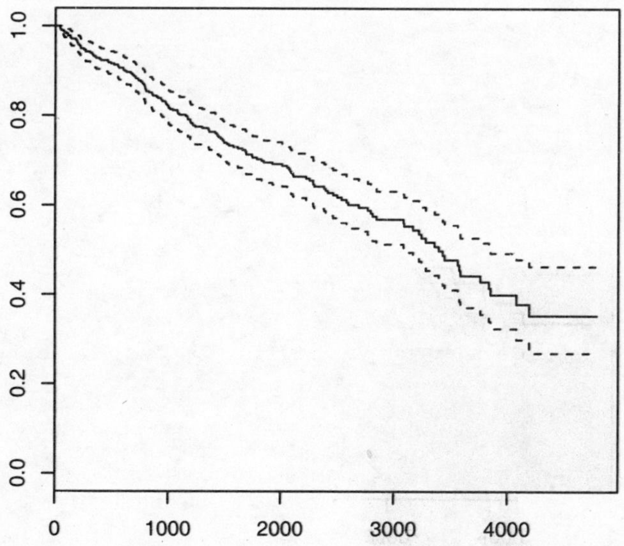

12.10 Conclusion

This Chapter covers a wide variety of advanced multivariate analysis techniques. Discriminant function analysis to predict a categorical dependent variable by one or more continuous or binary independent variables is illustrated. Exploratory Factor Analysis techniques used to identify the latent relational structure among a set of variables and narrow down to smaller number of variables is covered in this Chapter. Cluster analysis explains various methods of clustering like partitioning methods, hierarchical methods and model based methods for clustering in R. Correspondence analysis to find similarity, affinity, confusion, association, or interaction between the row and column variables are well explained in this Chapter. Other multivariate techniques include multidimensional scaling to visualize the level of similarity of individual cases of a dataset, conjoint analysis, decision tree for classification, random forest and survival analysis. All techniques are explained with appropriate data sets and functions in R.

13 Advanced Graphs

13.1 Introduction

This Chapter describes how to customize our graphs. Many statistically sophisticated graphs like lattice graphs, ggplot2, probability graphs, mosaic graphs, correlograms and interactive plots are covered in this Chapter. This is one of the most powerful features of R which many software is lacking. Graphical parameters describe how to change a graph's symbols, fonts, colors, and lines. Axes and text describe how to customize a graph's axes, add reference lines, text annotations and a legend. Combining plots describes how to organize multiple plots into a single graph.

The lattice package provides a comprehensive system for visualizing multivariate data, including the ability to create plots conditioned on one or more variables. The ggplot2 package offers an elegant system for generating univariate and multivariate graphs. Other graph types include probability plots, mosaic plots, and correlograms. Finally methods of interacting with graphs (e.g. linking multiple graphs with color brushing, or interactive rotation in real-time) are provided.

13.2 Graphical Parameters

We can customize many features of our graphs like font, color, axes and titles through graphic options. One way is to specify these options in through the `par( )` function. The syntax of par() function is as follows.

```
par(optionname=value, optionname=value, ...)
```

Once we set the parameter values in `par()` function, the changes will be in effect for the rest of the session or until we change them again. For example, we can save the copy of current settings to a variable. For example, we can change the color of the labels to blue while drawing the histogram for the built-in dataset `mtcars` as follows.

Program

```
par()                  # view current settings
opar <- par()          # make a copy of current settings
par(col.lab="blue")    # blue x and y labels
hist(mtcars$mpg)       # create a plot with these new settings
```

Output

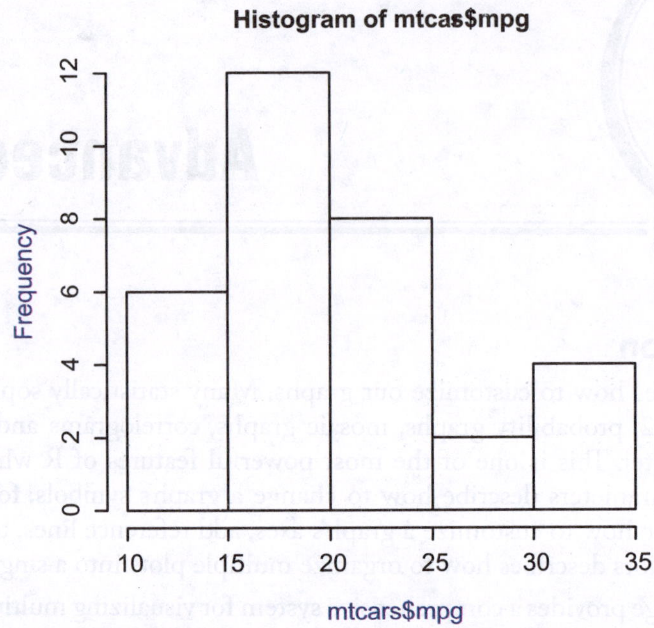

We can also produce the same histogram with the single line command as follows.

```
hist(mtcars$mpg, col.lab="blue")
```

The original settings can be restored by giving `par(opar)`.

Table 13.1 gives various options for controlling text and Figure 13.1 gives various plotting symbols. We can use the `pch` option to specify symbols to use when plotting points. For symbols 21 through 25, specify border color (`col`) and fill color (`bg`).

Table 13.1: Options for Controlling Text

Option	Description
cex	number indicating the amount by which plotting text and symbols should be scaled relative to the default. 1=default, 1.5 is 50% larger, 0.5 is 50% smaller, etc.
cex.axis	magnification of axis annotation relative to cex
cex.lab	magnification of x and y labels relative to cex
cex.main	magnification of titles relative to cex
cex.sub	magnification of subtitles relative to cex

Line type and width can be specified using the parameter `lty` and line width can be specified by the parameter `lwd`. The default value of `lwd` is 1 and 2 means twice the width. The following example for plotting a line chart for the rainfall illustrates the use of `lty` and `lwd` parameters.

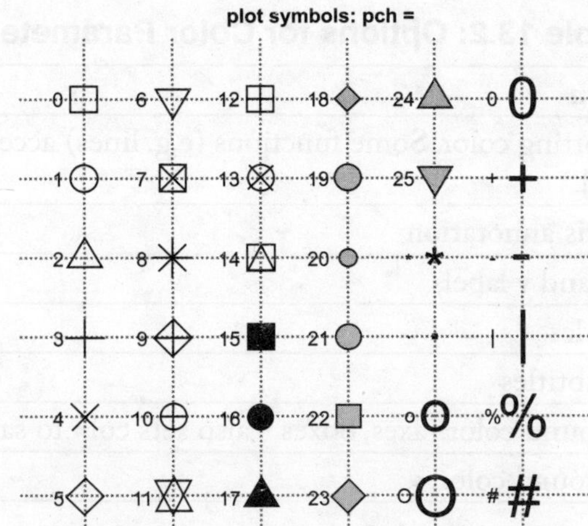

Fig.3.1: Options for Plotting Symbols

Program

```
y=c(14,12,18,10,15)
x=c(1,2,3,4,5)
# Plot the line chart.
plot(x,y,type = "o", lty=3, lwd=2,col = "red", xlab ="Month", ylab = "Rain
fall",main = "Rain fall chart")
```

Output

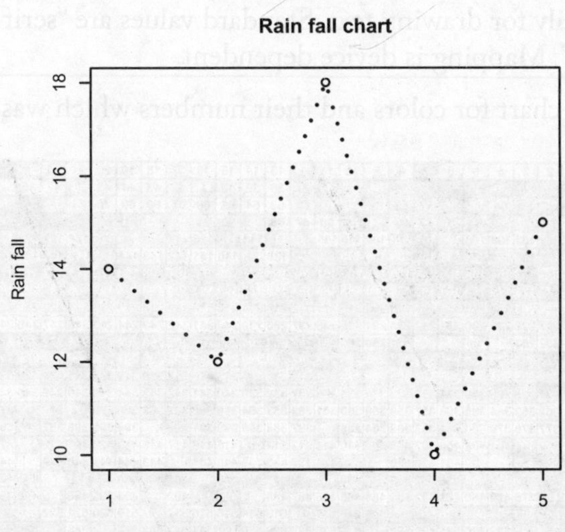

We can specify colors for the foreground, background, titles, x and y labels etc using the parameters given in Table 13.2.

Table 13.2: Options for Color Parameters

Option	Description
col	Default plotting color. Some functions (e.g. lines) accept a vector of values that are recycled.
col.axis	color for axis annotation
col.lab	color for x and y labels
col.main	color for titles
col.sub	color for subtitles
fg	plot foreground color (axes, boxes - also sets col= to same)
bg	plot background color

We can specify the font size, font style and font family as shown in Table 13.3.

Table 13.3: Options for Font Parameters

Option	Description
font	Integer specifying font to use for text. 1=plain, 2=bold, 3=italic, 4=bold italic, 5=symbol
font.axis	font for axis annotation
font.lab	font for x and y labels
font.main	font for titles
font.sub	font for subtitles
ps	font point size (roughly 1/72 inch). text size=ps*cex
family	font family for drawing text. Standard values are "serif", "sans", "mono", "symbol". Mapping is device dependent.

Figure 13.2 gives the chart for colors and their numbers which was created by Earl F. Glynn.

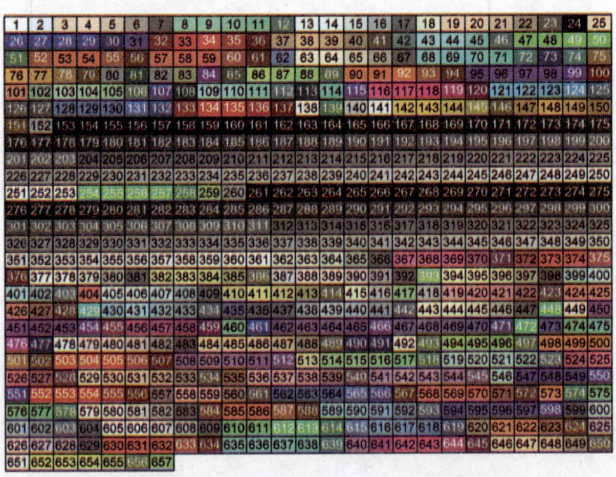

Fig.3.2: Color Chart with Numbers

13.3 Combining Graphs

R makes it easy to combine multiple plots into one overall graph, using either the `par()` or `layout( )` function. With the `par()` function, we can include the option `mfrow=c(nrows, ncols)` to create a matrix of `nrows x ncols` plots that are filled in by `row`. `mfcol=c(nrows, ncols)` fills in the matrix by columns.

Following example illustrates how to arrange 3 histograms in 2 rows and 2 column.

Program

```
attach(mtcars)
par(mfrow=c(2,2))
hist(wt);hist(mpg);hist(disp)
```

Output

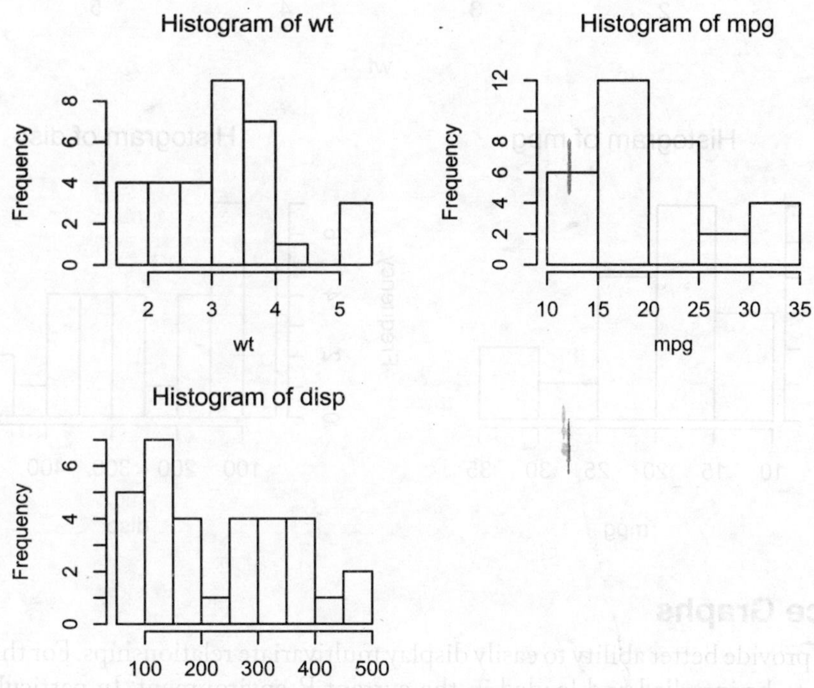

The `layout()` function has the form `layout(mat)` where `mat` is a matrix object specifying the location of the N figures to plot. Following program illustrates the use of `layout()` function.

Program

```
attach(mtcars)
layout(matrix(c(1,1,2,3), 2, 2, byrow = TRUE))
hist(wt)
```

```
hist(mpg)
hist(disp)
```

Output

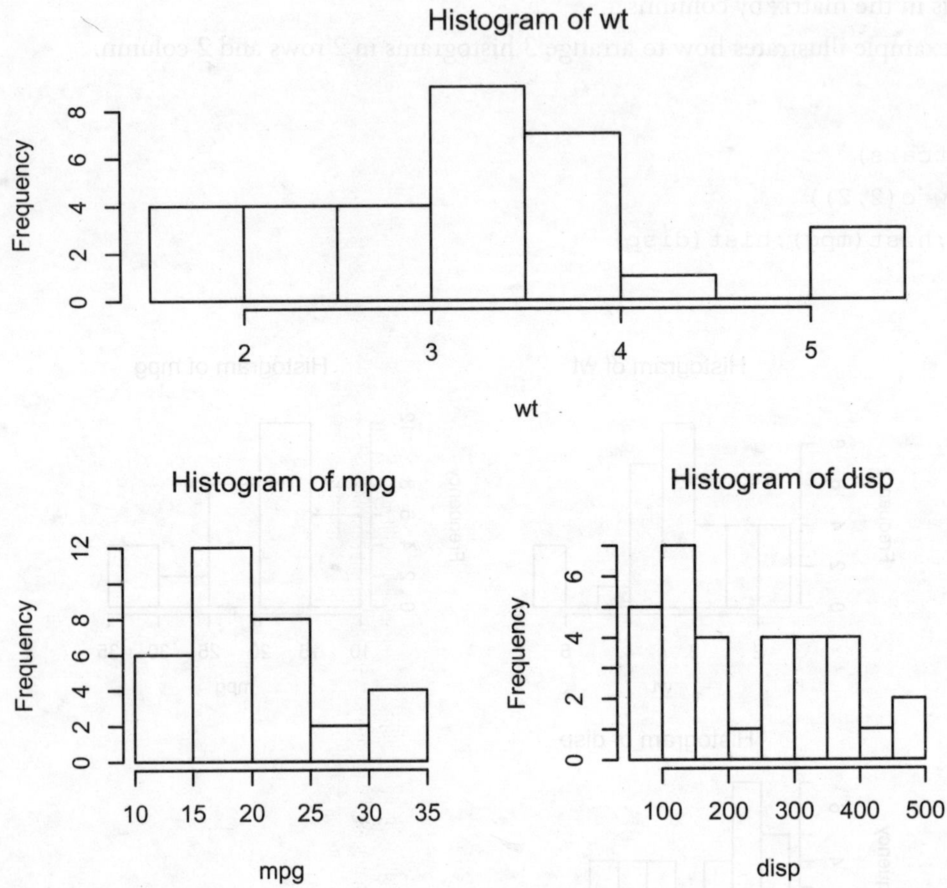

13.4 Lattice Graphs

Lattice graphs provide better ability to easily display multivariate relationships. For this the `lattice` package needs to be installed and loaded in the current R environment. In particular, the package supports the creation of trellis graphs - graphs that display a variable or the relationship between variables, conditioned on one or more other variables. The syntax is `graph_type(formula, data)`
where `graph_type` is selected from Table 13.4. The parameter `formula` specifies the variable(s) to display and any conditioning variables. For example `~x|A` means display numeric variable `x` for each level of factor `A`. `y~x | A*B` means display the relationship between numeric variables `y` and `x` separately for every combination of factor `A` and `B` levels. `~x` means display numeric variable `x` alone.

Table 13.4: Graph Types with Description and Example Formula

graph_type	Description	Formula Examples
barchart	bar chart	x~A or A~x
bwplot	boxplot	x~A or A~x
cloud	3D scatterplot	z~x*y|A
contourplot	3D contour plot	z~x*y
densityplot	kernal density plot	~x|A*B
dotplot	dotplot	~x|A
histogram	histogram	~x
levelplot	3D level plot	z~y*x
parallel	parallel coordinates plot	data frame
splom	scatterplot matrix	data frame
stripplot	strip plots	A~x or x~A
xyplot	scatterplot	y~x|A
wireframe	3D wireframe graph	z~y*x

Following programs illustrates the use of `lattice` package and various graphs. For this the built-in dataset `mtcars` is used. Program 1 illustrates a kernel density plot for `miles per gallon (mpg)` of `mtcars` dataset.

Program 1

```
#Lattice Examples
library(lattice)
attach(mtcars)
# create factors with value labels
gear.f<-factor(gear,levels=c(3,4,5),labels=c("3gears","4gears","5gea
rs"))
cyl.f <-factor(cyl,levels=c(4,6,8),labels=c("4cyl","6cyl","8cyl"))
# kernel density plot
densityplot(~mpg,main="Density Plot", xlab="Miles per Gallon")
```

Output 1

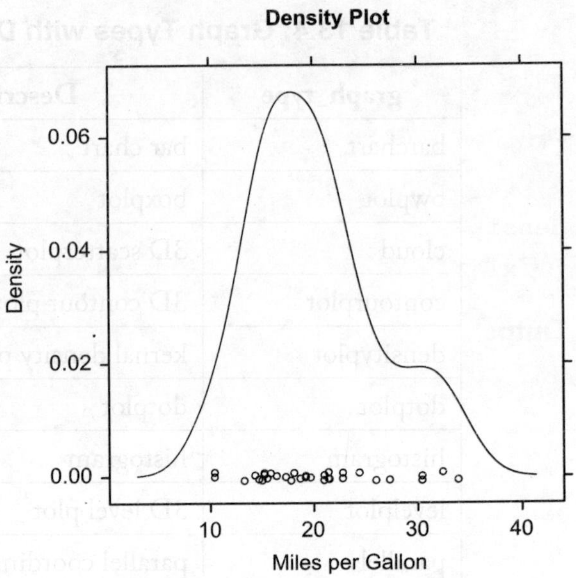

Program 2 illustrates a kernel density plot at factor levels (no: of cylinders) for `miles per gallon (mpg)` of `mtcars` dataset.

Program 2

```
# kernel density plots by factor level
densityplot(~mpg|cyl.f,main="Density Plot by Number of Cylinders",
   xlab="Miles per Gallon")
```

Output 2

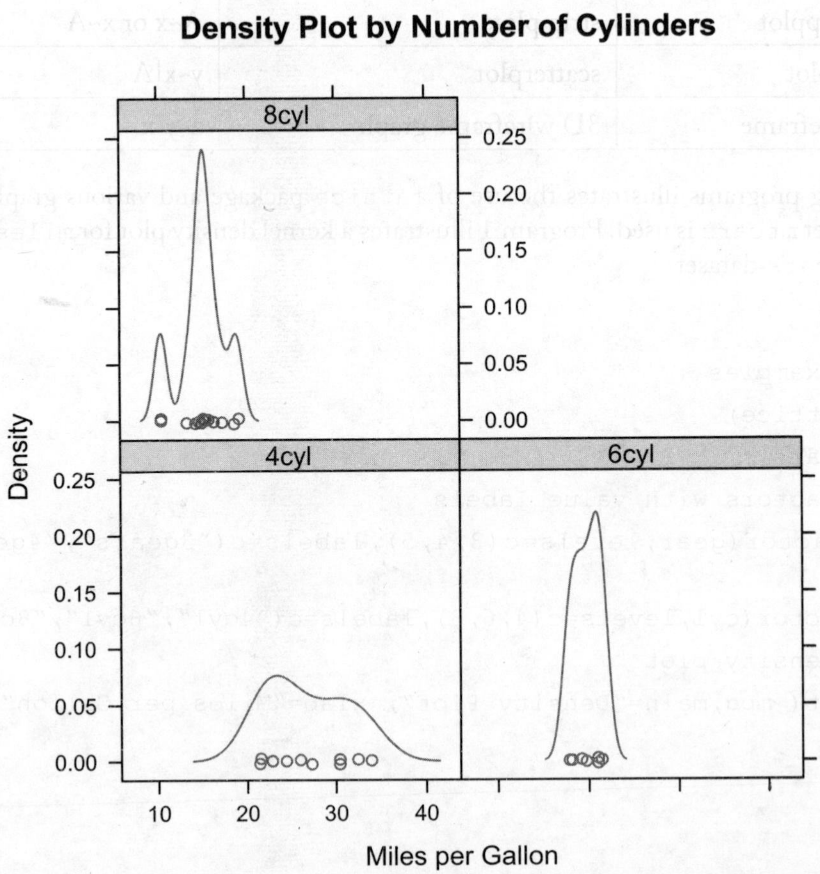

Program 3 illustrates a kernel density plot at factor levels (no: of cylinders) for `miles per gallon (mpg)` of `mtcars` dataset with `layout()` function.

Program 3

```
# kernel density plots by factor level (alternate layout)
densityplot(~mpg|cyl.f,main="Density Plot by Number of Cylinders",
   xlab="Miles per Gallon", layout=c(1,3))
```

Output 3

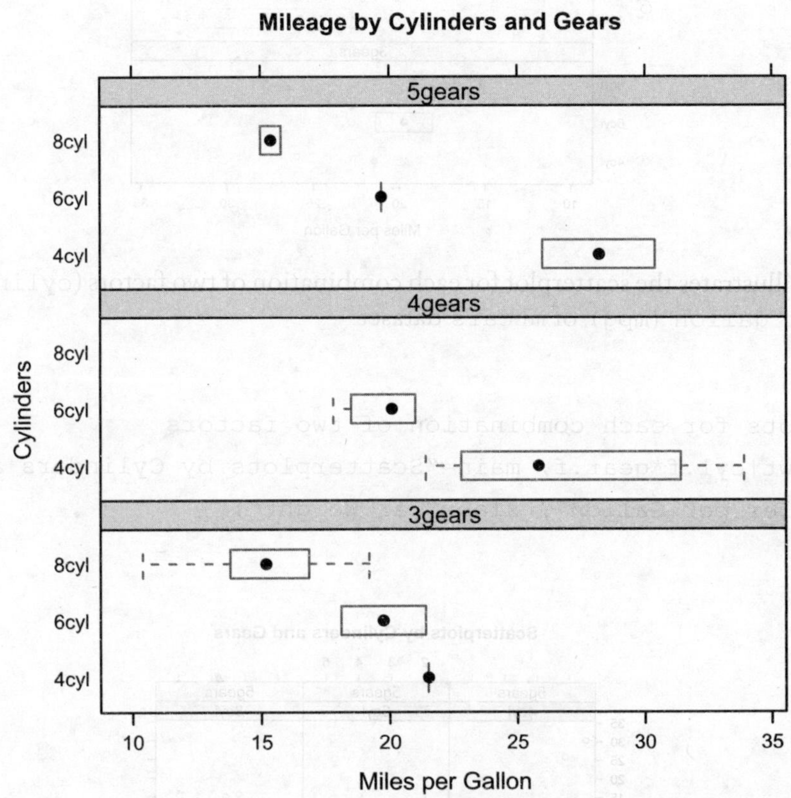

Program 4 illustrates the boxplot for each combination of two factors (`cylinders, gears`) for `miles per gallon (mpg)` of `mtcars` dataset.

Program 4

```
# boxplots for each combination of two factors
bwplot(cyl.f~mpg|gear.f,
   ylab="Cylinders", xlab="Miles per Gallon",
   main="Mileage by Cylinders and Gears",
   layout=c(1,3))
```

Output 4

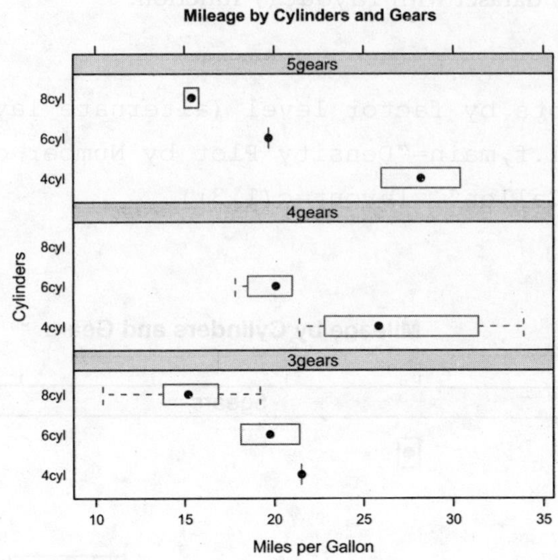

Program 5 illustrates the scatterplot for each combination of two factors (`cylinders, gears`) for `miles per gallon (mpg)` of `mtcars` dataset

Program 5

```
# scatterplots for each combination of two factors
xyplot(mpg~wt|cyl.f*gear.f, main="Scatterplots by Cylinders and Gears",
   ylab="Miles per Gallon", xlab="Car Weight")
```

Output 5

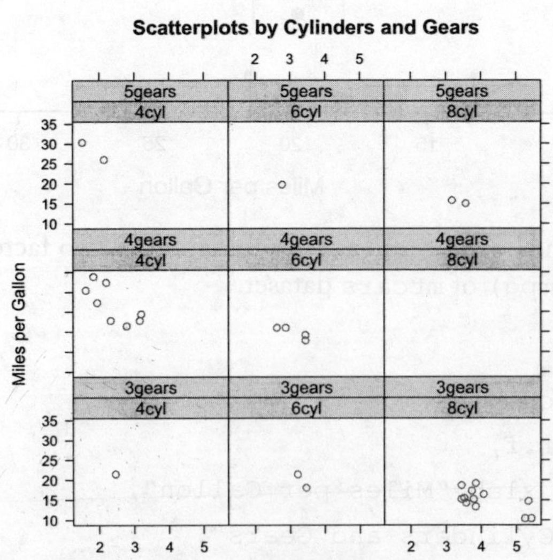

Program 6 illustrates the 3D scatterplot for factor level (`cylinders`) for `miles per gallon (mpg),wt,qsec` of `mtcars` dataset

Program 6

```
# 3d scatterplot by factor level
cloud(mpg~wt*qsec|cyl.f,main="3D Scatterplot by Cylinders")
```

Output 6

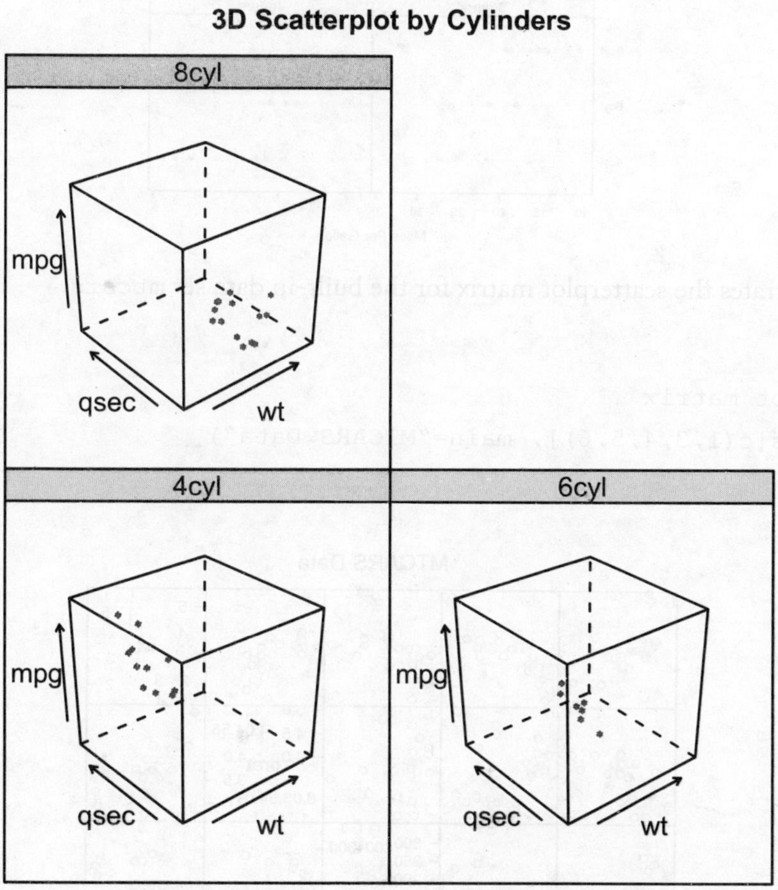

Program 7 illustrates the dot plot for each combination of two factors (`cylinder,gear`).

Program 7

```
# dotplot for each combination of two factors
dotplot(cyl.f~mpg|gear.f,main="Dotplot  Plot  by  Number  of  Gears  and
Cylinders",
   xlab="Miles Per Gallon")
```

Output 7

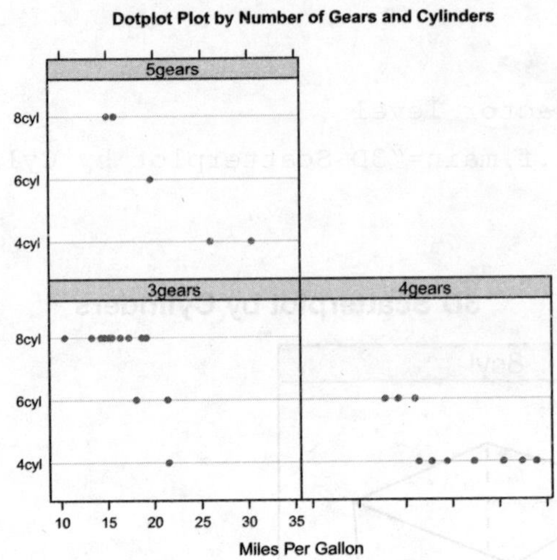

Program 8 illustrates the scatterplot matrix for the built-in data set mtcars.

Program 8

```
# scatterplot matrix
splom(mtcars[c(1,3,4,5,6)], main="MTCARS Data")
```

Output 8

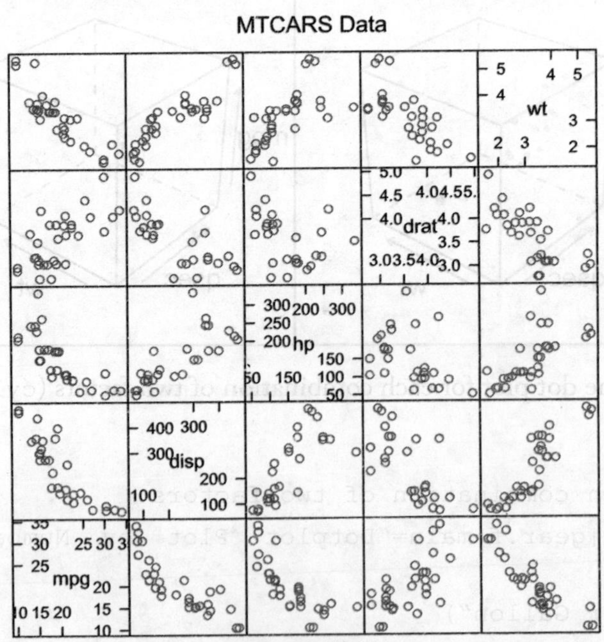

13.5 ggplot2 Graphs

The `ggplot2` package, created by Hadley Wickham, offers a powerful graphics language for creating elegant and complex plots. The `ggplot2` allows us to create graphs that represent both univariate and multivariate numerical and categorical data. Grouping can be represented by color, symbol, size, and transparency. The creation of trellis plots (conditioning) is relatively simple. The package `ggplot2` has a helper function called `qplot()` (for quick plot) that can hide much of this complexity when creating standard graphs.

`qplot()` – The `qplot()` function can be used to create the most common graph types. While it does not expose `ggplot's` full power, it can create a very wide range of useful plots. The format is as follows.

```
qplot(x, y, data, color, shape, size, fill, alpha, geom,
method, formula, facets, xlim, ylim, xlab, ylab, main, sub)
```

where

`x, y` – Specifies the variables placed on the horizontal and vertical axis. For univariate plots (eg: histograms), we can omit `y`.

`data` – Specifies a data frame.

`color, shape, size, fill` – Associates the levels of variable with symbol color, shape, or size. For line plots, color associates levels of a variable with line color. For density and box plots, `fill` associates fill colors with a variable. Legends are drawn automatically.

`alpha` – Alpha transparency for overlapping elements expressed as a fraction between 0 (complete transparency) and 1 (complete opacity).

`geom` – Specifies the geometric objects that define the graph type. The `geom` option is expressed as a character vector with one or more entries. `geom` values include `"point"`, `"smooth"`, `"boxplot"`, `"line"`, `"histogram"`, `"density"`, `"bar"` and `"jitter"`.

`method, formula` – If `geom="smooth"`, a loess fit line and confidence limits are added by default. When the number of observations is greater than 1,000, a more efficient smoothing algorithm is employed. Methods include `"lm"` for regression, `"gam"` for generalized additive models, and `"rlm"` for robust regression. The formula parameter gives the form of the fit. For example, to add simple linear regression lines, we would specify `geom="smooth", method="lm", formula=y~x`. Changing the formula to `y~poly(x,2)` would produce a quadratic fit. Note that the formula uses the letters x and y, not the names of the variables. For `method="gam"`, be sure to load the `mgcv` package. For `method="rml"`, load the `MASS` package.

`facets` – Creates a trellis graph by specifying conditioning variables. Its value is expressed as `rowvar ~ colvar`. To create trellis graphs based on a single conditioning variable, we need to use `rowvar~. or .~colvar`).

`xlim, ylim` – Two-element numeric vectors giving the minimum and maximum values for the horizontal and vertical axes, respectively.

`xlab, ylab` – Character vectors specifying horizontal and vertical axis labels.

`main, sub` – Character vectors specifying the title and subtitle.

Following are some examples using built-in data set `mtcars` (car mileage, weight, number of gears, number of cylinders, etc.). The library ggplot2 is loaded in the current R environment.

Program 1 illustrates kernel density plots for `mpg` in `mtcars` dataset grouped by number of `gears`.

Program 1

```
# ggplot2 examples
library(ggplot2)
# create factors with value labels
mtcars$gear <- factor(mtcars$gear,levels=c(3,4,5),
   labels=c("3gears","4gears","5gears"))
mtcars$am <- factor(mtcars$am,levels=c(0,1),
   labels=c("Automatic","Manual"))
mtcars$cyl <- factor(mtcars$cyl,levels=c(4,6,8),
   labels=c("4cyl","6cyl","8cyl"))
# Kernel density plots for mpg
# grouped by number of gears (indicated by color)
qplot(mpg, data=mtcars, geom="density", fill=gear, alpha=I(.5),
   main="Distribution of Gas Milage", xlab="Miles Per Gallon",
   ylab="Density")
```

Output 1

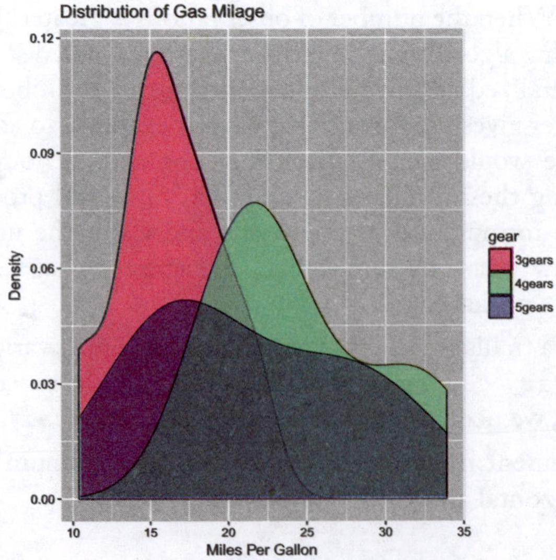

Program 2 illustrates the scatterplot of `mpg vs. hp` for each combination of gears and cylinders in `mtcars` dataset. In each facet, transmission type is represented by shape and color.

Program 2

```
# Scatterplot of mpg vs. hp for each combination of gears and cylinders
# in each facet, transmittion type is represented by shape and color
qplot(hp, mpg, data=mtcars, shape=am, color=am,
   facets=gear~cyl, size=I(3),
   xlab="Horsepower", ylab="Miles per Gallon")
```

Output 2

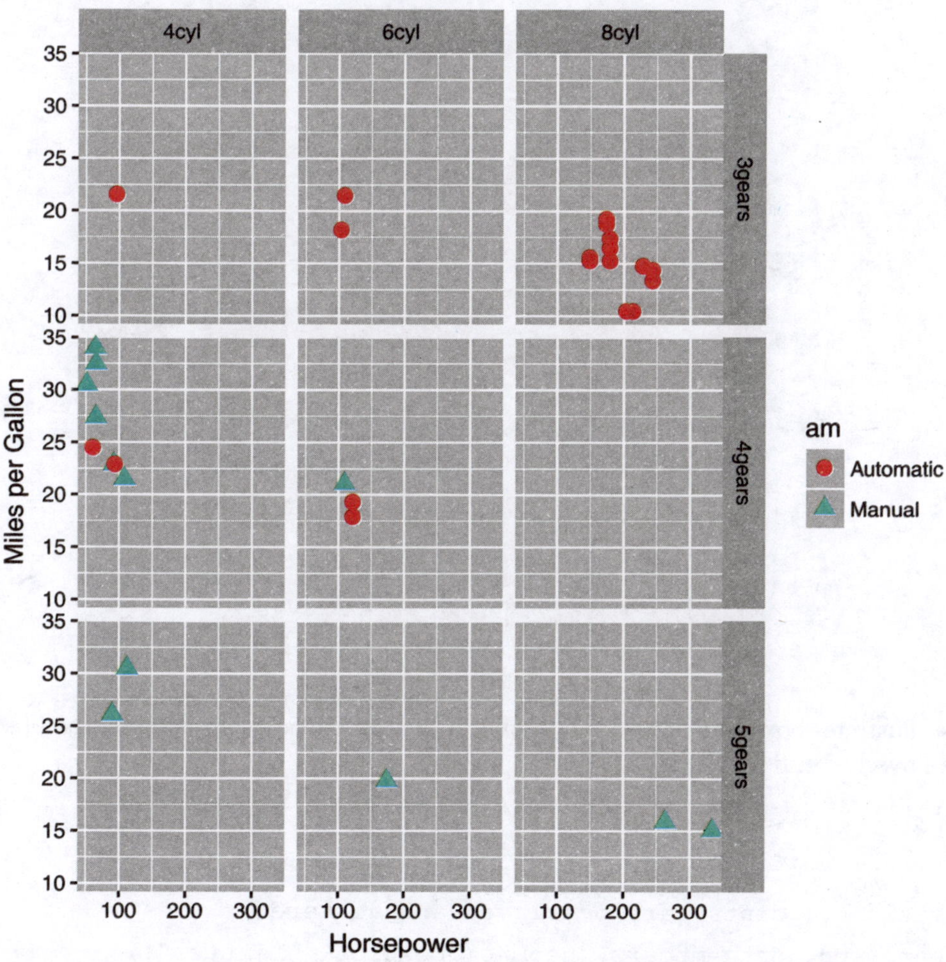

Program 3 illustrates separate regressions of `mpg` on `weight` for each number of cylinders in `mtcars` data set.

Program 3

```
# Separate regressions of mpg on weight for each number of cylinders
qplot(wt, mpg, data=mtcars, geom=c("point", "smooth"),
   method="lm", formula=y~x, color=cyl,
   main="Regression of MPG on Weight",
   xlab="Weight", ylab="Miles per Gallon")
```

Output 3

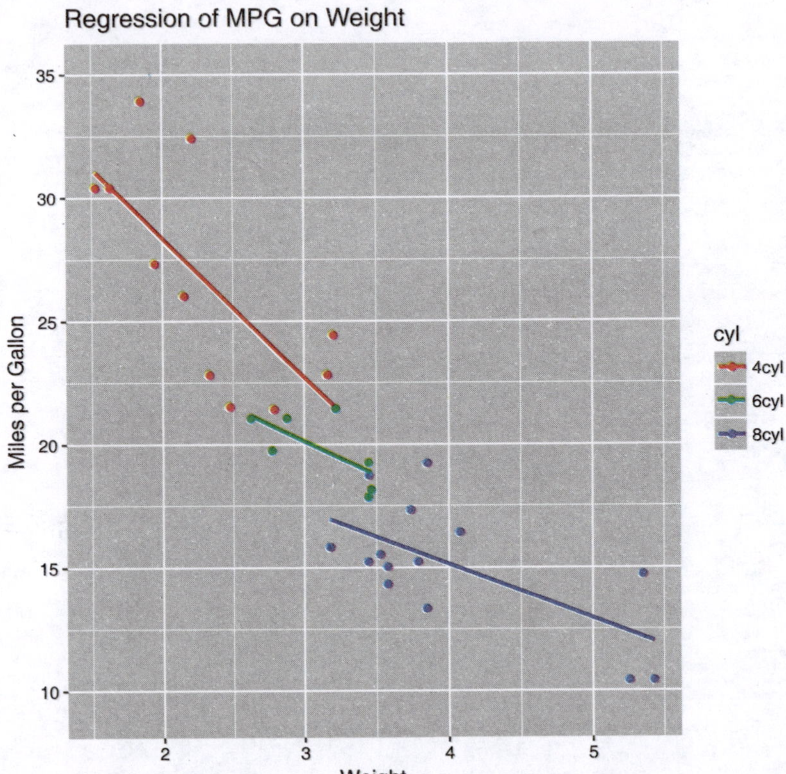

Program 4 illustrates box plots of `mpg` by number of `gears` in `mtcars` dataset. The observations (points) are overlaid and jittered.

Program 4

```
# Boxplots of mpg by number of gears
# observations (points) are overlayed and jittered
qplot(gear, mpg, data=mtcars, geom=c("boxplot", "jitter"),
   fill=gear, main="Mileage by Gear Number",
   xlab="", ylab="Miles per Gallon")
```

Output 4

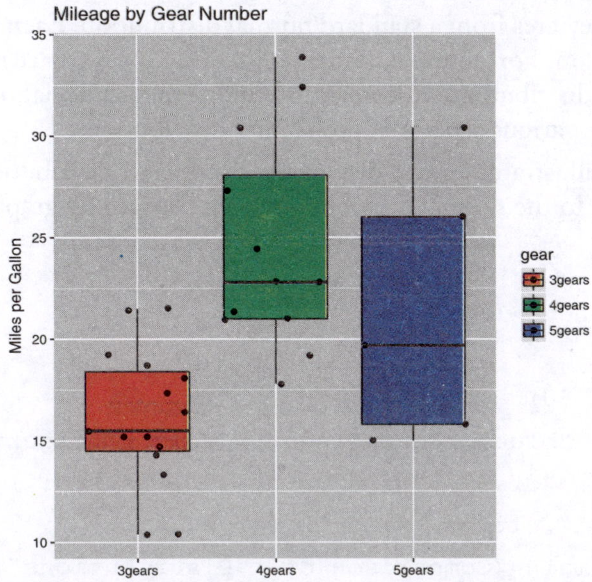

13.6 Probability Graphs

R makes it easy to draw probability distributions and demonstrate statistical concepts. Some of the more common probability distributions available in R are given below.

Distribution	R name	Distribution	R name
Beta	`beta`	Lognormal	`lnorm`
Binomial	`binom`	Negative Binomial	`nbinom`
Cauchy	`cauchy`	Normal	`norm`
Chisquare	`chisq`	Poisson	`pois`
Exponential	`exp`	Student t	`t`
F	`f`	Uniform	`unif`
Gamma	`gamma`	Tukey	`tukey`
Geometric	`geom`	Weibull	`weib`
Hypergeometric	`hyper`	Wilcoxon	`wilcox`
Logistic	`logis`		

The functions available for each distribution follow this format.

`dname()` -density or probability function

`pname()` -cumulative density function

`qname()` -quantile function

`rname()` -random deviates

For example, pnorm(0)=0.5 (the area under the standard normal curve to the left of zero). qnorm(0.9)=1.28 (1.28 is the 90th percentile of the standard normal distribution). rnorm(100) generates 100 random deviates from a standard normal distribution. Each function has parameters specific to that distribution. For example, rnorm(100, m=50, sd=10) generates 100 random deviates from a normal distribution with mean 50 and standard deviation 10. We can use these functions to demonstrate various aspects of probability distributions.

Following program illustrates how to display the Student's t distributions with various degrees of freedom and compare to the normal distribution using probability graphs.

Program

```
x <- seq(-4, 4, length=100)
hx <- dnorm(x)
degf <- c(1, 3, 8, 30)
colors <- c("red", "blue", "darkgreen", "gold", "black")
labels <- c("df=1", "df=3", "df=8", "df=30", "normal")
plot(x, hx, type="l", lty=2, xlab="x value",
  ylab="Density", main="Comparison of t Distributions")
for (i in 1:4){
  lines(x, dt(x,degf[i]), lwd=2, col=colors[i])
}
legend("topright", inset=.05, title="Distributions",
  labels, lwd=2, lty=c(1, 1, 1, 1, 2), col=colors)
```

Output

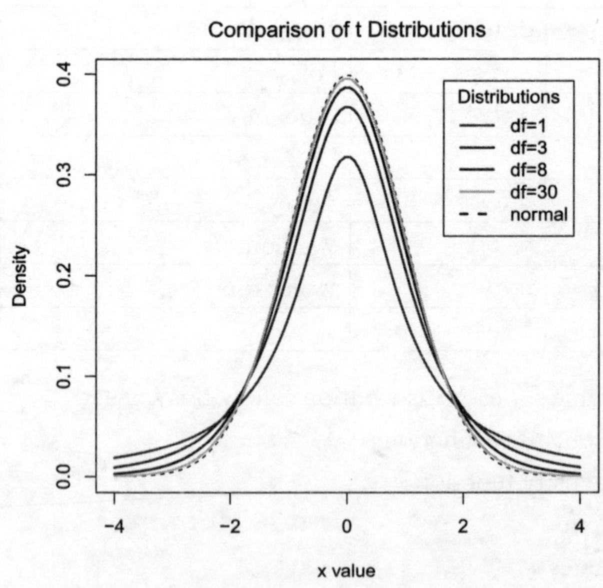

Suppose the children's IQ scores are normally distributed with a mean of 100 and a standard deviation of 15. We want to know what proportion of children is expected to have an IQ between 80 and 120. In such cases we can go with the probability plots. Following program illustrates this.

Program

```
# Children's IQ scores are normally distributed with a
# mean of 100 and a standard deviation of 15. What
# proportion of children are expected to have an IQ between
# 80 and 120?
mean=100; sd=15
lb=80; ub=120
x <- seq(-4,4,length=100)*sd + mean
hx <- dnorm(x,mean,sd)
plot(x, hx, type="n", xlab="IQ Values", ylab="",
  main="Normal Distribution", axes=FALSE)
i <- x >= lb & x <= ub
lines(x, hx)
polygon(c(lb,x[i],ub), c(0,hx[i],0), col="red")
area <- pnorm(ub, mean, sd) - pnorm(lb, mean, sd)
result <- paste("P(",lb,"< IQ <",ub,") =",
   signif(area, digits=3))
mtext(result,3)
axis(1, at=seq(40, 160, 20), pos=0)
```

Output

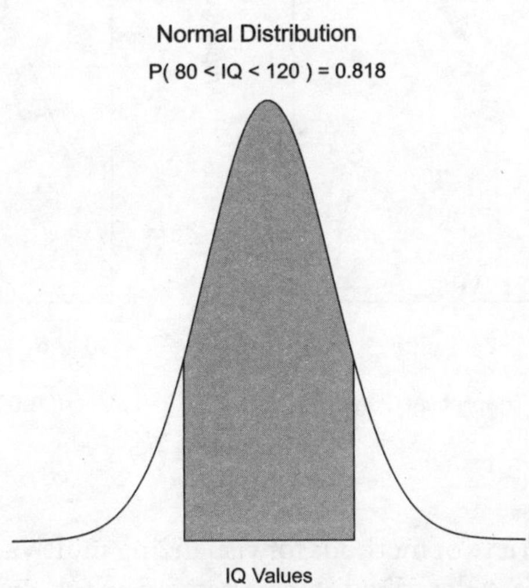

There are several methods of fitting distributions in R. We can use the `qqnorm()` function to create a Quantile-Quantile plot evaluating the fit of sample data to the normal distribution. More generally, the `qqplot()` function creates a Quantile-Quantile plot for any theoretical distribution. Following program illustrates this.

Program

```
# Q-Q plots
par(mfrow=c(1,2))
# create sample data
x <- rt(100, df=3)
# normal fit
qqnorm(x); qqline(x)
# t(3Df) fit
qqplot(rt(1000,df=3), x, main="t(3) Q-Q Plot",
   ylab="Sample Quantiles")
abline(0,1)
```

Output

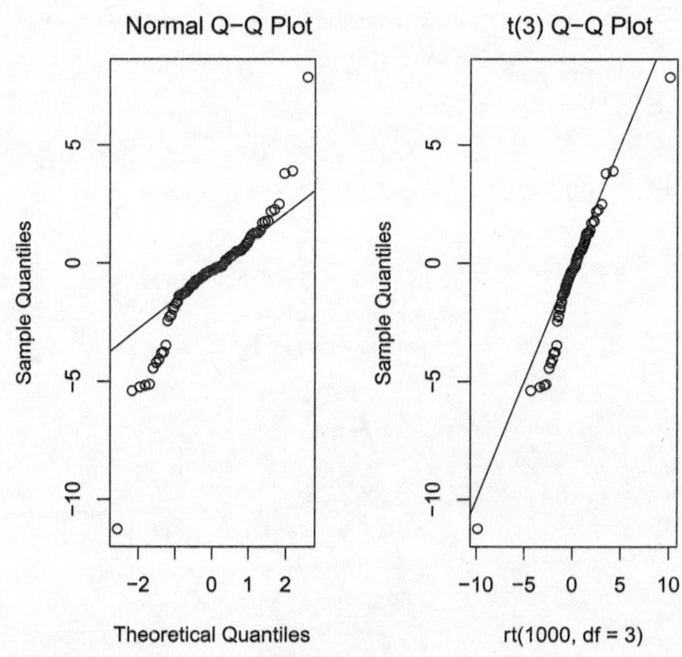

13.7 Mosaic Graphs

The `vcd` package provides a variety of methods for visualizing multivariate categorical data. Extended mosaic and association plots are described in this section. Each provides a method of visualizing complex data and evaluating deviations from a specified independence model. For extended mosaic plots, use `mosaic(x, condvar, data)` where `x` is a table or formula, `condvar` is an optional conditioning variable, and `data` specifies a data frame or a table. We can include `shade=TRUE` to color the figure, and `legend=TRUE` to display a legend for the Pearson residuals.

Following program illustrates the mosaic graph.

Program

```
#Mosaic Plot Example
library(vcd)
mosaic(HairEyeColor, shade=TRUE, legend=TRUE)
```

Output

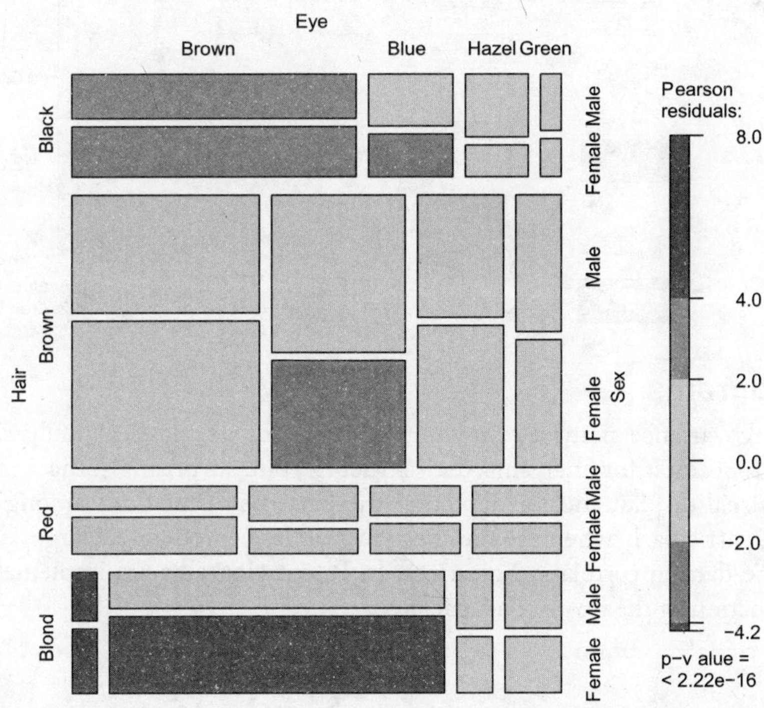

To produce an extended association plot, use `assoc(x, row_vars, col_vars)` where `x` is a contingency table, `row_vars` is a vector of integers giving the indices of the variables to be used for the rows, and `col_vars` is a vector of integers giving the indices of the variables to be used for the columns of the association plot. Following program illustrates this.

Program

```
# Association Plot Example
library(vcd)
assoc(HairEyeColor, shade=TRUE)
```

Output

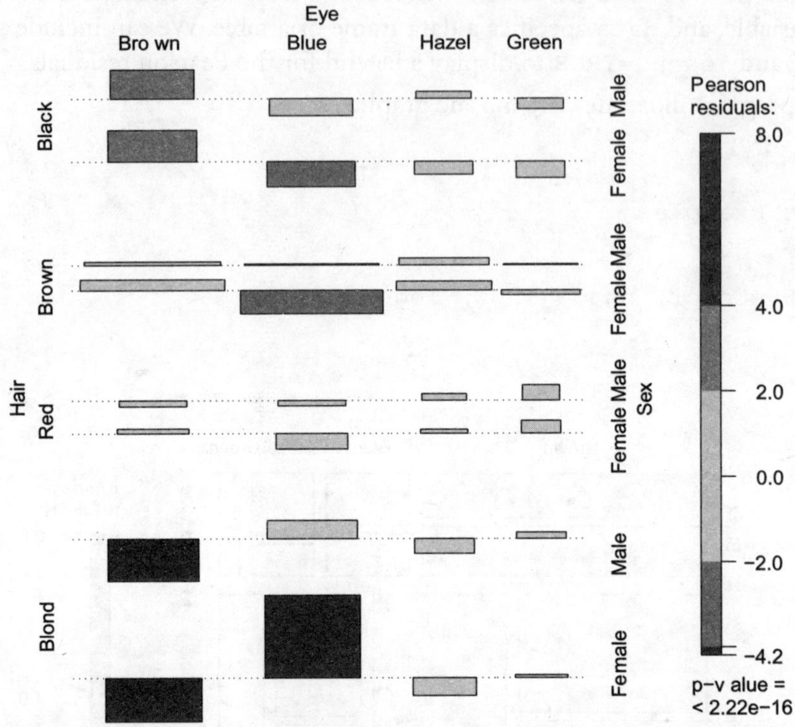

13.8 Correlograms

Correlation and covariance matrices provide the basis for all classical multivariate techniques. Many statistical tools exist for analyzing their structure, but, surprisingly, there are few techniques for exploratory visual display, and for depicting the patterns of relations among variables in such matrices directly, particularly when the number of variables is moderately large. Correlograms help us to visualize the data in correlation matrices. In R, correlograms are implemented through the `corrgram()` function in the `corrgram` package.

```
corrgram(x, order, panel, lower.panel, upper.panel, text.panel, diag.
panel)
```

where

x is a data frame with one observation per row.

`order=TRUE` will cause the variables to be ordered using principal component analysis of the correlation matrix.

`panel` refers to the off-diagonal panels. We can use `lower.panel` and `upper.panel` to choose different options below and above the main diagonal respectively. `text.panel` and `diag.panel` refer to the main diagonal. Allowable parameters are given below.

`off diagonal panels`

`panel.pie` (the filled portion of the pie indicates the magnitude of the correlation) `panel.shade` (the depth of the shading indicates the magnitude of the correlation)

`panel.ellipse` (confidence ellipse and smoothed line)

`panel.pts` (scatterplot)

`main diagonal panels`

`panel.minmax` (min and max values of the variable)

`panel.txt` (variable name).

Following programs illustrate the `corrgram()` function. Before using this function, the `corrgram` package needs to be installed and loaded into the current R environment. For this we are using the built-in data set `mtcars`.

Program 1

```
# First Correlogram Example
library(corrgram)
corrgram(mtcars, order=TRUE, lower.panel=panel.shade,
  upper.panel=panel.pie, text.panel=panel.txt,
  main="Car Milage Data in PC2/PC1 Order")
```

Output 1

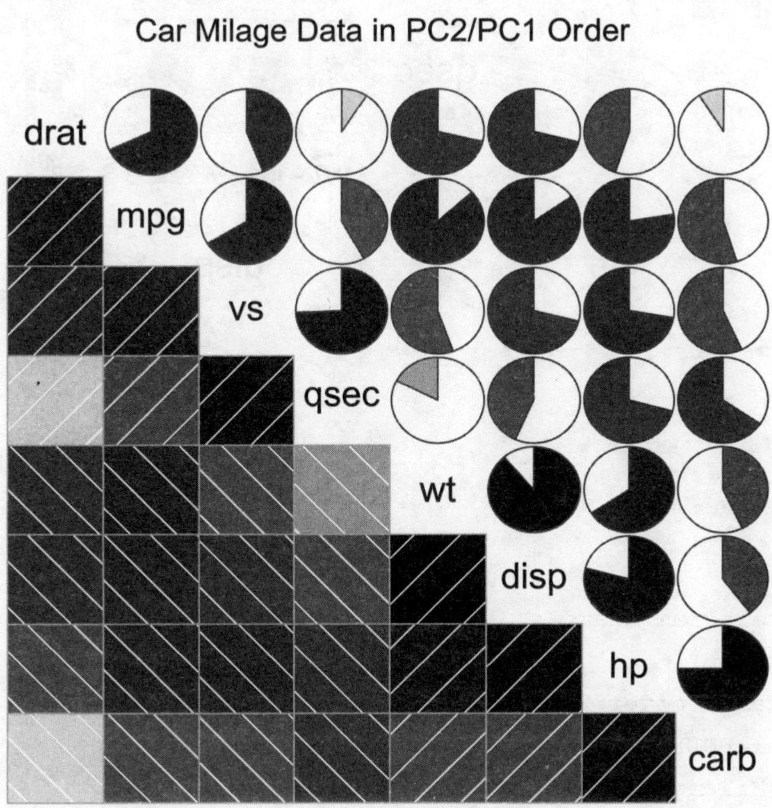

Program 2

```
# Second Correlogram Example
library(corrgram)
corrgram(mtcars, order=TRUE, lower.panel=panel.ellipse,
  upper.panel=panel.pts, text.panel=panel.txt,
  diag.panel=panel.minmax,
  main="Car Mileage Data in PC2/PC1 Order")
```

Output 2

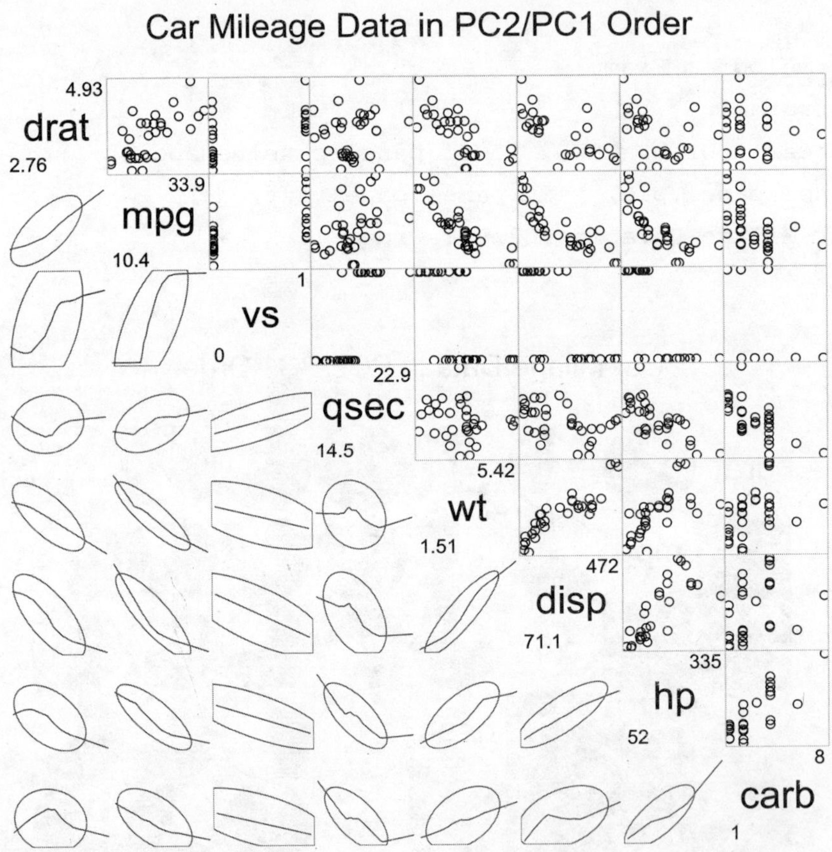

Program 3

```
# Third Correlogram Example
library(corrgram)
corrgram(mtcars, order=NULL, lower.panel=panel.shade,
  upper.panel=NULL, text.panel=panel.txt,
  main="Car Mileage Data (unsorted)")
```

Output 3

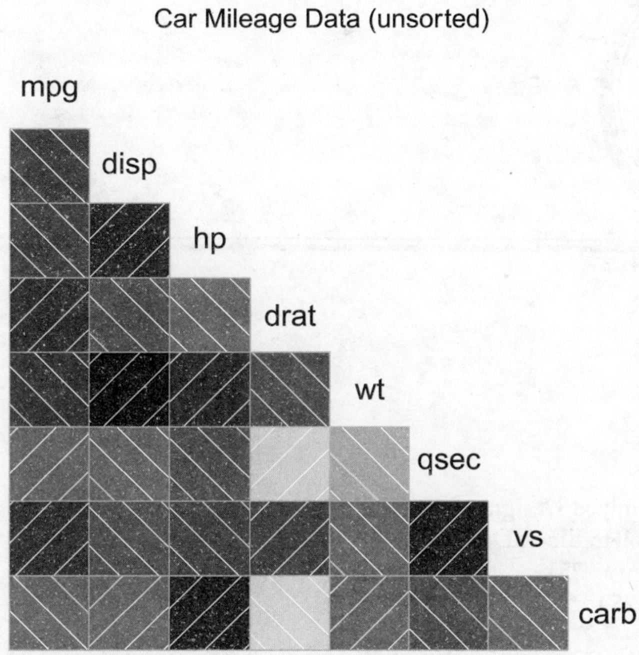

13.9 Conclusion

This Chapter gives a detailed explanation of advanced types of graphs used in R. Various graphical parameters and how to combine graphs are explained in this Chapter. Advanced graphs like lattice graphs, ggplot2 graphs, probability graphs, mosaic graphs and correlograms are illustrated with example program and output.

Index

S

T

U

V

W

X

Z